教育部高等学校电子信息类专业教学指导委员会规划教材

高等学校电子信息类专业系列教材

Technical English for Information Science and Electronic Engineering (Second Edition)

信息科学与电子工程专业英语

（第2版）

吴雅婷　王朔中　黄素娟　编著
Wu Yating　Wang Shuozhong　Huang Sujuan

清华大学出版社

北京

内 容 简 介

本书供高等院校信息科学、通信工程、电子技术、计算机应用等专业的本科生和研究生学习专业英语之用。选材兼顾经典题材和新兴技术，在编写中摈弃过分依赖语法、死记硬背的陈旧教学方法，注重培养学生以较高准确性和足够的速度阅读专业资料和文献的能力，兼顾一定的专业英语表达能力，从阅读、翻译、写作等角度提高学生对专业英语的应用能力。

全书共 17 单元，各单元包括课文、词汇、难点注释、课外阅读资料、习题。书后附有关于科技英语阅读、写作、克服中式英语等问题的指南和讨论。

图书在版编目（CIP）数据

信息科学与电子工程专业英语/吴雅婷，王朔中，黄素娟编著. —2 版. —北京：清华大学出版社，2019（2025.1重印）
（高等学校电子信息类专业系列教材）
ISBN 978-7-302-50620-1

Ⅰ．①信… Ⅱ．①吴… ②王… ③黄… Ⅲ．①信息技术－英语－高等学校－教材②电子技术－英语－高等学校－教材 Ⅳ．①G202②TN

中国版本图书馆 CIP 数据核字（2018）第 151320 号

责任编辑：黄　芝　李　晔
封面设计：李召霞
责任校对：梁　毅
责任印制：曹婉颖

出版发行：清华大学出版社
　　　　网　　　址：https://www.tup.com.cn，https://www.wqxuetang.com
　　　　地　　　址：北京清华大学学研大厦 A 座　　　邮　　　编：100084
　　　　社 总 机：010-83470000　　　邮　　　购：010-62786544
　　　　投稿与读者服务：010-62776969，c-service@tup.tsinghua.edu.cn
　　　　质量反馈：010-62772015，zhiliang@tup.tsinghua.edu.cn
　　　　课件下载：https://www.tup.com.cn，010-83470236
印 装 者：北京同文印刷有限责任公司
经　　　销：全国新华书店
开　　　本：185mm×260mm　　　印　　　张：22.25　　　字　　　数：543 千字
版　　　次：2008 年 2 月第 1 版　　　2019 年 1 月第 2 版　　　印　　　次：2025 年 1 月第 10 次印刷
印　　　数：16001～18000
定　　　价：59.50 元

产品编号：075794-01

Preface

This textbook of technical English is intended for teaching undergraduates and graduate students majoring in information technology, communication engineering, electronic engineering, computer and related subjects.

English as a medium of communication is important in students' future career. The graduates will face various scientific articles, technical documents, product manuals, commercials, and other materials in English. However, having learned English ever since they entered primary school, many university students in their junior and senior years still lack adequate experiences and abilities in using the language as a tool. They are unable to acquire information and knowledge in the fast-developing technological fields, let alone express themselves in English orally or in written form. The problem does not primarily lie in grammar or vocabulary. Indeed, many students have a good mastery of the knowledge about English, but perhaps not the English language itself. They may know almost every rule of the grammar as well as a fairly large quantity of words, even rarely used ones. Some show extraordinary skills in tackling various exams. When coming to practical uses, however, things become quite different. Many students find it difficult to read technical materials at a reasonable speed and catch the message accurately, and don't know how to write in English correctly.

In view of the above, we emphasize actual use of the language, rather than the grammar. Taking into account the limited classroom hours and the practical needs of most students, this course mainly focuses on teaching student to read. The book covers a range of topics including communications, signal and information processing, electronic circuits and systems, microwaves, optical fibers, biomedical engineering, computer science, etc. Each unit consists of a text of 2500~3500 words in two or three parts, a vocabulary, some notes on the text, materials for off-classroom reading, and exercises. The exercises are not designed for grammar review, but rather, should be used as a supplement in improving students' reading ability.

It should be noted that, without a substantial amount of reading practice outside the classroom and continuous efforts after this course, only attending the lectures is far from enough for a student to be able to use technical English proficiently. Therefore, students are strongly encouraged to read as much as possible, not confined to the materials in the textbook.

Writing is not the main objective of the course. Nonetheless, we believe that reading proficiency resulting from intensive practical use and a good habit of careful observation while reading will greatly help enhance writing ability. Some notes on technical English writing are included in the Appendix.

This textbook is a result of many years' teaching practice of the authors and all members of the teaching group. The authors wish to express their sincere thanks to Chen Quanlin, Shi Hai, Zhu Qiuyu, Shi Xuli and Li Yingjie for their contributions and invaluable help over the years.

Without doubt, this book needs further improvements. Therefore any comments or recommendations are sincerely welcome and highly appreciated.

Wang Shuozhong, Huang Sujuan, Wu Yating
October 8, 2017

前 言
PREFACE

本教材是为信息科学、通信工程、电子技术、计算机应用等专业的本科生、研究生学习科技英语而编写的。本书选材力求覆盖较广泛的专业方向，注重经典题材和新兴技术，对部分基本原理或新概念提供相关英文辅助资料，以便教师结合课文有选择地用英语讲述一些专业基础知识，或者供学生阅读，使他们在学习科技英语的同时扩大专业知识面。

英语是理工科学生必须掌握的实用工具。然而，不少学生在学了十多年英语以后，仍不能有效地运用英语获取专业知识和科技信息，更不要说用英语进行科技交流了。根据这种情况，结合大学英语教学现状，我们在本书编写中力求改革创新，拒绝应试教学，摒弃从语法到语法、死记硬背的陈旧教学方法，强调大量实践，主张阅读准确性和阅读速度并重，兼顾英语表达能力的提高。

我们认为大学高年级和研究生专业英语教学应以培养和提高英语运用能力为根本目的。学生并不缺少语法知识，而是缺少实践。他们很少甚至没有读过科技英语资料，不掌握丰富的表达形式，缺乏正确的语感。我国学生语法基础普遍较好，但在阅读中往往过分依赖语法分析。他们不了解语法的作用应是内在的和深层的，而不是表面的。依赖语法分析不仅阅读速度上不去，而且即使看懂了句子，读完全文可能还抓不住要点。这种现象相当普遍。实际上，理工科学生学外语并不是为了研究语言，而是要运用语言，因此应以感性认识和反复实践为主，语法知识学习为辅。基于这一认识，我们在课文注释中尽量避免使用语法术语，希望学生在阅读实践中提高阅读能力，最终甩掉语法拐棍。只有这样才能逐步做到顺序阅读而不用回头看，达到理解准确性和阅读速度的统一。

写作不是本教材的重点，但阅读能力的突破以及在阅读中的留心观察，对于写作能力的形成和提高具有关键性的作用。附录中收入了我们在科技英语阅读和写作方面的体会，其中包括一些探索性的研究心得和观点。此外，我们还讨论了普遍存在的中式英语问题，根据大量实例分析了一些典型情况，并就如何克服中式英语提出我们的看法，供读者参考并希望得到专家的指导。

本书是 2008 年版《信息科学与电子工程专业英语》的第 2 版，扩大了适用范围，充实了近年来如物联网、大数据、云计算等热点技术及其应用的内容，力求通过范文的阅读和翻译，培养学生以较高准确性和足够的速度阅读专业资料的能力，同时使学生通过学习科技英语的用词、句型和语言风格，提高专业英语写作和表达的应用能力。

　　本教材反映了教学小组全体教师多年来在教学中积累的经验，编者特别要感谢陈泉林、石海、朱秋煜、石旭利、李颖洁老师所提供的帮助和支持。

　　因编者水平所限，书中不当之处在所难免，敬请读者不吝指正。

编者

2017 年 10 月

Contents

Electronics: Analog and Digital

Unit 1

Signals in electronics may be of two types, analog or digital. Digital instruments are in general more precise than analog ones and they easily transmit information even over very long distances. However, most electronic designs include a combination of both real-world analog signals and digital signals.

Text

Part I: Ideal Operational Amplifiers and Practical Limitations

In order to discuss the ideal parameters of operational amplifiers, we must first define the terms, and then go on to describe what we regard as the ideal values for those terms. At first sight, the specification sheet for an operational amplifier seems to list a large number of values, some in strange units, some interrelated, and often confusing to those unfamiliar with the subject. Without a real appreciation of what each definition means, the designer is doomed to failure. The objective is to be able to design a circuit from the basis of the published data, and know that it will function as predicted when the prototype is constructed.[1] It is all too easy with linear circuits, which appear relatively simple when compared with today's complex logic arrangements, to ignore detailed performance parameters which can drastically reduce the expected performance.[2]

Let us take a very simple but striking example. Consider a requirement for an amplifier having a voltage gain of 10 at 50 kHz driving into a 10 kΩ load.[3] A common low-cost, internally frequency-compensated op amp is chosen; it has the required bandwidth at a closed-loop gain of 10, and it would seem to meet the bill.[4] The device is connected, and it is found to have the correct gain. But it will only produce a few volts output swing when the data clearly shows that the output should be capable of driving to within two or three volts of the power supply.[5] The designer has forgotten that the maximum output voltage swing is severely limited by frequency, and that the maximum low-frequency output swing becomes limited at about 10 kHz. This sort of problem occurs regularly for the inexperienced designer. So the moral is clear: always take the necessary time to write down the full operating requirements before attempting a design. Attention to the detail of the performance specification will always be beneficial. It is suggested the following list of performance details be considered:

- Closed loop gain accuracy, stability with temperature, time and supply voltage.
- Power supply requirements, source and load impedances, power dissipation.
- Input error voltages and bias currents. Input and output resistance, drift with time and temperature.
- Frequency response, phase shift, output swing, transient response, slew rate, frequency stability, capacitive load driving, overload recovery.
- Linearity, distortion and noise.
- Input, output or supply protection required. Input voltage range, common-mode rejection.
- External offset trimming requirement.

Not all of these terms will be relevant, but it is useful to remember that it is better to consider them initially rather than to be forced into retrospective modifications.

All parameters are subject to wide variations

Never forget this fact. How many times has a circuit been designed using typical values, only to find that the circuit does not work because the device used is not typical?[6] The above statement thus poses a tricky question: when should typical values and when should worst-case values be used in the design? This is where the judgment of the experienced designer must be brought to bear. Clearly, if certain performance requirements are mandatory, then worst-case values must be used. In many cases, however, the desirability of a certain defined performance will be a compromise between ease of implementation, degree of importance, and economic considerations.[7]

Do not over-specify or over-design

In the end, we are all controlled by cost. Simplicity is of the essence since the low parts count implementation is invariably cheaper and more reliable.[8]

As an example of this judgment about worst-case design, consider a low-gain DC transducer amplifier required to amplify 10 mV from a voltage source to produce an output of 1 V with an accuracy of ±1% over a temperature range of $0\sim70°C$.[9] Notice that the specification calls for an accuracy of ±1%. This implies that the output should be 1 V ±10 mV from $0\sim70°C$. The first step is, of course, to consider our list above, and decide which of the many parameters are relevant. Two of the most important to this specification are offset voltage drift and gain stability with temperature. We will assume that all initial errors are negligible (rarely the case in practice). The experienced designer would know that most op amps have a very large open-loop gain, usually very much greater than 10000. A closed-loop gain change of ±1% implies that the loop gain (as explained later) should change by less than ±100% for a closed-loop gain of 100.[10] This is clearly so easily fulfilled that the designer knows immediately that he can use typical open-loop gain values in his calculations. However, offset voltage drift is another matter. Many op amp specifications include only typical values for offset voltage drift; this may well be in the order of 5 $\mu V/°C$, with an unquoted maximum for any device of 30 $\mu V/°C$.[11] If by chance we use a device which has this worst-case drift, then the amplifier error could be $30 \times 70 = 2100\mu V = 2.1$ mV over temperature, which is a significant proportion of our total allowable error from all sources.

Part II: Data Registers and Counters

Data register

The simplest type of register is a data register, which is used for the temporary storage of a "word" of data. In its simplest form, it consists of a set of N D flip-flops, all sharing a common clock. All of the digits in the N bit data word are connected to the data register by an N-line "data bus". Figure 1.1 shows a 4 bit data register, implemented with four D flip-flops. The data register is said to be a synchronous device, because all the flip-flops change state at the same time.

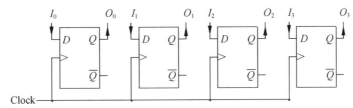

Figure 1.1   Four-bit D register

Shift registers

Another common form of register used in computers and in many other types of logic circuits is a shift register. It is simply a set of flip-flops (usually D latches or RS flip-flops) connected together so that the output of one becomes the input of the next, and so on in series.[1] It is called a shift register because the data is shifted through the register by one bit position on each clock pulse.[2] Figure 1.2 shows a 4 bit shift register, implemented with D flip-flops.

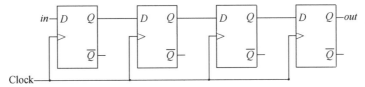

Figure 1.2   Four-bit serial-in serial-out shift register

On the leading edge of the first clock pulse, the signal on the DATA input is latched in the first flip-flop. On the leading edge of the next clock pulse, the contents of the first flip-flop is stored in the second flip-flop, and the signal which is present at the DATA input is stored in the first flip-flop, etc.[3] Because the data is entered one bit at a time, this called a serial-in shift register. Since there is only one output, and data leaves the shift register one bit at a time, then it is also a serial out shift register. (Shift registers are named by their method of input and output; either serial or parallel.) Parallel input can be provided through the use of the preset and clear inputs to the flip-flop. The parallel loading of the flip-flop can be synchronous (i.e., occurs with the clock pulse) or asynchronous (independent of the clock pulse) depending on the design of the shift register.[4] Parallel output can be obtained from the outputs of each flip-flop as shown in Figure 1.3.

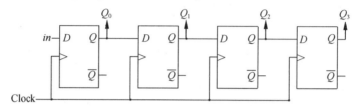

Figure 1.3   Four-bit serial-in parallel-out shift register

Communication between a computer and a peripheral device is usually done serially, while computation in the computer itself is usually performed with parallel logic circuitry. A shift register can be used to convert information from serial form to parallel form, and vice versa. Many different kinds of shift registers are available, depending upon the degree of sophistication required.

Counters — weighted coding of binary numbers

In a sense, a shift register can be considered a counter based on the unary number system. Unfortunately, a unary counter would require a flip-flop for each number in the counting range. A binary weighted counter, however, requires only flip-flops to count to N. A simple binary weighted counter can be made using T flip-flops. The flip-flops are attached to each other in a way so that the output of one acts as the clock for the next, and so on. In this case, the position of the flip-flop in the chain determines its weight; i.e., for a binary counter, the "power of two" it corresponds to.[5] A 3-bit (modulo 8) binary counter could be configured with T flip-flops as shown in Figure 1.4. A timing diagram corresponding to this circuit is shown in Figure 1.5.

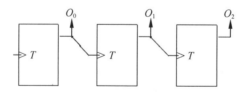

Figure 1.4   Three-bit binary counter

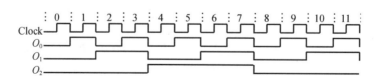

Figure 1.5   Three-bit counter timing diagram

Note that a set of lights attached to O_0, O_1, O_2 would display the numbers of full clock pulses which had been completed, in binary (modulo 8), from the first pulse.[6] As many T flip-flops as required could be combined to make a counter with a large number of digits.

Note that in this counter, each flip-flops changes state on the falling edge of the pulse from the previous flip-flop. Therefore there will be a slight time delay, due to the propagation delay of the flip-flops between the time one flip-flop changes state and the time the next one changes state, i.e., the change of state ripples through the counter, and these counters are therefore called ripple counters.[7] As in the case of a ripple carry adder, the propagation delay can become significant for large counters.

It is possible to make, or buy in a single chip, counters which will count up, count down, and which can be preset to any desired number. Counters can also be constructed which count in BCD and base 12 or any other number base.

A count down counter can be made by connecting the $\overline{Q}$ output to the clock input in the previous counter. By the use of preset and clear inputs, and by gating the output of each T flip flop with another logic level using AND gates (say logic 0 for counting down, logic 1 for counting up), then a presetable up-down binary counter can be constructed.[8] Figure 1.6 shows an up-down counter, without preset or clear.

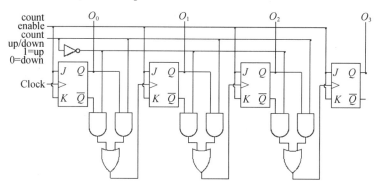

Figure 1.6   Programmable up-down counter*

Synchronous counters

The counters shown previously have been "asynchronous counters"; so called because the flip-flops do not all change state at the same time, but change as a result of a previous output. The output of one flip-flop is the input to the next; the state changes consequently "ripple through" the flip-flops, requiring a time proportional to the length of the counter.[9] It is possible to design synchronous counters, using JK flip-flops, where all flip flops change state at the same time; i.e., the clock pulse is presented to each JK flip-flop at the same time. This can be easily done by noting that, for a binary counter, any given digit changes its value (from 1 to 0 or from 0 to 1) whenever all the previous digits have a value of 1.[10]

---

*　本书所使用英文资料中的电路未改为国标符号。

Figure 1.7 shows an example of a 4-bit binary synchronous counter. A count down timer can be made by connecting the $\overline{Q}$ output to the J and K, through the AND gates. Preset and clear could also be provided, and the counter could be made "programmable" as in the previous case.

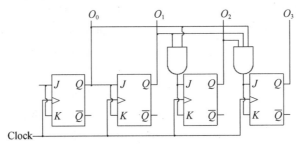

Figure 1.7   Four-bit synchronous counter

The timing diagram is similar to that shown for the asynchronous (ripple) counters, except that the ripple time is now zero; all counters clock at the same time. It is common for synchronous counters to trigger on the positive edge of the clock, rather than the trailing edge.

Part Ⅲ: Nature of Phase Lock

A phase lock loop contains three components (Figure 1.8):
- A phase detector (PD).
- A loop filter.
- A voltage-controlled oscillator (VCO) whose frequency is controlled by an external voltage.

The phase detector compares the phase of a periodic input signal against the phase of the VCO. Output of PD is a measure of the phase difference between its two inputs. The difference voltage is then filtered by the loop filter and applied to the VCO. Control voltage on the VCO changes the frequency in a direction that reduces the phase difference between the input signal and the local oscillator.[1]

When the loop is locked, the control voltage is such that the frequency of the VCO is exactly equal to the average frequency of the input signal.[2] For each cycle of input there is one, and only one, cycle of oscillator output. One obvious application of phase lock is in automatic frequency control (AFC). Perfect frequency control can be achieved by this method, whereas conventional AFC techniques necessarily entail some frequency error.

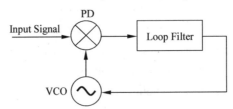

Figure 1.8   Basic phase lock loop

To maintain the control voltage needed for lock it is generally necessary to have a nonzero output from the phase detector. Consequently, the loop operates with some phase error present. As a practical matter, however, this error tends to be small in a well-designed loop.

A slightly different explanation may provide a better understanding of loop operation. Let us suppose that the incoming signal carries information in its phase or frequency; this signal is inevitably corrupted by additive noise. The task of a phase lock receiver is to reproduce the original signal while removing as much of the noise as possible.[3]

To reproduce the signal the receiver makes use of a local oscillator whose frequency is very close to that expected in the signal. Local oscillator and incoming signal waveforms are compared with one another by a phase detector whose error output indicates instantaneous phase difference. To suppress noise the error is averaged over some length of time, and the average is used to establish frequency of the oscillator.

If the original signal is well behaved (stable in frequency), the local oscillator will need very little information to be able to track, and that information can be obtained by averaging for a long period of time, thereby eliminating noise that could be very large.[4] The input to the loop is a noisy signal, whereas the output of the VCO is a cleaned-up version of the input. It is reasonable, therefore, to consider the loop as a kind of filter that passes signals and rejects noise.

Two important characteristics of the filter are that the bandwidth can be very small and that the filter automatically tracks the signal frequency. These features, automatic tracking and narrow bandwidth, account for the major uses of phase lock receivers. Narrow bandwidth is capable of rejecting large amounts of noise; it is not at all unusual for a PLL to recover a signal deeply embedded in noise.

The following applications represent some of the current uses of phase-lock.

(1) One method of tracking moving vehicles involves transmitting a coherent signal to the vehicle, offsetting the signal frequency, and re-transmitting back to the ground. The coherent transponder in the vehicle must operate so that the input and output frequencies are exactly related in the ratio m/n, where m and n are integers. Phase-lock techniques are often used to establish coherence.

(2) A phase-locked loop can be used as a frequency demodulator, in which it has superior performance to a conventional discriminator.

(3) Noisy oscillators can be enclosed in a loop and locked to a clean signal. If the loop has a wide bandwidth, the oscillator tracks out its own noise and its output is greatly cleaned up.

(4) Frequency multipliers and dividers can be built by using PLLs.

(5) Synchronization of digital transmission is typically obtained by phase-lock methods.

(6) Frequency synthesizers are conveniently built by phase-lock loops.

New Words

Part I

operational amplifier	运算放大器	op amp	运放的简写
parameters	参数	specification	指标
objective	目的	doom	注定
drastically	激烈地，彻底地	prototype	原型，样机
gain	增益	striking	惊人的，醒目的
output swing	输出电压变化范围	closed-loop gain	闭环增益
moral	道德，寓意	relevance	有关，适当
dissipation	消耗	impedance	阻抗
resistance	电阻	bias current	偏置电流
transient	瞬态的	drift	漂移
linearity	线性	slew rate*	转换率，斜率
retrospective	回顾的	offset	偏置，补偿
worst-case value	最不利的数值	trimming	微调
desirability	可取性，值得	mandatory	命令的，必需的
offset voltage drift	补偿电压的漂移	transducer	传感器，变换器
unquoted	未注明的	negligible	可忽略的
proportion	比例		

Part II

register	寄存器	shift register	移位寄存器
word of data	数据中的"字"	flip-flop	双稳态触发器
D flip-flop	D 触发器	bus	总线
synchronous	同步的	latch	锁存（器）
in series	串接	clock pulse	时钟脉冲
serial-in serial-out	串进串出	serial-in parallel-out	串进并出
leading edge	（脉冲的）前沿	falling edge	（脉冲的）下降沿
preset	预置	asynchronous	非同步的，异步的
peripheral	外围的，外围设备	parallel logic circuitry	并行逻辑电路
vice versa	反之亦然	sophistication	复杂性
weighted coding	加权编码	binary	二进制的

---

* In electronics, the slew rate represents the maximum rate of change of signal at any point in a circuit. Limitations in slew rate capability can give rise to nonlinear effects in electronic amplifiers. 转换率 (slew rate)：单位时间上升的电压幅度，单位为 V/μs，反映放大器对瞬态信号的跟踪能力，是一种瞬态特性。

unary	一元的	counter	计数器
power of two	2 的幂	modulo	模，取模的
configure	配置	timing diagram	时序图
light	灯	propagation	传播
ripple	波纹，波动，飘动	carry	进位
ripple carry adder	纹波进位加法器	chip	芯片
count up	向上计数	count down	向下计数
BCD*	二-十进制	number base	数制
clear input	清零端	gating	用门电路作逻辑运算
trigger	触发	up-down counter	可逆计数器
programmable	可编程的	trailing edge	后沿，下降沿

Part Ⅲ

detector	检测器，检波器	oscillator	振荡器
entail	引起	instantaneous	瞬时的
additive	相加的，加性的	track	跟踪
suppress	抑制	coherent	相干的
eliminate	消除，淘汰	transponder	应答器，转发器
superior	优越的	discriminator	鉴别器，鉴频器

Notes on the Text

Part I

1. The objective is to be able to design a circuit from the basis of the published data, and know that it will function as predicted when the prototype is constructed.
   目标是能够依据公布的数据设计电路，并知道构建的样机将具有预期的功能。

2. It is all too easy with linear circuits, which appear relatively simple when compared with today's complex logic arrangements, to ignore detailed performance parameters which can drastically reduce the expected performance.
   对于线性电路而言，它们与现在的复杂逻辑电路结构相比看起来较为简单，（因而在设计中）太容易忽视具体的性能参数了，这些参数可极大地削弱预期性能。
   * 本句主要结构：It is easy … to ignore …
   * 两个 which 从句分别修饰 circuits 和 parameters。

3. Consider a requirement for an amplifier having a voltage gain of 10 at 50 kHz driving into a 10 kΩ load.
   考虑对于一个在 50kHz 频率上电压增益为 10 的放大器驱动 10kΩ 负载时的要求。

4. A common low-cost, internally frequency-compensated op amp is chosen; it has the

---

* BCD: binary-coded decimal.

required bandwidth at a closed-loop gain of 10, and it would seem to meet the bill.

选择一个普通的带有内部频率补偿的低价运放，它在闭环增益为 10 时具有所要求的带宽，并且看来满足价格要求。

5. But it will only produce a few volts output swing when the data clearly shows that the output should be capable of driving to within two or three volts of the power supply.

但是它只能产生几伏的输出摆幅，然而数据表却清楚地显示输出应该能驱动达到电源的 2～3V 范围以内（例如供电电压是−10～+10V，则根据数据表输出应能达到−8～+8V 或−7～+7V）。

6. How many times has a circuit been designed using typical values, only to find that the circuit does not work because the device used is not typical?

有多少次是根据典型值设计好电路后却发现只是因为使用的器件不典型而不能工作呢？

7. Clearly, if certain performance requirements are mandatory, then worst-case values must be used. In many cases, however, the desirability of a certain defined performance will be a compromise between ease of implementation, degree of importance, and economic considerations.

显然，如果某些性能要求是强制性的，则一定要用最不利情况下的数值。然而在许多情况下，某一规定性能是否可取将在易实现性、重要性、经济性之间进行平衡。

8. Simplicity is of the essence since the low parts count implementation is invariably cheaper and more reliable.

简单极为重要，因为用较少元器件实现（的电路）必然更便宜也更可靠。

- low parts count implementation：采用零件少的实现方案。low count：低的计数，即数量少。parts：零件。

9. As an example of this judgment about worst-case design, consider a low-gain DC transducer amplifier required to amplify 10 mV from a voltage source to produce an output of 1 V with an accuracy of ±1% over a temperature range of 0～70℃.

作为最不利情况设计的例子，考虑一个低增益直流传感器放大器，要求将电压源输出的 10mV 信号放大，产生 1V 的输出，在 0～70℃范围内达到±1%的精度。

10. A closed-loop gain change of ±1% implies that the loop gain (as explained later) should change by less than ±100% for a closed-loop gain of 100.

闭环增益±1%的变化意味着环路增益（将在下面说明）的变化在闭环增益为 100 时应该小于 ±100%。

11. Many op amp specifications include only typical values for offset voltage drift; this may well be in the order of 5 μV/℃, with an unquoted maximum for any device of 30 μV/℃.

许多运放技术指标仅仅给出补偿电压偏移的典型值，这很可能会在 5 μV/℃的数量级，而未给出任何器件可以达到的最大值 30 μV/℃。

Part Ⅱ

1. It is simply a set of flip-flops (usually D latches or RS flip-flops) connected together so that the output of one becomes the input of the next, and so on in series.

   它就是一组触发器（通常是 D 锁存器或 RS 触发器）联在一起，使得其中一个触发器的输出成为下一个的输入，以此形成一串。

2. It is called a shift register because the data is shifted through the register by one bit position on each clock pulse.

   它被称为移位寄存器，因为数据在每一个时钟脉冲的作用下通过寄存器移动一位。

3. On the leading edge of the next clock pulse, the contents of the first flip-flop is stored in the second flip-flop, and the signal which is present at the DATA input is stored is the first flip-flop, etc.

   在下一个时钟脉冲的前沿，第一个触发器的内容被存放到第二个触发器中，而在数据输入端的信号则存放在第一个触发器中，以此类推。

4. The parallel loading of the flip-flop can be synchronous (i.e., occurs with the clock pulse) or asynchronous (independent of the clock pulse) depending on the design of the shift register.

   触发器的并行加载可以是同步的（即在时钟脉冲到达时发生），或者异步的（不依赖于时钟），取决于移位寄存器的设计。

5. The flip-flops are attached to each other in a way so that the output of one acts as the clock for the next, and so on. In this case, the position of the flip-flop in the chain determines its weight; i.e., for a binary counter, the "power of two" it corresponds to.

   触发器以这样的方式相互连接，使得一个触发器的输出成为下一个的时钟，以此类推。这样，触发器在链中的位置决定了它的权重，即对于二进制计数器而言就是它所对应的 2 的幂。

6. Note that a set of lights attached to Q_1, Q_2, Q_3 would display the numbers of full clock pulses which had been completed, in binary (modulo 8), from the first pulse.

   注意，一组接在 Q_1、Q_2、Q_3 上的灯泡将以二进制（模 8）形式显示从第一个脉冲开始已完成的完整时钟脉冲数。

7. Therefore there will be a slight time delay, due to the propagation delay of the flip-flops between the time one flip-flop changes state and the time the next one changes state, i.e., the change of state ripples through the counter, and these counters are therefore called ripple counters.

   因此将略有时延，这是由一个触发器改变状态到下一个触发器改变状态之间的传播延迟造成的，即状态的变化像波纹一样传过计数器，因而这些计数器被称为波纹计数器。

8. By the use of preset and clear inputs, and by gating the output of each T flip flop with another logic level using AND gates (say logic 0 for counting down, logic 1 for counting up), then a presetable up-down binary counter can be constructed.

利用预置和清零端，通过用与门将每一个 T 触发器的输出与另一个逻辑电平做逻辑运算（例如 0 为向下计数，1 为向上计数），则可构成可预置的可逆二进制计数器。

9. The output of one flip-flop is the input to the next; the state changes consequently "ripple through" the flip-flops, requiring a time proportional to the length of the counter.

一个触发器的输出是下一个的输入，因而状态的变化以波动形式通过各个触发器，所需时间与计数器的长度成正比。

10. This can be easily done by noting that, for a binary counter, any given digit changes its value (from 1 to 0 or from 0 to 1) whenever all the previous digits have a value of 1.

这很容易做到，注意到对于二进制计数器，只要所有前面的数字都是 1，任何给定的数字都会改变它的值（从 1 变为 0，或者从 0 变为 1）。

Part Ⅲ

1. Control voltage on the VCO changes the frequency in a direction that reduces the phase difference between the input signal and the local oscillator.

压控振荡器的控制电压使频率朝着减小输入信号与本地振荡器之间相位差的方向改变。

2. When the loop is locked, the control voltage is such that the frequency of the VCO is exactly equal to the average frequency of the input signal.

当锁相环处于锁定状态时，控制电压使得压控振荡器的频率正好等于输入信号频率的平均值。

3. The task of a phase-lock receiver is to reproduce the original signal while removing as much of the noise as possible.

锁相接收机的作用是重建原信号而尽可能地去除噪声。

4. If the original signal is well behaved (stable in frequency), the local oscillator will need very little information to be able to track, and that information can be obtained by averaging for a long period of time, thereby eliminating noise that could be very large.

如果原信号质量好（频率稳定），本地振荡器只需要极少信息就能实现跟踪，此信息可通过长时间的平均得到，从而消除可能很强的噪声。

Technical Tips

RS flip-flop

The most fundamental latch is the simple RS flip-flop, where S and R stand for set and reset. It can be constructed from a pair of cross-coupled NOR (negative OR) logic gates. The stored bit is present on the output marked Q. Normally, in storage mode, the S and R inputs are both low. If S is pulsed high while R is held low, then the Q output is forced high, and stays high even after S returns low; similarly, if R is pulsed high while S is held low, then the Q output is forced low, and stays low even after R returns low.

S	R	Action
0	0	Keep state
0	1	$Q = 0$
1	0	$Q = 1$
1	1	Unstable combination

JK flip-flop

The JK flip-flop augments the behavior of the RS flip-flop by interpreting the $S = R = 1$ condition as a "flip" or toggle command. Specifically, the combination $J = 1$, $K = 0$ is a command to set the flip-flop; the combination $J = 0$, $K = 1$ is a command to reset the flip-flop; and the combination $J = K = 1$ is a command to toggle the flip-flop, i.e., change its output to the logical complement of its current value. Setting $J = K = 0$ does NOT result in a D flip-flop, but rather, will hold the current state. To synthesize a D flip-flop, simply set K equal to the complement of J.

J	K	Q_{next}	Comment
0	0	Q_{prev}	hold state
0	1	0	reset
1	0	1	set
1	1	$\overline{Q}_{prev}$	toggle

D flip-flop

The Q output always takes on the state of the D input at the moment of a rising clock edge, and never at any other time. It is called the D flip-flop for this reason, since the output takes the value of the D input or Data input, and Delays it by one clock count. The D flip-flop can be interpreted as a primitive memory cell, zero-order hold, or delay line.

Clock	D	Q	Q_{prev}
Rising edge	0	0	X
Rising edge	1	1	X
Non-Rising	X	constant	

Supplementary Readings: Bridging the Gap between the Analog and Digital Worlds

Most applications require the co-existence of analog and digital functionality, and the benefits of combining this functionality on a single chip are significant. Such mixed-signal integration, however, also presents significant challenges. Furthermore, digital and analog developments tend to evolve at differing rates, yet mixed-signal solutions for markets such as industrial, automotive and medical, must remain available over significant time periods. The latest mixed-signal semiconductor processes are helping to address some of these issues, and this article will look at some of the issues designers should consider when specifying integrated mixed-signal solutions.

Mixed-signal solution for the real world

System designers often partition the digital portion from the analog section of a given design for a variety of reasons: the availability of mixing components for the two technologies, the complexity of the digital design or again because of the existence of pure digital processing parts as standard products. Placing the analog elements in an integrated circuit definitively allows the system designer to optimize the costs of its entire module.

This integration approach is usually difficult for advanced markets such as telecommunications or computers, but makes sense for more mature or conservative markets such as automotive, medical and industrial. For most of these mature market's applications, digital functions are finding their way onto what once were pure analog designs. Adding digital functions to an analog design is helped in part by the development of new process technologies that can handle both short-channel, fast-switching digital transistors as well as high-voltage analog transistors. For example, AMI Semiconductor's latest mixed-signal technology offers digital and analog integration capabilities on the same design platform. The I3T technology family is based on standard CMOS 0.35μm, limiting the maximum gate voltage to 3.3V. Some consider this technology outdated, from a pure digital designer's point of view, but it is at the forefront for the automotive, industrial and medical markets.

This list of optional features that enables the design of real SoCs includes high voltage interfacing up to 80V, microprocessing capabilities up to 32 bits, wireless capabilities up to 2.8GHz, and dense logic design up to 15K gates/mm^2. Beside these capabilities, NVM integration is possible: E^{2}PROM up to 4 Kbytes, Flash memory up to half a megabit or On-Time-Programmable (OTP) cells for application calibrations. The ability to integrate all these features on a chip gives the customer the possibility to be independent from the obsolescence of the stand-alone NVM market, which is more or less driven by the computer market. This advantage is quite relevant when we consider the cost of re-qualifying a module for the OEMs in automotive, for instance. It also makes sense when considering the long lifespan of the applications embedded into cars, the industrial environment or medical self-treatment devices where patient cost is an important consideration.

Nevertheless bridging the gap from digital to analog on a single chip does not occur without issues. Clocking noise from high-speed digital circuits, for instance, often interferes with noise-sensitive analog functions. In addition, switching currents from high-power analog functions can interfere with low-voltage digital processors. The goal is to protect low-voltage transistors from the electric field effects of voltages that are 10 to 30 times higher.

Basically, the chip integrates the system functionality from the sensor to the actuator, going through some digital processing. Conventional mixed-signal technology allows analog control and signal processing functions such as amplifiers, analog-to-digital converters (ADCs) and filters to be combined with digital functionality such as microcontrollers, memory, timers and logic control functions on a single, customized chip. All signals that process an algorithm or arithmetic calculation are digital, so conversion of analog to digital signals is mandatory when submitting data for comparison or processing by via a microcontroller, while conversion from digital output signals to analog high-voltage signals is required to drive an actuator or a load. The most recent mixed-signal technology AMIS developed, significantly simplifies the implementation of such driver functionality by allowing much higher voltage functionality to be integrated into an IC alongside the relatively low voltages required for conventional mixed-signal functions. This high-voltage mixed-signal technology is particularly relevant to automotive electronics applications where higher voltage outputs — to drive a motor or actuate a relay — need to be combined with analog signal conditioning functions and complex digital processing.

A growing trend in mixed-signal circuit design is to add some type of central processing circuit to the analog circuits. For many applications the suitable choice of processing intelligence is an 8-bit microcontroller core such as an 8051 or 6502. 8 bits remains the most popular choice as this type of SoC is not intended to replace complex high-end central microcontrollers but more decentralized or slave applications such as sensor conditioning circuitry with local (as close to the sensor as possible) simple intelligence to control relays or motors. An automotive example would be the lateral actuation of a car's headlamps when the steering wheel is turned to improve the driver's safety and improve field of vision. The sensor input would come from the steering angle via a serial link (most of the time with a LIN or I^2C protocol) and the SoC would be close to the motor with an on-board set of algorithms to command the motor's movement.

For higher end applications that require more calculation power, the move to ARM processors is possible. This creates a high-end solution (up to date for the mature markets) which could last over the application's lifespan because the microcontroller would be a small part of an integrated circuit that emulates the module's functionalities.

In order to understand how larger geometries can be better suited for some mixed-signal applications, one needs to understand all of the characteristics involved. Below we will discuss seven key characteristics, however this is by no means comprehensive.

1. Gate and memory size in mixed-signal applications generally drive cost.

Gate and memory size drive cost because most mixed-signal devices are core limited. This can be quite different than an all-digital circuit. Many times, the all-digital device will have so many I/Os that the number of pads on the device determines the periphery and therefore the area. This is rarely the case for mixed-signal devices. For the most part digital cells scale pretty closely to the expected area savings. One would expect a 0.25-micron cell to be 51 percent smaller than a 0.35-micron cell of equivalent function. This is illustrated by the following formula:

$$\text{Size Ratio} = \frac{(0.25)^2}{(0.35)^2} = \frac{0.0625}{0.1225} \approx 51\%$$

While this holds for digital cells we will see that analog cells are quite a different story. Therefore the amount of digital content (including memory) is the key in determining the best technology for the application.

2. Parasitic lessens as the geometry decreases.

This is good news for both the digital and analog designer. Understandably this will translate into high bandwidths and data rates. While the magnitude of the parasitic capacitance per gate or resistance of the interconnection is most assuredly lower as geometry decreases, it is also less predictable. This can cause analog modeling problems and highlights the need for careful understanding of the parasitic.

3. The trans-conductance characteristic is the relationship between a drain current and the voltage across the gate and source.

As the geometry decreases the trans-conductance gets higher. This is good news for both analog and digital domains in that smaller conductance interacts with capacitance to create smaller bandwidths and therefore lower data rates.

It is well understood that as geometry decreases the voltage limits of the device decrease as well. In the pure digital world this is beneficial in several ways: less power and less radiated emissions. The only downside is the need for multiple voltage rails on most digital circuits. In the analog domain, the power savings is there but reduced range of operation makes the design task harder. It is quite common for analog designers to bias their circuits at $V_T + 2V_{on}$ and $V_{dd} - (V_T + 2V_{on})$. Unfortunately, the threshold voltage, V_T, does not scale with the geometry. In other words, the operating range of voltages gets smaller as the technology shrinks. This means the analog portions of a circuit must be more tightly controlled which translates to larger, better matched transistors.

4. Channel resistance gets lower as the technology shrinks.

While this may sound like a good thing, and for digital circuits it generally is, this translates to transistors with lower gain in the analog domain. Lower gain may mean more stages in the circuit.

5. The linearity of smaller geometries also becomes a factor in analog designs.

Often non-linearity problems are solved by increasing the size of the circuit. An example of this can be seen in D/A and A/D converters where the performance of the converter is very much proportional to the size of the circuit.

6. Noise in circuits implemented in smaller technologies can cause problems for analog designers.

This is usually worsened by the fact that there is usually a large and fast digital circuit that is generating much of the noise. The smaller operating voltage range works against the designer as well. Signal to noise ratio in the analog circuit gets worse because the signal levels go down but the noise levels may actually go up.

7. Analog circuit modeling in smaller geometries is problematic.

Much of this is due to the lower levels of predictability and the nature of the parasitic. Some of it is due to the maturity of the technology as well. This, of course, will improve as the technology develops.

Because of these items listed above it is important to understand that as the process geometry shrinks, the analog actually gets bigger, and definitely harder. This has to be compensated by increasing the sizes of the transistors, capacitors and resistors used. Moving to smaller technologies should only be done when the performance requirements of the application demand it. For most mixed-signal SoC devices this will be driven by the digital gate count and the amount of memory in the design. Only when there is significant digital content should you consider smaller technologies.

Conclusion

The latest generation of mixed-signal process technologies has moved well into the deep sub-micron world where adding digital circuits and cores to an analog ASIC has become a cost-effective approach.

With the addition of digital process capability and the digital processing horsepower that becomes available, many analog functions are being converted to digital signals earlier in the signal path. The advantage of this approach is that digital filters and digital control elements are not sensitive to drift inaccuracies caused by aging, process changes or temperature changes. The result is a much more robust design than an analog-only approach.

Exercises

I. Translate the following sentences into Chinese.

1. As with series resonance, the greater the resistance in the circuit the lower the Q and, accordingly, the flatter and broader the resonance curve of either line current or circuit impedance.

2. A wire carrying a current looks exactly the same and weighs exactly the same as it does when it is not carrying a current.

3. Click mouse on the waveform and drag it to change the pulse repetition rate, or directly enter a new value of the period in the provided dialogue box, while keeping the pulse width unchanged.

4. Electronics is the science and the technology of the passage of charged particles in a gas, in a vacuum, or in a semiconductor. Please note that particle motion confined within a metal only is not considered electronics.

5. Hardware technologies have played vital roles in our ability to use electronic properties to process information, but software and data processing aspects have not developed at the same speed.

6. However, in a properly designed DC amplifier the effect of transistor parameter variation, other than Ico, may be practically eliminated if the operation point of each stage is adjusted so that it remains in the linear operation range of the transistor as temperature varies.

Ⅱ. **Fill in the blanks with the most appropriate choice.**

1. A message signal can _____ any amplitude value between 0 and A volts.

    A. assume   B. use   C. receive   D. accept

2. Each time a positive clock edge occurs, the flip-flop changes state, leading to half as many pulses at the output _____ to the clock input.

    A. as   B. compared   C. due   D. so as

3. In the previous section we discussed sine-wave or CW modulation systems in which the modulating signal _____ of a digital pulse train.

    A. made   B. consisted   C. contained   D. got

4. In this book we shall emphasize the limitations imposed on the information transmitted by the system through which it was _____ and shall attempt some comparison of different systems.

    A. put   B. traveled   C. passed   D. viewed

5. This signal either does not change, or it changes _____ by an amount equivalent to one or more quantum steps.

    A. interruptedly   B. rudely   C. abruptly   D. absolutely

6. We shall only be _____ with logical representations, not absolute values

    A. interested   B. caring   C. referred   D. concerned

Ⅲ. **Choose the phrase that is closest in meaning to the underlined part.**

1. It is all too easy with linear circuits, which appear relatively simple when compared with today's complex logic arrangements, to ignore detailed performance parameters which can drastically reduce the expected performance.

    A. which has bad influence upon the system performance

    B. which is important to ensure circuit linearity

    C. which is possible to enhance the system performance

    D. which is crucial for maintaining the desired performance

2. Therefore there will be a slight time delay, due to the propagation delay of the flip-flops between the time one flip-flop changes state and the time the next one changes state, i.e., the change of state ripples through the counter, and these counters are therefore called ripple counters.

    A. the state change is propagated through the counter like ripples

    B. the state changes cause ripples in the counter

C. passing through the counter, the state ripple changes

D. the state of the counter changes due to ripples

3. Instead of triggering on each pulse, a phase lock technique <u>examines the relative phase between each oscillator and many of its sync pulses</u> and adjusts oscillator frequency so that the average phase discrepancy is small.

A. checks each oscillator for many sync pulses

B. checks the phase relationship between individual oscillators and a collection of sync pulses

C. looks at the relations between the phase and the sync pulses

D. examines whether the phase is relative to the oscillator and the sync pulses

4. By <u>keeping the off state slightly below threshold</u>, the delay between the applied electrical pulse and the resulting optical output pulse is minimized; this delay must indeed not be more than the bit interval so that the optical pulse can accurately reproduce the input signal.

A. ensuring that the system is off the threshold by a small margin

B. maintaining the system's shut-down state somewhat below a prescribed level

C. making sure the system is below its threshold so that the state is kept off

D. keeping the system in a shut-down state that is under a given level with a tiny tolerance

5. If the original signal is well behaved, <u>the local oscillator will need very little information to be able to track</u>, and that information can be obtained by averaging for a long period of time, thereby eliminating noise that could be very large.

A. the LO will not require any information in order to keep tracking

B. the LO will make use of tracking information that is scarce in the system

C. the LO will require some information, but not much, so that the system can track

D. the LO will use no information other than some little one to maintain tracking

6. The third section describes quantization schemes that <u>take account of the characteristics of speech</u>.

A. take measure of the speech characteristics

B. take the speech characteristics into consideration

C. count the speech characteristics

D. make use of the speech characteristics

7. In a properly designed DC amplifier <u>the effect of transistor parameter variation</u> may be practically eliminated if the operating point of each stage is adjusted so that it remains in the linear operation range of the transistor as temperature varies.

A. the effective variation of the transistor parameters

B. the effort to change transistor parameters

C. the transistor parameters that effectively change

D. the results caused by transistor parameter changes

8. Stability and repeatability are fundamental attributes of digital circuits, however, and the necessary accuracy can be obtained in a digital version of the modulator <u>by an appropriate choice of word length to represent the signals</u>.

A. by expressing the signals with a suitable word length

B. by using a word long enough to describe the signals

C. by choose to characterize the signals in terms of word length appropriately

D. by appropriately representing the signals to choose a length of words

Integrated Circuits

The idea of putting transistors and other electronics wired together on a single chip was first conceived almost half century ago. This has been proven to initiate a revolution with far-reaching influences on the way of our life. With nearly a billion transistors on the latest microprocessor, it is predicted that several times as many transistors on a chip are theoretically possible in the foreseeable future.

Text

Part I: The Integrated Circuit

Digital logic and electronic circuits derive their functionality from electronic switches called transistor. Roughly speaking, the transistor can be likened to an electronically controlled valve whereby energy applied to one connection of the valve enables energy to flow between two other connections.[1] By combining multiple transistors, digital logic building blocks such as AND gates and flip-flops are formed. Transistors, in turn, are made from semiconductors. Consult a periodic table of elements in a college chemistry textbook, and you will locate semiconductors as a group of elements separating the metals and nonmetals.[2] They are called semiconductors because of their ability to behave as both metals and nonmetals. A semiconductor can be made to conduct electricity like a metal or to insulate as a nonmetal does. These differing electrical properties can be accurately controlled by mixing the semiconductor with small amounts of other elements. This mixing is called doping. A semiconductor can be doped to contain more electrons (N-type) or fewer electrons (P-type). Examples of commonly used semiconductors are silicon and germanium. Phosphorous and boron are two elements that are used to dope N-type and P-type silicon, respectively.[3]

A transistor is constructed by creating a sandwich of differently doped semiconductor layers. The two most common types of transistors, the bipolar-junction transistor (BJT) and the field-effect transistor (FET) are schematically illustrated in Figure 2.1. This figure shows both the silicon structures of these elements and their graphical symbolic representation as would be seen in a circuit diagram. The BJT shown is an NPN transistor, because it is composed of a sandwich of N-P-N doped silicon. When a small current is injected into the base terminal, a larger current is enabled to flow from the collector to the emitter. The FET shown is an N-channel FET, which is composed of two N-type regions separated by a P-type substrate. When a voltage is applied to the insulated gate terminal, a current is enabled to flow from the drain to the source. It is called N-channel, because the gate voltage induces an N-channel within the substrate, enabling current to flow between the N-regions.

Another basic semiconductor structure shown in Figure 2.1 is a diode, which is formed simply by a junction of N-type and P-type silicon. Diodes act like one-way valves by conducting current only from P to N. Special diodes can be created that emit light when a voltage is applied. Appropriately enough, these components are called light emitting diodes, or LEDs. These small lights are manufactured by the millions and are found in diverse applications from telephones to traffic lights.

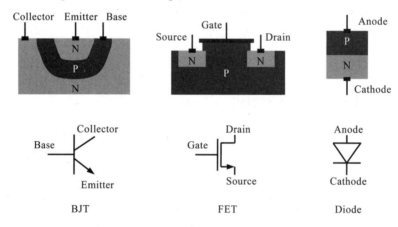

Figure 2.1   BJT, FET, and diode structural and symbolic representation

The resulting small chip of semiconductor material on which a transistor or diode is fabricated can be encased in a small plastic package for protection against damage and contamination from the outside world.[4] Small wires are connected within this package between the semiconductor sandwich and pins that protrude from the package to make electrical contact with other parts of the intended circuit. Once you have several discrete transistors, digital logic can be built by directly wiring these components together. The circuit will function, but any substantial amount of digital logic will be very bulky, because several transistors are required to implement each of the various types of logic gates.

At the time of the invention of the transistor in 1947 by John Bardeen, Walter Brattain, and William Shockley, the only way to assemble multiple transistors into a single circuit was to buy separate discrete transistors and wire them together. In 1959, Jack Kilby and Robert Noyce independently invented a means of fabricating multiple transistors on a single slab of semiconductor material. Their invention would come to be known as the integrated circuit, or IC, which is the foundation of our modern computerized world. An IC is so called because it integrates multiple transistors and diodes onto the same small semiconductor chip. Instead of having to solder individual wires between discrete components, an IC contains many small components that are already wired together in the desired topology to form a circuit.

A typical IC, without its plastic or ceramic package, is a square or rectangular silicon die measuring from 2 to 15 mm on an edge. Depending on the level of technology used to manufacture the IC, there may be anywhere from a dozen to tens of millions of individual transistors on this small chip. This amazing density of electronic components indicates that the transistors and the wires that connect them are extremely small in size. Dimensions on an IC are measured in units of micrometers, with one micrometer (1μm) being one millionth of a meter. To serve as a reference point, a human hair is roughly 100μm in diameter. Some modern ICs contain components and wires that are measured in increments as small as 0.1μm! Each year, researchers and engineers have been finding new ways to steadily reduce these feature sizes to pack more transistors into the same silicon area, as indicated in Figure 2.2. The era of "easy" scaling is over. We are now in a period where technology and device innovations are required. Beyond 2020, new currently unknown inventions will be required.

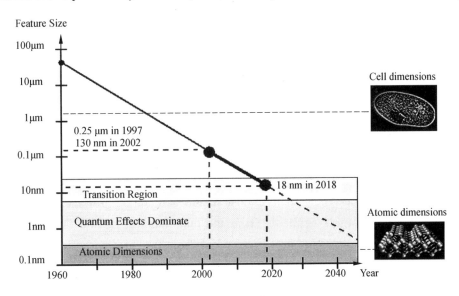

Figure 2.2　Device scaling over time

When an IC is designed and fabricated, it generally follows one of two main transistor technologies: bipolar or metal-oxide semiconductor (MOS). Bipolar processes create BJTs, whereas MOS processes create FETs. Bipolar logic was more common before the 1980s, but MOS technologies have since accounted the great majority of digital logic ICs. N-channel FETs are fabricated in an NMOS process, and P-channel FETs are fabricated in a PMOS process. In the 1980s, complementary-MOS, or CMOS, became the dominant process technology and remains so to this day. CMOS ICs incorporate both NMOS and PMOS transistors.

Part II: Application Specific Integrated Circuit

An application-specific integrated circuit (ASIC) is an integrated circuit (IC) customized for a particular use, rather than intended for general-purpose use. For example, a chip designed solely to run a cell phone is an ASIC. In contrast, the 7400 series and 4000 series integrated circuits are logic building blocks that can be wired together for use in many different applications.

As feature sizes have shrunk and design tools improved over the years, the maximum complexity (and hence functionality) possible in an ASIC has grown from 5,000 gates to over 100 million.[1] Modern ASICs often include entire 32-bit processors, memory blocks including ROM, RAM, EEPROM, Flash and other large building blocks. Such an ASIC is often termed a SoC (System-on-Chip). Designers of digital ASICs use a hardware description language (HDL), such as Verilog or VHDL, to describe the functionality of ASICs.

Field-programmable gate arrays (FPGA) are the modern day equivalent of 7400 series logic and a breadboard, containing programmable logic blocks and programmable interconnects that allow the same FPGA to be used in many different applications. For smaller designs and/or lower production volumes, FPGAs may be more cost effective than an ASIC design. The non-recurring engineering cost (the cost to setup the factory to produce a particular ASIC) can run into hundreds of thousands of dollars.[2]

The general term application specific integrated circuit includes FPGAs, but most designers use ASIC only for non-field programmable devices and make a distinction between ASIC and FPGAs.[3]

Standard cell design

In the mid 1980s a designer would choose an ASIC manufacturer and implement their design using the design tools available from the manufacturer. While third party design tools were available, there was not an effective link from the third party design tools to the layout and actual semiconductor process performance characteristics of the various ASIC manufacturers.[4] Most designers ended up using factory specific tools to complete the implementation of their designs. A solution to this problem that also yielded a much higher density device was the implementation of Standard Cells. Every ASIC manufacturer could create functional blocks with known electrical characteristics, such as propagation delay, capacitance and inductance; that could also be represented in third party tools.[5] Standard cell design is the utilization of these functional blocks to achieve very high gate density and good electrical performance. Standard cell design fits between Gate Array and Full Custom design in terms of both its NRE (Non-Recurring Engineering) and recurring component cost.[6]

By the late 1980s, logic synthesis tools, such as Design Compiler, became available. Such tools could compile HDL descriptions into a gate-level netlist. This enabled a style of design called standard-cell design. Standard-cell Integrated Circuits (ICs) are designed in the following conceptual stages, although these stages overlap significantly in practice.

These steps, implemented with a level of skill common in the industry, almost always produce a final device that correctly implements the original design, unless flaws are later introduced by the physical fabrication process.[7]

A team of design engineers starts with a non-formal understanding of the required functions for a new ASIC, usually derived from requirements analysis.

- The design team constructs a description of an ASIC to achieve these goals using an HDL. This process is analogous to writing a computer program in a high-level language. This is usually called the RTL (register transfer level) design.
- Suitability for purpose is verified by simulation. A virtual system created in software, using a tool such as Virtutech's Simics, can simulate the performance of ASICs at speeds up to billions of simulated instructions per second.
- A logic synthesis tool, such as Design Compiler, transforms the RTL design into a large collection of lower-level constructs called standard cells. These constructs are taken from a standard-cell library consisting of pre-characterized collections of gates such as 2 input nor, 2 input nand, inverters, etc.[8] The standard cells are typically specific to the planned manufacturer of the ASIC. The resulting collection of standard cells, plus the needed electrical connections between them, is called a gate-level netlist.
- The gate-level netlist is next processed by a placement tool which places the standard cells onto a region representing the final ASIC. It attempts to find a placement of the standard cells, subject to a variety of specified constraints.
- The routing tool takes the physical placement of the standard cells and uses the netlist to create the electrical connections between them. Since the search space is large, this process will produce a "sufficient" rather than "globally-optimal" solution. The output is a set of photomasks enabling semiconductor fabrication to produce physical ICs.
- Close estimates of final delays, parasitic resistances and capacitances, and power consumptions can then be made. In the case of a digital circuit, this will be further mapped into delay information. These estimates are used in a final round of testing. This testing demonstrates that the device will function correctly over all extremes of the process, voltage and temperature. When this testing is complete the photomask information is released for chip fabrication.

These design steps (or flow) are also common to standard product design. The significant difference is that Standard Cell design uses the manufacturer's cell libraries that have been used in hundreds of other design implementations and therefore are of much lower risk than full custom design.[9]

Gate array design

Gate array design is a manufacturing method in which the diffused layers, i.e. transistors and other active devices, are predefined and wafers containing such devices are held in stock prior to metallization, in other words, unconnected.[10] The physical design process then defines the interconnections of the final device. It is important to the designer that minimal propagation delays can be achieved in ASICs versus the FPGA solutions available in the marketplace. Gate array ASIC is a compromise as mapping a given design onto what a manufacturer held as a stock wafer never gives 100% utilization.[11]

Pure, logic-only gate array design is rarely implemented by circuit designers today, replaced almost entirely by field programmable devices such as FPGAs, which can be programmed by the user and thus offer minimal tooling charges, marginally increased piece part cost and comparable performance.[12] Today gate arrays are evolving into structured ASICs that consist of a large IP core* like a processor, DSP unit, peripherals, standard interfaces, integrated memories SRAM, and a block of reconfigurable uncommitted logic.[13] This shift is largely because ASIC devices are capable of integrating such large blocks of system functionality and "system on a chip" requires far more than just logic blocks.

Full-custom design

The benefits of full-custom design usually include reduced area, performance improvements and also the ability to integrate analog components and other pre-designed components such as microprocessor cores that form a System-on-Chip. The disadvantages can include increased manufacturing and design time, increased non-recurring engineering costs, more complexity in the CAD system and a much higher skill requirement on the part of the design team.[14] However for digital only designs, "standard-cell" libraries together with modern CAD systems can offer considerable performance/cost benefits with low risk. Automated layout tools are quick and easy to use and also offer the possibility to manually optimize any performance limiting aspect of the design.

Structured design

Structured ASIC design is an ambiguous expression, with different meanings in different contexts. This is a relatively new term in the industry, which is why there is some variation in its definition. However, the basic premise of a structured ASIC is that both manufacturing cycle time and design cycle time are reduced compared to cell-based ASIC by virtue of there being pre-defined metal layers and pre-characterization of what is on the silicon.[15] One definition states that, in a structured ASIC design, the logic mask-layers of a device are predefined by the ASIC vendor (or in some cases by a third party). Structured ASIC technology is seen as bridging the gap between field-programmable gate arrays and

---

* IP core: intellectual property core，预先设计好的硬件或软件内核。

"standard-cell" ASIC designs.

What makes a structured ASIC different from a gate array is that in a gate array the predefined metal layers serve to make manufacturing turnaround faster. In a structured ASIC the predefined metallization is primarily to reduce cost of the mask sets and is also used to make the design cycle time significantly shorter as well. Likewise, the design tools used for structured ASIC can substantially lower cost, and are easier to use than cell-based tools, because the tools do not have to perform all the functions that cell-based tools do.

One other important aspect about structured ASIC is that it allows IP that is common to certain applications to be "built in", rather than "designed in". By building the IP directly into the architecture the designer can again save both time and money compared to designing IP into a cell-based ASIC.

New Words

Part I

transistor	晶体管	valve	阀
flip-flop	触发器，	insulate	绝缘，隔离
	双稳态多谐振荡器	doping	掺杂（质）
silicon	硅	germanium	锗
phosphorous	磷的	boron	硼
bipolar	有两极的，双极的	field-effect	场效应
base	基极	collector	集电极
emitter	发射极	gate	栅极
drain	漏极	source	源极
diode	二极管	protrude	突出
slab	厚片，板层	solder	焊接，焊料
topology	拓扑，布局	ceramic	陶瓷
die	印模，模子	complementary	互补的，补充的

Part II

Application-Specific		customize	定制
Integrated Circuit	专用集成电路 (ASIC)	cell phone	蜂窝式电话
feature size	特征尺寸	functionality	功能
SoC (System on Chip)	片上系统	Hardware	
		Description	
Field-Programmable		Language (HDL)	硬件描述语言
Gate Array (FPGA)	现场可编程门阵列	breadboard	面包板
recurring	循环的	non-field	

generalized	通用化	programmable	非现场可编程的
propagation delay	传播延迟	layout	布局，布线
inductance	电感	capacitance	电容
netlist	电子设计中的联接性	synthesis	合成
analogous	类似的，相似的	flaw	缺陷，瑕疵
nand	与非	virtual system	虚拟系统
constraint	约束条件	nor	或非
routing	路由，联线	placement	放置
parasitic	寄生的	resistance	电阻
diffuse	扩散	active device	有源器件
wafer	晶片，薄酥饼	metallization	金属化
perpendicular	垂直的	marginally	有限度地
tooling	工具作业	peripheral	外围设备
reconfigurable	可重新设置的	uncommitted	未指定的，不受约束的
ambiguous	模糊的	premise	前提
by virtue of ...	凭借……		
vendor	供应商		

Notes on the Text

Part I

1. Roughly speaking, the transistor can be likened to an electronically controlled valve whereby energy applied to one connection of the valve enables energy to flow between two other connections.

   粗略地说，晶体管好似一种电子控制阀，由此加在阀一端的能量（电压）可以使能量（电流）在另外两个端之间流动。

2. Consult a periodic table of elements in a college chemistry textbook, and you will locate semiconductors as a group of elements separating the metals and nonmetals.

   查阅大学化学书中的元素周期表，你会查到半导体是介于金属与非金属之间的一类元素。

3. Phosphorous and boron are two elements that are used to dope N-type and P-type silicon, respectively.

   N 型硅半导体掺入磷元素，而 P 型硅半导体掺入硼元素。

4. The resulting small chip of semiconductor material on which a transistor or diode is fabricated can be encased in a small plastic package for protection against damage and contamination from the outside world.

   半导体材料上制作晶体管或二极管所形成的小芯片用塑料封装以防损伤和被外界污染。

Part II

1. As feature sizes have shrunk and design tools improved over the years, the maximum complexity (and hence functionality) possible in an ASIC has grown from 5000 gates to over 100 million.

   随着特征尺寸的逐年缩小和设计工具的改进，ASIC 中的最大复杂度从 5000 个门电路增长到了 1 亿个门电路，因而功能也有了极大的提高。

2. The non-recurring engineering cost (the cost to setup the factory to produce a particular ASIC) can run into hundreds of thousands of dollars.

   不能循环的工程费用（建立工厂生产特定 ASIC 的成本）可能会达到数十万美元。

3. The general term application specific integrated circuit includes FPGAs, but most designers use ASIC only for non-field programmable devices and make a distinction between ASIC and FPGAs.

   专用集成电路这一通用名词也包括 FPGA，但是大多数设计者仅将 ASIC 用于非现场可编程的器件，将 ASIC 和 FPGA 两者区别开来。

4. While third party design tools were available, there was not an effective link from the third party design tools to the layout and actual semiconductor process performance characteristics of the various ASIC manufacturers.

   尽管有第三方设计工具，但第三方设计工具和不同的 ASIC 制造商的布线以及实际半导体工艺过程的性能之间却缺乏有效的联系。

5. Every ASIC manufacturer could create functional blocks with known electrical characteristics, such as propagation delay, capacitance and inductance; that could also be represented in third party tools.

   每个 ASIC 制造商都可以创造他们自己的具有已知电性能的功能块，如传播延迟器、电容、电感，这些都可以用第三方工具来表示（实现）。

6. Standard cell design fits between Gate Array and Full Custom design in terms of both its NRE (Non-Recurring Engineering) and recurring component cost.

   标准单元设计使门阵列和全定制设计之间在一次性投入的工程费用和循环元件成本方面相互适应。

   - Non-recurring engineering (NRE) refers to the one-time cost of researching, designing, and testing a new product.

7. These steps, implemented with a level of skill common in the industry, almost always produce a final device that correctly implements the original design, unless flaws are later introduced by the physical fabrication process.

   以工业界普通的熟练水平实现的这些步骤几乎总是产生能正确实现原设计的最终器件，除非后来在物理制造过程中引入了缺陷。

8. These constructs are taken from a standard-cell library consisting of pre-characterized collections of gates such as 2 input nor, 2 input nand, inverters, etc.

   这些构成的元素是从一个标准单元库中得到的，这个库由事先规定好的门电路集合构成，例如 2 输入或非门、2 输入与非门、非门等。

9. The significant difference is that Standard Cell design uses the manufacturer's cell libraries that have been used in hundreds of other design implementations and therefore are of much lower risk than full custom design.

重要的差别在于标准单元设计使用制造商的单元库，这些库已用于数以百计的设计实现，因而比起全定制设计来风险小得多。

10. Gate array design is a manufacturing method in which the diffused layers, i.e. transistors and other active devices, are predefined and wafers containing such devices are held in stock prior to metallization, in other words, unconnected.

门阵列设计是一种制造方法，事先定义好扩散层（晶体管和其他有源器件），包含这些器件的晶片在金属化之前被库存，也就是说先不进行连接。

11. Gate array ASIC is a compromise as mapping a given design onto what a manufacturer held as a stock wafer never gives 100% utilization.

门阵列 ASIC 是一种折中方案，因为将某一给定的设计与制造商库存的晶片相对应总是不可能达到 100% 利用率的。

- as mapping … never gives … 表示原因。

12. Pure, logic-only gate array design is rarely implemented by circuit designers today, replaced almost entirely by field programmable devices such as FPGAs, which can be programmed by the user and thus offer minimal tooling charges, marginally increased piece part cost and comparable performance.

现在电路设计者已经很少采用纯粹的逻辑门阵列设计，而几乎都代之以 FPGA 之类的现场可编程器件了。这些器件可由用户编程，使工具作业费用最低，以略为提高的零件价格获得可比的性能。

13. Today gate arrays are evolving into structured ASICs that consist of a large IP core like a processor, DSP unit, peripherals, standard interfaces, integrated memories SRAM, and a block of reconfigurable uncommitted logic.

现在门阵列正在发展为结构化 ASIC，其中包含很大的 IP 内核，如处理器、DSP 单元、外围设备、标准接口、集成 SRAM 存储器以及一组可重新设置的未确定功能的逻辑单元。

- IP core (intellectual property core): 预先设计好、可复用、有知识产权的硬件或软件块。

14. The disadvantages can include increased manufacturing and design time, increased non-recurring engineering costs, more complexity in the CAD system and a much higher skill requirement on the part of the design team.

缺点包括增加的制造和设计时间，增加的不可循环工程成本，更复杂的 CAD 系统，以及对设计团队熟练程度高得多的要求。

15. However, the basic premise of a structured ASIC is that both manufacturing cycle time and design cycle time are reduced compared to cell-based ASIC by virtue of there being pre-defined metal layers and pre-characterization of what is on the silicon.

不过结构化 ASIC 的基本前提是，由于有事先定义的金属层和事先规定了硅片上包含的内容，制造周期和设计周期相对于基于单元的 ASIC 都有所减少。

Technical Tips

SoC

System on chip (SoC) is an idea of integrating all components of a computer or other electronic system into a single integrated circuit (chip). It may contain digital, analog, mixed-signal, and often radio frequency functions—all on one chip. A typical application is in the area of embedded systems. A typical SoC consists of the following components connected by either a proprietary or industry-standard bus such as the AMBA bus from ARM.

- One or more microcontroller, microprocessor or DSP core(s).
- Memory blocks including a selection of ROM, RAM, EEPROM and Flash.
- Timing sources including oscillators and phase-locked loops.
- Peripherals including counter-timers, real-time timers and power-on reset generators.
- External interfaces including industry standards such as USB, FireWire, Ethernet, USART, SPI.
- Analog interfaces including ADCs and DACs.
- Voltage regulators and power management circuits.

Netlist

The word netlist can be used in several different domains, but perhaps the most popular is in the electronic design domain. In this domain, a "netlist" describes the connectivity of an electronic design.

Netlists usually convey connectivity information and provide nothing more than instances, nets, and perhaps some attributes. If they express much more than this, they are usually considered to be a hardware description language such as Verilog, VHDL, or any one of several specific languages designed for input to simulators. Netlists can be either physical or logical; either instance-based or net-based; and flat or hierarchical. The latter can be either folded or unfolded.

Supplementary Readings

1. Integrated Circuits: the Past and the Future

As with many inventions, two people had the idea for an integrated circuit at almost the same time. Transistors had become commonplace in everything from radios to phones to computers, and now manufacturers wanted something even better. Sure, transistors were smaller than vacuum tubes, but for some of the newest electronics, they weren't small enough.

But there was a limit on how small you could make each transistor, since after it was made it had to be connected to wires and other electronics. The transistors were already at the limit of what steady hands and tiny tweezers could handle. So, scientists wanted to make a whole circuit — the transistors, the wires, everything else they needed — in a single blow. If they could create a miniature circuit in just one step, all the parts could be made much smaller.

One day in late July of 1958, Jack Kilby was sitting alone at Texas Instruments. It suddenly occurred to him that all parts of a circuit, not just the transistor, could be made out of silicon. At the time, nobody was making capacitors or resistors out of semiconductors. If it could be done then the entire circuit could be built out of a single crystal — making it smaller and much easier to produce. By September 12, Kilby had built a working model, and on February 6, Texas Instruments filed a patent. Their first "Solid Circuit" the size of a pencil point, was shown off for the first time in March.

But over in California, another man had similar ideas. In January of 1959, Robert Noyce was working at the small Fairchild Semiconductor startup company. He also realized a whole circuit could be made on a single chip. That spring, Fairchild began a push to build what they called "unitary circuits" and they also applied for a patent on the idea. Knowing that TI had already filed a patent on something similar, Fairchild wrote out a highly detailed application, hoping that it wouldn't infringe on TI's similar device.

All that detail paid off. On April 25, 1961, the patent office awarded the first patent for an integrated circuit to Robert Noyce while Kilby's application was still being analyzed. Today, both men are acknowledged as having independently conceived of the idea.

Today's predictions also say that there is a limit to just how much the transistor can do. This time around, the predictions are that transistors can't get substantially smaller than they currently are. Then again, in 1961, scientists predicted that no transistor on a chip could ever be smaller than 10 millionths of a meter — and on a modern Intel Pentium chip they are 100 times smaller than that.

With hindsight, such predictions seem ridiculous, and it's easy to think that current predictions will sound just as silly thirty years from now. But modern predictions of the size limit are based on some very fundamental physics — the size of the atom and the electron. Since transistors run on electric current, they must always, no matter what, be at least big enough to allow electrons through.

On the other hand, all that's really needed is a single electron at a time. A transistor small enough to operate with only one electron would be phenomenally small, yet it is theoretically possible. The transistors of the future could make modern chips seem as big and bulky as vacuum tubes seem to us today. The problem is that once devices become that tiny, everything moves according to the laws of quantum mechanics — and quantum mechanics allows electrons to do some weird things. In a transistor that small, the electron would act more like a wave than a single particle. As a wave it would smear out in space, and could even tunnel its way through the transistor without truly acting on it.

Researchers are nevertheless currently working on innovative ways to build such tiny devices — abandoning silicon, abandoning all of today's manufacturing methods. Such transistors are known, not surprisingly, as single electron transistors, and they'd be considered "on" or "off" depending on whether they were holding an electron. In fact, such a tiny device might make use of the quantum weirdness of the ultra-small. The electron could be coded to have three positions — instead of simply "on" or "off" it could also have "somewhere between on and off." This would open up doors for entirely new kinds of computers. At the moment, however, there are no effective single electron transistors.

Even without new technologies, there's room for miniaturization. Moore's law continues and transistors double every two years toward the billion-transistor microprocessor. Chips like this would allow computers to be much "smarter" than they currently are.

2. A Top-Down Approach to IC Design

The challenges facing the electronics design community today are significant. Advances in semiconductor technology have increased the speed and complexity of designs in tandem with growing time-to-market pressures. The companies that have remained competitive are those that are able to adapt to changing methodology requirements and develop a broad range of products quickly and accurately.

Successful product development environments (PDEs) streamline the design process by creating the best practices involving people, process, and technology. Developing these best practices is based on a thorough understanding of the needed design methods and how to apply them to the system project. This document reviews the basic principles of top-down design for ASIC and FPGA-intensive systems, and provides guidelines for developing best practices based on both semiconductor and EDA technology advances.

The strategy of most successful PDEs is to build advanced, high quality products based on a system platform architecture that effectively incorporates leading-edge hardware and software algorithms as well as core technology. This strategy provides integration density, performance, and packaging advantages and enables product differentiation in features, functions, size, and cost. In most cases, to fully exploit these opportunities, this strategy requires a transition from a serial or bottom-up product development approach to top-down design.

In a bottom-up design approach, the design team starts by partitioning the system design into various subsystem and system components (blocks). The subsystems are targeted to ASICs, FPGAs, or microprocessors. Since these subsystem designs are usually on the critical path to completing the design, the team starts on these immediately, developing the other system components in parallel. Each block is designed and verified based on its requirements. When all blocks are complete, system verification begins.

The bottom-up design approach has the advantages of focusing on the initial product delivery and of allowing work to begin immediately on critical portions of the system. With this approach, however, system-level design errors do not surface until late in the design cycle and may require costly design iterations. Furthermore, while related products can reuse lower-level components, they cannot leverage any system-level similarities in design architecture, intellectual property, or verification environment. Finally, bottom-up design requires commitment to a semiconductor technology process early on and hinders the ability to reuse designs in other technology processes.

The alternative approach is the top-down design approach. In this approach, the design team invests time up front in developing system-level models and verification environment. Using the system models, the team is able to analyze trade-offs in system performance, features set, partitioning, and packaging. Furthermore, a system-level verification environment ensures that system requirements are met and provides the infrastructure for verifying the subsystems and system components.

The top-down design approach results in higher confidence so that the completed design will meet the original schedule and system specifications. Basing the starting point of the system design on a single verified model ensures that critical design issues surface early in the process and reduces false starts in the concurrent design of ASICs, PCBs, and systems. The design team can discover and manage system-level issues up front, rather than having to redesign the system at the end of the design cycle. Because each subsystem is designed and verified within the context of the system verification environment, the overall system functionality is preserved.

Exercises

I. Translate the following sentences into Chinese.

1. If analog signals are to be transmitted digitally, they first have to be sampled at a specified rate and further converted to discrete amplitude samples by quantization.

2. Linear filters amplify or attenuate selected spatial frequencies, can achieve such effects as smoothing and sharpening, and usually form the basis of re-sampling and boundary detection algorithms.

3. Stability and repeatability are fundamental attributes of digital circuits, however, and the necessary accuracy can be obtained in a digital version of the modulator by an appropriate choice of word length to represent the signals.

4. The first observation is made on the fundamental relationship between the nature of system and the periodicity of its frequency response: a continuous system has an aperiodic frequency response, while a discrete system has a periodic frequency response.

5. The main function of the receiver is to extract the input message signal from the

degraded version of the transmitted signal coming from the channel.

Ⅱ. Choose the word or phrase that is closest in meaning to the underlined part.

1. Roughly speaking, the transistor can be <u>likened</u> to an electronically controlled valve whereby energy applied to one connection of the valve enables energy to flow between two other connections.

  A. related

  B. linked

  C. analogized

  D. viewed

2. <u>While</u> third party design tools were available, there was not an effective link from the third party design tools to the layout and actual semiconductor process performance characteristics of the various ASIC manufacturers.

  A. When

  B. Although

  C. As

  D. Since

3. These steps, <u>implemented with a level of skill common in the industry</u>, almost always produce a final device that correctly implements the original design, unless flaws are later introduced by the physical fabrication process.

  A. practiced using skills generally available in the industry

  B. commonly performed at levels of skilled personnel in the industry

  C. realized with the skillful common level in the industry

  D. carried out by skills commonly used in the industry

4. A second major step would be to <u>develop design specifications that consider the functionality of the human</u> with the same degree of care that has been given to the rest of the system.

  A. develop design procedures to account for the human behavior and activities

  B. promote design arrangements and take the human factors into consideration

  C. make used of design steps that respect the human functionality

  D. draft and effect design requirements that take into account the human functionality

5. Compared with most of the textbooks at the introductory level of RF analog design, <u>this book presents some hands-on experiences on the design issues</u> that really work and has been proved by manufactured chips.

  A. this book provides some experiences at hand on the issues encountered in design

  B. this book provides some actually working experiences about the design problems

  C. this book presents some available experiences over the design problems

  D. this book presents some issues concerning design experiences that are handed over

6. For a decade there has been a search for a programmable processor which, <u>given the cost and volume constraints</u>, is general enough to be programmed with different

algorithms.

A. with controlled measures of price and magnitude

B. given the condition of risk and number

C. given the constants of charge and weight

D. given the limits of price and size

7. In a properly designed DC amplifier the effect of transistor parameter variation, other than Ico, may be practically eliminated if the operating point of each <u>stage</u> is adjusted so that it remains in the linear operation range of the transistor as temperature varies.

A. transistor

B. amplifier

C. Ico

D. parameter

As a result of the growth of microwave technology and its applications, and especially with the rapid development of wireless communications in recent years, professionals who are working in the areas of microwaves as well as communication engineering are all faced with the need to understand the theoretical and experimental aspects of microwave devices and circuits, and the design of antennas.

Text

Part I: Electromagnetic Field

The electromagnetic field is a physical field produced by electrically charged objects. It affects the behavior of charged objects in the vicinity of the field. The electromagnetic field extends indefinitely throughout space and describes the electromagnetic interaction. It is one of the four fundamental forces in the nature (the others are gravitation, the weak interaction, and the strong interaction).

The field can be viewed as the combination of an electric field and a magnetic field. The electric field is produced by stationary charges, and the magnetic field by moving charges (currents); these two are often described as the sources of the field. The way in which charges and currents interact with the electromagnetic field is described by Maxwell's equations and the Lorentz force law.

From a classical point of view, the electromagnetic field can be regarded as a smooth, continuous field, propagated in a wavelike manner, whereas from a quantum mechanical point of view, the field can be viewed as being composed of photons.

Structure of the electromagnetic field

The electromagnetic field may be viewed in two distinct ways.

Continuous structure: Classically, electric and magnetic fields are thought of as being produced by smooth motions of charged objects. For example, oscillating charges produce electric and magnetic fields that may be viewed in a "smooth", continuous, wavelike manner. In this case, energy is viewed as being transferred continuously through the electromagnetic field between any two locations. For instance, the metal atoms in a radio transmitter appear to transfer energy continuously. This view is useful to a certain extent (radiation of low frequency), but problems are found at high frequencies (see ultraviolet catastrophe). This problem leads to another view.

Discrete structure: The electromagnetic field may be thought of in a more "coarse" way. Experiments reveal that electromagnetic energy transfer is better described as being carried away in photons with a fixed frequency. Planck's relation links the energy E of a photon to its frequency ν through the equation:

$$E = h\nu$$

where h is Planck's constant, named in honor of Max Planck, and ν is the frequency of the photon. For example, in the photoelectric effect—the emission of electrons from metallic surfaces by electromagnetic radiation—it is found that increasing the intensity of the incident radiation has no effect, and that only the frequency of the radiation is relevant in ejecting electrons.[1]

This quantum picture of the electromagnetic field has proved very successful, giving rise to quantum electrodynamics, a quantum field theory describing the interaction of electromagnetic radiation with charged matter.

Dynamics of the electromagnetic field

In the past, electrically charged objects were thought to produce two types of field associated with their charge property. An electric field is produced when the charge is stationary with respect to an observer measuring the properties of the charge and a magnetic field (as well as an electric field) is produced when the charge moves (creating an electric current) with respect to this observer. Over time, it was realized that the electric and magnetic fields are better thought of as two parts of a greater whole—the electromagnetic field.[2]

Once this electromagnetic field has been produced from a given charge distribution, other charged objects in this field will experience a force (in a similar way that planets experience a force in the gravitational field of the Sun). If these other charges and currents are comparable in size to the sources producing the above electromagnetic field, then a new net electromagnetic field will be produced.[3] Thus, the electromagnetic field may be viewed as a dynamic entity that causes other charges and currents to move, and which is also affected by them. These interactions are described by Maxwell's equations and the Lorentz force law.

Part Ⅱ: Microstrip Antenna

In telecommunication, there are several types of microstrip antennas (also known as printed antennas) the most common of which is the microstrip patch antenna or patch antenna. A patch antenna is a narrowband, wide-beam antenna fabricated by etching the antenna element pattern in metal trace bonded to an insulating dielectric substrate with a continuous metal layer bonded to the opposite side of the substrate which forms a ground plane.[1] Common microstrip antenna radiator shapes are square, rectangular, circular and elliptical, but any continuous shape is possible. Some patch antennas eschew a dielectric substrate and suspend a metal patch in air above a ground plane using dielectric spacers; the resulting structure is less robust but provides better bandwidth. Because such antennas have a very low profile, are mechanically rugged and can be conformable, they are often mounted on the exterior of aircraft and spacecraft, or are incorporated into mobile radio communications devices.[2]

Microstrip antennas are also relatively inexpensive to manufacture and design because of the simple 2-dimensional physical geometry. They are usually employed at UHF and higher frequencies because the size of the antenna is directly tied to the wavelength at the resonant frequency. A single patch antenna provides a maximum directive gain of around 6~9 dBi. It is relatively easy to print an array of patches on a single (large) substrate using lithographic techniques. Patch arrays can provide much higher gains than a single patch at little additional cost; matching and phase adjustment can be performed with printed microstrip feed structures, again in the same operations that form the radiating patches. The ability to create high gain arrays in a low-profile antenna is one reason that patch arrays are common on airplanes and in other military applications.

The most commonly employed microstrip antenna is a rectangular patch. The rectangular patch antenna is approximately a one-half wavelength long section of rectangular microstrip transmission line. When air is the antenna substrate, the length of the rectangular microstrip antenna is approximately one-half of a free-space wavelength. Since the antenna is loaded with a dielectric as its substrate, the length of the antenna decreases as the relative dielectric constant of the substrate increases. The resonant length of the antenna is slightly shorter because of the extended electric "fringing fields" which increase the electrical length of the antenna slightly. An early model of the microstrip antenna is a section of microstrip transmission line with equivalent loads on either end to represent the radiation loss.

The dielectric loading of a microstrip antenna affects both its radiation pattern and impedance bandwidth. As the dielectric constant of the substrate increases, the antenna bandwidth decreases which increases the Q factor of the antenna and therefore decreases the impedance bandwidth.[3] This relationship did not immediately follow when using the transmission line model of the antenna, but is apparent when using the cavity model which was introduced in the late 1970s. The radiation from a rectangular microstrip antenna may be understood as a pair of equivalent slots. These slots act as an array and have the highest directivity when the antenna has an air dielectric and decreases as the antenna is loaded by material with increasing relative dielectric constant.

An advantage inherent to patch antennas is the ability to have polarization diversity. Patch antennas can easily be designed to have various polarizations, using multiple feed points, or a single feed point with asymmetric patch structures.[4] This unique property allows patch antennas to be used in many areas types of communications links that may have varied requirements.

The half-wave rectangular microstrip antenna has a virtual shorting plane along its center. This may be replaced with a physical shoring plane to create a quarter-wavelength microstrip antenna. This is sometimes called a half-patch. The antenna only has a single radiation edge (equivalent slot) which lowers the directivity/gain of the antenna. The impedance bandwidth is slightly lower than a half-wavelength full patch as the coupling between radiating edges has been eliminated.

Part Ⅲ: Microwaves

Microwaves are electromagnetic waves with wavelengths longer than those of terahertz (THz) frequencies, but relatively short for radio waves. Microwaves have wavelengths approximately in the range of 30 cm (frequency = 1 GHz) to 1 mm (300 GHz). This range of wavelengths has led many to question the naming convention used for microwaves as the name suggests a micrometer wavelength.[1] However, the boundaries between far infrared light, terahertz radiation, microwaves, and ultra-high-frequency radio waves are fairly arbitrary and are used variously between different fields of study. The same equations of electromagnetic theory apply at all frequencies. Apparatus and techniques may be described as "microwave" when the wavelengths of signals are roughly the same as the dimensions of the equipment, so that lumped-element circuit theory is no longer accurate. The term microwave generally refers to "alternating current signals with frequencies between 300 MHz (3×10^8 Hz) and 300 GHz (3×10^{11} Hz)." However, both IEC standard 60050 and IEEE standard 100 define "microwave" frequencies starting at 1 GHz (30 cm wavelength).

The existence of electromagnetic waves, of which microwaves are part of the frequency spectrum, was predicted by James Clerk Maxwell in 1864 from his equations. In 1888, Heinrich Hertz was the first to demonstrate the existence of electromagnetic waves by building an apparatus that produced and detected microwaves in the UHF region. In 1894 J. C. Bose publicly demonstrated radio control of a bell using millimeter wavelengths, and conducted research into the propagation of microwaves.

The microwave range includes ultra-high frequency (UHF) (0.3~3 GHz), super high frequency (SHF) (3~30 GHz), and extremely high frequency (EHF) (30~300 GHz) signals.

Above 300 GHz, the absorption of electromagnetic radiation by Earth's atmosphere is so great that it is effectively opaque, until the atmosphere becomes transparent again in the so-called infrared and optical window frequency ranges.

Devices

Vacuum tube based devices operate on the ballistic motion of electrons in a vacuum under the influence of controlling electric or magnetic fields, and include the magnetron, klystron, traveling wave tube (TWT), and gyrotron.[2] These devices work in the density modulated mode, rather than the current modulated mode. This means that they work on the basis of clumps of electrons flying ballistically through them, rather than using a continuous stream.[3]

Uses

A microwave oven works by passing microwave radiation, usually at a frequency of 2450 MHz (a wavelength of 12.24 cm), through the food. Water, fat, and sugar molecules in the food absorb energy from the microwave beam in a process called dielectric heating. Many molecules (such as those of water) are electric dipoles, meaning that they have a positive charge at one end and a negative charge at the other, and therefore rotate as they try to align themselves with the alternating electric field induced by the microwave beam. This molecular movement creates heat as the rotating molecules hit other molecules and put them into motion. Microwave heating is most efficient on liquid water, and much less so on fats and sugars (which have less molecular dipole moment), and frozen water (where the molecules are not free to rotate). Microwave heating is sometimes incorrectly explained as a rotational resonance of water molecules: such resonance only occurs at much higher frequencies, in the tens of gigahertz. Moreover, large industrial/commercial microwave ovens operating in the 900 MHz range also heat water and food perfectly well.

A common misconception is that microwave ovens cook food from the "inside out". In reality, microwaves are absorbed in the outer layers of food in a manner somewhat similar to heat from other methods. The rays from a microwave electrically manipulate water particles to cook food. It is actually the friction caused by the movement that creates heat and warms the food. The misconception arises because microwaves penetrate dry nonconductive substances at the surfaces of many common foods, and thus often deposit initial heat more deeply than other methods. Depending on water content the depth of initial heat deposition may be several centimeters or more with microwave ovens, in contrast to broiling, which relies on infrared radiation, or the thermal convection of a convection oven, which deposit heat shallowly at the food surface. Depth of penetration of microwaves is dependent on food composition and the frequency, with lower microwave frequencies being more penetrating.

Microwave radio is used in broadcasting and telecommunication transmissions because, due to their short wavelength, highly directive antennas are smaller and therefore more practical than they would be at longer wavelengths (lower frequencies). There is also more bandwidth in the microwave spectrum than in the rest of the radio spectrum; the usable bandwidth below 300 MHz is less than 300 MHz while many GHz can be used above 300 MHz. Typically, microwaves are used in television news to transmit a signal from a remote location to a television station from a specially equipped van.

Before the advent of fiber optic transmission, most long distance telephone calls were carried via microwave point-to-point links through sites like the AT&T Long Lines facility. Starting in the early 1950's, frequency division multiplex was used to send up to 5,400 telephone channels on each microwave radio channel, with as many as ten radio channels combined into one antenna for the hop to the next site, up to 70 km away.[4]

Radar also uses microwave radiation to detect the range, speed, and other characteristics of remote objects.

Wireless LAN protocols, such as Bluetooth and the IEEE 802.11 specifications, also use microwaves in the 2.4 GHz ISM band, although 802.11a uses ISM band and UNII* frequencies in the 5 GHz range. Licensed long-range (up to about 25 km) Wireless Internet Access services can be found in many countries (but not the USA) in the 3.5～4.0 GHz range.

Metropolitan Area Networks: MAN protocols, such as WiMAX (Worldwide Interoperability for Microwave Access) based in the IEEE 802.16 specification. The IEEE 802.16 specification was designed to operate between 2 to 11 GHz. The commercial implementations are in the 2.5 GHz, 3.5 GHz and 5.8 GHz ranges.

Wide Area Mobile Broadband Wireless Access: MBWA protocols based on standards specifications such as IEEE 802.20 or ATIS/ANSI HC-SDMA (e.g. iBurst) are designed to operate between 1.6 and 2.3 GHz to give mobility and in-building penetration characteristics similar to mobile phones but with vastly greater spectral efficiency.

Cable TV and Internet access on coax cable as well as broadcast television use some of the lower microwave frequencies. Some mobile phone networks, like GSM, also use the lower microwave frequencies.

Many semiconductor processing techniques use microwaves to generate plasma for such purposes as reactive ion etching and plasma-enhanced chemical vapor deposition (PECVD).

Microwaves can be used to transmit power over long distances, and post-World War II research was done to examine possibilities. NASA worked in the 1970s and early 1980s to research the possibilities of using Solar Power Satellite (SPS) systems with large solar arrays that would beam power down to the Earth's surface via microwaves.[5]

Microwave frequency bands

The microwave spectrum is usually defined as electromagnetic energy ranging from approximately 1 GHz to 1000 GHz in frequency, but older usage includes lower frequencies. Most common applications are within the 1 to 40 GHz range. Microwave Frequency Bands as defined by the Radio Society of Great Britain in Table 3.1.

Table 3.1　Microwave frequency bands

Designation	Frequency range	Designation	Frequency range
L band	1～2 GHz	Q band	30～50 GHz
S band	2～4 GHz	U band	40～60 GHz
C band	4～8 GHz	V band	50～75 GHz
X band	8～12 GHz	E band	60～90 GHz
Ku band	12～18 GHz	W band	75～110 GHz
K band	18～26.5 GHz	F band	90～140 GHz
Ka band	26.5～40 GHz	D band	110～170 GHz

* ISM bands: industrial, scientific and medical radio bands. UNII: Unlicensed National Information Infrastructure.

New Words

Part I

vicinity	邻近，附近	stationary	静止的，不变的
charge	电荷	quantum	量子
photon	光子	oscillate	振荡
atom	原子	ultraviolet	紫外线的
catastrophe	大灾难，大祸	photoelectric effect	光电效应
emission	发射，散发	metallic	金属的
incident	入射的	eject	喷射，强制离开
electrodynamics	电动力学	dynamics	动力学
gravitational	重力的	entity	实体

Part II

microstrip antenna	微带天线	patch	片
fabricate	制造，	etch	蚀刻
insulate	绝缘	dielectric	介电的，电介质
substrate	基底	rectangular	矩形的
elliptical	椭圆的	eschew	避开
spacer	定位架子	robust	牢固，稳健
profile	轮廓，姿态	conformable	适合的，顺从的
UHF (ultra-high frequency)	特高频	dBi (decibel isotropic)	全向性分贝
resonant	谐振的	lithographic	平板印刷的
transmission line	传输线	fringe	加边饰，条纹
impedance	阻抗	cavity	空腔
polarization	极化，偏振	diversity	多样，差异性
asymmetric	非对称的	virtual shorting plane	虚拟短路平面

Part III

terahertz	特赫，10^{12} Hz	boundary	边界，分界线
infrared	红外线	apparatus	设备，装置，仪器
lumped element	集总元件	opaque	不透（明）的
transparent	透明的，可透过的	vacuum tube	真空管，电子管
ballistic motion	冲击运动	magnetron	磁电管，磁控管
klystron	速调管	traveling wave tube	行波管
gyrotron	振动陀螺仪	clump	簇，团

dipole	偶极子	moment	矩
friction	摩擦，摩擦力	resonance	谐振，共振
convection	对流	penetrate	穿透，渗透
deposit	存放，堆积	antenna	天线
van	货车，篷车	advent	到来
multiplex	复用	Bluetooth	蓝牙
metropolitan	都市的	interoperability	互操作性
coax cable	同轴电缆	plasma	等离子体
reactive ion etching	反应离子刻蚀	vapor deposition	汽相淀积，蒸镀
beam	发送，传送，光束		

Notes on the Text

Part I

1. For example, in the photoelectric effect—the emission of electrons from metallic surfaces by electromagnetic radiation—it is found that increasing the intensity of the incident radiation has no effect, and that only the frequency of the radiation is relevant in ejecting electrons.

   例如，在光电效应（即因电磁辐射而从金属表面发射电子的现象）中，我们发现入射辐射强度的增强是没有影响的，只有辐射频率与发射的电子有关。

2. Over time, it was realized that the electric and magnetic fields are better thought of as two parts of a greater whole—the electromagnetic field.

   随着时间的推移，电场和磁场可以更好地被认为是电磁场这一整体的两个部分。

3. If these other charges and currents are comparable in size to the sources producing the above electromagnetic field, then a new net electromagnetic field will be produced.

   如果另外这些电荷和电流的大小与产生上述电磁场的源是可比的，那么将产生一个新的净电磁场。

Part II

1. A patch antenna is a narrowband, wide-beam antenna fabricated by etching the antenna element pattern in metal trace bonded to an insulating dielectric substrate with a continuous metal layer bonded to the opposite side of the substrate which forms a ground plane.

   片状天线是一种窄带宽波束的天线，通过将天线单元图样蚀刻到粘贴在绝缘基底上的金属轨迹而制成，基底的另一面则粘贴连续的金属层形成接地平面。

2. Because such antennas have a very low profile, are mechanically rugged and can be conformable, they are often mounted on the exterior of aircraft and spacecraft, or are incorporated into mobile radio communications devices.

   因为这种天线外形低矮，机械强度大，并且形状上适应性强，通常装在飞机或太空飞行器外表，或组合在移动无线电通信设备上。

- conformable，有适应性的，指能适应形状。

3. As the dielectric constant of the substrate increases, the antenna bandwidth decreases which increases the Q factor of the antenna and therefore decreases the impedance bandwidth.

随着基底介电常数的增大，天线的带宽减小，其 Q 值提高，因而阻抗带宽减小。

4. Patch antennas can easily be designed to have various polarizations, using multiple feed points, or a single feed point with asymmetric patch structures.

片状天线能很容易地通过多个馈点或在非对称片结构上采用单一馈点设计成具有各种偏振特性。

- various polarizations：包括 vertical polarization（垂直偏振），horizontal polarization（水平偏振），right hand circular polarization（RHCP，右旋圆偏振），left hand circular polarization（LHCP，左旋圆偏振）。

Part Ⅲ

1. This range of wavelengths has led many to question the naming convention used for microwaves as the name suggests a micrometer wavelength.

这个波长范围令人对命名习惯提出了疑问，因为微波使人联想到微米波长。

2. Vacuum tube based devices operate on the ballistic motion of electrons in a vacuum under the influence of controlling electric or magnetic fields, and include the magnetron, klystron, traveling wave tube (TWT), and gyrotron.

基于电子管的器件是在受控制电场和磁场影响的真空内由电子的冲击运动而工作的，包括磁控管、速调管、行波管和振动陀螺仪。

3. This means that they work on the basis of clumps of electrons flying ballistically through them, rather than using a continuous stream.

这意味着它们是基于真空管发出的电子簇工作的，而不是用连续的电子流。

4. Starting in the early 1950's, frequency division multiplex was used to send up to 5,400 telephone channels on each microwave radio channel, with as many as ten radio channels combined into one antenna for the hop to the next site, up to 70 km away.

从 20 世纪 50 年代开始，人们用频分复用在每一个微波无线电信道中传送多达 5400 路电话，将 10 路无线电信道组合起来送到一个天线，发送到 70 km 以外的下一个中继站。

- hop to the next site：直译"跳到下一个地点"，指传送到下一个中继站。

5. NASA worked in the 1970s and early 1980s to research the possibilities of using Solar Power Satellite (SPS) systems with large solar arrays that would beam power down to the Earth's surface via microwaves.

美国宇航局在 20 世纪 70 年代和 80 年代初期研究利用太阳能卫星系统 SPS 的可能性，这种系统装有大型太阳能阵列，通过微波向地球表面送回发射能量。

- beam power down to the Earth's surface：将功率（电能）波束射向地球表面。

Technical Tips

Fundamental forces

There are 4 fundamental forces that have been identified. In our present Universe they have rather different properties.

The **strong interaction** is very strong, but very short-ranged. It acts only over ranges of order $10 \sim 13$ centimeters and is responsible for holding the nuclei of atoms together. It is basically attractive, but can be effectively repulsive in some circumstances.

The **electromagnetic force** causes electric and magnetic effects such as the repulsion between like electrical charges or the interaction of bar magnets. It is long-ranged, but much weaker than the strong force. It can be attractive or repulsive, and acts only between pieces of matter carrying electrical charge.

The **weak force** is responsible for radioactive decay and neutrino interactions. It has a very short range and, as its name indicates, it is very weak.

The **gravitational force** is weak, but very long ranged. Furthermore, it is always attractive, and acts between any two pieces of matter in the Universe since mass is its source.

dBi

dB (isotropic) — the forward gain of an antenna compared to a fictitious isotropic antenna, which uniformly distributes energy in all directions.

The decibel (dB) is a logarithmic unit that expresses the magnitude of a physical quantity relative to a specified or implied reference level. Its logarithmic nature allows very large or very small ratios to be represented by a convenient number, in a similar manner to scientific notation. Decibels are useful for a wide variety of measurements in acoustics, physics, electronics and other disciplines.

The idea of decibel is to linearize a physical value which is exponential but perceived as linear (in fact as a logarithm of the original) by human. This concerns a lot of common stuff, such as intensity of light, level of noise, frequency of sound.

A decibel is one tenth of a bel (B). Devised by engineers of the Bell Telephone Laboratory to quantify the reduction in audio level over a 1 mile (approximately 1.6 km) length of standard telephone cable, the bel was originally called the transmission unit or TU, but was renamed in 1923 or 1924 in honor of the Bell System's founder and telecommunications pioneer Alexander Graham Bell. In many situations, however, the bel proved inconveniently large, so the decibel has become more common.

Supplementary Readings: What Are Microwaves?

"Microwaves" is a descriptive term used to identify electromagnetic waves in the frequency spectrum ranging approximately from 1 Giga Hertz (10^9 Hertz) to 30 Giga Hertz. This corresponds to wavelengths from 30 cm to 1 cm. Higher frequencies (extending up to 600 GHz) are also called "microwaves". These waves present several interesting and unusual features not found in other portions of the electromagnetic frequency spectrum. These features make "microwaves" uniquely suitable for several useful applications.

Characteristic features of microwaves

The main characteristic features of microwaves originate from the small size of wavelengths (1 cm to 30 cm) in relation to the sizes of components or devices commonly used. Since the wavelengths are small, the phase varies rapidly with distance; consequently the techniques of circuit analysis and design, of measurements and of power generation and amplification at these frequencies are distinct from those at lower frequencies.

For dealing with these small wavelengths, methods of circuit representation and analysis need to be modified. The phase difference caused by the interconnection between various components or various parts of a single component is not negligible. Consequently, analysis based on Kirchhoff's laws and voltage current concepts are not adequate to describe the circuit behavior at microwave frequencies. It is necessary to analyze the circuit or the component in terms of electric and magnetic fields associated with it. For this reason microwave engineering is also known as electromagnetic engineering or applied electromagnetics. A background of electromagnetic theory is a prerequisite for understanding microwaves.

Not only analytical techniques, the methods of measurement also become specialized at microwave frequencies. Measurements are carried out in terms of field amplitudes, phase differences and powers carried by the waves. A very commonly used method of microwave measurements is based on the study of a standing wave pattern formed along the line because of the interference of incident and reflected waves. Ratio of the amplitudes and phase relationship between incident and reflected waves tell us about impedance characteristics of the components causing the reflection. Several other special techniques have been developed for use at microwave frequencies.

Microwave circuit components also have a different look. Use of lumped elements at microwave frequencies becomes difficult because of small wavelengths involved. For realizing the lumped behavior of a capacitor, an inductor or a resistor, the component size must be much smaller than the wavelength. Because of this reason microwave systems employ distributed circuit elements very often. These elements are made up of small sections of transmission lines and waveguides. For example, a quarter wavelength section of a transmission line is used as an impedance transformer. A half wavelength section, on the other hand, constitutes a resonant circuit to be used in place of an L-C resonator. Use of miniature lumped elements at microwave frequencies has been made possible by the advancement in microelectronics technology during the last ten years. These techniques allow us to fabricate inductors, capacitors and resistors that are about a millimeter or two in size; much smaller than small wavelengths at microwave frequencies. Another aspect unique to microwave circuits is the possibility of radiation from discontinuities in distributed circuits. This necessitates a more careful and accurate circuit design.

The challenge of generating microwaves has resulted in a variety of devices—both in vacuum tube and in semiconductor device areas. When an attempt is made to use a lower frequency source at microwave frequencies, the operation is limited by the fact that transit time of the carriers through the device (i.e., electrons in triodes and electrons or holes in transistors) becomes comparable to the time period of the wave. This problem has been solved by technological innovations (in case of transistors) and by totally novel ideas (as in case of klystrons, magnetrons, transferred electron devices and avalanche diodes).

Applications of microwaves

Study and research in microwaves has not only been an interesting and challenging academic endeavor, it has led to several useful applications in communications, in radar, in physical research, in medicine and in industrial measurements and also for heating and drying of agricultural and food products.

A significant advantage associated with the use of microwaves for communications is their large bandwidth. A ten percent bandwidth at 3 GHz implies availability of 300 MHz spectrum. This means all the radio, television and other communications that are transmitted in the frequency spectrum from DC to 300MHz can be accommodated in a 10% bandwidth around 3 GHz (say from 2850 to 3150 MHz). Since the lower frequency part of the radio spectrum is getting crowded, there is a trend to use more and more of microwave region (and beyond) for various different services.

Short wavelengths also simplify the design and installation of high directivity antennae. Antenna directivity depends on the ratio of antenna aperture to the wavelength of the signal to be transmitted. At 10 GHz, a pencil beam with 1° beamwidth can be obtained by using a 6.9 feet diameter antenna. At 10 MHz, this will require an antenna diameter of 6,900 feet. This becomes impractical, especially if it is desired to rotate the antenna so that the beam can look in various directions.

Small antenna size and the property of reflection of microwaves from metallic surfaces make it practical to operate radar systems at these frequencies. Radar is an electronic method of detecting the presence of aircraft (or other objects) at ranges and in circumstances where other means of detection are not possible. Operation of the radar is based on the measurement of the time it takes for a pulse transmitted from an antenna to get reflected by the object to be detected and to return at the antenna and the receiver. Also, in many radar systems, a shift in the frequency of reflected signal caused by the Doppler effect can be recorded. Velocity of the target can be calculated from this measurement. The reflection from the object to be measured is significant only when the wavelength is much smaller than the size of the object. For this reason, the radar could not become practicable at lower frequency and had to wait for the development of microwave technology during the

Second World War period. Today, radars constitute about 70% of microwave equipment. There are a whole variety of radars: early-warning radar, missile-tracking radar, missile-guidance radar, fire-control radar, weather-detection radar, air-traffic control radar and even radars to detect and control the speed of automobiles.

There are other advantages associated with the small wavelengths at microwave frequencies. Unlike lower radio frequencies, these waves are not reflected and practically not absorbed by the ionosphere. This has led radio astronomers to use these frequencies to study electromagnetic radiations originating from stars and other astronomical objects. Also, this property makes microwaves suitable for space communication and satellite communication.

Microwaves exhibit another interesting feature. Molecular, atomic, and nuclear systems display various resonance phenomena when placed in periodic electromagnetic fields. Several of these resonance absorption lines lie in the microwave frequency range. The resonance absorption is due to rotational transitions in the molecules and the absorption spectra provide information on the molecular structure and intramolecular energies. Thus microwaves become a very powerful experimental tool for the study of some of the basic properties of materials. Besides scientific research, absorption of microwaves by molecular resonances is well suited for various industrial measurements. It can be used to measure the concentration of different gases, e.g., in an exhaust chimney in order to control the emission of pollutants, or in chemical processes in order to record continuously the concentration of gases evolved in the process.

The study of microwave resonances in molecules has led to several useful devices. The most significant ones are the non-reciprocal devices employing ferrites and solid-state microwave amplifiers and oscillators called masers. The magnetic properties of microwave ferrites are due to the electron spins in solids. The coupling between spins is such as to divide the magnetic atoms into groups having oppositely oriented magnetic dipoles. When placed in an external static magnetic field these materials exhibit non-reciprocal behavior at microwave frequencies. The maser is a microwave amplifier or oscillator which employs, as its working substance, a paramagnetic material having a suitable set of electron-spin energy levels separated by energy intervals that correspond to the frequencies in the microwave range. Stimulated transition from a higher energy state to a lower state results in radiation at microwave frequencies. Masers have lower noise figure than any other type of amplifier known and are used in the communication systems where extremely low noise characteristics are desired.

Just like any other form of energy, microwave energy can also be used for heating. Thermal effects produced by microwaves have a variety of industrial applications. Microwave ovens for cooking follow the principle of dielectric heating. Cooking is done very quickly and uniformly by microwaves since the food is cooked by the waves on the inside at the same time as on the outside. Like transfer of heat by conduction, convection and radiation, microwave heating can be considered as another mode of heat transfer. In this mode, heat is produced directly at the locations of the dielectric losses. Water has higher dielectric loss than the other ingredients in food products. Thus water pockets get heated first which is exactly where heat is required for cooking purposes. Microwave diathermy machines produce heat inside the muscles without heating the tissues and skin outside. Also, microwave drying machines are used in printing, textile, and paper industries.

Exercises

I. Translate the following sentences into Chinese.

1. A very commonly used method of microwave measurements is based on the study of a standing wave pattern formed along the line because of the interference of incident and reflected waves.

2. Computations show a reduction of 6dB in the EM field intensity with the distance doubled, and an increase of 3dB in the intensity with the transmitted power doubled. This result provides verification to the algorithm used.

3. Like transfer of heat by conduction, convection and radiation, microwave heating can be considered as another mode of heat transfer, in which heat is produced directly at the location of the dielectric losses.

4. Operation of the radar is based on the measurement of the time it takes for a pulse transmitted from an antenna to get reflected by the object to be detected and to return at the antenna and the receiver.

5. Other motivations for using CAD in circuit design includes the wish to acquire confidence in a design that was accomplished by other means, and, not least in importance, a sense of curiosity or perhaps a desire to discover the unexpected.

6. The spacing between the repeating amplifiers is a function of the cable attenuation and the system bandwidth so that the gain provided by these amplifiers compensates for the loss introduced by the cable.

7. When the cut-off frequency is no less than the maximal frequency of the original signal, nor is it greater than the difference between the sampling frequency and the maximal frequency, the original signal may be completely rebuilt.

II. Choose the word or phrase that is closest in meaning to the underlined part.

1. If these other charges and currents <u>are comparable in size to the sources</u> producing the above electromagnetic field, then a new net electromagnetic field will be produced.

   A. make comparison with the size of the sources

   B. are compared with the size of the sources

   C. have similar size to the sources

   D. take a common size of the sources

2. This range of wavelengths <u>has led many to question the naming convention</u> used for microwaves as the name suggests a micrometer wavelength.

A. has raised many questions about the naming habit

B. has caused many people to challenge the naming rules

C. has led many questions of the naming convention

D. has resulted in many problems in the naming tradition

3. NASA worked in the 1970s and early 1980s to research the possibilities of using Solar Power Satellite (SPS) systems with large solar arrays that would <u>beam power down to the Earth's surface</u> via microwaves.

A. shed solar energy to the Earth's surface from the satellite

B. set the satellite down to the Earth's surface with power

C. shut down the power on the Earth's surface from the satellite

D. switch off power to the Earth's surface from the satellite

4. As DoD urgently wanted military command and control networks that could <u>survive a nuclear war</u>, ARPA was charged with inventing a technology that could get data to its destination reliably even if arbitrary parts of the network disappeared without warning as a result of a nuclear attack.

A. win a nuclear war

B. be used in preparation of a nuclear war

C. avoid a nuclear war

D. be still operational after a nuclear war

5. At the present, <u>state of the art</u> microwave amplifiers and oscillator tubes can operate in a frequency range up to 40GHz and solid-state microwave devices up to 100GHz.

A. recent and most advanced

B. high tech related

C. sophisticated

D. artistically manufactured

6. In such a fiber rays traveling at larger angles with respect to the axis <u>have to traverse a longer path</u> and hence take a longer time than those rays which propagate with smaller angles to the axis.

A. have transmitted over a longer distance

B. are bound to treat a longer way

C. must travel through a longer route

D. must deal with a longer trace

7. By keeping the off state slightly below threshold, the delay between the applied electrical pulse and the resulting optical output pulse is minimized; <u>this delay must indeed not be more than the bit interval</u> so that the optical pulse can accurately reproduce the input signal.

A. this delay must indeed be no more than one internal bit

B. indeed, this delay must exceed the bit of interval

C. as a matter of fact, this delay interval must be a little bit less

D. this delay must indeed be kept less than the spacing between data bits

8. Computations show <u>a reduction of 6dB in the EM field intensity with the distance doubled,</u> and an increase of 3dB in the intensity with the transmitted power doubled. This result provides verification to the algorithm used.

A. that, with a 6dB reduction, the EM field intensity is twice as strong

B. that the EM field intensity is decreased by 6dB as the range is doubled

C. that, in the EM field, intensity with double distance leads to a 6dB reduction

D. a 6dB intensity reduction causes a double distance in the EM field

Unit 4

Communication and Information Theory

Communication systems are designed to transmit information, which is unknown to the recipient until after it is received. More information is communicated to the recipient when he/she is "surprised" by the transmitted message. Information theory is a mathematical theory of communication as indicated by the title of Claude Shannon's seminal work.

Text

Part I: Telecommunication

Telecommunication is the transmission of signals over a distance for the purpose of communication. In modern times, this process typically involves the sending of electromagnetic waves by electronic transmitters, but in earlier times telecommunication may have involved the use of smoke signals, drums or semaphore. Today, telecommunication is widespread and devices that assist the process such as television, radio and telephone are common in many parts of the world. There are also many networks that connect these devices, including computer networks, public telephone networks, radio networks and television networks. Computer communication across the Internet is one of many examples of telecommunication.

Telecommunication systems are generally designed by telecommunication engineers. Early inventors in the field include Alexander Graham Bell, Guglielmo Marconi and John Logie Baird. Telecommunication is an important part of the world economy with the telecommunication industry's revenue being placed at just under 3 percent of the gross world product.

Basic elements

Each telecommunication system consists of three basic elements: a transmitter that takes information and converts it to a signal, a transmission medium over which the signal is transmitted, and a receiver that receives the signal and converts it back into usable information.

Consider a radio broadcast for example. The broadcast tower is the transmitter, the radio is the receiver and the transmission medium is free space. Often telecommunication systems are two-way, and a single device acts as both a transmitter and receiver, or transceiver. For example, a mobile phone is a transceiver.

Telecommunication over a phone line is called point-to-point communication because it is between one transmitter and one receiver. Telecommunication through radio broadcasts is called broadcast (or point-to-multipoint) communication because it is between one powerful transmitter and numerous receivers.

Analog or digital

Signals can either be analog or digital. In an analog signal, the signal is varied continuously with respect to the information. In a digital signal, the information is encoded as a set of discrete values (for example, ones and zeros). During transmission, the information contained in analog signals will be degraded by noise. Conversely, unless the noise exceeds a certain threshold, the information contained in digital signals will remain intact. This represents a key advantage of digital signals over analog signals.

Networks

A collection of transmitters, receivers or transceivers that communicate with each other is known as a network.[1] Digital networks may consist of one or more routers that route data to the correct user. An analog network may consist of one or more switches that establish a connection between two or more users. For both types of network, repeaters may be necessary to amplify or recreate the signal when it is being transmitted over long distances. This is to combat attenuation that can render the signal indistinguishable from noise.[2]

Channels

A channel is a division in a transmission medium so that it can be used to send multiple streams of information.[3] For example, a radio station may broadcast at 96 MHz while another radio station may broadcast at 94.5 MHz. In this case, the medium has been divided by frequency and each channel received a separate frequency to broadcast on. Alternatively, one could allocate each channel a recurring segment of time over which to broadcast — this is known as time-division multiplexing and is sometimes used in digital communication.[4]

Modulation

The shaping of a signal to convey information is known as modulation. Modulation can be used to represent a digital message as an analog waveform. This is known as keying and several keying techniques exist (these include phase-shift keying, frequency-shift keying and amplitude-shift keying). Bluetooth, for example, uses phase-shift keying to exchange information between devices.

Modulation can also be used to transmit the information of analog signals at higher frequencies. This is helpful because low-frequency analog signals cannot be effectively transmitted over free space. Hence the information from a low-frequency analog signal must be superimposed on a higher-frequency signal (known as a carrier wave) before transmission. There are several different modulation schemes available to achieve this (two of the most basic being amplitude modulation and frequency modulation). An example of this process in action is a DJ's voice being superimposed on a 96 MHz carrier wave using frequency modulation (the voice would then be received on a radio as the channel "96 FM").

Part Ⅱ: Data Transmission

Data transmission is the conveyance of any kind of information from one space to another. Historically this could be done by a courier, a chain of bonfires or semaphores, and later by Morse code over copper wires.

In recent computer terms, it means sending a stream of bits or bytes from one location to another using any number of technologies, such as copper wire, optical fiber, laser, radio, or infra-red light. Practical examples include moving data from one storage device to another and accessing a website, which involves data transfer from web servers to a user's browser.

A related concept to data transmission is the data transmission protocol used to make the data transfer legible. Current protocols favor packet based communication.

Types of data transmission

Serial transmission: Bits are sent over a single wire individually. Whilst only one bit is sent at a time, high transfer rates are possible. This can be used over longer distances as a check digit or parity bit can be sent along it easily.

Parallel transmission: Multiple wires are used to transmit bits simultaneously. It is much faster than serial transmission as one byte can be sent rather than one bit. This method is used internally within the computer, for example the internal buses, and sometimes externally for such things as printers. However this method of transmission is only available over short distances as the signal will degrade and become unreadable since there is more interference between many wires than between one.

Asynchronous and synchronous data transmission

Asynchronous transmission uses start and stop bits to signify the beginning and end of a transmission. This means that an 8 bit ASCII character would actually be transmitted using 10 bits, e.g., A "0100 0001" would become "**1** 0100 0001 **0**". The extra one (or zero depending on parity bit) at the start and end of the transmission tells the receiver first that a character is coming and secondly that the character has ended. This method of transmission is used when data is sent intermittently as opposed to in a solid stream.[1] In the previous example the start and stop bits are in bold. The start and stop bits must be of opposite polarity. This allows the receiver to recognize when the second packet of information is being sent.

Synchronous transmission uses no start and stop bits but instead synchronizes transmission speeds at both the receiving and sending end of the transmission using clock signals built into each component.[2] A continual stream of data is then sent between the two nodes. Due to the absence of start and stop bits the data transfer rate is quicker although more errors will occur as the clocks will eventually get out of sync, and the receiving device would have the wrong time that had been agreed in the protocol for sending/receiving data, so some bytes could become corrupted by losing bits.[3] Ways to get around this problem include re-synchronization of the clocks and use of check digits to ensure the byte is correctly interpreted and received.

Protocols and handshaking

Protocol: A protocol is an agreed-upon format for transmitting data between two devices, e.g., computer and printer. All communications between devices require that the devices agree on the format of the data. The set of rules defining a format is called a protocol.

The protocol determines the following:

- The type of error checking to be used if any, e.g., check digit (and what type/formula to be used).
- Data compression method, if any, e.g., zipped files if the file is large, like transfer across the Internet, LANs and WANs.
- How the sending device indicates that it has finished sending a message, e.g., in a communications port a spare wire would be used for serial (USB) transfer start and stop digits may be used.[4]
- How the receiving device indicates that it has received a message.
- Rate of transmission (in baud or bit rate).
- Whether transmission is to be synchronous or asynchronous.

In addition, protocols can include sophisticated techniques for detecting and recovering from transmission errors and for encoding and decoding data.

Handshaking is the process by which two devices initiate communications, e.g., a certain ASCII character or an interrupt signal/request bus signal to the processor along the control bus.[5] Handshaking begins when one device sends a message to another device indicating that it wants to establish a communications channel. The two devices then send several messages back and forth that enable them to agree on a communications protocol. Handshaking must occur before data transmission as it allows the protocol to be agreed.

Part Ⅲ: Information Theory

Information theory is a branch of applied mathematics and engineering involving the quantification of information to find fundamental limits on compressing and reliably communicating data.[1] A key measure of information that comes up in the theory is known as information entropy, which is usually expressed by the average number of bits needed for storage or communication. Intuitively, entropy quantifies the uncertainty involved in a random variable. For example, a fair coin flip will have less entropy than a roll of a die.[2]

Applications of fundamental topics of information theory include lossless data compression (e.g. ZIP files), lossy data compression (e.g. MP3s), and channel coding (e.g. for DSL lines). The field is at the crossroads of mathematics, statistics, computer science, physics, neurobiology, and electrical engineering. Its impact has been crucial to success of the Voyager missions[*] to deep space, the invention of the CD, the feasibility of mobile phones, the development of the Internet, the study of linguistics and of human perception, the understanding of black holes, and numerous other fields. Important sub-fields of information theory are source coding, channel coding, algorithmic complexity theory, algorithmic information theory, and measures of information.

Overview

The main concepts of information theory can be grasped by considering the most widespread means of human communication: language. Two important aspects of a good language are as follows: First, the most common words (e.g., "a," "the," "I") should be shorter than less common words (e.g., "benefit," "generation," "mediocre"), so that sentences will not be too long. Such a tradeoff in word length is analogous to data compression and is the essential aspect of source coding. Second, if part of a sentence is unheard or misheard due to noise (e.g., a passing car), the listener should still be able to collect the meaning of the underlying message. Such robustness is as essential for an electronic communication system as it is for a language. Properly building such robustness into communications is done by channel coding. Source coding and channel coding are the fundamental concerns of information theory.

Note that these concerns have nothing to do with the importance of messages. For example, a platitude such as "Thank you; come again" takes about as long to say or write as the urgent plea, "Call an ambulance!" while clearly the latter is more important and more meaningful. Information theory, however, does not involve message importance or meaning, as these are matters of the quality of data rather than the quantity of data, the latter of which is determined solely by probabilities.[3]

Information theory is generally considered to have been founded in 1948 by Claude Shannon (Figure 4.1) in his seminal work, "A Mathematical Theory of Communication." The central paradigm of classical information theory is the engineering problem of the transmission of information over a noisy channel. The most fundamental results of this theory are Shannon's source coding theorem, which establishes that, on average, the number of bits needed to represent the result of an uncertain event is given by its entropy; and Shannon's noisy-channel coding theorem, which states that reliable communication is possible over noisy channels provided that the rate of communication is below a certain

---

* Voyager 1 is a space probe launched September 5, 1977. It visited Jupiter and Saturn and was the first to provide detailed images of the moons of these planets. It is the farthest human-made object, traveling away from both the Earth and the Sun. Voyager 2 was launched earlier on August 20, 1977. The Voyager mission was supposed to last just five years, and is now celebrating its 30th anniversary. Scientists continue to receive data from the spacecrafts as they approach interstellar space.

threshold called the channel capacity.[4] The channel capacity can be approached by using appropriate encoding and decoding systems.

Figure 4.1　Claude Shannon

Information theory is closely associated with a collection of pure and applied disciplines that have been investigated and reduced to engineering practice throughout the world under a variety of titles over the past half century or more: adaptive systems, anticipatory systems, artificial intelligence, complex systems, complexity science, cybernetics, informatics, machine learning, along with systems sciences of many descriptions. Information theory is a broad and deep mathematical theory, with equally broad and deep applications, amongst which is the vital field of coding theory.

Coding theory is concerned with finding explicit methods, called codes, of increasing the efficiency and reducing the net error rate of data communication over a noisy channel to near the limit that Shannon proved is the maximum possible for that channel.[5] These codes can be roughly subdivided into data compression (source coding) and error-correction (channel coding) techniques. In the latter case, it took many years to find the methods Shannon's work proved were possible. A third class of information theory codes is cryptographic algorithms (both codes and ciphers). Concepts, methods and results from coding theory and information theory are widely used in cryptography and cryptanalysis.

Information theory is also used in information retrieval, intelligence gathering, gambling, statistics, and even in musical composition.

Quantities of information

Information theory is based on probability theory and statistics. The most important quantities of information are entropy, the information in a random variable, and mutual information, the amount of information in common between two random variables. The former quantity indicates how easily message data can be compressed while the latter can be used to find the communication rate across a channel.[6]

The choice of logarithmic base determines the unit of information entropy that is used. The most common unit of information is the bit, based on the binary logarithm.

Coding theory

Coding theory is the most important and direct application of information theory. It can be subdivided into source coding theory and channel coding theory. Using a statistical description for data, information theory quantifies the number of bits needed to describe the data, which is the information entropy of the source.

Data compression (source coding). There are two formulations for the compression problem:

- Lossless data compression — the data must be reconstructed exactly;
- Lossy data compression—allocates bits needed to reconstruct the data, within a specified fidelity level measured by a distortion function. This subset of Information theory is called rate-distortion theory.[7]

Error-correcting codes (channel coding). While data compression removes as much redundancy as possible, an error correcting code adds just the right kind of redundancy (i.e. error correction) needed to transmit the data efficiently and faithfully across a noisy channel.

This division of coding theory into compression and transmission is justified by the information transmission theorems, or source-channel separation theorems that justify the use of bits as the universal currency for information in many contexts. However, these theorems only hold in the situation where one transmitting user wishes to communicate to one receiving user. In scenarios with more than one transmitter (the multiple-access channel), more than one receiver (the broadcast channel) or intermediary "helpers" (the relay channel), or more general networks, compression followed by transmission may no longer be optimal. Network information theory refers to these multi-agent communication models.

New Words

Part I

semaphore	旗语	gross product	总产值，总产量
revenue	收入，税收	degrade	退化，降级
transceiver	收发器	intact	完好的，完整的
threshold	阈值，上限，下限	switch	交换器，交换
router	路由器	combat	抗击
repeater	中继器，转发器	render	表示，表现，再现
attenuation	衰减	allocate	分派
indistinguishable	难以分辨的	keying	键控（法）
recur	复发，再发生	superimpose	叠加，重叠

Part II

		courier	信使，送急件的人
conveyance	运送，运输	Morse code	莫尔斯电码

bonfire	篝火	laser	激光
optical fiber	光纤	browser	浏览器
infra-red	红外线的，红外线	favor	支持
legible	可识别的，清楚的	parity	奇偶性
serial	串行	asynchronous	异步
parallel	并行	intermittently	间歇地
signify	告知，预示	synchronous	同步
bold	黑体的，粗体的	baud	波特
handshaking	握手		

Part Ⅲ

entropy	熵，平均信息量	quantify	量度，表示数量
uncertainty	不确定性	die	骰子
lossless	无损的	lossy	有损耗的
neurobiology	神经生物学	voyager	旅行者，探索者
feasibility	可行性，可能性	perception	感知，感觉
mediocre	不好不坏的，通常	measure	测度，度量
analogous	类比的，相似的	tradeoff	折中，权衡
robustness	稳健性，鲁棒性	platitude	陈词滥调，老生常谈
plea	请求，恳求	seminal	开创性的
paradigm	范例，样式	theorem	定理
channel capacity	信道容量	artificial	人工的
anticipatory system	预知系统	logarithmic	对数的
intelligence	智能，情报	fidelity	保真度，逼真
informatics	信息科学	context	背景，上下文
cipher	密码	scenario	情况，情景
cryptanalysis	密码分析	intermediary	中间的，媒介的
mutual information	互信息	redundancy	冗余，多余
faithfully	如实地，正确地		

Notes on the Text

Part I

1. Digital networks may consist of one or more routers that route data to the correct user. An analog network may consist of one or more switches that establish a connection between two or more users.

   数字网络由一个或多个路由器组成，路由器把数据发送给恰当的用户。模拟网路由一个或多个交换器组成，交换器在两个或多个用户间建立连接。

2. This is to combat attenuation that can render the signal indistinguishable from noise.

（中继器）用来抗击衰减，再现噪声中难以分辨的信号。

3. A channel is a division in a transmission medium so that it can be used to send multiple streams of information.

信道是传输媒介中的一部分，可用于使传输媒介传送多个信息流。

4. Alternatively, one could allocate each channel a recurring segment of time over which to broadcast — this is known as time-division multiplexing and is sometimes used in digital communication.

另一种方法是给每个信道分配重复的时间段，在这种时间段中进行广播，称为时分多路技术，有时用于数字通信中。

Part Ⅱ

1. This method of transmission is used when data is sent intermittently as opposed to in a solid stream.

当数据是间歇地发送而不是连续流时，使用这种传输方式。

2. Synchronous transmission uses no start and stop bits but instead synchronizes transmission speeds at both the receiving and sending end of the transmission using clock signals built into each component.

同步传输不使用起始和结束位，而是用插入各数据单元中的时钟信号使接收端和发送端传输速度同步。

3. Due to the absence of start and stop bits the data transfer rate is quicker although more errors will occur as the clocks will eventually get out of sync, and the receiving device would have the wrong time that had been agreed in the protocol for sending/receiving data, so some bytes could become corrupted by losing bits.

由于没有起始和结束位，数据传输速率较快，尽管会出现更多差错，因为时钟最后将失去同步，接收设备就要发生时间错误，这种时间关系是由发送/接收数据的协议所规定的，因此一些字节因丢失数据比特而被破坏。

4. How the sending device indicates that it has finished sending a message, e.g., in a communications port a spare wire would be used, for serial (USB) transfer start and stop digits may be used.

发送设备如何表示已完成一个消息的发送，例如在通信端口可用一根空闲的导线，对于串行（USB）传输用开始和结束字来表示。

5. Handshaking is the process by which two devices initiate communications, e.g., a certain ASCII character or an interrupt signal/request bus signal to the processor along the control bus.

握手是两个设备开始建立通信的过程，例如沿控制总线送给处理器的某个ASCII 字符或是中断信号/请求总线信号。

Part Ⅲ

1. Information theory is a branch of applied mathematics and engineering involving the quantification of information to find fundamental limits on compressing and reliably communicating data.

信息论是应用数学和工程学的一个分支，涉及信息的定量，用以确定数据压缩和可靠通信的基本界限。

2. Intuitively, entropy quantifies the uncertainty involved in a random variable. For example, a fair coin flip will have less entropy than a roll of a die.

直观地说，熵定量地表示一个随机变量所包含的不确定性。例如，掷硬币比掷骰子的熵小。

- a fair coin flip：这里 fair 表示公平，硬币两面出现的概率相等。

3. Information theory, however, does not involve message importance or meaning, as these are matters of the quality of data rather than the quantity of data, the latter of which is determined solely by probabilities.

然而，信息论不涉及消息的重要性或者意义，因为这些是关于数据的质而不是数据的量，数据的量完全取决于概率。

4. The most fundamental results of this theory are Shannon's source coding theorem, which establishes that, on average, the number of bits needed to represent the result of an uncertain event is given by its entropy; and Shannon's noisy-channel coding theorem, which states that reliable communication is possible over noisy channels provided that the rate of communication is below a certain threshold called the channel capacity.

这个理论最基本的结论是香农信源编码定理：在平均意义上表示一个不确定事件的结果所需要的比特数由其熵给出，以及香农有噪信道编码定理：只要通信速率低于某个阈值，即信道容量，就可能在有噪信道上进行可靠通信。

5. Coding theory is concerned with finding explicit methods, called codes, of increasing the efficiency and reducing the net error rate of data communication over a noisy channel to near the limit that Shannon proved is the maximum possible for that channel.

编码理论是有关寻找一些明确的方法，称为编码，这些方法会提高效率，降低有噪信道数据通信的净误码率，以接近香农所证明的该信道最大可能达到的极限。

6. The former quantity indicates how easily message data can be compressed while the latter can be used to find the communication rate across a channel.

前者（信息熵）指出消息数据压缩的难易程度，而后者（互信息）用来确定信道的通信速率。

7. Lossy data compression allocates bits needed to reconstruct the data within a specified fidelity level measured by a distortion function. This subset of Information theory is called rate-distortion theory.

有损数据压缩是在给定保真度条件下分配重建数据所需比特数，保真度由失真函数来度量。信息论的这个分支称为率-失真理论。

Technical Tips

Baud

In telecommunications and electronics, baud is a measure of the symbol rate, the number of distinct symbol changes made to the transmission medium per second in a digitally modulated signal. The baud (symbol rate) is distinct from the bit rate since one symbol can carry more than one bit of information. In voice band modems, where spectral efficiency is important, it is common for one symbol to carry 3 or more bits. A 3,000 bps modem that transmits symbols that each carries 3 bits should be described as operating at 1,000 baud. Early modems operated at one bit per symbol. Baud and bit rate for those devices were equivalent, leading many to believe the two terms are synonymous. They are not.

DSL

DSL or xDSL is a family of technologies that provide digital data transmission over the wires of a local telephone network. DSL originally stood for digital subscriber loop, although in recent years, many have adopted digital subscriber line as a more marketing-friendly term for the most popular version of consumer-ready DSL, ADSL.

Typically, the download speed of consumer DSL services ranges from 256 kbps to 24,000 kbps, depending on DSL technology, line conditions and service level implemented. Typically, upload speed is lower than download speed for Asymmetric Digital Subscriber Line (ADSL) and equal to download speed for Symmetric Digital Subscriber Line (SDSL).

Rate-distortion theory

Rate-distortion theory addresses the problem of determining the minimal amount of entropy (or information) that should be communicated over a channel, so that the source can be approximately reconstructed at the receiver without exceeding a given distortion. Rate-distortion theory gives theoretical bounds for how much compression can be achieved using lossy data compression methods. Many of the existing audio, speech, image, and video compression techniques have transforms, quantization, and bit-rate allocation procedures based on the general shape of rate-distortion functions.

Supplementary Readings

1. Telephone

In a conventional telephone system, the caller is connected to the person he wants to talk to by switches at various telephone exchanges. The switches form an electrical connection between the two users and the setting of these switches is determined electronically when the caller dials the number. Once the connection is made, the caller's voice is transformed to an electrical signal using a small microphone in the caller's handset. This electrical signal is then sent through the network to the user at the other end where it transformed back into sound by a small speaker in that person's handset. There is a separate electrical connection that works in reverse, allowing the users to converse.

The fixed-line telephones in most residential homes are analog — that is, the speaker's voice directly determines the signal's voltage. Although short-distance calls may be handled from end-to-end as analog signals, usually telephone service providers transparently convert the signals to digital for switching and transmission before converting them back to analog for reception. The advantage of this is that digitized voice data can travel side-by-side with data from the Internet and can be perfectly reproduced in long distance communication (as opposed to analog signals that are inevitably impacted by noise).

Mobile phones have had a significant impact on telephone networks. Mobile phone subscriptions now outnumber fixed-line subscriptions in many markets. Sales of mobile phones in 2005 totaled 816.6 million with that figure being almost equally shared amongst the markets of Asia/Pacific (204m), Western Europe (164m), CEMEA (Central Europe, the Middle East and Africa) (153.5m), North America (148m) and Latin America (102m). In terms of new subscriptions over the five years from 1999, Africa has outpaced other markets with 58.2% growth. Increasingly these phones are being serviced by systems where the voice content is transmitted digitally such as GSM or W-CDMA with many markets choosing to depreciate analog systems such as AMPS.

There have also been dramatic changes in telephone communication behind the scenes. Starting with the operation of TAT-8 in 1988, the 1990s saw the widespread adoption of systems based on optic fibres. The benefit of communicating with optic fibers is that they offer a drastic increase in data capacity. TAT-8 itself was able to carry 10 times as many telephone calls as the last copper cable laid at that time and today's optic fiber cables are able to carry 25 times as many telephone calls as TAT-8. This drastic increase in data capacity is due to several factors. First, optic fibers are physically much smaller than competing technologies. Second, they do not suffer from crosstalk which means several hundred of them can be easily bundled together in a single cable. Lastly, improvements in multiplexing have lead to an exponential growth in the data capacity of a single fiber.

2. Radio and Television

In a broadcast system, a central high-powered broadcast tower transmits a high-frequency electromagnetic wave to numerous low-powered receivers. The high-frequency wave sent by the tower is modulated with a signal containing visual or audio information. The antenna of the receiver is then tuned so as to pick up the high-frequency wave and a demodulator is used to retrieve the signal containing the visual or audio information. The broadcast signal can be either analog (signal is varied continuously with respect to the information) or digital (information is encoded as a set of discrete values).

The broadcast media industry is at a critical turning point in its development, with many countries moving from analog to digital broadcasts. This move is made possible by the production of cheaper, faster and more capable integrated circuits. The chief advantage of digital broadcasts is that they prevent a number of complaints with traditional analog broadcasts. For television, this includes the elimination of problems such as snowy pictures, ghosting and other distortion. These occur because of the nature of analog transmission, which means that perturbations due to noise will be evident in the final output. Digital transmission overcomes this problem because digital signals are reduced to binary data upon reception and hence small perturbations do not affect the final output. In a simplified example, if a binary message 1011 was transmitted with signal amplitudes [1.0 0.0 1.0 1.0] and received with signal amplitudes [0.9 0.2 1.1 0.9] it would still decode to the binary message 1011 — a perfect reproduction of what was sent. From this example, a problem with digital transmissions can also be seen in that if the noise is great enough it can significantly alter the decoded message. Using forward error correction a receiver can correct a handful of bit errors in the resulting message but too much noise will lead to incomprehensible output and hence a breakdown of the transmission.

3. The Internet

The Internet is a worldwide network of computers and computer networks that can communicate with each other using the Internet Protocol. Any computer on the Internet has a unique IP address that can be used by other computers to route information to it. Hence, any computer on the Internet can send a message to any other computer using its IP address. These messages carry with them the originating computer's IP address allowing for two-way communication. In this way, the Internet can be seen as an exchange of messages between computers.

The Internet works in part because of protocols that govern how the computers and routers communicate with each other. The nature of computer network communication lends itself to a layered approach where individual protocols in the protocol stack run more-or-less independently of other protocols. This allows lower-level protocols to be customized for the network situation while not changing the way higher-level protocols operate. A practical example of why this is important is because it allows an Internet browser to run the same code regardless of whether the computer it is running on is connected to the Internet through an Ethernet or Wi-Fi connection. Protocols are often talked about in terms of their place in the OSI reference model, which emerged in 1983 as the first step in an unsuccessful attempt to build a universally adopted networking protocol suite.

For the Internet, the physical medium and data link protocol can vary several times as packets traverse the globe. This is because the Internet places no constraints on what physical medium or data link protocol is used. This leads to the adoption of media and protocols that best suit the local network situation. In practice, most intercontinental communication will use the Asynchronous Transfer Mode (ATM) protocol (or a modern equivalent) on top of optic fiber. This is because for most intercontinental communication the Internet shares the same infrastructure as the public switched telephone network.

At the network layer, things become standardized with the Internet Protocol (IP) being adopted for logical addressing. For the World Wide Web, these "IP addresses" are derived from the human readable form using the Domain Name System (e.g. 72.14.207.99 is derived from www.google.com). At the moment, the most widely used version of the Internet Protocol is version four but a move to version six is imminent.

At the transport layer, most communication adopts either the Transmission Control Protocol (TCP) or the User Datagram Protocol (UDP). TCP is used when it is essential every message sent is received by the other computer where as UDP is used when it is merely desirable. With TCP, packets are retransmitted if they are lost and placed in order before they are presented to higher layers. With UDP, packets are not ordered or retransmitted if lost. Both TCP and UDP packets carry port numbers with them to specify what application or process the packet should be handled by. Because certain application-level protocols use certain ports, network administrators can restrict Internet access by blocking the traffic destined for a particular port.

Above the transport layer, there are certain protocols that are sometimes used and loosely fit in the session and presentation layers, most notably the Secure Sockets Layer (SSL) and Transport Layer Security (TLS) protocols. These protocols ensure that the data transferred between two parties remains completely confidential and one or the other is in use when a padlock appears at the bottom of your web browser. Finally, at the application layer, are many of the protocols Internet users would be familiar with such as HTTP (web browsing), POP3 (e-mail), FTP (file transfer), BitTorrent (file sharing) and OSCAR (instant messaging).

Exercises

I. Translate the following passages into Chinese.

1. Communication may be broadly defined as the transfer of information from one point to another. When the information is to be conveyed over any distance a communication system is usually required. Within a communication system the information transfer is frequently achieved by superimposing or modulating the information on to an electromagnetic wave which acts as a carrier for the information signal. This modulated carrier is then transmitted to the required destination where it is received and the original information signal is obtained by demodulation. Sophisticated techniques have been developed for this process by using electromagnetic carrier waves operating at radio frequencies as well as microwave and millimeter wave frequencies. However, communication may also be achieved by using an electromagnetic carrier that is selected from the optical range of frequencies.

2. Electronic communications is the transfer and movement of data between locations through the use of computers. An electronic communication system includes the equipment needed to support the movement of information, the communication lines and media to carry the information, the computer software and programs to control the flow of information, the personnel to plan, implement, and operate communications, and the management of all these resources. Electronic communications establishes links between people as well as computers.

3. First generation communications systems can be characterized by the use of analog transmission techniques, and the use of simple multiplex access techniques such as frequency division multiple access (FDMA). They suffered from a low user capacity, and security problems due to the simple radio interface used. Second generation systems were introduced in the early 1990's, and all use digital technology. This provided an increase in the user capacity of around three times, achieved by compressing the voice waveforms before transmission. Third generation systems are an extension on the complexity of second-generation systems and are to be introduced after the year 2000. The system capacity will be increased to over ten times original first generation systems, achieved by using complex multiplex access techniques such as code division multiplex access (CDMA), or an extension of TDMA, and by improving flexibility of services available.

4. For each combination of communication (modulation/detection) type, channel fading model, and diversity type, the average bit error rate (BER) and/or symbol error rate (SER) of the system is obtained and represented by an expression in a form that can readily be evaluated. All cases considered correspond to real practical channels, and in many instances the BER and SER expressions obtained can be evaluated numerically on a hand-held calculator.

5. Modulation is the systematic variation of some attribute of a carrier waveform such as the amplitude, phase, or frequency in accordance with a function of the message signal. It is used in communication systems for matching signal characteristics to channel characteristics, for reducing noise and interference, for simultaneously transmitting several signals over a single channel, and for overcoming some equipment limitations. A considerable portion of this book is devoted to the study of how modulation schemes are deigned to achieve the above tasks. The success of a communication system depends to a large extent on the modulation.

Ⅱ. **Choose the word or phrase that is closest in meaning to the underlined part.**

1. The receiving device would have the wrong time that had been agreed in the protocol for sending/receiving data, so some bytes could become corrupted by losing bits.

   A. that had been consistent with the protocol of data exchange

   B. that had been the same as the protocol for sending/receiving data

      C. that had been in agreement with the protocol of data transmission

      D. that had been defined in the data transmission protocol

2. Synchronous transmission uses no start and stop bits but instead synchronizes transmission speeds at both the receiving and sending end of the transmission <u>using clock signals built into each component</u>.

      A. using synchronization signals to build each component

      B. using timing pulses that are incorporated in each component

      C. using timing signals in order to build each component

      D. using clocks that can build signal components

3. Information theory, however, does not involve message importance or meaning, as these are matters of the quality of data rather than the quantity of data, <u>the latter of which is determined solely by probabilities</u>.

      A. which is the later one of the determined probabilities

      B. the later one being probably deterministic

      C. in which the later one is deterministic rather than probabilistic

      D. the data quantity being determined by probabilities only

4. Any small deformations in the height or width of the pulses are irrelevant since it is only necessary to know whether the pulse is present or absent in order <u>to retrieve the original message</u>.

      A. to reform the original information

      B. to recover the original signal

      C. to re-obtain the original information

      D. to represent the original signal

5. Consequently, electronic equipment is constantly subjected to unwanted sources of energy and is <u>constantly producing energy that adjacent equipment is not designed to accept</u>.

      A. continually making unaccepted interference to adjacent equipment

      B. continuously causing neighboring equipment not to accept expected energy

      C. constantly producing energy that is acceptable only to neighboring equipment

      D. ceaselessly generating energy that is considered acceptable in the design of adjacent equipment

6. Earlier we introduced the concept that the identity of an amplitude modulated message signal <u>may under certain circumstances be communicated by transmitting regular samples of the message</u>, rather than the continuous signal.

      A. may transmit samples that are regular in communications under some conditions

      B. may be in the circumstances that regular message samples are communicated

      C. may be conveyed by sending signal sampled at regular intervals under some conditions

      D. may communicate with certain customers by sending regular samples of the message

7. For <u>each of the building blocks of the RF transceiver</u>, which has been broken into

separate chapters, a list of essential reference publications also guarantees depth and academic value of the research achievements presented.

A. each of the basic components of the RF transceiver

B. each of the groups that are built into the RF transceiver

C. the individual elements in the RF transceiver

D. each of the buildings that blocks the RF transceiver

8. We are to develop a code such that fewer bits are assigned to code words representing gray levels having higher probability of occurrence, <u>and vice versa</u>.

A. in other words, gray levels that more frequently occur are given more bits

B. and more bits are used for gray levels of lower probability of occurrence

C. otherwise, more bits are needed in the similar case

D. in other words, more probable gray levels require shorter code words

Unit 5 | Multiple Access Techniques

Today the rapidly increasing communications systems are operating in an increasingly crowded frequency spectrum. The only solution appears to be sharing the precious frequency resources among different users, and there comes the need for developing various multiple access techniques.

Text

Part I: Multiple Access Techniques: FDMA, TDMA and CDMA

Multiple access schemes are used to allow many simultaneous users to use the same fixed bandwidth radio spectrum. In any radio system, the allocated bandwidth is always limited. For mobile phone systems the total bandwidth is typically 50MHz, which is split in half to provide the forward and reverse links of the system. Sharing of the spectrum is required in order to increase the user capacity of any wireless network. FDMA, TDMA and CDMA are the three major methods of sharing the available bandwidth to multiple users in wireless system. There are many extensions, and hybrid techniques for these methods, such as OFDM, and hybrid TDMA and FDMA systems. However, an understanding of the three major methods is required for understanding of any extensions to these methods.

Frequency division multiple access

In Frequency Division Multiple Access (FDMA), the available bandwidth is subdivided into a number of narrower bands. Each user is allocated a unique frequency band in which to transmit and receive. During a call, no other user can use the same frequency band. Each user is allocated a forward link channel (from the base station to the mobile phone) and a reverse channel (back to the base station), each being a single way link. The transmitted signal on each of the channels is continuous allowing analog transmissions. The bandwidths of FDMA channels are generally low (30 kHz) as each channel only supports one user. FDMA is used as the primary breakup of large allocated frequency bands and is used as part of most multi-channel systems. Figures 5.1 and 5.2 show the allocation of the available bandwidth into several channels.

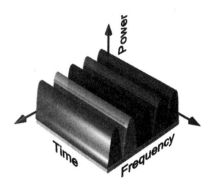

Figure 5.1   FDMA showing that the each narrow band channel is allocated to a single user

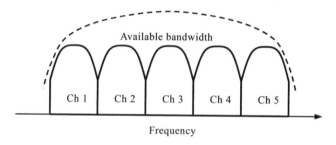

Figure 5.2   FDMA spectrum, where the available bandwidth is subdivided into narrower band channels

Time division multiple access

Time Division Multiple Access (TDMA) divides the available spectrum into multiple time slots, by giving each user a time slot in which they can transmit or receive. Figure 5.3 shows how the time slots are provided to users in a round robin fashion, with each user being allotted one time slot per frame.[1]

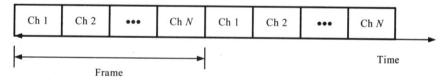

Figure 5.3   TDMA scheme where each user is allocated a small time slot

TDMA systems transmit data in a buffer and burst method, thus the transmission of each channel is non-continuous. The input data to be transmitted is buffered over the previous frame and burst transmitted at a higher rate during the time slot for the channel.[2] TDMA cannot send analog signals directly due to the buffering required, thus is only used for transmitting digital data. TDMA can suffer from multipath effects as the transmission rate is generally very high. This leads the multipath signals causing inter-symbol interference.

TDMA is normally used in conjunction with FDMA to subdivide the total available bandwidth into several channels. This is done to reduce the number of users per channel allowing a lower data rate to be used. This helps reduce the effect of delay spread on the transmission. Figure 5.4 shows the use of TDMA with FDMA. Each channel based on FDMA, is further subdivided using TDMA, so that several users can transmit over one channel. This type of transmission technique is used by most digital second generation mobile phone systems. For GSM, the total allocated bandwidth of 25MHz is divided into 125 channels using FDMA, each having a bandwidth of 200 kHz. These channels are then subdivided further by using TDMA so that each 200 kHz channel allows 8～16 users.

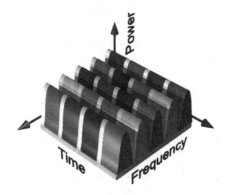

Figure 5.4   TDMA/FDMA hybrid in which the bandwidth is split into frequency channels and time slots

Code division multiple access

Code Division Multiple Access (CDMA) is a spread spectrum technique that uses neither frequency channels nor time slots. In CDMA, the narrow band message (typically digitized voice data) is multiplied by a large bandwidth signal which is a pseudo random noise code (PN code). All users in a CDMA system use the same frequency band and transmit simultaneously. The transmitted signal is recovered by correlating the received signal with the PN code used by the transmitter. Figure 5.5 shows the general use of the spectrum using CDMA.

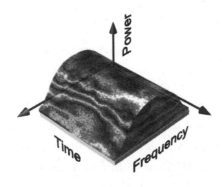

Figure 5.5   Code division multiple access (CDMA)

CDMA technology was originally developed by the military during World War Ⅱ.

Researches were spurred into looking at ways of communicating that would be secure and work in the presence of jamming. Some of the properties that have made CDMA useful are:

- Signal hiding and non-interference with existing systems..
- Anti-jam and interference rejection.
- Information security.
- Accurate ranging.
- Multiple user access.
- Multipath tolerance.

For many years, spread spectrum technology was considered solely for military applications. However, with rapid developments in LSI and VLSI designs, commercial systems are starting to be used.

CDMA process gain

One of the most important concepts required in order to understand spread spectrum techniques is the idea of process gain. The process gain of a system indicates the gain or signal to noise improvement exhibited by a spread spectrum system by the nature of the spreading and despreading process.[3] The process gain of a system is equal to the ratio of the spread spectrum bandwidth used, to the original data bit rate. Thus, the process gain can be written as:

$$G_p = \frac{BW_{RF}}{BW_{info}}$$

where BW_{RF} is the transmitted bandwidth after the data is spread, and BW_{info} is the bandwidth of the information data being sent.

Figure 5.6 shows the process of a CDMA transmission. The data to be transmitted (a) is spread before transmission by modulating the data using a PN code. This broadens the spectrum as shown in (b). In this example the process gain is 125 as the spread spectrum bandwidth is 125 times greater than the data bandwidth. Part (c) shows the received signal. This consists of the required signal, plus background noise, and any interference from other CDMA users or radio sources. The received signal is recovered by multiplying the signal by the original spreading code. This process causes the wanted received signal to be despread back to the original transmitted data. However, all other signals uncorrelated to the PN spreading code used become more spread. The wanted signal in (d) is then filtered removing the wide spread interference and noise signals.

CDMA generation

CDMA is achieved by modulating the data signal by a pseudo random noise sequence (PN code), which has a chip rate higher than the bit rate of the data. The PN code sequence is a sequence of ones and zeros (called chips), which alternate in a random fashion. The data is modulated by modular-2 adding the data with the PN code sequence. This can also be done by multiplying the signals, provided the data and PN code are represented by 1 and

−1 instead of 1 and 0. Figure 5.7 shows a basic CDMA transmitter.

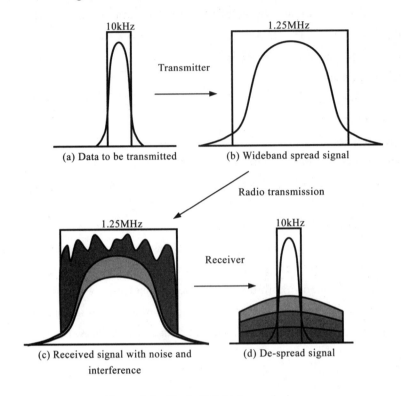

Figure 5.6   Basic CDMA transmission

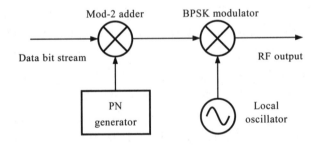

Figure 5.7   Simple direct sequence modulator

The PN code used to spread the data can be of two main types. A short PN code (typically 10～128 chips in length) can be used to modulate each data bit. The short PN code is then repeated for every data bit allowing for quick and simple synchronization of the receiver. Figure 5.8 shows the generation of a CDMA signal using a 10-chip length short code. Alternatively a long PN code can be used. Long codes are generally thousands to millions of chips in length, thus are only repeated infrequently. Because of this they are useful for added security as they are more difficult to decode.

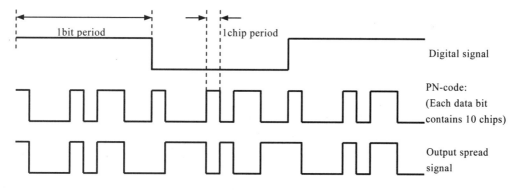

1bit period

1chip period

Digital signal

PN-code:
(Each data bit
contains 10 chips)

Output spread
signal

Figure 5.8　Direct sequence signals

CDMA forward link encoding

The forward link, from the base station to the mobile, of a CDMA system can use special orthogonal PN codes called Walsh code, for separating the multiple users on the same channel. These are based on a Walsh matrix, which is a square matrix with binary elements, and dimensions which are a power of two. It is generated from the basis $W_1 = 0$ and that:

$$W_{2n} = \begin{bmatrix} W_n & W_n \\ W_n & \bar{W}_n \end{bmatrix}$$

where W_n is the Walsh matrix of dimension n. For example:

$$W_2 = \begin{bmatrix} 0 & 0 \\ 0 & 1 \end{bmatrix} \qquad W_4 = \begin{bmatrix} 0 & 0 & 0 & 0 \\ 0 & 1 & 0 & 1 \\ 0 & 0 & 1 & 1 \\ 0 & 1 & 1 & 0 \end{bmatrix}$$

Walsh codes are orthogonal, which means that the dot product of any two rows is zero. This is due to the fact that for any two rows exactly half the number of bits match and half do not.

Each row of a Walsh matrix can be used as the PN code of a user in a CDMA system. By doing this the signals from each user is orthogonal to every other user, resulting in no interference between the signals.[4] However, in order for Walsh codes to work the transmitted chips from all users must be synchronized. If the Walsh code used by one user is shifted in time by more than about 1/10 of a chip period with respect to all the other Walsh codes, it loses its orthogonal nature, resulting in inter-user interference.[5] For the forward link signals for all the users originate from the base station, allowing the signals to be easily synchronized.

CDMA reverse link encoding

The reverse link is different to the forward link because the signals from each user do not originate from a same source as in the forward link. The transmission from each user will arrive at a different time, due to propagation delay and synchronization errors. Due to the unavoidable timing errors between the users, there is little point in using Walsh codes as they will no longer be orthogonal.[6] For this reason simple pseudo random sequence which are uncorrelated, but not orthogonal are used for the PN codes of each user.

The capacity is different for the forward and the reverse links because of the differences in modulation. The reverse link is not orthogonal, resulting in significant inter-user interference. For this reason the reverse channel sets the capacity of the system.[7]

Part II: Orthogonal Frequency Division Multiplexing

Orthogonal Frequency Division Multiplexing (OFDM)—essentially identical to Coded OFDM (COFDM)—is a digital multi-carrier modulation scheme, which uses a large number of closely-spaced orthogonal sub-carriers. Each sub-carrier is modulated with a conventional modulation scheme (such as quadrature amplitude modulation) at a low symbol rate, maintaining data rates similar to conventional single-carrier modulation schemes in the same bandwidth. In practice, OFDM signals are generated using the fast Fourier transform algorithm.

OFDM has developed into a popular scheme for wideband digital communication systems with a wide range of applications. The primary advantage of OFDM over single-carrier schemes is its ability to cope with severe channel conditions—for example, attenuation of high frequencies at a long copper wire, narrowband interference and frequency-selective fading due to multipath — without complex equalization filters.[1] Channel equalization is simplified because OFDM may be viewed as using many slowly-modulated narrowband signals rather than one rapidly-modulated wideband signal. Low symbol rate makes the use of a guard interval between symbols affordable, making it possible to handle time-spreading and eliminate inter-symbol interference (ISI).

A major disadvantage of OFDM is the high peak-to-average-power ratio (PAPR), requiring more expensive transmitter circuitry, and possibly lowering power efficiency. In addition, it is sensitive to Doppler shift and frequency synchronization problems.

Orthogonality

In OFDM, the sub-carrier frequencies are chosen so that the sub-carriers are orthogonal to each other, meaning that cross-talk between the sub-channels is eliminated and inter-carrier guard bands are not required. This greatly simplifies the design of both the transmitter and the receiver; unlike conventional FDM, a separate filter for each sub-channel is not required.

The orthogonality also allows high spectral efficiency, near the Nyquist rate.[2] Almost the whole available frequency band can be utilized. OFDM generally has a nearly "white" spectrum, giving it benign electromagnetic interference properties with respect to other co-channel users.[3]

The orthogonality allows for efficient modulator and demodulator implementation using the FFT algorithm. Although the principles and some of the benefits have been known since the 1960s, OFDM is popular for wideband communications today by way of low-cost digital signal processing components that can efficiently calculate the FFT.

OFDM requires very accurate frequency synchronization between the receiver and the transmitter; with frequency deviation, the sub-carriers shall no longer be orthogonal, causing inter-carrier interference (ICI), i.e. cross-talk between the sub-carriers. Frequency offsets are typically caused by mismatched transmitter and receiver oscillators, or by Doppler shift due to movement. Whilst Doppler shift alone may be compensated for by the receiver, the situation is worsened when combined with multipath, as reflections will appear at various frequency offsets, which is much harder to correct.[4] This effect typically worsens as speed increases, and is an important factor limiting the use of OFDM in high-speed vehicles. Several techniques for ICI suppression are suggested, but they may increase the receiver complexity.

Guard interval for elimination of inter-symbol interference

One key principle of OFDM is that since low symbol rate modulation schemes (i.e. where the symbols are relatively long compared to the channel time characteristics) suffer less from intersymbol interference caused by multipath, it is advantageous to transmit a number of low-rate streams in parallel instead of a single high-rate stream.[5] Since the duration of each symbol is long, it is feasible to insert a guard interval between the OFDM symbols, thus eliminating the intersymbol interference.

The guard interval also eliminates the need for a pulse-shaping filter, and it reduces the sensitivity to time synchronization problems.

A simple example: If one sends a million symbols per second using conventional single-carrier modulation over a wireless channel, then the duration of each symbol would be one microsecond or less. This imposes severe constraints on synchronization and necessitates the removal of multipath interference. If the same million symbols per second are spread among one thousand sub-channels, the duration of each symbol can be longer by a factor of thousand, i.e. one millisecond, for orthogonality with approximately the same bandwidth. Assume that a guard interval of 1/8 of the symbol length is inserted between each symbol. Intersymbol interference can be avoided if the multipath time-spreading (the time between the reception of the first and the last echo) is shorter than the guard interval, i.e. 125 microseconds. This corresponds to a maximum difference of 37.5 kilometers between the lengths of the paths. The last 125 microseconds of each symbol are copied and sent in advance of the symbol as a cyclic prefix.

The cyclic prefix, which is transmitted during the guard interval, consists of the end of the OFDM symbol copied into the guard interval, and the guard interval is transmitted followed by the OFDM symbol.[6] Although the guard interval only contains redundant data, which means that it reduces the capacity, some OFDM-based systems, such as some of the broadcasting systems, deliberately use a long guard interval in order to allow the transmitters to be spaced farther apart in a single frequency network (SFN), and longer guard intervals allow larger SFN cell-sizes. A rule of thumb for the maximum distance between transmitters in an SFN is equal to the distance a signal travels during the guard interval — for instance, a guard interval of 200 microseconds would allow transmitters to be spaced 60 km apart.

Simplified equalization

The effects of frequency-selective channel conditions, for example fading caused by multipath propagation, can be considered as constant (flat) over an OFDM sub-channel if the sub-channel is sufficiently narrow-banded, i.e. if the number of sub-channels is sufficiently large. This makes equalization far simpler at the receiver in OFDM in comparison to conventional single-carrier modulation. The equalizer only has to multiply each sub-carrier by a constant value, or a rarely changed value.

Our example: The OFDM equalization in the above numerical example would require $N = 1000$ complex multiplications per OFDM symbol, i.e. one million multiplications per second, at the receiver. The FFT algorithm requires $N\log_2N = 10000$ complex-valued multiplications per OFDM symbol, i.e. 10 million multiplications per second, at both the receiver and transmitter side. This should be compared with the corresponding one million symbols/second single-carrier modulation case mentioned in the example, where the equalization of 125 microseconds time-spreading using a FIR filter would require 125 multiplications per symbol, i.e. 125 million multiplications per second.

Some of the sub-carriers in some of the OFDM symbols may carry pilot signals for measurement of the channel conditions, i.e. the equalizer gain for each sub-carrier. Pilot signals may also be used for synchronization.

If differential modulation such as DPSK or DQPSK is applied to each sub-carrier, equalization can be completely omitted, since these schemes are insensitive to slowly changing amplitude and phase distortion.

Channel coding and interleaving

OFDM is invariably used in conjunction with channel coding (forward error correction), and almost always uses frequency and/or time interleaving.

Frequency (subcarrier) interleaving increases resistance to frequency-selective channel conditions such as fading. For example, when a part of the channel bandwidth is faded, frequency interleaving ensures that the bit errors that would result from those subcarriers in the faded part of the bandwidth are spread out in the bit-stream rather than being concentrated.[7] Similarly, time interleaving ensures that bits that are originally close together in the bit-stream are transmitted far apart in time, thus mitigating against severe fading as would happen when traveling at high speed.

However, time interleaving is of little benefit in slowly fading channels, such as for stationary reception, and frequency interleaving offers little to no benefit for narrowband channels that suffer from flat-fading (where the whole channel bandwidth is faded at the same time).

Interleaving is used in OFDM to spread the errors out in the bit-stream that is presented to the error correction decoder, because when such decoders are presented with a high concentration of errors the decoder is unable to correct all the bit errors, and a burst of uncorrected errors occurs.

A common type of error correction coding used with OFDM-based systems is convolutional coding, which is often concatenated with Reed-Solomon coding. Convolutional coding is used as the inner code and Reed-Solomon coding is used for the outer code — usually with additional interleaving (on top of the time and frequency interleaving mentioned above) in between the two layers of coding. The reason why this combination of error correction coding is used is that the Viterbi decoder used for convolutional decoding produces short errors bursts when there is a high concentration of errors, and Reed-Solomon codes are inherently well-suited to correcting bursts of errors.

New Words

Part I

simultaneous	同时的	hybrid	混合的
allocate	分配，指派	time slot	时隙
round robin	循环（复用）	allot	分配
frame	帧	buffer	缓冲器
burst	爆发	multipath	多径
pseudo random noise	伪随机噪声	correlate	相关，作相关处理
spur	刺激，激励	jamming	干扰
tolerance	容忍，宽容	gain	增益
despread	解除扩频	chip	码片
alternate	交替	modular-2	模 2 的
synchronization	同步	orthogonal	正交的
matrix	矩阵	dimension	维数
power	幂	dot product	点积，标量积
originate	发源	propagation	传播

Part II

multi-carrier	多载波	sub-carrier	子载波
quadrature	正交，90°相位差	algorithm	算法

attenuation	衰减	fading	衰落
equalization	均衡	guard interval	保护间隔
orthogonality	正交性	Doppler shift	多普勒频移
cross-talk	窜音，干扰	benign	良好的，有利的
mismatch	失配，不匹配	offset	偏移
deviation	偏移，偏差	parallel	并行，平行
duration	持续时间	sensitivity	敏感性，灵敏度
prefix	前缀	cell-size	蜂窝大小
redundant	冗余的，多余的	pilot signal	导频信号
numerical	数值的	mitigate	使缓和，减轻
interleaving	交织，交错	concatenate	连在一起，级联
convolutional coding	卷积编码	sinusoid	正弦曲线

Notes on the Text

Part I

1. Figure 5.3 shows how the time slots are provided to users in a round robin fashion, with each user being allotted one time slot per frame.

   图 5.3 显示如何以一种循环复用的方式把时隙分配给用户，每个用户每帧分得一个时隙。

2. The input data to be transmitted is buffered over the previous frame and burst transmitted at a higher rate during the time slot for the channel.

   待发送的输入数据在前一帧期间被缓存，在分配给该信道的时隙中以较高速率爆发式发送出去。

3. The process gain of a system indicates the gain or signal to noise improvement exhibited by a spread spectrum system by the nature of the spreading and despreading process.

   系统的处理增益是指扩频系统通过扩频和反扩频的性质所表现出来的增益或信噪比的提高。

4. By doing this the signals from each user is orthogonal to every other user, resulting in no interference between the signals.

   这一处理过程使每一用户的信号与所有其他用户的信号正交，因而相互之间没有干扰。

5. If the Walsh code used by one user is shifted in time by more than about 1/10 of a chip period with respect to all the other Walsh codes, it loses its orthogonal nature, resulting in inter-user interference.

   如果一个用户使用的 Walsh 码在时间上相对于其他所有 Walsh 码移动了超过约十分之一的码片周期，就失去了正交性，导致用户间干扰。

6. Due to the unavoidable timing errors between the users, there is little point in using Walsh codes as they will no longer be orthogonal.

由于用户之间不可避免的定时偏差，Walsh 码几乎没用，因为它们之间不再正交。

7. The reverse link is not orthogonal, resulting in significant inter-user interference. For this reason the reverse channel sets the capacity of the system.

反向链接是非正交的，导致用户间的严重干扰。由于这一原因，反向信道限制了系统的容量。

Part Ⅱ

1. The primary advantage of OFDM over single-carrier schemes is its ability to cope with severe channel conditions—for example, attenuation of high frequencies at a long copper wire, narrowband interference and frequency-selective fading due to multipath—without complex equalization filters.

OFDM（正交频分复用）与单载波方案相比的主要优点是不需要复杂的均衡滤波器就能应对严重的信道问题，如：在长铜线中的高频衰减、窄带干扰以及由于多路径而引起的频率选择性衰落。

2. The orthogonality also allows high spectral efficiency, near the Nyquist rate.

正交性也使 OFDM 的频谱利用率到接近于 Nyquist 频率。

3. OFDM generally has a nearly "white" spectrum, giving it benign electromagnetic interference properties with respect to other co-channel users.

OFDM 信号一般具有"白的"频谱，使之在与其他用户使用同一信道的情况下具有良好的抗电磁干扰性质。

4. Whilst Doppler shift alone may be compensated for by the receiver, the situation is worsened when combined with multipath, as reflections will appear at various frequency offsets, which is much harder to correct.

当只有多普勒频移时可以用接收机来补偿，当多普勒频移和多路径结合在一起时，情况就变得更糟，因为反射会出现在不同的频率偏移上，这种偏移很难校正。

5. One key principle of OFDM is that since low symbol rate modulation schemes (i.e. where the symbols are relatively long compared to the channel time characteristics) suffer less from intersymbol interference caused by multipath, it is advantageous to transmit a number of low-rate streams in parallel instead of a single high-rate stream.

OFDM 的一个关键的特性是因为低符号速率调制方案（也就是与信道时间特性相比，符号的持续时间相对较长）很少受到由多径引起的符号间干扰的影响，并行地传输许多低速率数据流要比传输一个高速率数据流有利。

6. The cyclic prefix, which is transmitted during the guard interval, consists of the end of the OFDM symbol copied into the guard interval, and the guard interval is transmitted followed by the OFDM symbol.

在保护间隔中传输的循环前缀是由复制到保护间隔中的 OFDM 符号的尾部组成

的，保护间隔是在 OFDM 符号之前传输的。

7. For example, when a part of the channel bandwidth is faded, frequency interleaving ensures that the bit errors that would result from those subcarriers in the faded part of the bandwidth are spread out in the bit-stream rather than being concentrated.

例如，当一部分信道带宽衰减时，频率交织将确保由带宽衰减部分的那些子载波产生的比特误差会分散在整个比特流上而不是集中起来。

Technical Tips

GSM

Global System for Mobile communications is the most popular standard for mobile phones in the world. The GSM Association estimates that 82% of the global mobile market uses the standard. GSM is used by over 2 billion people across more than 212 countries and territories. Its ubiquity makes international roaming very common between mobile phone operators, enabling subscribers to use their phones in many parts of the world. GSM differs from its predecessors in that both signaling and speech channels are digital call quality, and so is considered a second generation (2G) mobile phone system. The key advantage of GSM systems to consumers has been better voice quality and low-cost alternatives to making calls, such as the Short message service. The advantage for network operators has been the ease of deploying equipment from any vendors that implement the standard.

QAM

Quadrature amplitude modulation (QAM) is a modulation scheme which conveys data by changing (modulating) the amplitude of two carrier waves. These two waves, usually sinusoids, are out of phase with each other by 90° and are thus called quadrature carriers — hence the name of the scheme.

Like all modulation schemes, QAM conveys data by changing some aspect of a carrier signal, or the carrier wave, (usually a sinusoid) in response to a data signal. In the case of QAM, the amplitude of two waves, 90 degrees out-of-phase with each other (in quadrature) are changed to represent the data signal.

Phase modulation (analog PM) and phase-shift keying (digital PSK) can be regarded as a special case of QAM, where the amplitude of the modulating signal is constant, with only the phase varying. This can also be extended to frequency modulation (FM) and frequency-shift keying (FSK), for these can be regarded a special case of phase modulation.

Supplementary Readings: Wavelength-Division Multiplexing

In fiber-optic communications, wavelength-division multiplexing (WDM) is a technology which multiplexes multiple optical carrier signals on a single optical fibre by using different wavelengths (colors) of laser light to carry different signals. This allows for a multiplication in capacity, in addition to making it possible to perform bidirectional communications over one strand of fiber. The true potential of optical fiber is fully exploited when multiple beams of light at different frequencies are transmitted on the same fiber. This is a form of frequency division multiplexing (FDM) but is commonly called wavelength division multiplexing. The term wavelength-division multiplexing is commonly applied to an optical carrier (which is typically described by its wavelength), whereas frequency-division multiplexing typically applies to a radio carrier (which is more often described by frequency). However, since wavelength and frequency are inversely proportional, and since radio and light are both forms of electromagnetic radiation, the two terms are equal.

WDM system

A WDM system uses a multiplexer at the transmitter to join the signals together, and a demultiplexer at the receiver to split them apart. With the right type of fiber it is possible to have a device that does both simultaneously, and can function as an optical add-drop multiplexer. The optical filtering devices used in the modems are usually etalons, stable solid-state single-frequency Fabry-Perot interferometers in the form of thin-film-coated optical glass.

The concept was first published in 1970, and by 1978 WDM was realized in the laboratory. The first WDM systems only combined two signals. Modern systems can handle up to 160 signals and can thus expand a basic 10 Gbps fiber system to a theoretical total capacity of over 1.6 Tbps over a single fiber pair.

WDM systems are popular with telecommunications companies because they allow them to expand the capacity of the network without laying more fiber. By using WDM and optical amplifiers, they can accommodate several generations of technology development in their optical infrastructure without having to overhaul the backbone network. Capacity of a given link can be expanded by simply upgrading the multiplexers and demultiplexers at each end. This is often done by using optical-to-electrical-to-optical translation at the very edge of the transport network, thus permitting interoperation with existing equipment with optical interfaces.

Most WDM systems operate on single mode fiber optical cables, which have a core diameter of 9 μm. Certain forms of WDM can also be used in multi-mode fiber cables (also known as premises cables) which have core diameters of 50 or 62.5 μm.

Early WDM systems were expensive and complicated to run. However, recent standardization and better understanding of the dynamics of WDM systems have made WDM much cheaper to deploy.

Optical receivers, in contrast to laser sources, tend to be wideband devices. Therefore the demultiplexer must provide the wavelength selectivity of the receiver in the WDM system.

WDM systems are divided in different wavelength patterns, conventional, dense and coarse WDM. Conventional WDM systems provide up to 16 channels in the 3rd transmission window (C-band) of silica fibers around 1550 nm with a channel spacing of 100 GHz. DWDM uses the same transmission window but with less channel spacing enabling up to 31 channels with 50 GHz spacing, 62 channels with 25 GHz spacing sometimes called ultra dense WDM. New amplification options (Raman amplification) enable the extension of the usable wavelengths to the L-band, more or less doubling these numbers.

CWDM in contrast to conventional WDM and DWDM uses increased channel spacing to allow less sophisticated and thus cheaper transceiver designs. To again provide 16 channels on a single fiber CWDM uses the entire frequency band between second and third transmission window (1310/1550 nm respectively) including both windows (minimum dispersion window and minimum attenuation window) but also the critical area where OH scattering may occur, recommending the use of OH-free silica fibers in case the wavelengths between second and third transmission window shall also be used. Avoiding this region, the channels 31, 49, 51, 53, 55, 57, 59, 61 remain and these are the most commonly used.

WDM, DWDM and CWDM are based on the same concept of using multiple wavelengths of light on a single fiber, but differ in the spacing of the wavelengths, number of channels, and the ability to amplify the multiplexed signals in the optical space. EDFA provide efficient wideband amplification for the C-band, Raman amplification adds a mechanism for amplification in the L-band. For CWDM wideband optical amplification is not available, limiting the optical spans to several tens of kilometers.

Coarse WDM

Originally, the term "Coarse Wavelength Division Multiplexing" was fairly generic, and meant a number of different things. In general, these things shared the fact that the choice of channel spacings and frequency stability was such that Erbium Doped Fibre Amplifiers (EDFAs) could not be utilized. Prior to the relatively recent ITU standardization of the term, one common meaning for Coarse WDM meant two (or possibly more) signals multiplexed onto a single fiber, where one signal was in the 1550-nm band, and the other in the 1310-nm band.

Recently the ITU has standardized a 20 nanometer channel spacing grid for use with CWDM, using the wavelengths between 1310 nm and 1610 nm. Many CWDM wavelengths below 1470 nm are considered "unusable" on older G.652 specification fibers, due to the increased attenuation in the 1310~1470 nm bands. Newer fibers which conform to the G.652.C and G.652.D standards, such as Corning SMF-28e and Samsung Widepass nearly eliminate the "water peak" attenuation peak and allow for full operation of all twenty ITU

CWDM channels in metropolitan networks.

The Ethernet LX-4 physical layer standard is an example of a CWDM system in which four wavelengths near 1310 nm, each carrying a 3.125 gigabit-per-second (Gbps) data stream, are used to carry 10 gigabit-per-second of aggregate data.

The main characteristic of the recent ITU CWDM standard is that the signals are not spaced appropriately for amplification by EDFAs. This therefore limits the total CWDM optical span to somewhere near 60 km for a 2.5 Gbps signal, which is suitable for use in metropolitan applications. The relaxed optical frequency stabilization requirements allow the associated costs of CWDM to approach those of non-WDM optical components.

CWDM is also being used in cable television networks, where different wavelengths are used for the downstream and upstream signals. In these systems, the wavelengths used are often widely separated, for example the downstream signal might be at 1310 nm while the upstream signal is at 1550 nm.

Dense WDM

Dense Wavelength Division Multiplexing, or DWDM for short, refers originally to optical signals multiplexed within the 1550 nm band so as to leverage the capabilities (and cost) of erbium doped fibre amplifiers (EDFAs), which are effective for wavelengths between approximately 1525~1565 nm (C band), or 1570~1610 nm (L band). EDFAs were originally developed to replace SONET/SDH optical-electrical-optical (OEO) regenerators, which they have made practically obsolete. EDFAs can amplify any optical signal in their operating range, regardless of the modulated bit rate. In terms of multi-wavelength signals, so long as the EDFA has enough pump energy available to it, it can amplify as many optical signals as can be multiplexed into its amplification band (though signal densities are limited by choice of modulation format). EDFAs therefore allow a single-channel optical link to be upgraded in bit rate by replacing only equipment at the ends of the link, while retaining the existing EDFA or series of EDFAs along a long haul route. Furthermore, single-wavelength links using EDFAs can similarly be upgraded to WDM links at reasonable cost. The EDFAs cost is thus leveraged across as many channels as can be multiplexed into the 1550 nm band.

Exercises

I. Translate the following passage into Chinese.

OFDM consists of a large number of subcarriers equally spaced in a frequency band. Each band may be digitally modulated by a same scheme such as PSK, QAM, etc., or by different schemes. A serially transmitted sequence is divided into a number of sections, each having N symbols, and the N symbols in each section are used to modulate N carriers for simultaneous transmission. Therefore OFDM is essentially a parallel modulation system. When the number of subcarriers is sufficiently large, the system can resist multipath interference. This is because that, in the time domain, a symbol duration longer than the multipath delay can be chosen, while in the frequency domain, each symbol only occupies a small portion of the channel's frequency band. Thus, the effect of multipath fading spreads over many symbols, resulting in slight distortion to many symbols rather than complete destroy of a few symbols. In this way, correct demodulation is not affected so that the signal can be accurately recovered at the receiver.

In an OFDM system, the principle of choosing the subcarrier interval is to make the subcarriers mutually orthogonal within the entire symbol period. Thus, even if spectral overlap exists between the subcarriers, the symbols can still be recovered without loss. In order to realize maximum spectral efficiency, the interval between subcarriers is usually chosen to equal the reciprocal of the symbol duration T. Therefore the subcarrier frequencies in the base band are $f_n = n/T$ ($n = 0, 1, \cdots, N-1$). Denoting the n-th modulating symbol as $X(n)$, the OFDM waveform within a symbol duration can be expressed as:

$$x(t) = \sum_{n=0}^{N-1} X(n)\exp\left(j2\pi\frac{n}{T}t\right), \quad 0 \leqslant t < T \tag{1}$$

Sampling this waveform at $t = T/N$ yields

$$x(k) = \sum_{n=0}^{N-1} X(n)\exp\left(j2\pi\frac{kT}{N}\right) = \sum_{n=0}^{N-1} X(n)\exp\left(j2\pi\frac{nk}{N}\right), \quad k = 1,2,\ldots,N-1 \tag{2}$$

It is observed from the above expression that $x(k)$ and $X(n)$ form a discrete Fourier transform pair, therefore the baseband OFDM waveform can be generated from the discrete Fourier transform of N modulating symbols. When $N=2^m$ where m is an integer, the fast algorithm of IDFT is easy to implement.

II. Choose the word or phrase that is closest in meaning to the underlined part.

1. The process gain of a system indicates the gain or signal to noise improvement exhibited by a spread spectrum system <u>by the nature of the spreading and despreading process</u>.
    A. by virtue of the spreading/dispreading process
    B. by processing the spreading/despreading naturally
    C. according to the spreading/despreading characteristics
    D. using the natural spreading/dispreading process
2. Due to the unavoidable timing errors between the users, <u>there is little point in using Walsh codes as they will no longer be orthogonal</u>.
    A. using Walsh codes will have some point due to the absence of orthogonality
    B. using Walsh codes is meaningless since orthogonality will not exist any more
    C. Walsh code cannot be used since they are not orthogonal
    D. it is unnecessary to use Walsh codes because orthogonality is lost
3. For example, when a part of the channel bandwidth is faded, frequency interleaving ensures that the bit errors <u>that would result from those subcarriers in the faded part of the bandwidth</u> are spread out in the bit-stream rather than being concentrated.

A. that would be produced in those subcarriers suffering from frequency selective fading

B. that would cause some subcarriers being faded in some part of the bandwidth

C. that would came from the fading subcarriers falling in part of the bandwidth

D. that would result in those faded subcarrier of the part of the bandwidth

4. Earlier we introduced the concept that the identity of an amplitude modulated message signal <u>may under certain circumstances be communicated by transmitting regular samples of the message</u>, rather than the continuous signal.

A. may transmit samples that are regular in communications under some conditions

B. may be in the circumstances that regular message samples are communicated

C. may be conveyed by sending signal values sampled at regular intervals under certain conditions

D. may communicate with certain customers by sending regular samples of the message

5. Early we introduced the concept that the identity of an amplitude modulated message signal may under certain circumstances be communicated by transmitting <u>regular samples of the message</u>, rather than the continuous signal.

A. values of the message signal taken at regular intervals

B. formally obtained message samples

C. samples of the message produced in a specific manner

D. samples of the regularly obtained message

6. Having defined these functions, we will proceed to show how they can be used to <u>evaluate certain integrals characteristic of system error performance</u>.

A. evaluate characteristics of certain integrals in system error performance

B. assess certain integrals that are typical in describing error performance of the systems

C. decide the value of some characteristic integrals of error performance of the systems

D. carry out evaluations on the integrated characteristics of system error performance

7. Modulation is the systematic variation of some attribute of a carrier waveform such as the amplitude, phase, or frequency <u>in accordance with a function of the message signal</u>.

A. in terms of a message carried by the signal

B. according to the behavior of the signal

C. due to the performance of the signal

D. in relation with a quantity derived from the signal

8. Over recent years this potential has largely been realized in the costs of the optical fiber transmission medium <u>that for bulk purchases is now becoming competitive with copper wires</u>.

A. that is specifically for purchases, and is becoming superior to copper wires

B. that is bulkily comparable in price with copper wires

C. that is competing with copper wires in terms of the scale of purchases

D. that is becoming a challenge to copper wires when bought in a large quantity

Unit 6

Mobile Communications

The future mobile communications is expected to develop towards "any time, any where, any service", and provide completely open environments for interconnection with the external world.

Text

Part I: Mobile Communications

A mobile system is one in which users can physically move while communicating with one another. Examples include pagers, cellular phones, and cordless phones. It is the mobility that has made RF communications powerful and popular. The transceiver carried by the user is called the "mobile unit" (or simply the "mobile"), the "terminal," or the "hand-held unit." The complexity of the wireless infrastructure often demands that the mobiles communicate only through a fixed, relatively expensive unit called the "base station." Each mobile receives and transmits information from and to the base station via two RF channels called the "forward channel" or "downlink" and the "reverse channel" or "uplink," respectively. Most of our treatment relates to the mobile unit because, compared to the base station, hand-held units constitute a much larger portion of the market and their design is much more similar to other types of RF systems.

Cellular system

With the limited available spectrum (e.g., 25 MHz around 900 MHz), how do hundreds of thousands of people communicate in a crowded metropolitan area? To answer this question, we first consider a simpler case: thousands of FM radio broadcasting stations may operate in a country in the 88-108 MHz band. This is possible because stations that are physically far enough from each other can use the same carrier frequency (frequency reuse) with negligible mutual interference, except at some point in the middle where the stations are received with comparable signal levels.[1] The minimum distance between two stations that can employ equal carrier frequencies depends on the signal power produced by each.

In mobile communications, the concept of frequency reuse is implemented in a "cellular" structure, where each cell is configured as a hexagon and surrounded by six other cells as shown in Figure 6.1(a). The idea is that, if the center cell uses a frequency f_1 for communication, the six neighboring cells cannot utilize this frequency but the cells beyond the immediate neighbors may.[2] In practice, more efficient frequency assignment leads to the "7-cell" reuse pattern shown in Figure 6.1(b). Note that in reality each cell utilizes a group of frequencies.

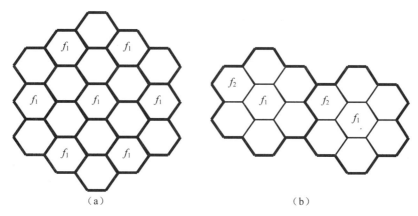

(a)   (b)

Figure 6.1   (a) Simple cellular system   (b) 7-cell reuse pattern

The mobile units in each cell of Figure 6.1(b) are served by a base station, and all of the base stations are controlled by a "mobile telephone switching office" (MTSO).

Co-channel interference

An important issue in a cellular system is how much two cells that use the same frequency interfere with each other. Called co-channel interference (CCI), this effect depends on the ratio of the distance between two co-channel cells to the cell radius and is independent of the transmitted power. Given by the frequency reuse plan, this ratio is approximately equal to 4.6 for the 7-cell pattern of Figure 6.1(b). It can be shown that this value yields a signal-to-co-channel interference ratio of 18 dB.

Handoff

What happens when a mobile unit "roams" from cell A to cell B? Since the power level received from the base station in cell A is insufficient to maintain communication, the mobile must change its server to the base station in cell B. Furthermore, since adjacent cells do not use the same group of frequencies, the channel must also change. Called "handoff," this process is performed by the MTSO. Once the level received by the base station in cell A drops below a threshold, the MTSO hands off the mobile to the base station in cell B, hoping that the latter is close enough. This strategy fails with relatively high probability, resulting in dropped calls.

To improve the handoff process, second-generation cellular systems allow the mobile unit to measure the received signal level from different base stations, thus performing handoff when the path to the second base station has sufficiently low loss.

Path loss and multipath fading

Propagation of signals in a mobile communication environment is quite complex. We briefly describe some of the important concepts here. Signals propagating through free space experience a power loss proportional to the square of the distance, d, from the source.[3] In reality, however, the signal travels through both a direct path and an indirect, reflective path (Figure 6.2). It can be shown that in this case, the loss increases with the fourth power of the distance. In crowded areas, the actual loss profile maybe proportional to d^2 for some distance and d^4 for another.

In addition to the overall loss profile depicted in Figure 6.2, another mechanism gives rise to fluctuations in the received signal level as a function of distance. Since the two signals shown in Figure 6.2 generally experience different phase shifts, possibly arriving at the receiver with opposite phases and roughly equal amplitudes, the net received signal may be very small.[4] Called "multipath fading," this phenomenon introduces enormous variations in the signal level as the receiver moves by a fraction of the wavelength. In reality, since the transmitted signal is reflected by many buildings and moving cars, the fluctuations are quite irregular.

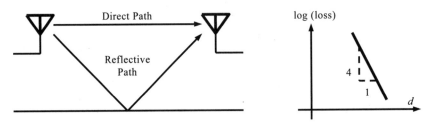

Figure 6.2   Indirect signal propagation and resulting loss profile

Diversity

The effect of fading can be lowered by adding redundancy to the transmission or reception of the signal. "Space diversity" or "antenna diversity" employs two or more antennas spaced apart by a significant fraction of the wavelength so as to achieve a higher probability of receiving a non-faded signal.[5]

"Frequency diversity" refers to the case where multiple carrier frequencies are used, with the idea that fading is unlikely to occur simultaneously at two frequencies sufficiently far from each other.

"Time diversity" is another technique whereby the data is transmitted or received more than once to overcome short-term fading.

Delay spread

Suppose two signals in a multipath environment experience roughly equal attenuation but different delays. This is possible because the absorption coefficient and phase shift of reflective or refractive materials vary widely, making it likely for two paths to exhibit equal loss and unequal delays.

In a multipath environment, many signals arrive at the receiver with different delays, yielding RMS delay spreads as large as several microseconds and hence fading bandwidths of several hundreds of kilohertz.[6] Thus, an entire communication channel may be suppressed during such a fade.

Large delay spreads introduce another difficulty as well: if the delay spread is comparable with the bit period of the digital modulating waveform, then multiple replicas of the signal are received with different delays, giving rise to considerable inter-symbol interference.

Interleaving

The nature of multipath fading and the signal processing techniques used to alleviate this issue is such that errors occur in clusters of bits.[7] In order to lower the effect of these errors, the baseband bit stream in the transmitter undergoes "interleaving" before modulation. An interleaver in essence scrambles the time order of the bits according to an algorithm known by the receiver.[8] Interleaving can also be viewed as a type of time diversity with no overhead (although it entails some latency).

Part II: Fourth Generation Wireless Networks

4G is the fourth generation of broadband cellular network technology, succeeding 3G. A 4G system must provide capabilities defined by International Telecommunication Union (ITU) in International Mobile Telecommunications-Advanced (IMT-Advanced Standard). Potential and current applications include amended mobile web access, IP telephony, gaming services, high-definition mobile TV, video conferencing, and 3D television.

In March 2008, the ITU-Radio communications sector (ITU-R) specified a set of requirements for 4G standards, named the IMT-Advanced specification, setting peak speed requirements for 4G service at 100 megabits per second (Mbit/s) for high mobility communication (such as from trains and cars) and 1 gigabit per second (Gbit/s) for low mobility communication (such as pedestrians and stationary users).[1]

Since the first-release versions of Mobile WiMAX and LTE support much less than 1 Gbit/s peak bit rate, they are not fully IMT-Advanced compliant. According to operators, a generation of the network refers to the deployment of a new non-backward-compatible technology. On December 6, 2010, ITU-R recognized that these two technologies, as well as other beyond-3G technologies that do not fulfill the IMT-Advanced requirements, could nevertheless be considered "4G", provided they represent forerunners to IMT-Advanced compliant versions and "a substantial level of improvement in performance and capabilities with respect to the third generation systems now deployed".

As opposed to earlier generations, a 4G system does not support traditional circuit-switched telephony service, but all-Internet Protocol (IP) based communication such as IP telephony. The spread spectrum radio technology used in 3G systems, is abandoned in all 4G candidate systems and replaced by OFDMA multi-carrier transmission and other frequency-domain equalization (FDE) schemes, making it possible to transfer very high bit rates despite extensive multi-path radio propagation.[2] The peak bit rate is further improved by smart antenna arrays for multiple-input multiple-output (MIMO) communications.

Background

In the field of mobile communications, a "generation" generally refers to a change in the fundamental nature of the service, non-backwards-compatible transmission technology, higher peak bit rates, new frequency bands, wider channel frequency bandwidth in Hertz, and higher capacity for many simultaneous data transfers (higher system spectral efficiency in bit/second/Hertz/site).

New mobile generations have appeared about every ten years since the first move from 1981 analog (1G) to digital (2G) transmission in 1992. This was followed, by 3G multi-media support in 2001, spread spectrum transmission and, at least 200 kbit/s peak bit rate, in 2011/2012 to be followed by "real" 4G, which refers to all-Internet Protocol (IP) packet-switched networks giving mobile ultra-broadband (gigabit speed) access.

While the ITU has adopted recommendations for technologies that would be used for future global communications, they do not actually perform the standardization or development work themselves. Instead, they rely on the work of other standard bodies such as IEEE, The WiMAX Forum, and 3GPP.

In the mid-1990s, the ITU-R standardization organization released the IMT-2000 requirements as a framework for what standards should be considered 3G systems, requiring 200 kbit/s peak bit rate. In 2008, ITU-R specified the IMT-A requirements for 4G systems. The fastest 3G-based standard in the UMTS family is the HSPA+ standard, which is commercially available since 2009 and offers 28 Mbit/s downstream (22 Mbit/s upstream) without MIMO, i.e. only with one antenna, and in 2011 accelerated up to 42 Mbit/s peak bit rate downstream using either DC-HSPA+ (simultaneous use of two 5 MHz UMTS carriers) or 2×2 MIMO. In theory speeds up to 672 Mbit/s are possible, but have not been deployed yet. The fastest 3G-based standard in the CDMA2000 family is the EV-DO Rev. B, which is available since 2010 and offers 15.67 Mbit/s downstream.

IMT-Advanced requirements

An IMT-Advanced cellular system must fulfill the following requirements:
- Be based on an all-IP packet switched network.
- Have peak data rates of up to approximately 100 Mbit/s for high mobility such as mobile access and up to approximately 1 Gbit/s for low mobility such as nomadic or local wireless access.
- Be able to dynamically share and use the network resources to support more simultaneous users per cell.
- Use scalable channel bandwidths of 5～20 MHz, optionally up to 40 MHz.
- Have peak link spectral efficiency of 15 bit/s/Hz in the downlink, and 6.75 bit/s/Hz in the uplink (meaning that 1 Gbit/s in the downlink should be possible over less

than 67 MHz bandwidth).

- System spectral efficiency is, in indoor cases, 3-bit/s/Hz/cell for downlink and 2.25-bit/s/Hz/cell for uplink.
- Smooth handovers across heterogeneous networks.

System Standards

In September 2009, technology proposals were submitted to the International Telecommunication Union (ITU) as 4G candidates. Basically all proposals are based on two technologies: LTE-A standardized by the 3GPP and 802.16m standardized by the IEEE (i.e. WiMAX).

Implementations of Mobile WiMAX and first-release LTE are largely considered a stopgap solution that will offer a considerable boost until WiMAX 2 (based on the 802.16m spec) and LTE Advanced are deployed. The latter's standard versions were ratified in spring 2011. Some sources consider first-release LTE and Mobile WiMAX implementations as pre-4G or near-4G, as they do not fully comply with the planned requirements of 1 Gbit/s for stationary reception and 100 Mbit/s for mobile.

Confusion has been caused by some mobile carriers who have launched products advertised as 4G but which according to some sources are pre-4G versions, commonly referred to as "3.9G", which do not follow the ITU-R defined principles for 4G standards, but today can be called 4G according to ITU-R.[3] Vodafone NL for example, advertised LTE as "4G", while advertising now LTE Advanced as their "4G+" service which actually is True 4G. A common argument for branding 3.9G systems as new-generation is that they use different frequency bands from 3G technologies; that they are based on a new radio-interface paradigm; and that the standards are not backwards compatible with 3G, whilst some of the standards are forwards compatible with IMT-2000 compliant versions of the same standards.

Just as LTE and WiMAX are being vigorously promoted in the global telecommunications industry, the former is also the most powerful 4G mobile communications leading technology and has quickly occupied the Chinese market. Time Division Long Term Evolution (TD-LTE) is not the first 4G wireless mobile broadband network data standard, but it is China's 4G standard that was amended and published by China's largest telecom operator—China Mobile. Whether this standard advocated by China Mobile will be widely recognized by the international market remains to be seen.

Principal technologies in all candidate systems

The physical layer transmission techniques of 4G systems include MIMO, frequency domain equalization and Turbo error-correcting codes.

The performance of radio communications depends on an antenna system, termed smart or intelligent antenna. Multiple antenna technologies are emerging to achieve the goal of 4G systems such as high rate, high reliability, and long range communications. In the early 1990s, to cater for the growing data rate needs of data communication, many transmission schemes were proposed. Spatial multiplexing, which involves deploying multiple antennas at the transmitter and at the receiver, gained importance for its bandwidth conservation and power efficiency. Independent streams can then be transmitted simultaneously from all the antennas.

Multiple-input and multiple-output, or MIMO, is a method for multiplying the capacity of a radio link using multiple transmit and receive antennas to exploit multipath propagation.[4] Apart from capacity gain, reliability in transmitting high speed data in the fading channel can be improved by using more antennas at the transmitter or at the receiver. This is called transmit or receive diversity. Both transmit/receive diversity and spatial multiplexing are categorized into the space-time coding techniques, which does not necessarily require the channel knowledge at the transmitter.[5] The other category is closed-loop multiple antenna technologies, which require channel knowledge at the transmitter.

One of the key technologies for 4G and beyond is called Open Wireless Architecture (OWA), supporting multiple wireless air interfaces in an open architecture platform. Software-defined radio (SDR) is one form of OWA. Since 4G is a collection of wireless standards, the final form of a 4G device will constitute various standards. This can be efficiently realized using SDR technology, which is categorized to the area of the radio convergence.

Unlike 3G, which is based on two parallel infrastructures consisting of circuit switched and packet switched network nodes, 4G will be based on packet switching only. This will require low-latency data transmission. In the context of 4G, IPv6 is essential to support a large number of wireless-enabled devices. By increasing the number of IP addresses available, IPv6 removes the need for network address translation (NAT), a method of sharing a limited number of addresses among a large group of devices, although NAT will still be required to communicate with devices that are on existing IPv4 networks.[6]

New Words

Part I

pager	寻呼机	cellular	蜂窝状的
cordless phone	无绳电话	mobility	移动性
transceiver	收发器	infrastructure	基础设施
carrier	载波	hexagon	六边形
handoff	切换，移交	roam	漫游
threshold	阈值，门限	power	幂
multipath fading	多径衰落	fluctuation	波动，起伏
irregular	不规则的，无规律的	diversity	分集，多样性
redundancy	冗余	fraction	小部分，分数

delay spread	延迟扩展	attenuation	衰减
reflective	反射的	refractive	折射的
RMS (Root Mean		intersymbol	符号间，码间
Square)	均方根	alleviate	减轻
replica	复制品	interleaving	交叉，交织
scramble	打乱，使混杂	overhead	开销
entail	需要，使必要	latency	等待时间，时间延迟

Part Ⅱ

specification	规范	megabit	兆比特
gigabit	千兆比特	compliant	符合的
operator	运营商	deployment	部署
compatible	兼容的	fulfill	履行
provided	在……的条件下	forerunner	先驱
opposed to	区别于	candidate	候选者
multi-carrier	多载波	equalization	均衡
propagation	传播	antenna	天线
peak	峰值	spectral	频谱的
protocol	协议	standardization	标准化

Notes on the Text

Part I

1. This is possible because stations that are physically far enough from each other can use the same carrier frequency (frequency reuse) with negligible mutual interference, except at some point in the middle where the stations are received with comparable signal levels.

这是可能的，因为在物理位置上相隔足够远的电台可使用同一载波频率（频率重用），而相互干扰可以忽略，除了两个电台的中间位置以外，这里接收到的两个电台信号强度相近。

- with comparable signal levels：指收到来自两个电台的信号电平可相比，即强度差不多。

2. The idea is that, if the center cell uses a frequency f_1 for communication, the six neighboring cells cannot utilize this frequency but the cells beyond the immediate neighbors may.

频率重用的概念是：如果位于中央的蜂窝使用频率 f_1 进行通信，那么与其相邻的 6 个蜂窝就不能使用这个频率，但外面不直接相邻的蜂窝可再次使用这个频率。

3. Signals propagating through free space experience a power loss proportional to the

square of the distance, d, from the source.

在自由空间里传播的信号会有功率损耗，其值正比于离开发射源的距离 d 的平方。

4. Since the two signals shown in Figure 6.2 generally experience different phase shifts, possibly arriving at the receiver with opposite phases and roughly equal amplitudes, the net received signal may be very small.

由于图 6.2 所示的两个信号通常经受不同的相移，因此有可能到达接收端时相位相反，而幅度却大致相等，这样净接收的信号就可能非常弱。

5. "Space diversity" or "antenna diversity" employs two or more antennas spaced apart by a significant fraction of the wavelength so as to achieve a higher probability of receiving a non-faded signal.

空间分集或天线分集是采用两个或更多的天线间隔波长的几分之一放置，这样便能以较高的概率接收到无衰落的信号。

6. In a multipath environment, many signals arrive at the receiver with different delays, yielding RMS delay spreads as large as several microseconds and hence fading bandwidths of several hundreds of kilohertz.

在多径环境中，许多信号以不同的延迟到达接收机，产生的均方根延迟扩散可大到几微秒，因而衰落带宽达数百千赫。

7. The nature of multipath fading and the signal processing techniques used to alleviate this issue is such that errors occur in clusters of bits.

多径衰落的性质，以及用于减轻这一问题的信号处理技术使得差错以比特串的形式出现。

8. An interleaver in essence scrambles the time order of the bits according to an algorithm known by the receiver.

交织器实质上根据接收端已知的某种算法打乱比特位的时间顺序。

Part Ⅱ

1. In March 2008, the ITU-Radio communications sector (ITU-R) specified a set of requirements for 4G standards, named the IMT-Advanced specification, setting peak speed requirements for 4G service at 100 megabits per second (Mbit/s) for high mobility communication (such as from trains and cars) and 1 gigabit per second (Gbit/s) for low mobility communication (such as pedestrians and stationary users).

2008 年 3 月，ITU 无线电通信部（ITU-R）规定了一系列对 4G 标准的要求，命名为 IMT-Advanced 规范，设置了 4G 服务的峰值速度要求：要求在高速移动通信中（如火车和汽车）达到 100 Mbps（Mbit/s），在低移动性通信中（如行人和固定用户）达到 1 Gbps（Gbit/s）。

2. The spread spectrum radio technology used in 3G systems, is abandoned in all 4G candidate systems and replaced by OFDMA multi-carrier transmission and other frequency-domain equalization (FDE) schemes, making it possible to transfer very high bit rates despite extensive multi-path radio propagation.

所有的 4G 候选系统都弃用了 3G 使用的扩频无线技术，而转向 OFDMA 多载波传输和其他频域均衡（FDE）方案，从而在存在大量多径的电波传播环境下仍能达到很高的比特率。

3. Confusion has been caused by some mobile carriers who have launched products advertised as 4G but which according to some sources are pre-4G versions, commonly referred to as "3.9G", which do not follow the ITU-R defined principles for 4G standards, but today can be called 4G according to ITU-R.

有些移动运营商已经推出了标榜是 4G 的产品，但有些人认为这实际上是通常称为"3.9G"的准 4G，从而造成一些混淆。这些版本并不符合 ITU-R 4G 规范的定义原则，但根据 ITU-R（制定的原则），今天我们也可称之为 4G。

4. Multiple-input and multiple-output, or MIMO, is a method for multiplying the capacity of a radio link using multiple transmit and receive antennas to exploit multipath propagation.

多输入多输出（MIMO）技术采用多个发射和接收天线，从而利用多径传播以增加无线链路的容量。

5. Both transmit/receive diversity and transmit spatial multiplexing are categorized into the space-time coding techniques, which does not necessarily require the channel knowledge at the transmitter.

发射/接收分集和发射空间复用均被归类为空时编码技术，它们不一定要求发射端已知信道信息。

6. By increasing the number of IP addresses available, IPv6 removes the need for network address translation (NAT), a method of sharing a limited number of addresses among a large group of devices, although NAT will still be required to communicate with devices that are on existing IPv4 networks.

通过增加可用的 IP 地址数量，IPv6 不再需要网络地址转换（NAT），尽管在现有 IPv4 网络中仍然需要通过 NAT 与设备进行通信。NAT 是一种在一大组设备之间共享有限数量地址的方法。

Technical Tips

Fading

In wireless communications, the presence of reflectors in the environment surrounding a transmitter and receiver create multiple paths that a transmitted signal can traverse. As a result, the receiver sees the superposition of multiple copies of the transmitted signal, each traversing a different path. Each signal copy will experience differences in attenuation, delay and phase shift while traveling from the source to the receiver. This can result in either constructive or destructive interference, amplifying or attenuating the signal power seen at the receiver. Strong destructive interference is frequently referred to as a deep fade and may result in temporary failure of communication due to a severe drop in the channel signal-to-noise ratio.

A common example of multipath fading is the experience of stopping at a traffic light and hearing an FM broadcast degenerate into static, while the signal is re-acquired if the vehicle moves only a fraction of a meter. The loss of the broadcast is caused by the vehicle stopping at a point where the signal experienced severe destructive interference. Cellular phones can also exhibit similar momentary fades.

Interleaving in data transmission

Interleaving is mainly used in digital data transmission technology, to protect the transmission against burst errors. These errors overwrite a lot of bits in a row, but seldom occur. Interleaving is used to solve this problem. All data is transmitted with some control bits, such as error correction bits, that enable the channel decoder to correct a certain number of altered bits. If a burst error occurs, and more than this number of bits is altered, the codeword cannot be correctly decoded. So the bits of a number of codewords are interleaved and then transmitted. That way, a burst error affects only a correctable number of bits in each codeword, so the decoder can decode the codewords correctly.

Also, the complexity, required cost and effort for error correction of the communication can be reduced by employing interleaving method since that the data errors can be controlled to reasonable range.

Supplementary Readings: The Road to 5G

The 5th generation mobile networks or the 5th generation wireless systems, abbreviated 5G, are the proposed next telecommunications standards beyond the current 4G/IMT-Advanced standards.

What will 5G be? What it will not be is an incremental advance on 4G. The previous four generations of cellular technology have each been a major paradigm shift that has broken backward compatibility. Indeed, 5G will need to be a paradigm shift that includes very high carrier frequencies with massive bandwidths, extreme base station and device densities, and unprecedented numbers of antennas. However, unlike the previous four generations, it will also be highly integrative: tying any new 5G air interface and spectrum together with LTE and WiFi to provide universal high-rate coverage and a seamless user experience. To support this, the core network will also have to reach unprecedented levels of flexibility and intelligence, spectrum regulation will need to be rethought and improved, and energy and cost efficiencies will become even more critical considerations.

As the long-term evolution (LTE) system embodying 4G has now been deployed and is reaching maturity, where only incremental improvements and small amounts of new spectrum can be expected, it is natural for researchers to ponder "what's next?" However, this is not a mere intellectual exercise. Driven largely by smartphones, tablets, and video streaming, the most recent VNI report and forecast makes plain that an incremental approach will not come close to meeting the demands that networks will face by 2020. In just a decade, the amount of IP data handled by wireless networks will have increased by well over a factor of 100. In addition to the sheer volume of data, the number of devices and the data rates will continue to grow exponentially. The number of devices could reach the tens or even hundreds of billions by the time 5G comes to fruition, due to many new applications beyond personal communications.

Engineering Requirements for 5G

In order to more concretely understand the engineering challenges facing 5G, and to plan to meet them, it is necessary to first identify the requirements for a 5G system. The following items are requirements in each key dimension, but it should be stressed that not all of these need to be satisfied simultaneously. Different applications will place different requirements on the performance, and peak requirements that will need to be satisfied in certain configurations are mentioned below. For example, very-high-rate applications such as streaming high-definition video may have relaxed latency and reliability requirements compared to driverless cars or public safety applications, where latency and reliability are paramount but lower data rates can be tolerated.

(1) **Data Rate:** The need to support the mobile data traffic explosion is unquestionably the main driver behind 5G. Data rate can be measured in several different ways, and there will be a 5G goal target for each such metric:

(a) *Aggregate data rate* or *area capacity* refers to the total amount of data the network can serve, characterized in bits/s per unit area. The general consensus is that this quantity will need to increase by roughly 1000× from 4G to 5G.

(b) *Edge rate* or 5% rate is the worst data rate that a user can reasonably expect to receive when in range of the network, and so is an important metric and has a concrete engineering meaning. Goals for the 5G edge rate range from 100 Mbps (easily enough to support high-definition streaming) to as much as 1 Gbps. Meeting 100 Mbps for 95% of users will be extraordinarily challenging, even with major technological advances. This requires about a 100× advance since current 4G systems have a typical 5% rate of about 1 Mbps, although the precise number varies quite widely depending on the load, the cell size, and other factors.

(c) *Peak rate* is the best-case data rate that a user can hope to achieve under any conceivable network configuration. The peak rate is a marketing number, devoid of much meaning to engineers and likely to be in the range of tens of Gbps.

Meeting the requirements in (a), (b), which are about 1000× and 100× current 4G technology, respectively.

(2) **Latency:** Current 4G roundtrip latencies are on the order of about 15 ms, and are based on the 1 ms subframe time with necessary overheads for resource allocation and access. Although this latency is sufficient for most current services, anticipated

5G applications include two-way gaming, novel cloud-based technologies such as those that may be touch-screen activated (the "tactile Internet"), and virtual and enhanced reality (e.g., Google glass or other wearable computing devices). As a result, 5G will need to be able to support a roundtrip latency of about 1 ms, an order of magnitude faster than 4G. In addition to shrinking down the subframe structure, such severe latency constraints may have important implications on design choices at several layers of the protocol stack and the core network.

(3) Energy and Cost: As we move to 5G, costs and energy consumption will, ideally, decrease, but at least they should not increase on a per-link basis. Since the per-link data rates being offered will be increasing by about 100 times, this means that the Joules per bit and cost per bit will need to fall by at least 100 times. For example, mmWave spectrum should be $10\sim100$ times cheaper per Hz than the 3G and 4G spectrum below 3 GHz. Similarly, small cells should be $10\sim100$ times cheaper and more power efficient than macrocells. A major cost consideration for 5G, even more so than in 4G due to the new BS densities and increased bandwidth, is the backhaul from the network edges into the core.

Key Technologies to Get to 1000× Data Rate

Of the requirements outlined above, certainly the one that gets the most attention is the need for radically higher data rates across the board. Our view is that the required 1000× will, for the most part, be achieved through combined gains in three categories:

(a) Extreme densification and offloading to improve the area spectral efficiency. Put differently, more active nodes per unit area and Hz.

(b) Increased bandwidth, primarily by moving toward and into mmWave spectrum but also by making better use of WiFi's unlicensed spectrum in the 5-GHz band. Altogether, more Hz.

(c) Increased spectral efficiency, primarily through advances in MIMO, to support more bits/s/Hz per node.

The combination of more nodes per unit area and Hz, more Hz, and more bits/s/Hz per node, will compound into many more bits/s per unit area. The "big three" 5G technologies includes ultra-densification, mmWave, and massive multiple-input multiple-output (MIMO).

A. Extreme Densification and Offloading

A straightforward but extremely effective way to increase the network capacity is to make the cells smaller. Networks are now rapidly evolving to include nested small cells such as picocells (range under 100 meters) and femtocells (WiFi-like range), as well as distributed antenna systems that are functionally similar to picocells from a capacity and coverage standpoint but have all their baseband processing at a central site and share cell IDs.

Cell shrinking has numerous benefits, the most important being the reuse of spectrum across a geographic area and the ensuing reduction in the number of users competing for resources at each BS. Contrary to widespread belief, as long as power-law path-loss models hold the signal-to-interference ratio (SIR) is preserved as the network densifies. Thus, in principle, cells can shrink almost indefinitely without a sacrifice in SIR, until nearly every BS serves a single user (or is idle). This allows each BS to devote its resources, as well as its backhaul connection, to an ever-smaller number of users.

B. Millimeter Wave

Although beachfront bandwidth allocations can be made significantly more efficient by modernizing regulatory and allocation procedures, to put large amounts of new bandwidth into play there is only one way to go: up in frequency. Fortunately, vast amounts of relatively idle spectrum do exist in the mmWave range of 30~300 GHz, where wavelengths are 1~10 mm. There are also several GHz of plausible spectrum in the 20-30 GHz range.

The main reason that mmWave spectrum lies idle is that, until recently, it had been deemed unsuitable for mobile communications because of rather hostile propagation qualities, including strong pathloss, atmospheric and rain absorption, low diffraction around obstacles and penetration through objects, and, further, because of strong phase noise and exorbitant equipment costs. The dominant perception had therefore been that such frequencies, and in particular the large unlicensed band around 60 GHz, were suitable mainly for very-short-range transmission. However, semiconductors are maturing, their costs and power consumption rapidly falling and the other obstacles related to propagation are now considered increasingly surmountable given time and focused effort.

C. Massive MIMO

Well-established by the time LTE was developed, MIMO was a native ingredient thereof with two-to-four antennas per mobile device and as many as eight per BS sector. Marzetta was instrumental in articulating a vision in which the number of antennas increased by more than an order of magnitude, first in a 2007 presentation with the details formalized in a landmark paper. The proposal was to equip BSs with a number of antennas much larger than the number of active users per time-frequency signaling resource, and given that under reasonable time-frequency selectivities accurate channel estimation can be conducted for at most some tens of users per resource, this condition puts the number of antennas per BS into the hundreds. This bold idea, initially termed "large-scale antenna systems" but now more popularly known as "massive MIMO," offers enticing benefits including enormous enhancements in spectral efficiency without the need for increased BS densification and simple transmit/receive structures because of the quasi-orthogonal nature of the channels between each BS and the set of active users sharing the same signaling resource.

The promise of these benefits has elevated massive MIMO to a central position in preliminary 5G discussions, with a foreseen role of providing a high-capacity umbrella of ubiquitous coverage in support of underlying tiers of small cells.

Exercises

I. Translate the following sentences into Chinese.

1. Communication is the transmission of information from one point to another. This transmission requires the ability to vary signals with time in a manner which is unpredictable to the receiver.

2. It is true of any communication system that the shape and amplitude of the transmitted signal will be continuously degraded by the introduction of noise, and the attenuation along the transmission path.

3. Since the very beginning, communications systems have consisted of three major parts, namely, the equipment, the medium, and the protocol. It is still the case today. However, the close link of telecommunications with the computer technology has brought about tremendous changes in communications, from the concepts, to the contents and the methods.

4. The availability of such a large collection of system performance curves in a single compilation allows the researcher or system designer to perform trade-off studies among the various communication type/fading channel/diversity combinations so as to determine the optimum choice in the face of his or her available constraints.

5. The channel provides the electrical connection between the information source and the user. The channel can have many different forms such as a microwave radio link over free space, a pair of wires, or an optical fiber.

6. The degradation of the transmitted signal is a result of signal distortion due to imperfect response of the channel and due to undesirable electrical signals (noise) and interference. Noise and signal distortion are two basic problems of electrical communication.

II. Choose the phrase that is closest in meaning to the underlined part.

1. This is possible because stations that are physically far enough from each other can use the same carrier frequency (frequency reuse) with negligible mutual interference, except at some point in the middle <u>where the stations are received with comparable signal levels</u>.

   A. where the signals received from the stations are relatively strong

   B. where the signals from different stations are similar in level

   C. where the receiving stations can be compared with the signal levels

   D. where the stations can receive comparatively high level signals

2. Space diversity or antenna diversity employs two or more antennas <u>spaced apart by a significant fraction of the wavelength</u> so as to achieve a higher probability of receiving a non-faded signal.

   A. placed sufficiently apart measured by the wavelength

　　B. far enough to make the wavelength only a fraction of the spacing

　　C. separated by a distance less than a wavelength but not too small

　　D. divided by a few wavelengths

3. While the subject of coding <u>often carries an air of secrecy</u>, a more important motive in many modern coding systems is the improved efficiency in conveying information.

　　A. always brings secret information in the air

　　B. is generally transmitted through air and kept secret

　　C. often uses secret carriers

　　D. is considered mysterious and often used in secret communication

4. Our reliance on computer technology <u>has left us vulnerable to attack</u>, and the vulnerability creates difficult political dilemmas that must be dealt with should we wish to continue following the currents of the Third Wave.

　　A. has left us to launch attack

　　B. has made us immune against hostile actions

　　C. has made us susceptible to assault

　　D. has left us voluntary in offense

5. Our reliance on computer technology and our quick transition into a knowledge-based economy have left us vulnerable to attack, and that vulnerability creates difficult political dilemmas that must be dealt with <u>should we wish to continue following the current</u> of the Third Wave.

　　A. we should wish to go on after the following current

　　B. so that we should carry on the current

　　C. only if we want to continue following the current

　　D. if we wish to go ahead to follow the current

6. We shall use this parameter as <u>a measure of degradation</u> during the evaluation of different quantization systems later in this chapter.

　　A. an action of processing

　　B. a degree of enhancement

　　C. an amount of impairment

　　D. an effect of interference

Unit 7 Optical Communications

A major principle in communications systems has been that the higher the frequency, the greater the technical complexity. Sending more information would cost more. However, for optical carriers, which have frequencies in the hundreds of terahertz, information bandwidth is in some sense free.

Text

Part I: Electromagnetic Spectrum

Various observations relating to the potential of optical technology for transmission of information can be made from the frequency line of Table 7.1.

Table 7.1   A frequency line which gives the wavelengths λ, the frequencies ν, and the photon energy ε_p for the various regions of the frequency spectrum

Name	audio	radio	μwave	mmwave	IR	OPT/UV	x-ray	Gamma
λ	300km	300m	30cm	3mm	30μm	0.3μm	30Å	0.03Å
ν(Hz)	10^3	10^6	10^9	10^{11}	10^{13}	10^{15}	10^{17}	10^{20}
ε_p	—	—	3μeV	0.3meV	30meV	3eV	300eV	0.3MeV

The information rates in which one is interested in conventional "modern-day" communications systems generally correspond to audio rates in telephone systems, radio rates in commercial broadcast systems, or digital television rates in the most advanced video distribution systems.[1] These rates are generally below several GHz. If one were to transmit such information without impressing it on an optical carrier but instead on a radio frequency (RF) carrier a bit higher than the maximum rate, the transmission wavelength of the RF carrier would be centimeters or larger.[2] There can, however, be great advantages to using optical carriers. An obvious one is the low loss and directionality of the optical fiber. Clearly, the carrier must have a higher rate than the information rate. A major principle that has appeared in communications systems has been that the higher the frequency, the greater the technical complexity. Microwaves are harder to handle than are radio waves. As wavelengths decrease to approach the size of circuit components, circuit elements are no longer lumped, and leads can act as reflective components and/or antennas and lumped elements as electromagnetic resonators.[3] This has generally meant that sending more information would cost more and there was therefore a cost per bit/sec (bps) of transmitted information in the sense that going to a higher information rate requires a higher frequency. Thus, the first observation from the frequency line would be that, for optical carriers, which have frequencies in the hundreds of THz, information bandwidth is in some sense free. That is to say, the optical wavelength is so small compared to most devices that the technology has changed drastically from electrical and microwave. Once we assume that we have such technology, no matter how high an information rate one might want it will not be necessary to change the carrier, as the carrier frequency is higher than any realistic information rate could become. Bandwidth is not completely free, though, as encoders and decoders must necessarily operate at the information rate, but much of the rest of the system must necessarily handle only the carrier plus modulation. If a component can handle a frequency of 5×10^{14} Hz, an information shift in that frequency of a part in a thousand (corresponding to a 500 GHz information rate) will have little or no effect on device performance. Therefore, once the system is already set up, one can upgrade system speed more or less at will without the kind of costs incurred by changing the electromagnetic carrier in conventional systems.

A consequence of the size of the optical bandwidth is that the optical carrier can be used to carry many different telephone conversations, television programs, etc., simultaneously. The process by which this is generally carried out (at least in synchronous format) is called time division multiplexing (TDM). The idea is that, if one wishes to multiplex 16 different channels each transmitting at 1 Mbps, one could perform this by dividing each bit period by 16 and then interleaving the bits into a composite 1μsec bit (1 Mbps rate) which actually carries 16 bits of information on it.[4] With telephone conversations representing a rate of 64 kbps, the 100s of Tbps bandwidth of the optical carrier holds great promise for TDM. Of course, TDM is not the only multiplexing scheme one can imagine using. One could imagine impressing a number of subcarriers, spaced by perhaps some GHz, onto the optical carrier. Each of these carriers could then be modulated at an information rate and then re-separated according to their different carrier wavelengths at the output. Such a scheme is referred to as wavelength-division multiplexing (WDM) or subcarrier modulation, depending on the implementation. Many of the present-day schemes for increasing link throughput with increasing traffic involve combining many TDM signals onto WDM carriers. In fact, the limitation on density of WDM turns out to be not bandwidth but power. That is, each channel requires some amount of power. The more channels, then, the higher the power requirement. At some power level, optical fiber nonlinearity becomes important, and this nonlinearity tends to mix the signals together. There is presently much effort going on in trying to find ways to equalize such nonlinearities.

The high carrier frequency of the optical carrier also has drawbacks, especially as it relates, through the speed of light, to the optical wavelength. The optical period corresponds to less than two femtoseconds. This means that phase control corresponds to manipulation of sub-femtosecond periods of time. Although techniques to do such are emerging, they are complicated—much more complicated than manipulating microwave or radio frequency waveforms. For this reason, coherent optical reception is still a laboratory technology. The development of the rare earth-doped optical fiber amplifier seems to have obviated the need for coherent techniques in telecommunication as far as improved signal-to-noise ratio goes.

The short period of the optical wave also implies a short wavelength centered around half of a micron. The smallness of the optical wavelength, therefore, allows for the miniaturization of transmit and receive modules, which should allow considerable reduction in size, weight, and cost of optical communication systems with respect to microwave/radio wave counterparts.[5] In the case of microwaves, the higher the packaging density of open microwave channels, the worse the crosstalk. No matter how tightly one packs fiber, on the other hand, the crosstalk is essentially zero if the cladding is properly designed. This leads to the characteristic that fiber is an excellent medium for space division multiplexing (SDM)—that is, packaging a number of channels with different information streams in close proximity.

Although all the advantages of coherent optical communication systems have yet to be brought to fruition, another property of optical radiation has made today's optical communication systems not desirable for applications.[6] The important property here is that of photon energy. As is seen from Table 7.1, the photon energy ranges from roughly 2 eV to roughly 4 eV. This would seem to be an advantage in efficiency. However, there is a penalty to be paid for having such photon energy. Because single photons are detectable, the emission/reception process must take on a granular nature. As is well-known, even in a steady rain, the probability of a raindrop landing (as a function of time) follows a Poisson distribution, implying that there is raindrop bunching.[7] A raindrop would rather fall right after the one before. Raindrops are impatient and don't like to wait. In much the same manner, a laser likes to spit bunches of photons even under constant bias current. Such behavior leads to a type of noise commonly referred to as shot noise or quantum noise.

Optical quantum detectors can operate at room temperature, as single photons are measurable. Therefore, optical direct detection can be quite sensitive if shot noise-limited. Direct detection, further, is totally compatible with intensity modulation schemes—schemes in which the source is essentially just turned on and off.[8] Such modulation schemes are the easiest to implement. When coupled with light's short wavelength which allows for miniature sources and detectors and micron-sized waveguides, direct detection schemes have allowed for small, lightweight, high bandwidth systems which are competitive in many areas, most notably to the present telecommunications transmission, although a myriad of other applications are continually opening up.[9] As mentioned previously, these applications have tended to open up more slowly than originally predicted, as cost was really not much of a consideration in telecommunications, where equipment costs are swamped by other considerations.[10] With consumer electronics, one need not worry about right of way or installation. At present, the cost of connecting to personal computers a few meters from each other optically is so expensive that fiber has not yet come to the consumer market. The high cost of the link in such a case, though, is not fundamental but more historical. Present-day developments in millimeter core plastic is an example of a much cheaper technology than, for example, glass fiber. The costs of components to go into fiber links as well as packaging costs are presently being reduced and new applications are opening up.

Part II: Optical Fiber

An optical fiber (or fiber) is a glass or plastic fiber designed to guide light along its length by confining as much light as possible in a propagating form.[1] In fibers with large core diameter, the confinement is based on total internal reflection. In smaller diameter core fibers, (widely used for most communication links longer than 200 meters) the confinement relies on establishing a waveguide. Fiber optics is the overlap of applied science and engineering concerned with such optical fibers. Optical fibers are widely used in fiber-optic communication, which permits transmission over longer distances and at higher data rates than other forms of wired and wireless communications. They are also used to form sensors, and in a variety of other applications.

The term optical fiber covers a range of different designs including graded-index optical fibers and step-index optical fibers. Based on the way in which lights are propagated though the fiber, there are single mode fibers including nonzero dispersion-shifted fibers and dispersion-shifted fibers, and multimode fibers. A fiber may either be single-mode or multimode, dictated by the specific design and the wavelength of the light propagating in the fiber.[2] Because of the mechanical properties of the more common glass optical fibers, special methods of splicing fibers and of connecting them to other equipment are needed. Manufacture of optical fibers is based on partially melting a chemically doped preform and pulling the flowing material on a draw tower.[3] Fibers are built into different kinds of cables depending on how they will be used.

Optical fiber communication

Optical fiber can be used as a medium for telecommunication and networking because it is flexible and can be bundled as cables. It is especially advantageous for long-distance communications, because light propagates through the fiber with little attenuation compared to electrical cables. This allows long distances to be spanned with few repeaters. Additionally, the light signals propagating in the fiber can be modulated at rates as high as 40 Gbps, and each fiber can carry many independent channels, each by a different wavelength of light (wavelength-division-multiplex WDM).[4] In total, a single fiber-optic cable can carry data at rates as high as 14.4 Pbps (around 14 million Gbps). Over short distances, such as networking within a building, fiber saves space in cable ducts because a single fiber can carry much more data than a single electrical cable. Fiber is also immune to electrical interference, which prevents cross-talk between signals in different cables and pickup of environmental noise.[5] Also, wiretapping is more difficult compared to electrical connections, and there are concentric dual core fibers that are said to be tap-proof. Because they are non-electrical, fiber cables can bridge very high electrical potential differences and can be used in environments where explosive fumes are present, without danger of ignition.[6]

Although fibers can be made out of transparent plastic, glass, or a combination of the two, the fibers used in long-distance telecommunications applications are always glass, because of the lower optical attenuation. Both multi-mode and single-mode fibers are used in communications, with multi-mode fiber used mostly for short distances (up to 500 m), and single-mode fiber used for longer distance links. Because of the tighter tolerances required to couple light into and between single-mode fibers (core diameter about 10 micrometers), single-mode transmitters, receivers, amplifiers and other components are generally more expensive than multi-mode components.[7]

Fiber optic sensors

Optical fibers can be used as sensors to measure strain, temperature, pressure and other parameters. The small size and the fact that no electrical power is needed at the remote location give the fiber optic sensor advantages to conventional electrical sensor in certain applications.

Optical fibers are used as hydrophones for seismic or sonar applications. Hydrophone systems with more than 100 sensors per fiber cable have been developed. Hydrophone sensor systems are used by the oil industry as well as a few countries' navies. Both bottom mounted hydrophone arrays and towed streamer systems are in use. The German company Sennheiser developed a microphone working with a laser and optical fibers.

Optical fiber sensors for temperature and pressure have been developed for downhole measurement in oil wells. The fiber optic sensor is well suited for this environment as it is functioning at temperatures too high for semiconductor sensors.

Another use of the optical fiber as a sensor is the optical gyroscope which is in use in the Boeing 767 and in some car models (for navigation purposes) and the use in hydrogen microsensors.

Fiber-optic sensors have been developed to measure co-located temperature and strain simultaneously with very high accuracy. This is particularly useful to acquire information from small complex structures.

Other uses of optical fibers

Fibers are widely used in illumination applications. They are used as light guides in medical and other applications where bright light needs to be shone on a target without a clear line-of-sight path. In some buildings, optical fibers are used to route sunlight from the roof to other parts of the building. Optical fiber illumination is also used for decorative applications, including signs, art, and artificial Christmas trees.

Optical fiber is also used in imaging optics. A coherent bundle of fibers is used, sometimes along with lenses, for a long, thin imaging device called an endoscope, which is used to view objects through a small hole. Medical endoscopes are used for minimally invasive exploratory or surgical procedures (endoscopy). Industrial endoscopes are used for inspecting anything hard to reach, such as jet engine interiors.

An optical fiber doped with certain rare-earth elements such as erbium can be used as the gain medium of a laser or optical amplifier. Rare-earth doped optical fibers can be used to provide signal amplification by splicing a short section of doped fiber into a regular (undoped) optical fiber line. The doped fiber is optically pumped with a second laser wavelength that is coupled into the line in addition to the signal wave.[8] Both wavelengths of light are transmitted through the doped fiber, which transfers energy from the second pump wavelength to the signal wave. The process that causes the amplification is stimulated emission.

Optical fiber can be used to supply a low level of power (around one watt) to electronics situated in a difficult electrical environment. Examples of this are electronics in high-powered antenna elements and measurement devices used in high voltage transmission equipment.

Principle of operation

An optical fiber is a cylindrical dielectric waveguide that transmits light along its axis, by the process of total internal reflection. The fiber consists of a core surrounded by a cladding layer (Figure 7.1). To confine the optical signal in the core, the refractive index of the core must be greater than that of the cladding. The boundary between the core and cladding may either be abrupt, in step-index fiber, or gradual, in graded-index fiber.

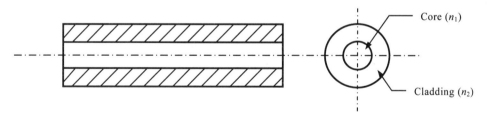

Figure 7.1　A typical optical fiber consisting of a transparent material of refractive index n_1 and surrounded by a cladding of a slightly lower refractive index n_2. Most of the propagating energy is confined to the core region and the field decays exponentially in the cladding.

Multimode fiber

Fiber with large (greater than 10 μm) core diameter may be analyzed by geometric optics. Such fiber is called multimode fiber, from the electromagnetic analysis. In a step-index multimode fiber (Figure 7.2), rays of light are guided along the fiber core by total internal reflection. Rays that meet the core-cladding boundary at a high angle (measured relative to a line normal to the boundary), greater than the critical angle for this boundary, are completely reflected.[9] The critical angle (minimum angle for total internal reflection) is determined by the difference in index of refraction between the core and cladding materials. Rays that meet the boundary at a low angle are refracted from the core into the cladding, and do not convey light and hence information along the fiber.[10] The critical angle determines the acceptance angle of the fiber, often reported as a numerical aperture. A high numerical aperture allows light to propagate down the fiber in rays both close to the axis and at various angles, allowing efficient coupling of light into the fiber.[11] However, this high numerical aperture increases the amount of dispersion as rays at different angles have different path lengths and therefore take different times to traverse the fiber.[12] A low numerical aperture may therefore be desirable.

In a graded-index fiber (Figure 7.3), the index of refraction in the core decreases continuously between the axis and the cladding. This causes light rays to bend smoothly as they approach the cladding, rather than reflecting abruptly from the core-cladding boundary. The resulting curved paths reduce multi-path dispersion because high angle rays pass more through the lower-index periphery of the core, rather than the high-index center. The index profile is chosen to minimize the difference in axial propagation speeds of the various rays in the fiber. This ideal index profile is very close to a parabolic relationship between the index and the distance from the axis.

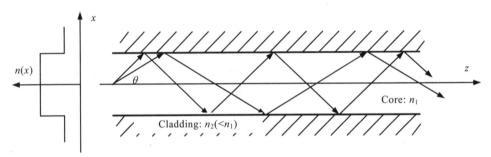

Figure 7.2   A step-index multimode fiber in which the refractive index in the core is constant. Light rays impinging on the core-cladding interface at an angle greater than the critical angle are trapped inside the core of the waveguide. In such a fiber rays traveling at larger angles to the axis have to traverse a larger path and hence take a longer time than those rays which propagate with lesser angles to the axis. This leads to a substantial amount of broadening in a pulse propagating through the fiber.

Singlemode fiber

Fiber with a core diameter less than about ten times the wavelength of the propagating light cannot be modeled using geometric optics. Instead, it must be analyzed as an electromagnetic structure, by solution of Maxwell's equations as reduced to the electromagnetic wave equation.[13] The electromagnetic analysis may also be required to understand behaviors such as speckle that occur when coherent light propagates in multi-mode fiber. As an optical waveguide, the fiber supports one or more confined transverse modes by which light can propagate along the fiber. Fiber supporting only one mode is called single-mode or mono-mode fiber. The behavior of larger-core multimode fiber can also be modeled using the wave equation, which shows that such fiber supports more than one mode of propagation (hence the name). The results of such modeling of multi-mode fiber approximately agree with the predictions of geometric optics, if the fiber core is large enough to support more than a few modes.

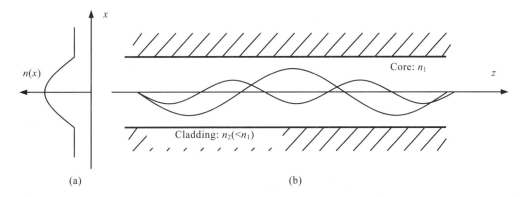

Figure 7.3　A graded-index optical fiber in which the refractive index in the core decreases continuously away from the axis. Figure (a) shows a typical variation of refractive index across the core of the optical fiber. Light rays in such a fiber are trapped by a continuous refraction towards the center of the core, which leads to a periodic focusing of the rays, as illustrated in (b). In such a fiber, even though rays making larger angles with the axis traverse a longer path length, they do so in a region with a lower refractive index and hence at a higher speed of propagation: this leads to a smaller value of pulse dispersion in such fibers as compared to homogeneous core fibers.

The waveguide analysis shows that the light energy in the fiber is not completely confined in the core. Instead, especially in single-mode fibers, a significant fraction of the energy in the bound mode travels in the cladding as an evanescent wave.

The most common type of single-mode fiber has a core diameter of 8 to 10 μm and is designed for use in the near infrared. The mode structure depends on the wavelength of the light used so that this fiber actually supports a small number of additional modes at visible wavelengths. Multi-mode fiber, by comparison, is manufactured with core diameters as small as 50 microns and as large as hundreds of microns.

New Words

Part I

impress	印，铭刻，加载	directionality	方向性
resonator	谐振器	terahertz	特赫（10^{12}Hz）
synchronous	同步的	incur	招致，蒙受，引起
throughput	吞吐量	interleave	交织
femtosecond	毫微微秒（10^{-15}s）	nonlinearity	非线性
obviate	避免，使成为不必要	coherent	相干的
miniature	小型的	micron	微米
counterpart	对等物，对等的角色	miniaturization	小型化

proximity	接近，亲近	cladding	光纤包层
photon	光子	fruition	结果实，成就
bias	偏置	granular	颗粒状

Part Ⅱ

core	纤芯	diameter	直径
confinement	限制	waveguide	波导
graded-index	渐变（梯度）折射率	step-index	阶跃（突变）折射率
single mode fiber	单模光纤	dispersion	色散
multimode fibers	多模光纤	polarization	偏振，极化
crystal	晶体	splice	结合，焊接
bundle	捆，包扎	doped	掺杂质的
repeater	中继器，转发器	attenuation	衰减
duct	管道	immune	免疫的，不受影响的
wiretapping	搭线窃听	concentric	同心的
tap-proof	防窃听的	ignition	燃烧，点火
strain	应力	hydrophone	水听器
seismic	地震的	sonar	声呐
towed streamer	拖曳式水听器阵	gyroscope	陀螺仪
co-located	位于同一地方的	endoscope	内窥镜，内诊镜
invasive	入侵的，侵略性的	erbium	铒
cylindrical	圆柱形的	dielectric	介电的，电介质的
abrupt	突然的	index of refraction	折射率
normal	垂直的，法线的	aperture	孔径，光圈
refractive	折射的	profile	轮廓，分布
parabolic	抛物线的	speckle	散斑，斑点
coherent	相干的	transverse	横向的
evanescent	渐逝的	micron	微米

Notes on the Text

Part I

1. The information rates in which one is interested in conventional "modern-day" communications systems generally correspond to audio rates in telephone systems, radio rates in commercial broadcast systems, or digital television rates in the most advanced video distribution systems.

人们所感兴趣的"现代"常规通信系统的信息传输速率通常对应于电话系统中的音频，商用广播系统中的无线电频率，或是在最先进的视频节目分配系统中的数字电视信息速率。

2. If one were to transmit such information without impressing it on an optical carrier but instead on a radio frequency (RF) carrier a bit higher than the maximum rate, the transmission wavelength of the RF carrier would be centimeters or larger.

如果要传输这样的信息而不将它加载于光纤上，而是加载在略高于最大速率的射频载波上，则此射频载波就会是厘米波或波长再长一些的波。

3. As wavelengths decrease to approach the size of circuit components, circuit elements are no longer lumped, and leads can act as reflective components and/or antennas and lumped elements as electromagnetic resonators.

随着波长减小到接近于电路元件的尺寸，电路单元就不再是集总的，导线可起到反射元件以及（或）天线的作用，这些集总单元则成为电磁谐振器。

4. The idea is that, if one wishes to multiplex 16 different channels each transmitting at 1 Mbps, one could perform this by dividing each bit period by 16 and then interleaving the bits into a composite 1μsec bit (1 Mbps rate) which actually carries 16 bits of information on it.

其原理是：如果要复用 16 个 1 Mbps 的不同信道，可将每一比特所占时间除以 16，然后将 16 个数据比特交织成一个持续 1 μs 的复合比特（即比特率为 1 Mbps），这一复合比特实际上带有 16 比特的信息。

5. The smallness of the optical wavelength, therefore, allows for the miniaturization of transmit and receive modules, which should allow considerable reduction in size, weight, and cost of optical communication systems with respect to microwave/radio wave counterparts.

光波波长之小使发射和接收模块得以小型化，这就使光通信系统的尺寸、重量以至价格与相应的微波、无线电波通信系统相比都大为降低。

6. Although all the advantages of coherent optical communication systems have yet to be brought to fruition, another property of optical radiation has made today's optical communication systems not desirable for applications.

虽然相干光通信系统的所有优点还有待于落实在具体成果中，光辐射的另一性质却使目前的光通信系统不利于应用。

7. As is well-known, even in a steady rain, the probability of a raindrop landing (as a function of time) follows a Poisson distribution, implying that there is raindrop bunching.

众所周知，即使在一场稳定的降雨中，雨滴落地的概率（作为时间的函数）服从 Poisson 分布，意味着有成串的雨滴。

8. Direct detection, further, is totally compatible with intensity modulation schemes—schemes in which the source is essentially just turned on and off.

进一步来说，直接检测与强度调制方案完全兼容，在这些方案中电源实质上只是简单地接通或断开。

9. When coupled with light's short wavelength which allows for miniature sources and detectors and micron-sized waveguides, direct detection schemes have allowed for

small, lightweight, high bandwidth systems which are competitive in many areas, most notably to the present telecommunications transmission, although a myriad of other applications are continually opening up.

光的波长很小，可以使用小型的光源和检测器以及微米级的波导，于是用直接检测方案可实现在许多领域具有竞争力的小巧的宽带系统。特别引人注目的是当前在电信传输中的应用，尽管无数其他应用也在不断涌现出来。

10. As mentioned previously, these applications have tended to open up more slowly than originally predicted, as cost was really not much of a consideration in telecommunications, where equipment costs are swamped by other considerations.

如前所述，（线路）成本并非电信系统中真正重要的考虑因素，通信设备的成本主要受到其他因素的制约，因此这些应用比预料的出现得慢。

Part Ⅱ

1. An optical fiber (or fiber) is a glass or plastic fiber designed to guide light along its length by confining as much light as possible in a propagating form.

光纤是一种玻璃的或塑料的纤维，用来沿其长度方向引导光，把尽可能多的光限制于一种传播的形式。

2. An optical fiber may either be single-mode or multimode, dictated by the specific design and the wavelength of the light propagating in the fiber.

一根光纤根据其设计和在其中传播的光的波长，可以是单模的也可以是多模的。

3. Manufacture of optical fibers is based on partially melting a chemically doped preform and pulling the flowing material on a draw tower.

光纤制造过程是将化学掺杂的预制棒部分融化，并在一个抽丝塔上拉长流动的原料。

4. Additionally, the light signals propagating in the fiber can be modulated at rates as high as 40 Gbps, and each fiber can carry many independent channels, each by a different wavelength of light (wavelength-division-multiplex WDM).

此外在光纤中传播的光信号可以调制高达 40 Gbps 的速率，每一根光纤都能作为许多独立的信道，每个信道用不同波长的光来调制（波分复用）。

  • each by a different wavelength of light：each 后面省略了 modulated

5. Fiber is also immune to electrical interference, which prevents cross-talk between signals in different cables and pickup of environmental noise.

光纤也不会受电干扰的影响，防止了不同光缆中信号之间的串话以及环境噪声的介入。

6. Because they are non-electrical, fiber cables can bridge very high electrical potential differences and can be used in environments where explosive fumes are present, without danger of ignition.

因为光纤是不用电的，它能横跨很高的电位差，能用于存在爆炸烟雾的环境下而没有燃烧的危险。

7. Because of the tighter tolerances required to couple light into and between

single-mode fibers (core diameter about 10 micrometers), single-mode transmitters, receivers, amplifiers and other components are generally more expensive than multi-mode components.

由于将光耦合到单模光纤或在单模光纤之间耦合（纤芯直径大约为 10 μm）的允差较小，单模发射器、接受器、放大器和其他元件的价格通常比多模元件的贵。

8. The doped fiber is optically pumped with a second laser wavelength that is coupled into the line in addition to the signal wave.

除了信号波外，耦合到光纤线路的另一个激光波长被泵浦（注入）到掺杂介质的光纤中。

9. Rays that meet the core-cladding boundary at a high angle (measured relative to a line normal to the boundary), greater than the critical angle for this boundary, are completely reflected.

当射线射到纤芯和包层之间界面的角度（与垂直于边界的直线之间的夹角）大于临界角时，射线被完全反射。

10. Rays that meet the boundary at a low angle are refracted from the core into the cladding, and do not convey light and hence information along the fiber.

以小角度射到分界面上的射线被折射，从纤芯进入包层，它们并不沿着光纤传输光，因而也不传输信息。

11. A high numerical aperture allows light to propagate down the fiber in rays both close to the axis and at various angles, allowing efficient coupling of light into the fiber.

大的数值孔径使光能以接近于轴线的方式沿光纤传播，也能以不同的角度传输，从而使得光能有效地耦合进入光纤。

12. However, this high numerical aperture increases the amount of dispersion as rays at different angles have different path lengths and therefore take different times to traverse the fiber.

然而，大的数值孔径增加了色散的总量，因为以不同角度传播的光线具有不同的光程长度，因而花了不同的时间穿过光纤。

13. Instead, it must be analyzed as an electromagnetic structure, by solution of Maxwell's equations as reduced to the electromagnetic wave equation.

而它必须作为电磁结构通过解 Maxwell 方程组来分析，Maxwell 方程组可化为电磁波的波动方程。

- reduce：公式的化简，这里是将 Maxwell 方程组的 4 个方程化为一个波动方程。

Technical Tips

Crosstalk

Crosstalk is the disturbance caused by electromagnetic interference. In electronics, the term crosstalk means undesired capacitive, inductive, or conductive coupling from one circuit, part of a circuit, or channel, to another. Any phenomenon by which a signal transmitted on one circuit or channel of a transmission system creates an undesired effect in another circuit or channel.

In telecommunication or telephony, crosstalk is often distinguishable as pieces of speech or signaling tones leaking from other people's connections. If the connection is analog, twisted pair cabling can often be used to reduce the effects of crosstalk. Alternatively, the signals can be converted to digital form, which is much less susceptible to crosstalk. In wireless communication, crosstalk is often denoted co-channel interference, and is related to adjacent-channel interference.

Total internal reflection

Total internal reflection (TIR) is the phenomenon which involves the reflection of all the incident light off the boundary. TIR only takes place when both of the following two conditions are met:

- the light is in the more dense medium and approaching the less dense medium.
- the angle of incidence is greater than the so-called critical angle.

Total internal reflection will not take place unless the incident light is traveling within the more optically dense medium towards the less optically dense medium. TIR will happen for light traveling from water towards air, but it will not happen for light traveling from air towards water. TIR would happen for light traveling from water towards air, but it will not happen for light traveling from water (n=1.333) towards crown glass (n=1.52). TIR occurs because the angle of refraction reaches a 90-degree angle before the angle of incidence reaches a 90-degree angle. The only way for the angle of refraction to be greater than the angle of incidence, is for light to bend away from the normal. Since light only bends away from the normal when passing from a more dense medium into a less dense medium, then this would be a necessary condition for total internal reflection.

Supplementary Readings: Optical Systems

An optical system model

A schematic depiction of the organization of an archetypical optical system is given in Figure 7.4. The model used here, as we will see in the subsequent discussion, is quite general and applies to practically all-optical systems that exist, including communications as well as sensing systems. For example, the earliest types of optical communication systems were probably ones in which a lamp was sequentially hidden from sight for fixed periods between periods of being in plain view. Such a system was employed by Paul Revere in 1776, but it is very likely that such systems had been in operation since the times of the early Greeks or Egyptians. In such a system, the information source is the lamp holder, the encoder is his arms together with the occluding sheet, the receiver optics are the eyes of the beholder, the detector is the beholder's retinae, the receiver is the brain of the beholder, and the information out is the response of the beholder.

Perhaps a major point in having a model such as in Figure 7.4 is that such a model is so general that we can use it as a basis for comparing widely differing systems that at first may appear incomparable. Certainly, however, any two systems can be compared by comparing the data launched into the system with that exiting the system (bit error rate (BER) counting in digital systems or noise figure measurement in analog systems). Other figures of merit can, indeed, also allow comparison of the specific blocks of the model. Such comparison will be a major occupation of this course—to compare performance of the various Mehdi Au LLPschemes for performing the various functions of the blocks of Figure 7.4. The following four subsections will discuss first sources, then fibers, and then detectors. The last section will give some systems architecture perspective, as the other types of components which make up the blocks of Figure 7.4 in the archetypical "modern-day" optical communication systems are very architecture-dependent. The discussion that follows will be given from a somewhat historical perspective.

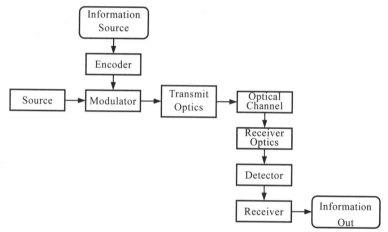

Figure 7.4   A schematic depiction of the organization of an optical communications system in which the square blocks are the optical system itself and the circular blocks denote the system input and output, respectively.

Optical paths

The second major development to occur during 1970 was the development of the low loss optical fiber. The idea of communicating through free space is well and good, but as was previously stated, a major advantage of optical transmitters was their directivity. For broadcasting, it is hard to beat radio waves. For point to point, it is hard to beat optics. But there are problems with using free space as a transmission medium. The first one is very practical. Usually, one is trying to communicate with someone else on the face of the Earth. Two major problems arise from this. One problem is that the Earth is round. Once line-of-sight distances are exceeded, one needs to increase link length by a quantum leap in order to include a satellite repeater. This is a problem for both microwave and optical transmission. As was shown by Hertz, although the first definitive trans-Atlantic demonstration was made by Marconi some years later around the turn of the century, low-frequency waves (AM band, ≤1 MHz) will cling to the ground for some distance. Already by the shortwave band (~10 MHz), the waves begin to skip off the Earth, although up to roughly 100 MHz they still reflect off the ionosphere. At higher frequencies, one needs an orbiting reflector and/or repeater.

Another problem with free-space optical transmission is that, unfortunately, there is a thing surrounding the Earth called the atmosphere. Radio waves don't care too much what is happening in the atmosphere, but optical waves do. Rain, snow, fog, and even wind affect optical transmission. There are free-space optical links still in use, especially between buildings in cities and on campuses, but for any but the shortest, most protected of these links, weather interference does occur. Many sensors, though, by nature, use free space and always will as they are measuring the weather. An example is the LIDAR, or laser radar.

A third problem with free-space communication is more fundamental. That problem is diffraction. Coherent waves in free space will expand at an angle that is roughly equal to the wavelength of the radiation divided by the effective radiating aperture. One can minimize the diffraction effect only by using larger and larger focusing lenses. In fact, one can project a 600m spot on the moon, but this requires using a 2.7m telescope as the transmitter. The diffraction effect, therefore, puts fundamental bounds on distances and powers necessary in free-space systems.

The optical fiber is a solution to the above-mentioned problems, at least in telecommunications systems and in some sensor systems as well.

A "modern-day" archetypical telecommunications optical transmitter, such as the one employed in today's telephone network, is depicted in Figure 7.5. The idea is that the laser diode can be "pigtailed" with an optical fiber, therefore obviating the need for any focusing optics whatsoever. The transmitter module therefore needs no alignment. One need only hook up the laser to a current source and hook up the fiber output into a transmission fiber by means of an optical connector.

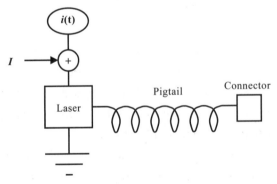

Figure 7.5　Schematic depiction of an optical transmitter as used in the telephone network

Exercises

I. Translate the following sentences into Chinese.

1. Early in the twentieth century, it was found that light could cause atoms to emit electrons and that, when light released an electron from an atom, the energy possessed by the electron very greatly exceeded that which the atom could, according to the electromagnetic wave theory, have received.

2. Pulse broadening determines the minimum separation between adjacent pulses, which in turn determines the maximum information-carrying capacity of the optical fiber.

3. If one were to transmit such information without impressing it on an optical carrier but instead on a radio frequency (RF) carrier a bit higher than the maximum rate, the transmission wavelength of the RF carrier would be centimeters or larger.

4. The smallness of the optical wavelength, therefore, allows for the miniaturization of transmit and receive modules, which should allow considerable reduction in size, weight, and cost of optical communication systems with respect to microwave/radio wave counterparts.

5. Although all the advantages of coherent optical communication systems have yet to be brought to fruition, another property of optical radiation has made today's optical communication systems not desirable for applications.

6. When coupled with light's short wavelength which allows for miniature sources and detectors and micron-sized waveguides, direct detection schemes have allowed for small, lightweight, high bandwidth systems which are competitive in many areas, most notably to the present telecommunications transmission, although a myriad of other applications are continually opening up.

7. As mentioned previously, these applications have tended to open up more slowly than originally predicted, as cost was really not much of a consideration in telecommunications, where equipment costs are swamped by other considerations.

8. As wavelengths decrease to approach the size of circuit components, circuit elements are no longer lumped as such, and leads can act as reflective components and/or antennas and lumped elements as electromagnetic resonators.

II. Choose the word or phrase that is closest in meaning to the underlined part.

1. If one were to transmit such information <u>without impressing it on an optical carrier but instead on a radio frequency carrier</u>, the transmission wavelength of the RF carrier would be centimeters or larger

   A. without the impression that an optical carrier can replace a radio frequency carrier

   B. without pressing an optical carrier but instead pressing a radio frequency carrier on it

C. without modulating an optical wave but instead a radio frequency wave

D. this delay must indeed be no more than one internal bit

2. As mentioned previously, <u>these applications have tended to open up more slowly than originally predicted</u>, as cost was really not much of a consideration in telecommunications, where equipment costs are swamped by other considerations.

A. the intended applications are open and slow in the original prediction

B. there is a trend that these applications have not become available quickly enough as expected

C. these applications are likely not to be valid gradually, but will be open as predicted

D. these originally predicted applications will be open to the public slowly

3. Because of the <u>tighter tolerances required to couple light into and between single-mode fibers</u>, single-mode transmitters, receivers, amplifiers and other components are generally more expensive than multi-mode components

A. smaller errors in light coupling between single-mode fibers

B. serious coupling effect between different single-mode fibers

C. high difference between single-mode fibers

D. tougher requirements for feeding light into the fiber and mutual transferring between fibers

4. <u>The microwave band designation</u> has never been officially sanctioned by any industrial, professional or governmental organizations.

A. The design of microwave devices

B. The frequency of microwave band

C. The division of microwave spectrum

D. The bandwidth of microwaves

5. By keeping the off state slightly below threshold, the delay between the applied electrical pulse and the resulting optical output pulse is minimized; <u>this delay must indeed not be more than the bit interval</u> so that the optical pulse can accurately reproduce the input signal.

A. this delay must indeed be kept within the width of one bit

B. indeed, this delay must not exceed the bit of interval

C. as a matter of fact, this delay interval must be a bit less than an interval

D. this delay must indeed be no more than one internal bit

6. It may be mentioned here that in optical fibers having very small core radii and small index difference between the core and cladding, it can be so arranged that only one <u>mode of propagation</u> exists in the fiber.

A. pattern of field distribution

B. method of transmission

C. model of transmission line

D. propagation property

7. The development of optical fiber over the last twenty years has resulted in the production of optical fiber cables that <u>exhibit very low attenuation and transmission loss</u> in comparison with the best copper conductors.

A. cause very small reduction in the power of signals traveling over them

B. make very severe enhancement resulting in loss of transmission

C. show very weak coupling and infrequent transmission failure

D. attract very little attention so as to cause transmission degradation

8. Both intermodal and intramodel dispersions arise as a result of (a) waveguide effects and (b) material effects; <u>the latter due to the finite bandwidth of the source</u> and the fact that at different wavelengths the refractive indices are different.

A. the later is caused by the fine bandwidth of the source

B. the latter effects being confined to the finite bandwidth of the source

C. the material effects being a result of the restricted source bandwidth

D. both effects being the cause of the limited source bandwidth

Unit 8

Digital Signals and Signal Processing

There have been tremendous demands in the use of computers and special-purpose digital circuitry for performing varied signal processing functions that were originally achieved with analog equipment. Digital signal processing has grown to be a subject covering a very wide range of applications such as in audio and speech processing, image processing, telecommunications, and biomedicine.

Text

Part I: Digital Signal Processing

Digital signal processing (DSP) is the study of signals in a digital representation and the processing methods of these signals. DSP and analog signal processing are sub-fields of signal processing. DSP includes sub-fields like audio and speech signal processing, sonar and radar signal processing, sensor array processing, spectral estimation, statistical signal processing, image processing, signal processing for communications, biomedical signal processing, etc.

Since the goal of DSP is usually to measure or filter continuous real-world analog signals, the first step is usually to convert the signal from an analog to a digital form, by using an analog to digital converter. Often, the required output signal is another analog output signal, which requires a digital to analog converter.

The algorithms required for DSP are sometimes performed using specialized computers, which make use of specialized microprocessors called digital signal processors (also abbreviated DSP). These process signals in real time, and are generally purpose-designed application-specific integrated circuits (ASICs).[1] When flexibility and rapid development are more important than unit costs at high volume, DSP algorithms may also be implemented using field-programmable gate arrays (FPGAs).[2]

DSP domains

In DSP, engineers usually study digital signals in one of the following domains: time domain (one-dimensional signals), spatial domain (multidimensional signals), frequency domain, autocorrelation domain, and wavelet domains. They choose the domain in which to process a signal by making an informed guess (or by trying different possibilities) as to which domain best represents the essential characteristics of the signal.[3] A sequence of samples from a measuring device produces a time or spatial domain representation, whereas a discrete Fourier transform produces the frequency domain information, that is, the frequency spectrum.[4] Autocorrelation is defined as the cross-correlation of the signal with itself over varying intervals of time or space.

Signal sampling

With the increasing use of computers the usage and need of digital signal processing has increased. In order to use an analog signal on a computer it must be digitized with an analog to digital converter (ADC). Sampling is usually carried out in two stages, discretization and quantization. In the discretization stage, the space of signals is partitioned into equivalence classes and discretization is carried out by replacing the signal with representative signal of the corresponding equivalence class.[5] In the quantization stage the representative signal values are approximated by values from a finite set.

In order for a sampled analog signal to be exactly reconstructed, the Nyquist-Shannon sampling theorem must be satisfied. This theorem states that the sampling frequency must be greater than twice the bandwidth of the signal. In practice, the sampling frequency is often significantly more than twice the required bandwidth. The most common bandwidth scenarios are: DC-BW ("baseband"); and $f_c \pm BW$, a frequency band centered on a carrier frequency ("direct demodulation").

A digital to analog converter (DAC) is used to convert the digital signal back to analog. The use of a digital computer is a key ingredient into digital control systems.

Time and space domains

The most common processing approach in the time or space domain is enhancement of the input signal through a method called filtering. Filtering generally consists of some transformation of a number of surrounding samples around the current sample of the input or output signal. There are various ways to characterize filters; for example:

- A "linear" filter is a linear transformation of input samples; other filters are "non-linear." Linear filters satisfy the superposition condition, i.e., if an input is a weighted linear combination of different signals, the output is an equally weighted linear combination of the corresponding output signals.[6]
- A "causal" filter uses only previous samples of the input or output signals; while a "non-causal" filter uses future input samples. A non-causal filter can usually be changed into a causal filter by adding a delay to it.
- A "time-invariant" filter has constant properties over time; other filters such as adaptive filters change in time.
- Some filters are "stable", others are "unstable". A stable filter produces an output that converges to a constant value with time, or remains bounded within a finite

interval. An unstable filter produces output which diverges.

- A "finite impulse response" (FIR) filter uses only the input signal, while an "infinite impulse response" filter (IIR) uses both the input signal and previous samples of the output signal. FIR filters are always stable, while IIR filters may be unstable.

Most filters can be described in Z-domain (a superset of the frequency domain) by their transfer functions. A filter may also be described as a difference equation, a collection of zeroes and poles or, if it is an FIR filter, an impulse response or step response.[7] The output of an FIR filter to any given input may be calculated by convolving the input signal with the impulse response. Filters can also be represented by block diagrams which can then be used to derive a sample processing algorithm to implement the filter using hardware instructions.

Frequency domain

Signals are converted from time or space domain to the frequency domain usually through the Fourier transform. The Fourier transform converts the signal information to a magnitude and phase component of each frequency. Often the Fourier transform is converted to the power spectrum, which is the magnitude of each frequency component squared.

The most common purpose for analysis of signals in the frequency domain is analysis of signal properties. The engineer can study the spectrum to get information of which frequencies are present in the input signal and which are missing.

There are some commonly used frequency domain transformations. For example, the cepstrum converts a signal to the frequency domain through Fourier transform, takes the logarithm, and then applies another Fourier transform. This emphasizes the frequency components with smaller magnitude while retaining the order of magnitudes of frequency components.[8]

Applications

The main applications of DSP are audio signal processing, audio compression, digital image processing, video compression, speech processing, speech recognition, digital communications, radar, sonar, and biomedicine. Specific examples are speech compression and transmission in digital mobile phones, room matching equalization of sound in HiFi and sound reinforcement applications, weather forecasting, economic forecasting, seismic data processing, analysis and control of industrial processes, computer-generated animations in movies, medical imaging such as CAT scans and MRI, image manipulation, high fidelity loudspeaker crossovers and equalization, and audio effects for use with electric guitar amplifiers.

Implementation

Digital signal processing is often implemented using specialized microprocessors such as the MC56000 and the TMS320. These often process data using fixed-point arithmetic, although some versions are available which use floating point arithmetic and are more powerful. For faster applications FPGAs might be used. Beginning in 2007, multicore implementations of DSPs have started to emerge. For faster applications with vast usage, ASICs might be designed specifically. For slow applications, a traditional slower processor such as a microcontroller can cope.

Part Ⅱ: General Concepts of Digital Signal Processing

There have been tremendous demands in the use of digital computers and special-purpose digital circuitry for performing varied signal processing functions that were originally achieved with analog equipment. The continued evolution of inexpensive integrated circuits has led to a variety of microcomputers and minicomputers that can be used for various signal processing functions. It is now possible to build special-purpose digital processors within much smaller size and lower cost constraints of systems previously all analog in nature.[1]

We will provide a general discussion of the basic concepts associated with digital signal processing. To do so, it is appropriate to discuss some common terms and assumptions. Wherever possible, the definitions and terminology will be established in accordance with the recommendations of the IEEE Group on Audio and Electroacoustics.

An analog signal is a function that is defined over a continuous range of time and in which the amplitude may assume a continuous range of values. Common examples are the sinusoidal function, the step function, the output of a microphone, etc. The term *analog* apparently originated from the field of analog computation, in which voltages and currents are used to represent physical variables, but it has been extended in usage.

Continuous-time signal is a function that is defined over a continuous range of time, but in which the amplitude may either have a continuous range of values or a finite number of possible values. In this context, an analog signal could be considered as a special case of a continuous-time signal. In practice, however, the terms *analog* and *continuous-time* are interchanged casually in usage and are often used to mean the same thing. Because of the association of the term *analog* with physical analogies, preference has been established for the term *continuous-time*. Nevertheless, there will be cases in which the term *analog* will be used for clarity, particularly where it relates to the term *digital*.[2]

The term quantization describes the process of representing a variable by a set of distinct values. A quantized variable is one that may assume only distinct values.

A discrete-time signal is a function that is defined only at a particular set of values of time. This means that the independent variable, time, is quantized. If the amplitude of a discrete-time signal is permitted to assume a continuous range of values, the function is said to be a sampled-data signal. A sampled-data signal could arise from sampling an analog signal at discrete values of time.

A digital signal is a function in which both time and amplitude are quantized. A digital signal may always be represented by a sequence of numbers in which each number has a finite number of digits.

The terms *discrete-time* and *digital* are often interchanged in practice and are often used to mean the same thing. A great deal of the theory underlying discrete-time signals is applicable to purely digital signals, so it is not always necessary to make rigid distinctions. The term *discrete-time* will more often be used in pursuing theoretical developments, and the term *digital* will more often be used in describing hardware or software realizations.

A system can be described by any of the preceding terms according to the type of hardware or software employed and the type of signals present. Thus, reference can be made to *analog systems*, *continuous-time systems*, *discrete-time systems*, *digital systems*, etc.

A linear system is one in which the principle of superposition applies. A linear system can be described by linear differential or difference equations. A time-invariant linear system is one in which the parameters are fixed and do not vary with time.

A lumped system is one that is composed of finite nonzero elements satisfying ordinary differential or difference equation relationships, as opposed to a distributed system, satisfying partial differential equation relationships.[3]

The standard form for numerical processing of a digital signal is the binary number system. The binary number system makes use only of the values 0 and 1 to represent all possible numbers. The number of levels m that can be represented by a number having n binary digits (bits) is given by

$$m = 2^n \tag{8-1}$$

Conversely, if m is the number of possible levels required, the number of bits required is the smallest integer greater than or equal to $\log_2 m$.[4]

The process by which digital signal processing is achieved will be illustrated by a simplified system in which the signal is assumed to vary from 0 to 7 volts and in which 8 possible levels (at 1 V increments) are used for the binary numbers.[5] A block diagram is shown in Figure 8.1, and some waveforms of interest are shown in Figure 8.2. The signal is first passed through a continuous-time presampling filter whose function will be discussed later. The signal is then read at intervals of T seconds by a sampler. These samples must then be quantized to one of the standard levels. Although there are different strategies employed in the quantization process, one common approach, which will be assumed here, is that a sample is assigned to the nearest level. Thus, a sample of value 4.2 V would be quantized to 4 V, and a sample of value 4.6 V would be quantized to 5 V.

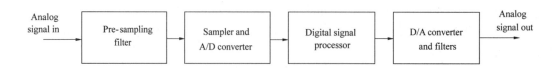

Figure 8.1   Block diagram of a possible digital processing system

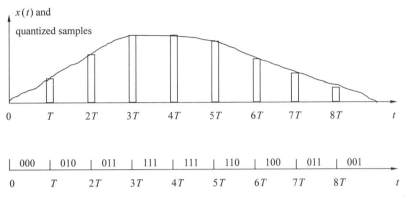

Figure 8.2 Sampling and digital conversion process

This process for the signal given is illustrated in Figure 8.2. The pulses representing the signal have been made very narrow to illustrate the fact that other signals may be inserted, or multiplexed, in the empty space. These pulses may then be represented as binary numbers. In order that these numbers could be seen on the figure, each has been shown over much of the space in a given interval. In practice, if other signals are to be inserted, the pulses representing the bits of the binary numbers could be made very short. A given binary number could then be read in a very short interval at the beginning of a sampling period, thus leaving most of the time available for other signals.

The process by which an analog sample is quantized and converted to a binary number is called analog-to-digital (A/D) conversion. In general, the dynamic range of the signal must be compatible with that of the A/D converter employed, and the number of bits employed must be sufficient for the required accuracy.

The signal can now be processed by the type of unit appropriate for the application intended. This unit may be a general-purpose computer or minicomputer, or it may be a special unit designed specifically for this purpose. At any rate, it is composed of some combination of standard digital circuits capable of performing the various arithmetic functions of addition, subtraction, multiplication, etc. In addition, it has logic and storage capability.

At the output of the processor, the digital signal can be converted to analog form again. This is achieved by the process of digital-to-analog (D/A) conversion. In this step, the binary numbers are first successively converted back to continuous-time pulses. The *gaps* between the pulses are then filled in by a reconstruction filter. This filter may consist of a holding circuit, which is a special circuit designed to hold the value of a pulse between successive sample values. In some cases, the holding circuit may be designed to interpolate the output signal between successive points according to some prescribed curve-fitting strategy.[6] In addition to a holding circuit, a basic continuous-time filter may be employed to provide additional smoothing between points.

A fundamental question that may arise is whether or not some information has been lost in the process. After all, the signal has been sampled only at discrete intervals of time; is there something that might be missed in the intervening time intervals? Furthermore, in the process of quantization, the actual amplitude is replaced by the nearest standard level, which means that there is a possible error in amplitude.

In regard to the sampling question, it will be shown that, if the signal is bandlimited, and if the sampling rate is greater than or equal to twice the highest frequency, the signal can theoretically be recovered from its discrete samples.[7] This corresponds to a minimum of two samples per cycle at the highest frequency. In practice, this sampling rate is usually chosen to be somewhat higher than the minimum rate (say, three or four times the highest frequency) in order to ensure practical implementation. For example, if the highest frequency of the analog signal is 5 kHz, the theoretical minimum sampling rate is 10,000 samples per second, and a practical system would employ a rate somewhat higher. The input continuous-time signal is often passed through a low-pass analog presampling filter to ensure that the highest frequency is within the bounds for which the signal can be recovered.[8]

If a signal is not sampled at a sufficiently high rate, a phenomenon known as aliasing results. This concept results in a frequency being mistaken for an entirely different frequency upon recovery. For example, suppose a signal with frequencies ranging from dc to 5 kHz is sampled at a rate of 6 kHz, which is clearly too low to ensure recovery. If recovery is attempted, a component of the original signal at 5 kHz now appears to be at 1 kHz, resulting in an erroneous signal. A common example of this phenomenon is one we will call the *wagon wheel effect*, probably noticed by the reader in western movies as the phenomenon in which the wheels appear to be rotating backwards.[9] Since each individual frame of a film is equivalent to a discrete sampling operation, if the rate of spokes passing a given angle is too large for a given movie frame rate, the wheels appear to be turning either backwards or at a very slow speed.[10] The effect of a presampling filter removes the possibility that a spurious signal whose frequency is too high for the system will be mistaken for one in the proper frequency range.[11]

With respect to the quantization error, it can be seen that the error can be made as small as one chooses if the number of bits can be made arbitrarily large. Of course, there is a practical maximum limit, so it is necessary to tolerate some error from this phenomenon. Even in continuous-time systems, there may be noise present which would introduce uncertainty in the actual magnitude. In fact, the uncertainty present in the digital sampling process is called quantization noise.

Let E_{max} and E_{min} represent the maximum and minimum values of the signal, and let q represent the vertical distance between successive quantum levels. Using n and m as previously defined, we have

$$q = \frac{E_{max} - E_{min}}{2^n} = \frac{E_{max} - E_{min}}{m} \qquad (8\text{-}2)$$

Assuming that a sample between two successive quantum levels is assigned to the nearest quantum level, the peak quantization noise and peak percentage quantization noise values are

$$\text{Peak Quantization Noise} = \frac{q}{2} \qquad (8\text{-}3)$$

$$\text{Peak Percentage Quantization Noise} = \frac{100\%}{2m} \qquad (8\text{-}4)$$

In many cases, the *variance* of the quantization noise is more important than the maximum value. The variance is directly proportional to the *average power* associated with the noise. If the signal is assumed to be uniformly distributed between quantum levels, it can be shown by statistical analysis that the noise variance σ^2 is

$$\sigma^2 = \frac{q^2}{12} \qquad (8\text{-}5)$$

The root-mean-square (RMS) (or standard deviation) value of this noise component is

$$\sigma = \frac{q}{2\sqrt{3}} \qquad (8\text{-}6)$$

Comparing (8-6) with (8-3), it is seen that the RMS noise component is $1/\sqrt{3}$ times the peak noise component.

In view of the preceding discussion, it appears that no information is lost in the sampling operation provided that the sampling rate is high enough, and the quantization error can be reduced to an insignificantly small level by choosing a sufficient number of bits to represent each binary number. These concepts then permit us to represent a continuous-time signal in terms of a series of discrete binary numbers, which may be processed directly with digital circuits.

The rather involved procedure of A/D conversion, processing, and final D/A conversion may seem like a lot of effort in order to handle one signal channel. Indeed, in many cases such a complex process may not be economically feasible for a single signal. One of the great advantages of the digital concept is the possibility of processing a number of channels with the same arithmetic unit. This process can be achieved by a process called *time-division multiplexing* (TDM). It was observed in the sampled signal shown in Figure 8.2 that there was a relatively long period between successive samples of the signal. During this period, samples of additional signals are fed into the processor.

This concept is illustrated in Figure 8.3. Each channel is read in a sequential order, and the corresponding values are converted into binary numbers in the same sequence. These numbers enter into the processing unit and, after suitable processing, appear at the output in the appropriate order. This composite digital signal must first be separated into the original different channels by means of a demltiplexer, which is synchronized with the input sampling signal. The channels then undergo the D/A conversion required for output.

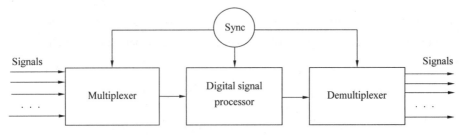

Figure 8.3　Multiplexed digital processing system

In the preceding discussions, we have assumed that both the starting and final signals in the system are in continuous-time form. Actually, there are many systems in which one or both are already digital in form. In such cases the A/D conversion and/or the D/A conversion may not be required, thus simplifying the system. For example, assume that a number of continuous-time telemetry signals are to be processed by a digital unit, but the output data is to be kept in digital form for scientific data reduction and computation. In this case, the A/D unit at the input is required, but no conversion is needed at the output.

New Words

Part I

sub-field	分领域，子领域	sonar	声呐
sensor array	传感器阵列	biomedical	生物特征的
algorithm	算法	abbreviate	缩写，缩略
purpose-designed	针对具体目的设计的	application-specific	面向应用的
Field-Programmable		integrated circuits	集成电路
Gate Array (FPGA)	现场可编程门阵列	autocorrelation	自相关
wavelet	小波	baseband	基带
informed	有知识的，有见闻的	spatial domain	空间域
cross-correlation	互相关	interval	间隔
discretization	离散化	quantization	量化
partition	分割，分区	finite set	有限的集
theorem	定理	scenario	情节，方案
carrier	载波	ingredient	成分，因素
demodulation	解调	enhancement	增强
filtering	滤波	weighted	加权的
characterize	描绘，刻画性质	superposition	叠加
causal	因果关系的	converge	收敛
diverge	发散	bounded	有界的
FIR (Finite Impulse		IIR (Infinite Impulse	

Response filter)	有限冲击响应滤波器	Response Filter)	无限冲击响应滤波器
transfer functions	传递函数	block diagram	方框图
derive	推导	magnitude	大小
cepstrum	倒谱	logarithm	对数
hifi (high fidelity)	高保真（音乐）	equalization	均衡
Magnetic Resonance		reinforcement	加强
Imaging (MRI)	磁共振成像	Computer Aided	
animation	动画	Tomography (CAT)	计算机断层扫描
crossover*	交叉，频率分割	loudspeaker	扬声器
fixed-point arithmetic	定点运算，整数运算	arithmetic	算术

Part Ⅱ

special-purpose	专用	terminology	术语
sinusoidal	正弦的	context	上下文，背景
casually	随便地	rigid	坚硬的，刚性的
pursue	追求，从事	excitation	激励
differential equation	微分方程	difference equation	差分方程
time-invariant	时不变的	lumped system	集总系统
increment	增量	presampling	预采样
waveform	波形	strategy	策略
multiplex	复用	dynamic range	动态范围
compatible	兼容	subtraction	减法
multiplication	乘法	reconstruction	重建
holding circuit	保持电路	extrapolate	外推
interpolate	内插	curve-fitting	曲线拟合
prescribed	预定的	intervene	插入，干预
intervening	期间的	bandlimited	限带的
aliasing	混叠	erroneous	错误的
wagon	四轮马车	spoke	轮辐
spurious	假的，伪造的	arbitrarily	任意地
uncertainty	不确定性	quantum	量子，量化
variance	方差	root-mean-square	均方根
preceding	前面的	composite	复合的
demultiplexer	解复用器	telemetry	遥测

---

* Audio crossover: a type of electronic filter used to separate audio signals into frequency bands.

Notes on the Text

Part I

1. These process signals in real time, and are generally purpose-designed application-specific integrated circuits (ASICs).

   这些（DSP 处理器）实时处理信号，通常是针对具体目的而设计的专用集成电路（ASIC）。

2. When flexibility and rapid development are more important than unit costs at high volume, DSP algorithms may also be implemented using field-programmable gate arrays (FPGAs).

   当灵活性和快速开发比大批量生产的成本更重要时，DSP 算法也可以用现场可编程门阵列来实现。

3. They choose the domain in which to process a signal by making an informed guess (or by trying different possibilities) as to which domain best represents the essential characteristics of the signal.

   他们按照某些依据来猜测（或试验不同的可能性）哪一个域能够最好地表示信号的本质特性来选择在其中进行信号处理的域。

   - making an informed guess：进行有根据的猜测，明智的猜测。

4. A sequence of samples from a measuring device produces a time or spatial domain representation, whereas a discrete Fourier transform produces the frequency domain information, that is, the frequency spectrum.

   从测量设备得到的样本序列产生（信号的）时域或空域表示，而离散 Fourier 变换则产生频域表示即频谱。

5. In the discretization stage, the space of signals is partitioned into equivalence classes and discretization is carried out by replacing the signal with representative signal of the corresponding equivalence class.

   在离散化阶段，信号空间被分割为相等的区间，用相应区间的代表性信号值代替信号本身。

6. Linear filters satisfy the superposition condition, i.e., if an input is a weighted linear combination of different signals, the output is an equally weighted linear combination of the corresponding output signals.

   线性滤波器满足叠加条件，就是说，如果输入是不同信号的加权线性组合，输出就是（各信号）相应输出的同样加权线性组合。

7. A filter may also be described as a difference equation, a collection of zeroes and poles or, if it is an FIR filter, an impulse response or step response.

   滤波器也可以用差分方程或一组零极点表示，对于 FIR 滤波器还可以用冲击响应或阶跃响应表示。

8. For example, the cepstrum converts a signal to the frequency domain through Fourier transform, takes the logarithm, and then applies another Fourier transform. This emphasizes the frequency components with smaller magnitude while retaining the order of magnitudes of frequency components.

例如倒谱用 Fourier 变换将信号转换到频域，取对数，然后再作第二次 Fourier 变换。这就在强调幅度较小的频率成分的同时保持了频率分量的数量级。

Part Ⅱ

1. It is now possible to build special-purpose digital processors within much smaller size and lower cost constraints of systems previously all analog in nature.

现在有可能在比以往全模拟系统小得多，而且成本也低得多的限制下构成专用数字处理器。

2. Because of the association of the term *analog* with physical analogies, preference has been established for the term *continuous-time*. Nevertheless, there will be cases in which the term *analog* will be used for clarity, particularly where it relates to the term *digital*.

由于"模拟"一词与物理类比的关联，已经确立了优先使用"连续时间"这一术语。不过有时为了清楚起见也用"模拟"一词，特别是与"数字"相联系时。

3. A lumped system is one that is composed of finite nonzero elements satisfying ordinary differential or difference equation relationships, as opposed to a distributed system, satisfying partial differential equation relationships.

集总系统是由有限非零元素构成，满足常微分（或差分）方程的系统，与满足偏微分方程的分布式系统相对应。

4. The number of levels m that can be represented by a number having n binary digits (bits) is given by $m = 2^n$. Conversely, if m is the number of possible levels required, the number of bits required is the smallest integer greater than or equal to $\log_2 m$.

可用 n 位二进制（n 比特）表示的等级数 m 由 $m = 2^n$ 给出。反过来，如果 m 是要求的等级数，所需的比特数是大于等于 $\log_2 m$ 的最小整数。

- 第一句的主句：The number of levels … is given by $m = 2^n$.

5. The process by which digital signal processing is achieved will be illustrated by a simplified system in which the signal is assumed to vary from 0 to 7 volts and in which 8 possible levels (at 1 V increments) are used for the binary numbers.

实现数字处理的过程将用一个简化系统来说明，假定信号在 0～7V 之间变化，以 1V 为增量，可用 8 种可能的值表示成二进制数。

6. In some cases, the holding circuit may be designed to interpolate the output signal between successive points according to some prescribed curve-fitting strategy.

在某些情况下，可设计保持电路，将输出信号在连续样点之间按照设定的曲线拟合方法进行内插。

7. In regard to the sampling question, it will be shown that, if the signal is bandlimited,

and if the sampling rate is greater than or equal to twice the highest frequency, the signal can theoretically be recovered from its discrete samples.

关于采样的问题，我们将表明，如果信号带宽有限，并且采样率大于或等于最高频率的两倍，理论上信号就能从离散的样本中恢复。

8. The input continuous-time signal is often passed through a low-pass analog presampling filter to ensure that the highest frequency is within the bounds for which the signal can be recovered.

常将输入的连续时间信号通过一个低通模拟预采样滤波器，以确保最高频率落在信号能够完全恢复的界限之内。

9. A common example of this phenomenon is one we will call the *wagon wheel effect*, probably noticed by the reader in western movies as the phenomenon in which the wheels appear to be rotating backwards.

一个普通例子就是我们称之为"车轮效应"的现象，就是读者可能在西部电影中注意到的车轮看起来向后转动的情况。

10. Since each individual frame of a film is equivalent to a discrete sampling operation, if the rate of spokes passing a given angle is too large for a given movie frame rate, the wheels appear to be turning either backwards or at a very slow speed.

因为影片的每一帧相当于一次离散的采样，如果相对于电影帧频而言轮辐越过的给定角度过大，轮子看起来就会向后转动或以很慢的速度转动。

11. The effect of a presampling filter removes the possibility that a spurious signal whose frequency is too high for the system will be mistaken for one in the proper frequency range.

采样前预滤波消除了这种对系统而言频率过高的伪信号被错误地当作适当频率范围内的另一信号的可能性。

- spurious signal 指频率高于系统所能处理范围（采样频率的一半）的信号。
- proper frequency range 是指满足采样定理的频率范围。

Technical Tips

ASIC

An application-specific integrated circuit (ASIC) is an integrated circuit (IC) customized for a particular use, rather than intended for general-purpose use. For example, a chip designed solely to run a cell phone is an ASIC. In contrast, the 7400 series and 4000 series integrated circuits are logic building blocks that can be wired together for use in many different applications.

FPGA

A field-programmable gate array (FPGA) is a semiconductor device containing programmable logic components called logic blocks, and programmable interconnects. Logic blocks can be programmed to perform the function of basic logic gates such as AND, and XOR, or more complex combinational functions such as decoders or simple mathematical functions. In most FPGAs, the logic blocks also include memory elements, which may be simple flip-flops or more complete blocks of memories.

A hierarchy of programmable interconnects allows logic blocks to be interconnected as needed by the system designer, somewhat like a one-chip programmable breadboard. Logic blocks and interconnects can be programmed by the customer/designer, after the FPGA is manufactured, to implement any logical function, hence the name *field-programmable*.

FPGAs are usually slower than their application-specific integrated circuit (ASIC) counterparts, as they cannot handle as complex a design, and draw more power. But their advantages include a shorter time to market, ability to re-program in the field to fix bugs, and lower non-recurring engineering costs.

Supplementary Readings: Designing Digital Filters

Compared to their analog counterparts, digital filters offer outstanding performance and flexibility. Designing digital filters can seem a daunting task, however, because of its seemingly endless range of implementation choices. The wide range of digital signal processing (DSP) design tools available can handle many of the details. What you need is a good handle on the basics of filter design to get the tools jump-started.

The place to start is by knowing type of information a signal contains. Information typically comes from one of two domains. It may lie in the frequency domain, where the spectral content of the signal is of interest. Information may also lie in the time domain, where the amplitude and phase of the signal is of interest. The term time domain is somewhat misleading, however, in that not all such signals relate to time. For example, a single sample from each element in an array of strain sensors on an aircraft ring yields a "signal" that can be processed using time-domain filters.

A second consideration is the type of filter implementation you want to use. As described in Digital Filters: an Introduction, by Iain A. Robin, digital filters come in two types: convolution and recursive. Convolution filters, also called Finite Impulse Response (FIR) filters, have the attribute of exhibiting no phase distortion. There is a delay, of course, but all incoming samples receive the same treatment so that signal phase relationships are preserved. High-order FIR filters can be readily implemented and will achieve extremely high performance, although they may require many resources to implement.

Recursive filters, also called Infinite Impulse Response (IIR) filters, can be implemented with far fewer resources than a corresponding FIR. This makes them both easier to implement and an order of magnitude faster in execution as a DSP algorithm. IIRs do, however, exhibit a non-linear phase response unless specifically designed for zero phase. They also suffer from performance limitations because finite word length arithmetic restricts the maximum IIR filter order that can be implemented.

Step response

With these two considerations in mind, you can begin evaluating filter characteristics against your application. Filters are most easily understood from either their step response or their frequency response. The step response, important in time domain applications, is the filter's output given an abrupt change in the input signal as illustrated in Figure 8.4. Step responses have three important parameters: risetime, overshoot, and phase linearity.

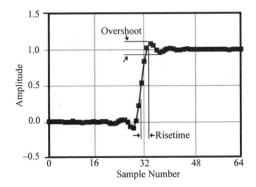

Figure 8.4　Step response is the filter's output given an abrupt change in the input signal

Risetime is the number of output samples between 10% of the output change and 90% of the change. Because time domain filters are typically used to help identify events in the signal (such as a bit boundary), the faster the risetime the better the filter.

Overshoot is a filter-generated distortion of the time domain information, which shows up as ripples at the edges of the output step. It is a distortion that should be eliminated if possible because it could mask critical system performance information. When the filter has overshoot, it becomes impossible to determine whether the signal is being distorted by the system that generates it, or by the filter.

Phase linearity for step responses refers to the symmetry of the step response above and below the 50% mark. As shown in Figure 8.5, a linear phase is symmetric about the halfway point while asymmetry occurs with non-linear phase. Linear phase ensures that rising edges of the filtered signal look like falling edges.

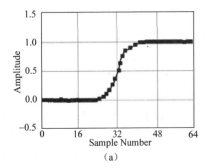
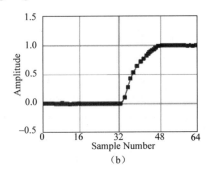

（a）　　　　　　　　　　　　　　　（b）

Figure 8.5　(a) Graph illustrating the symmetric linear phase (b) The asymmetric non-linear phase

Frequency response

Frequency response is important in frequency domain applications. The response, shown in Figure 8.6, has a passband and a stopband to select the frequencies of interest and discard all others. The boundary between the passband and stopband is the transition band, which occurs around the filter's cutoff frequency. The width of this transition band is the filter's roll-off, which is one of the important parameters of a frequency domain filter. In general, a faster roll-off is better.

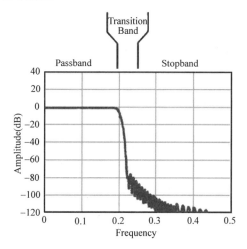

Figure 8.6   Illustration of the passband, stopband, and transition band in a filter with good stopband attenuation

Passband ripple is a second important parameter. It represents a distortion of signals occurring in the passband. Ideally, there should be no passband ripple so that the desired signals pass through unaltered.

The ideal filter also completely eliminates signals in the stopband. In practice, however, some energy in stopband frequencies will pass through. The amount by which the filter reduces the stopband signal is the filter's stopband attenuation, the third important time domain filter parameter.

There are four common types of frequency-domain filters:

- Low-pass
- High-pass
- Band-pass
- Band-reject

All of them can be evaluated using the three parameters.

Impulse response

Although the step and frequency responses are important for evaluating a digital filter, there is a third type of response that is important in implementing the filter: the impulse response. The impulse response, illustrated in Figure 8.7, is the filter's output upon receiving a signal that has only one non-zero sample, called a delta function ($\delta(n)$). The most straightforward way of implementing a digital filter is to create an FIR that convolves an impulse response $h(n)$ (also called the filter kernel) with the input signal $x(n)$ using:

$$y(n) = x(n) * h(n) = \sum_{i=0}^{M-1} x(n-i)h(n)$$

where M is the number of points used to express the filter kernel.

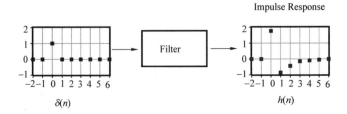

Figure 8.7   Illustration of the impulse response

Each of the three responses contains complete information about the filter, so knowing one gives you the other two. The step response is the discrete integration of the impulse response. The frequency response comes from the Discrete Fourier Transform (DFT) of the impulse response. A filter design can, therefore, begin with a response description in any of the forms.

These designs don't necessarily have to be complex. One of the most useful FIR time-domain filters, the moving average filter, is ideal for removing random (white) noise from a time-domain signal such as a serial bit stream. The transfer function of a moving average of length M is

$$y(n) = \frac{1}{M}\left[x(n) + x(n-1) + x(n-2) + \cdots + x(n-M-1)\right]$$

This is easily implemented in an FIR simply by storing the last M samples and adding them together. For an IIR the thing to realize is that the moving average takes in one new sample and drops the oldest sample each sample period, so

$$y(n) = \frac{1}{M}\left[x(n) + y(n-1) - x(n-M-1)\right]$$

The moving average filter reduces random noise in a signal by a factor square root M. So, a 100-point filter would reduce noise by a factor of 10. Unfortunately, the step response of a moving average filter has a risetime that increases with the M, which is undesirable. As it turns out, however, it has the fastest risetime for a given level of noise reduction of any time-domain filter. No matter what, then, you'll have to compromise between noise reduction and risetime.

The moving average is an excellent smoothing filter, but its frequency roll-off is slow and its stopband attenuation is ghastly, making it a terrible low-pass filter. This is typical; a digital filter can be optimized for time domain performance or frequency domain performance, but not both.

Windowed sinc low-pass filter

An appropriate FIR filter for frequency domain is the windowed-sinc filter. This low-pass filter uses the sinc function (sin x /x) for its filter kernel, where the value of the kernel components is given by:

$$h(i) = \frac{\sin(2\pi f_c i)}{i\pi}$$

where f_c is the desired cutoff frequency expressed as a fraction of the sampling frequency. If the filter kernel had an infinite number of points the result would be an ideal low-pass filter with no passband ripple, infinite attenuation in the stopband, and an infinitesimal transition band.

Unfortunately, an infinite number of points are not a good size for a filter kernel. One simple solution is to limit the number of points in the kernel by choosing $M+1$ points around the center of symmetry and ignoring all the rest. This, in effect, sets the remaining values to zero.

Choosing a window

The value of M sets the filter's roll-off characteristics. With an infinite number of points, the roll-off is infinitely steep: the output goes from one to zero in a single sample. With a finite number, the transition band bandwidth is given by:

$$BW \approx \frac{4}{M}$$

where the bandwidth is expressed as a fraction of the sampling frequency and must be between 0 and 0.5.

Simply truncating the sinc function to limit the number of points introduces some problems in the resulting frequency response, however, as shown in Figure 8.8. The discontinuity in the impulse response causes ripple in the passband and reduces stopband attenuation. To solve that problem, the windowed-sinc filter uses a filter kernel that is the product of the sinc function and a smoothly tapered window function.

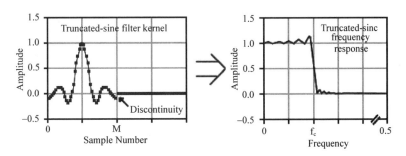

Figure 8.8   Truncating the sinc function to limit the number of points introduces some problems in the resulting frequency response

A variety of such window functions are possible, but two of the most useful are the Blackman and Hamming windows. Both are mathematically derived functions that bring the function and its first derivative to zero at the endpoints, resulting in a much smoother frequency response. The Blackman window has the better stopband attenuation of the two: −74 dB versus −53 dB for the Hamming window. The Hamming window, on the other hand, has about a 20% faster roll-off.

Forming other filters

With a good low-pass filter in hand, the other common types of frequency-domain filters are easy to obtain. You can, for instance, design a high-pass filter directly from the impulse response of a low-pass filter. There are two ways of handling this conversion: spectral inversion and spectral reversal.

Spectral inversion gives a frequency response that is an inversion (flipped top to bottom) of the corresponding low-pass filter. You calculate the coefficients by reversing the sign of all kernel components except the center one. The new center component is simply (1— the old center component). Figure 8.9 shows schematically how this works. The high-pass filter output is simply the low-pass filter's output subtracted from an all-pass filter (the delta function).

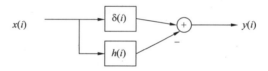

Figure 8.9   High-pass filter

Spectral reversal is less intuitive. In this approach, you change the sign of alternate kernel components. In effect, you have multiplied the filter kernel by a sinusoid with a frequency one half the sampling rate, which shifts the filter's frequency response by $f_s/2$. This results in a frequency response that is "flipped" left to right. The approach works because the frequency response of any digital filter is symmetric around zero frequency and repeats at the sampling frequency. As shown in Figure 8.10, spectral reversal effectively slides the frequency response of the low-pass filter over.

With both low-pass and high-pass filters in hand, it is easy to see how to build a band-reject filter. Simply add the results of the two filters together to get the total response. The band-reject kernel is the vector sum of the two filter kernels.

You can use spectral inversion or spectral reversal on the band-reject filter to obtain a band-pass filter. You can also create a band-pass filter by cascading the low-and high-pass filters, as shown in Figure 8.11. If you need a single filter with the same characteristics, you have to convolve the kernels of the two filters to generate the band-pass filter kernel.

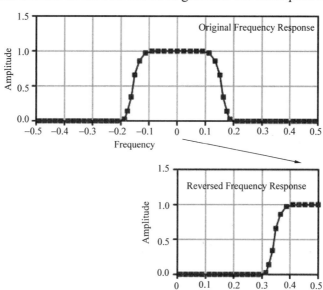

Figure 8.10   Spectral reversal effectively slides the frequency response of the low-pass filter over

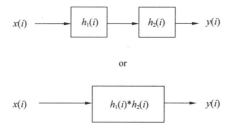

Figure 8.11   Bandpass filter

Exercises

I. Read the following passage and briefly answer the subsequent questions.

Now, more than ever, electrical engineers require information technology to manage their electronic design automation infrastructure. In the past, the lack of a comprehensive team-based design and process information management infrastructure for electronic design has had a negative effect on productivity. Today, information technology (IT) is used by several organizational disciplines to improve productivity.

Yet it is ironic that the electronics industry that enabled the information revolution has not taken fuller advantage of IT to improve its own productivity. The rapid growth in the use of IT — the Internet, corporate intranets, decentralized client/server computing environments — has dramatically changed the ways in which organizations manage and disseminate computer-based information. Work group interactions were once office-centered and characterized by a static, same time, same place information exchange paradigm. Today, they are increasingly taking place between geographically dispersed "virtual offices." This shift in the complexion of the workplace is compounding difficulties associated with managing information within and across organizational and geographical boundaries. Nowhere is this more prevalent than in design organizations within the electronics industry.

Over the past two decades, advances in EDA enabled electronic design teams to develop increasingly sophisticated and complex products. High-level design methods have come at the expense of explosive increases in the amount of design information that must be managed.

Additionally, widespread corporate initiatives to downsize and improve efficiencies, coupled with shrinking design cycles, have resulted in a demand for changes in the way design teams work. A shift toward concurrent, team-based approaches has taken place, in which large designs are hierarchically decomposed into functional blocks and developed by teams. This new way of working requires the ability to automate design process tasks and provide unobtrusive ways of allowing designers to communicate and share design information, as well as track design changes and manage the design process.

EDA vendors foster increases in designer productivity through the development of automation tools. Yet secondary importance has been placed on the capabilities needed to manage the design environment. Complicating the issue of design environment management is the wide-scale adoption of design processes which employ "best-in-class" design tools from multiple EDA vendors. While EDA standards for design description and tool interoperability have eased problems with tool connectivity, a lack of standards for how electronic design information is stored, accessed, distributed, tracked, and shared makes design environment management difficult and time consuming.

The current lack of an EDA-independent design management groupware infrastructure will continue to limit the productivity gains that might otherwise have been achieved through the adoption of new design methods and tools. The inability of electronic design engineering organizations to efficiently manage and reuse design and information is adversely affecting their ability to meet time-to-market goals and corporate initiatives to improve quality. It's time for the electronics industry to fully reap the benefits of IT.

- Why does the author say that it is the electronics industry that enabled the information revolution?
- How do you understand that electronics has not taken fuller advantage of IT to improve its own productivity?
- According to the passage, what particular information techniques have significantly influenced the organizations' ways of managing information?

- What does it mean by "a static, same time, same place information exchange paradigm"?
- Give your definition to "virtual office" based on the contents in this passage.
- What does EDA mean? What are its advantages?
- Why is it necessary for the design team to change their way of design?
- In which aspects the way of design has been changed?
- What in EDA have been standardized, and what have not?
- Give some of you views on the further development and improvement of EDA.

Ⅱ. **Choose the phrase that is closest in meaning to the underlined part.**

1. When flexibility and rapid development are more important than <u>unit costs at high volume</u>, DSP algorithms may also be implemented using field-programmable gate arrays (FPGAs).

   A. costs of large quantity of unit

   B. unit that costs when tuned to high volume

   C. price per unit under the condition of batch production

   D. costs per unit paid for a laud sound

2. Linear filters satisfy the superposition condition, i.e., if <u>an input is a weighted linear combination of different signals</u>, the output is an equally weighted linear combination of the corresponding output signals.

   A. an input is the sum of different signals, each being multiplied by a different weight

   B. an input is weighted and linearly combined with different signals

   C. an input is linearly weighted by combining different signals

   D. an input is linear with a weight to combine different signals

3. Since each individual frame of a film is equivalent to a discrete sampling operation, <u>if the rate of spokes passing a given angle is too large for a given movie frame rate</u>, the wheels appear to be turning either backwards or at a very slow speed.

   A. if the movie frame rate is too high with respect to the rate of spokes

   B. if the time interval between movie frames is too short with respect to the rate of spokes

   C. if the spokes move across a large angle to give the rate of movie frames

   D. if the rate of the movie frame is too low with respect to the rate of spokes

4. Although some communication signals <u>are inherently digital in nature</u>, many signals are analog, or smooth, function of time.

   A. are essentially of digital characteristics

   B. are inevitably in a digital form existing in the nature

   C. are naturally considered as digital

   D. are mainly in a digital nature

5. Bear in mind that the design is aimed at <u>a signal with a prescribed time domain</u>

amplitude envelope to meet the maximum power delivery requirement, and a specified spectral magnitude to achieve a desirable time resolution at the receiver.

    A. a signal having an envelope amplified in the time domain so that maximum power is delivered

    B. a signal whose waveform has a predefined envelope so that maximum power can be output

    C. a signal with a described amplitude envelope in the time domain, transmitting maximum power

    D. a signal requiring a set waveform amplification leading to maximum power transmission

6. Matched filters have been studied for more than thirty years, but only recently have they become easy enough to produce to be thought of as off-the-shelf elements.

    A. very easy to produce and one could think as if they were to be taken off-shelf

    B. quite simple as well as plentiful in production therefore regarded as items on the shelf

    C. sufficiently easily produced so as to be regarded as readily available components

    D. easy enough to produce one that is consider as an off-shore installation

7. Noise interference occurs and this is commonly due to lack of good audio practice, and in most cases can be cured or dramatically reduced by properly locating of microphones and loudspeakers.

    A. can be accused or successfully deducted

    B. can be remedied or greatly improved

    C. can be excluded or significantly avoided

    D. can be avoided or considerably lowered

8. The analysis filter bank spectral resolution may be dynamically altered so as to better match the time/frequency characteristic of each audio block.

    A. The filter bank for signal analysis may be modified dynamically in terms of the frequency domain resolution

    B. The analyzed spectrum is changed to provide dynamic resolution of the filter bank

    C. Analysis of the filter bank alters the spectral resolution in a dynamical fashion

    D. Dynamic authorization of the filter bank may be performed for better spectral resolution

Digital Audio Compression

Digital audio is obtained by sampling sound waveforms at a given rate, and quantizing the resulting amplitude samples into discrete values. The amount of digital information is very large for transmission or storage. Compression coding is therefore important to reduce the digitized audio data while maintaining the quality of the reproduced sound.

Text

Part I: MPEG Audio Layer 3

With the advent of the Internet, there is a desire for more and more information to be transmitted across phone lines. Audio information is one form that is increasingly downloaded, be it a sampler for a band's album, a radio program, or sound as part of a video.[1] As bandwidth in a telephone wire is limited, this has led to a need for information (including audio) to be compressed.

The traditional method of storing digital audio, used in CDs and digital TV, samples the amplitude of the sound a set number of times per second, and records this.[2] The precision of the amplitude is determined by the number of bits used to store the amplitude. So the bandwidth (or memory) consumed by the audio signal is dependent on three factors: the number of samples taken per second (Frequency), the number of bits used to store the amplitude (Bit Depth) and the length of the signal (Time). When we know these three things, the memory used becomes simple to calculate:

$$\text{Memory} = \text{Frequency} \times \text{Bit Depth} \times \text{Time}.$$

Additionally, if the signal is in stereo, then this must be doubled as two signals are in fact used.

This equation can be used to demonstrate why transmitting high-quality audio across the Internet requires compression. CD audio uses 16-bit stereo sampled at 44,100 Hz. This means that one minute of CD audio uses $44,100 \times 16 \times 60 \times 2 = 84,672,000$ bits, or slightly over 10 megabytes. A standard 56 kbps modem would take $84,672,000/57,344 = 1477$ seconds or about 25 minutes! 25 minutes is a long time to wait for one minute of audio, so an alternative is imperative. That alternative was MPEG Audio Layer 3, or MP3.

The codec

The human ear can only hear a limited range of frequencies. The codec therefore removes all sounds outside this range, as they will not be heard anyway.

A psycho-acoustic model is then applied to the sound. If a high-pitched sound is played, then the decibel threshold for sounds of lower frequencies to be made audible is increased.[3] The psycho-acoustic model removes any and all sounds that will be "masked" in this way.

The next stage is Joint Stereo. The human brain is unable to place the directions of sounds at low frequencies, so sounds below this threshold are encoded in mono. If some sections of the signal are still above the required bitrate, then the quality of these sections will be decreased. Finally, Huffman encoding is applied. This replaces all bitcodes with unique bitcodes of varying length according to the frequency of the pattern occurrence.[4] For instance, the most commonly occurred bit pattern would be encoded as "01", while the next common would be "010" and the next would be "011", and so on.

Social and economic effects

The social effects of MP3 cannot be underestimated. It is allowing new, unsigned bands to distribute free music over the Internet. Those with minority tastes can obtain experimental or alternative music far more easily than previously, as mainstream record shops do not tend to stock these genres of music.[5] Portable hardware MP3 players may now be purchased at low prices, and the price is still falling. Sites such as MP3.com distribute free MP3s from a multitude of unsigned bands. Others sell albums from unsigned bands, with a free MP3 track from some albums, allowing the consumer to sample the band's music before purchase. Some mainstream acts have also taken to distributing some free tracks in order to promote albums. There is, unfortunately, a darker side to this revolution. Illegal sites distribute tracks illegally "ripped" from the albums of established artists, who subsequently lose out on royalties.[6]

The economic implications of MP3 are closely tied to its social effects. The major record companies are essentially running scared of the effect this is likely to have.[7] They refuse to sell MP3 albums, except in those cases where the artist has enough clout to force them. They are hurriedly trying to establish a standard for a "secure" music format that cannot be used on more than one machine.[8] Microsoft recently attempted, and failed, to do just that. Their format, WMT4, was "cracked" within less than 24 hours of its release. In fact, the same techniques used to crack WMT4 can be applied to any music format, no matter how secure. People believe that MP3 may spell the end for the traditional record company. Most, however, foresee the record companies realizing that they cannot win this particular war, and beginning to distribute MP3 albums themselves. In fact, in this age MP3 is probably not that much less secure than the CD itself.

Conclusion

In conclusion, MP3 can compress digital audio by a high factor. This makes it ideal for the distribution of audio across the Internet. It has found popularity among unsigned and experimental bands, as well as some established artists who are advocates of the technology. Although the record companies refuse to back it, there is little they can do to stem the tide. They have found themselves very much in the position of King Canute[*], although this will undoubtedly change in the long term.

The MP3 file format is an extremely efficient compression standard, which has already seen off challenges from WMT4 and other rival standards.[9] Due to its extremely lax licensing terms, MP3 seems unlikely to lose its popularity.

Part II : Digital Audio Compression Standard AC3[†]

Foreword

The United States Advanced Television Systems Committee (ATSC)[†] was formed by the member organizations of the Joint Committee on InterSociety Coordination (JCIC)[‡], recognizing that the prompt, efficient and effective development of a coordinated set of national standards is essential to the future development of domestic television services.

One of the activities of the ATSC is exploring the need for and, where appropriate, coordinating the development of voluntary national technical standards for Advanced Television Systems (ATV).[1] The ATSC Executive Committee assigned the work of documenting the U.S. ATV standard to a number of specialist groups working under the Technology Group on Distribution (T3). The Audio Specialist Group (T3/S7) was charged with documenting the ATV audio standard.

This document was prepared initially by the Audio Specialist Group as part of its efforts to document the United States Advanced Television broadcast standard. It was approved by the Technology Group on Distribution on September 26, 1994, and by the full ATSC Membership as an ATSC Standard on November 10, 1994. Annex A, "AC-3 Elementary Streams in an MPEG-2 Multiplex," was approved by the Technology Group on Distribution on February 23, 1995, and by the full ATSC Membership on April 12, 1995. Annex B, "AC-3 Data Stream in IEC958 Interface," and Annex C, "AC-3 Karaoke Mode,"

---

[*] King Canute was a British monarch who believed that he could force the tide back. Funnily enough, he failed.

[†] The United States Advanced Television Systems Committee, December 20, 1995

[‡] The JCIC is presently composed of: the Electronic Industries Association (EIA), the Institute of Electrical and Electronic Engineers (IEEE), the National Association of Broadcasters (NAB), the National Cable Television Association (NCTA), and the Society of Motion Picture and Television Engineers (SMPTE).

NOTE: The user's attention is called to the possibility that compliance with this standard may require use of an invention covered by patent rights. By publication of this standard, no position is taken with respect to the validity of this claim, or of any patent rights in connection therewith. The patent holder has, however, filed a statement of willingness to grant a license under these rights on reasonable and nondiscriminatory terms and conditions to applicants desiring to obtain such a license. Details may be obtained from the publisher.

were approved by the Technology Group on Distribution on October 24, 1995 and by the full ATSC Membership on December 20, 1995. ATSC Standard A/53, *Digital Television Standard for HDTV Transmission*, references this document and describes how the audio coding algorithm described herein is applied in the U.S. ATV standard.

At the time of release of this document, the system description contained herein had not been verified by the transmission of signals from independently developed encoders to separately developed decoders.

Motivation

In order to more efficiently broadcast or record audio signals, the amount of information required to represent the audio signals may be reduced. In the case of digital audio signals, the amount of digital information needed to accurately reproduce the original pulse code modulation (PCM) samples may be reduced by applying a digital compression algorithm, resulting in a digitally compressed representation of the original signal.[2] (The term compression used in this context means the compression of the amount of digital information which must be stored or recorded, and not the compression of dynamic range of the audio signal.) The goal of the digital compression algorithm is to produce a digital representation of an audio signal which, when decoded and reproduced, sounds the same as the original signal, while using a minimum of digital information (bitrate) for the compressed (or encoded) representation. The AC-3 digital compression algorithm specified in this document can encode from 1 to 5.1 channels of source audio from a PCM representation into a serial bit stream at data rates ranging from 32 kbps to 640 kbps. The 0.1 channel refers to a fractional bandwidth channel intended to convey only low frequency (subwoofer) signals.

A typical application of the algorithm is shown in Figure 9.1. In this example, a 5.1 channel audio program is converted from a PCM representation requiring more than 5 Mbps (6 channels × 48 kHz × 18 bits = 5.184 Mbps) into a 384 kbps serial bit stream by the AC-3 encoder. Satellite transmission equipment converts this bit stream to an RF transmission which is directed to a satellite transponder. The amount of bandwidth and power required by the transmission has been reduced by more than a factor of 13 by the AC-3 digital compression. The signal received from the satellite is demodulated back into the 384 kbps serial bit stream, and decoded by the AC-3 decoder. The result is the original 5.1 channel audio program.

Digital compression of audio is useful wherever there is an economic benefit to be obtained by reducing the amount of digital information required to represent the audio. Typical applications are in satellite or terrestrial audio broadcasting, delivery of audio over metallic or optical cables, or storage of audio on magnetic, optical, semiconductor, or other storage media.

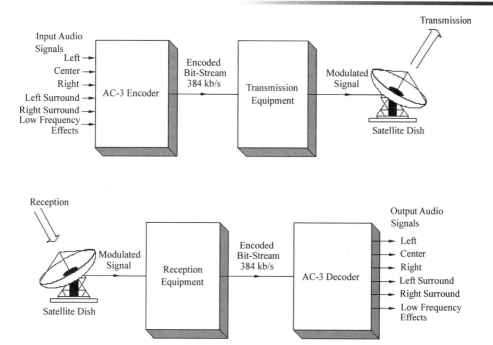

Figure 9.1   Example application of AC-3 to satellite audio transmission

Encoding

The AC-3 encoder accepts PCM audio and produces an encoded bit stream consistent with this standard. The specifics of the audio encoding process are not normative requirements of this standard. Nevertheless, the encoder must produce a bit stream matching the syntax described in Section 5, which, when decoded according to Sections 6 and 7, produces audio of sufficient quality for the intended application. Section 8 contains informative information on the encoding process. The encoding process is briefly described below.

The AC-3 algorithm achieves high coding gain (the ratio of the input bit-rate to the output bit-rate) by coarsely quantizing a frequency domain representation of the audio signal. A block diagram of this process is shown in Figure 9.2. The first step in the encoding process is to transform the representation of audio from a sequence of PCM time samples into a sequence of blocks of frequency coefficients. This is done in the analysis filter bank. Overlapping blocks of 512 time samples are multiplied by a time window and transformed into the frequency domain. Due to the overlapping blocks, each PCM input sample is represented in two sequential transformed blocks. The frequency domain representation may then be decimated by a factor of two so that each block contains 256 frequency coefficients. The individual frequency coefficients are represented in binary exponential notation as a binary exponent and a mantissa.[3] The set of exponents is encoded into a coarse representation of the signal spectrum which is referred to as the spectral envelope. This spectral envelope is used by the core bit allocation routine which determines how many bits to use to encode each individual mantissa. The spectral envelope and the coarsely quantized mantissas for 6 audio blocks (1536 audio samples) are formatted into an AC-3 frame. The AC-3 bit stream is a sequence of AC-3 frames.

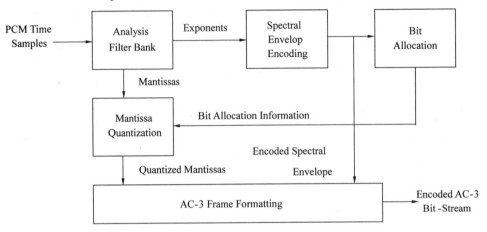

Figure 9.2　The AC-3 encoder

The actual AC-3 encoder is more complex than indicated in Figure 9.2. The following functions not shown above are also included:

- A frame header is attached which contains information (bit-rate, sample rate, number of encoded channels, etc.) required to synchronize to and decode the encoded bit stream.[4]
- Error detection codes are inserted in order to allow the decoder to verify that a received frame of data is error free.
- The analysis filter bank spectral resolution may be dynamically altered so as to better match the time/frequency characteristic of each audio block.[5]
- The spectral envelope may be encoded with variable time/frequency resolution.
- A more complex bit allocation may be performed, and parameters of the core bit allocation routine modified so as to produce a more optimum bit allocation.
- The channels may be coupled together at high frequencies in order to achieve higher coding gain for operation at lower bit-rates.
- In the two-channel mode a rematrixing process may be selectively performed in order to provide additional coding gain, and to allow improved results to be obtained in the event that the two-channel signal is decoded with a matrix surround decoder.[6]

Decoding

The decoding process is basically the inverse of the encoding process. The decoder, shown in Figure 9.3, must synchronize to the encoded bit stream, check for errors, and de-format the various types of data such as the encoded spectral envelope and the quantized mantissas. The bit allocation routine is run and the results used to unpack and de-quantize the mantissas. The spectral envelope is decoded to produce the exponents. The exponents and mantissas are transformed back into the time domain to produce the decoded PCM time samples.

The actual AC-3 decoder is more complex than indicated in Figure 9.3. The following functions not shown above are included:

- Error concealment or muting may be applied in case a data error is detected.
- Channels which have had their high-frequency content coupled together must be decoupled.
- Dematrixing must be applied (in the 2-channel mode) whenever the channels have been rematrixed.
- The synthesis filter bank resolution must be dynamically altered in the same manner as the encoder analysis filter bank had been during the encoding process.

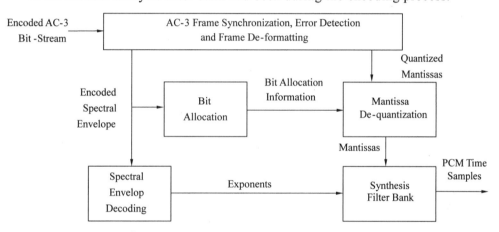

Figure 9.3　The AC-3 decoder

New Words

Part I

advent	到来，来临	sampler	样品
album	照相簿，歌曲集	amplitude	幅度，广阔
precision	精度，精确的	stereo	立体声
megabyte	兆字节	modem	调制解调器
imperative	势在必行的	psycho-acoustic	心理声学的
pitch	音调，程度	threshold	门限，阈值
mono	单一，单声道	bitrate	比特率
Huffman encoding	Huffman 编码	bitcode	比特字，比特码
underestimate	低估	minority	少数

mainstream	主流	genre	流派，类型
multitude	多数，大众	a multitude of ...	种种的，众多的
unsigned band	未签约的乐队	promote	推销，促进
rip	撕，拉，劈	royalty	版税，庄严，王权
clout	权力，影响，力量	spell	拼写，迷住
advocate	提倡者，拥护者	stem	阻止，堵住
rival	对手	lax	宽松的，不严格的

Part II

coordination	协调	voluntary	自发的，自愿的
executive	执行的，执行者	annex	附件
multiplex	多样的，多路复用	herein	在此，如此
motivation	动机，推动力	algorithm	算法
dynamic range	动态范围	fractional	部分的，分数的
woofer	低音喇叭	transponder	应答器，转发器
demodulate	解调	terrestrial	地面的，地球上的
consistent	一致的	normative	规范的，标准的
syntax	句法	informative	提供信息的
overlap	重叠	decimate	抽取
coefficient	系数	exponent	指数
mantissa	尾数	envelope	包络
allocation	分配，指定	synchronize	使同步，同时发生
resolution	分辨率	parameter	参数
inverse	反转的，逆	unpack	解开
conceal	隐藏	mute	无声，使无声
rematrix	重新进行矩阵变换	dematrix	求矩阵反变换

Notes on the Text

Part I

1. Audio information is one form that is increasingly downloaded, be it a sampler for a band's album, a radio program, or sound as part of a video.

   音频信息是一种愈来愈多被下载的（多媒体）形式，无论是乐队的唱片选曲、无线电节目，还是视频伴音。

   - be ... or ... 不管是……还是……

   Send me those sessions, <u>be it video or audio</u>, is a great idea to spread the spirit of an event.

   Only thus do you get him to lay aside his weapons, <u>be he friend or enemy</u>.

2. The traditional method of storing digital audio, used in CDs and digital TV, samples

the amplitude of the sound a set number of times per second, and records this.

用于 CD 和数字电视中存储数字音频的传统方法是每秒抽取并记录一定次数的声音幅度值。

- 本句主要成分：… method … samples the amplitude …

3. If a high-pitched sound is played, then the decibel threshold for sounds of lower frequencies to be made audible is increased.

在播放音调高的声音时，要提高使低频声能被听到的临界分贝数（分贝阈值）。

4. This replaces all bitcodes with unique bitcodes of varying length according to the frequency of the pattern occurrence.

将所有比特码根据其出现的频率换成独特的变长比特码。

5. Those with minority tastes can obtain experimental or alternative music far more easily than previously, as mainstream record shops do not tend to stock these genres of music.

具有非主流口味（喜好）的人获取实验性或不同寻常的音乐比以往容易得多，主流唱片店一般不经销这些流派的音乐。

6. Illegal sites distribute tracks illegally "ripped" from the albums of established artists, who subsequently lose out on royalties.

非法网站发行从已成名艺术家的唱片中非法窃取的音乐，这些艺术家因而失去版税。

7. The major record companies are essentially running scared of the effect this is likely to have.

主要的唱片公司差不多因为这可能产生的社会影响而惊恐万状。

8. They are hurriedly trying to establish a standard for a "secure" music format that cannot be used on more than one machine.

他们急欲建立一种"安全"音乐格式标准，使之不能用于一台以上的机器（仅能在一台机器上播放）。

9. The MP3 file format is an extremely efficient compression standard, which has already seen off challenges from WMT4 and other rival standards.

MP3 文件格式是一种效率极高的压缩标准，它已经赢得（告别）了 WMT4 和其他对手发起的挑战。

Part Ⅱ

1. One of the activities of the ATSC is exploring the need for and, where appropriate, coordinating the development of voluntary national technical standards for Advanced Television Systems (ATV).

ATSC（先进电视系统委员会）的工作之一就是寻求开发 ATV（先进电视系统）的非强制性国家技术标准的需要并在适当的情况下协调这种开发工作。

- 这里 exploring the need for 和 coordinating the development of 并列，后面的 voluntary national technical standards…是它们的共同宾语。

2. In the case of digital audio signals, the amount of digital information needed to accurately reproduce the original pulse code modulation (PCM) samples may be reduced by applying a digital compression algorithm, resulting in a digitally compressed representation of the original signal.

对于数字音频信号，用于精确重建原始脉冲编码调制样本所需要的数字信息量可以通过应用数字压缩算法来减少，由此产生原信号的数字压缩形式。

- 本句主要成分：...the amount ... may be reduced ..., resulting in ...

3. The individual frequency coefficients are represented in binary exponential notation as a binary exponent and a mantissa.

各频域系数以二进制指数形式表示成二进制指数和二进制尾数。

- 关于浮点数的二进制指数和尾数表示形式见 Technical Tips。

4. A frame header is attached which contains information (bit-rate, sample rate, number of encoded channels, etc.) required to synchronize to and decode the encoded bit stream.

在每一帧前面加上头部，其中包含与编码比特流实现同步并将它解码所需的信息，如比特率、采样频率、编码声道数等。

- the encoded bit stream 是 synchronize to 和 decode 的共同宾语。

5. The analysis filter bank spectral resolution may be dynamically altered so as to better match the time/frequency characteristic of each audio block.

分析滤波器组的频谱分辨率可以动态地改变以便更好地匹配每一音频（信号）块的时频特性。

6. In the two-channel mode a rematrixing process may be selectively performed in order to provide additional coding gain, and to allow improved results to be obtained in the event that the two-channel signal is decoded with a matrix surround decoder.

在双声道模式中，可以选择执行一个重新进行矩阵变换的过程以便提供附加的编码增益，并在使用矩阵环绕声解码器解码双声道信号时给出改进的效果。

Technical Tips

Huffman coding

There are many different reasons for and ways of encoding data, and one of these ways is Huffman coding. This is used as a compression method in digital imaging and video as well as in other areas. The idea behind Huffman coding is simply to use shorter bit patterns for more common characters, and longer bit patterns for less common characters. This way, the coded bit sequence is shorter than the original data without loss of any information as the original data can be obtained after decoding.

Floating point representation: the IEEE standard 754

IEEE floating point numbers have three basic components: sign, exponent, and mantissa. The mantissa is composed of the fraction and an implicit leading digit as explained below. The exponent base 2 is implicit and need not be stored. The exponent field needs to represent both positive and negative exponents. To do this, a *bias* is added to the actual exponent in order to get the stored exponent. For IEEE single-precision floats, this value is 127. Thus, an exponent of zero means that 127 is stored in the exponent field. A stored value of 200 indicates an exponent of $(200 - 127) = 73$. Exponents of -127 (all 0s) and $+128$ (all 1s) are reserved for special numbers. For double precision, the exponent field is 11 bits, and has a bias of 1023.

The following figure shows the layout for single (32-bit) and double (64-bit) precision floating-point values. The number of bits for each field are shown (bit ranges are in square brackets):

	Sign	Exponent	Fraction	Bias
Single Precision	1 [31]	8 [30-23]	23 [22-00]	127
Double Precision	1 [63]	11 [62-52]	52 [51-00]	1023

Consider single precision:

- The sign bit: 1 for negative and 0 for positive
- The mantissa: 23 bits
- The exponent: 8 bits

Using binary, the value of the number is: $(+/-)1.\text{mantissa} \times 2^{\text{exponent}}$. For example, -1.1011001101×2^8:

- Sign: 1
- Exponent: <u>10000111</u>, which is 00001000 (8) + 01111111 (127) = <u>10000111</u> (decimal 135).
- Mantissa: 10110011010000000000000

Supplementary Readings: Audio Compression Algorithm Overview

The goal of digital compression algorithms is to produce a digital representation of an audio signal which, when decoded and reproduced, sounds the same as the original signal, while using a minimum of digital information for the compressed representation. Different types of compression algorithms exist. This article provides an introduction to the AC-3 and MP3 algorithms. Any application using compression needs two steps at a minimum: a coder for compression and a decoder for decompression.

For example, consider a 1D (audio) signal to demonstrate the two different domains. Consider a complicated sound such as an ambulance alarm. We can describe this sound in two related ways:

Sample the amplitude of the sound many times a second, which gives an approximation to the sound as a function of time (time domain).

Analyze the sound in terms of the pitches of the notes, or frequencies, and recording the amplitude of each frequency (frequency domain).

Another example of digital compression algorithms are the popular music files available on the Internet. What has made this possible is the reduction of download time and file size of the transmitted song. The introduction of MP3 to the market made this possible. What once took hours to download and occupied huge amounts of space could be downloaded with the same speed modem much faster and stored in around one-tenth the disk space. At the same time, the high quality sound reproduction was retained. Thus music downloads have become popular on the Internet. However, it is worth mentioning that it's the file content and not the file type that may breach copyrights.

Introduction to MP3 and AC-3 algorithms

We will compare how these different algorithms handle compression at a high-level in this section.

MP3

MP3 (MPEG-1 Audio Layer 3) is a form of compression that was standardized by MPEG in 1991. The MP3 compression technique is based on the psycho-acoustic model of compression of human sensitivity to frequencies. This model selects audible frequencies and rejects all other frequencies. Human beings can hear frequencies in the range between 20 Hz and 20 kHz, and it is most sensitive between 2 to 4 kHz. MP3 files thus consist of frequencies in the audible range and reject frequencies which cannot be heard. This is known as destructive compression. The disadvantage is that frequencies once rejected or eliminated in the creation of an MP3 cannot be replaced.

While encoding a file into MP3, you can choose different compression levels. Audio quality is directly proportional to the file size. That is, the larger the size, the higher the quality. An MP3 file created with 128 kbps compression will be of greater quality and larger file size than that of a 56 kbps compression. The advantage of MP3 compression is that people can back up their own collection of songs and save it to their hard drive or CDs.

The MP3 format uses, at its heart, a "hybrid transform" to transform a time domain signal into a frequency domain signal. This basic model is the same for all three layers of audio defined by MPEG, but codec complexity increases with each layer. The codec divides data into frames, and each frame contains 384 samples, 12 samples from each of the 32 filtered sub-bands.

Steps in the MP3 algorithm:

- Use convolution filters to divide the audio signal (for example, 48 kHz sound) into frequency sub-bands that approximate the 32 critical bands (sub-band filtering).
- Determine amount of masking for each band caused by nearby band (the psychoacoustic model).
- If the power in a band is below the masking threshold, it is rejected.
- If the power is within acceptable limits, determine number of bits needed to

represent the coefficient such that noise introduced by quantization is below the masking effect (1-bit of quantization introduces about 6 dB of noise).

- Format bitstream.

A high-quality critical band filter is used for MP3. In addition, the psychoacoustic model includes temporal masking effects, takes into account stereo redundancy, and uses a Huffman coder.

AC-3

AC-3, developed by the Digital Coder group at Dolby Laboratories, is a high-quality, low-complexity multi-channel audio coder. You can obtain a lower net data rate by coding multiple channels as a single entity than by coding individual channels. By coding a multiplicity of channels as a single entity, it is able to operate at lower data rates for a given level of audio quality than an ensemble of equivalent single channel coders.

Although AC-3 algorithms are independent of the number of channels coded, current implementations have standardized on the SMPTE-recommended 5.1 channel arrangement: five full bandwidth channels representing left, center, right, left-surround, and right-surround; plus a limited bandwidth low-frequency subwoofer channel. AC-3 conveys this channel arrangement with a high degree of transparency at data rates as low as 320 kbps. AC-3 has been implemented using available, cost-effective DSP hardware, and is designed to be readily ported to new DSP platforms.

The central philosophy behind AC-3 is that all channels are compressed together as an ensemble, where the total bits that can be accommodated by the media is distributed among the channels. The input to the AC-3 encoder is six-channel PCM audio (16- to 24-bit resolution and 48 kHz sampling rate).

Steps in the AC-3 algorithm:

- Transform each of the channels from the time to the frequency domain, using Time Domain Aliasing Cancellation (TDAC). Blocks of 512 samples, or 10.7 ms of audio, are normally used to yield 256 spectral coefficients. However, when a transient signal is detected, the block size is reduced to 5.4 ms duration to minimize pre-echo.

- A mantissa and an exponent are then obtained by converting each of the spectral coefficients from all of the channels from a fixed-point binary number to floating-point notation. The mantissa is a fractional amount of the fixed-point number, and the exponent is a scaling factor, to which the mantissa is multiplied to obtain the fixed-point number. Resolution is obtained from the word length of the mantissa, and the exponent determines the quantizing step size of the frequency component. Expressing spectral coefficients in floating-point form is advantageous because it allows for floating-point coding opportunities.

- The output compressed data stream consists of the mantissa and exponent information from all of the channels, plus auxiliary data for exponent coding, coupling coefficients, and bit allocation.

The decoder is the reverse process of encoding.

Different strategies have been used by AC-3 to code floating point numbers. For a steady audio signal, the exponent information is repeated over several blocks up to about 64 ms in a duration of six blocks. Dolby also determined that if the difference between exponents in adjacent frequencies were to be coded instead of the actual values of the exponents, only about two-bit resolution would be required.

Bit allocation measures are used to obtain more data reduction. The set of spectral coefficient exponents spanning the frequency range is a representation of the signal power along the spectrum. This set is grouped into bands, whose width increases with frequency, similar to the critical bands.

Each band has a common exponent. The word length of the mantissas within each of the bands is then determined by a bit allocation routine, which is based on a predicted masking curve over the entire spectral range. This masking curve is determined for each frequency band. If a band exponent lies above or below the masking curve (as calculated from a model), the value of the curve at that band frequency is accordingly incremented or decremented. The results from each of the bands are then combined to obtain the predicted masking curve. After making sure that all parts of this curve exceed the threshold of human auditory sensitivity, the mantissa for each frequency component (not for each band) is re-quantized, with the resolution corresponding to the extent to which its exponent exceeds the predicted masking value.

After the mantissas have been re-quantized, a count of the number of bits consumed for all of the channels is performed. If the total number of bits available has not been exceeded, then the mantissas can be quantized with greater accuracy. However, if the total has been surpassed, then two measures can be invoked. The first is to just decrease the resolution of the mantissas. Up until now, we have only been considering data reduction in AC-3 for each of the channels independently. A second way of meeting the total bit requirement is a technique known to Dolby as coupling.

In the coupling technique, the mantissa information for frequency bands across multiple channels is combined into a single coupling channel, based on the average signal power. For each band, the ratio between the signal power in the coupling channel and in each separate channel (known as the coupling coefficient) is substituted for the mantissa and exponent in each channel, which in turn requires fewer bits. Then, the original spectral coefficients for each channel are recovered upon decoding, by multiplying the mantissas from the coupling channel by the appropriate coupling coefficients. Coupling occurs only for frequency bands above 10 kHz.

Different coding strategies can be used to achieve low data rates. AC-3 is by far the most complex of the two codecs. Steps for decoding the data are those essentially the reverse for those of encoding, requiring the ancillary data for parameters and information on reconstructing the original channels.

Exercises

I. Translate the following passages into Chinese.

1. The principles which underlie almost all digital audio applications and devices, be they digital synthesis, sampling, digital recording or CD or iPod playback, are based on the basic concepts which follow in this chapter. New forms of playback, file formats, compression and storage of data are all changing on a seemingly daily basis, but the underlying mechanisms for converting real-world sound into digital values, manipulating those data and finally converting them back into real-world sound has not varied much since Max Mathews developed MUSIC I in 1957 at Bell Labs.

2. Sound is created by vibrations, such as those produced by a guitar string, vocal cords or a speaker cone. These vibrations move the air molecules near them, forcing molecules together, as a result raising the air pressure slightly. The air molecules that are under pressure then push on air molecules surrounding them, which push on the next set of air molecules, and so forth, causing a wave of high pressure to move through the air; as high pressure waves move through the air, they leave low pressure areas behind them. When these pressure lows and highs — or waves — reach us, they vibrate the receptors in our ears, and we hear the vibrations as sound.

3. Unlike analog storage media such as magnetic tape and vinyl records, computers store audio information digitally as a series of zeros and ones. In digital storage, the original waveform is broken up into individual samples. This is know as digitizing or sampling the audio, and is sometimes called analog-to-digital conversion. The sampling rate defines how often a sample is taken. For example, CD-quality sound has 44.100 samples for each second of a waveform.

4. The higher the sampling rate, the closer the shape of the digital waveform will be to the original analog waveform. Low sampling rates limit the range of frequencies that can be recorded, which can result in a recording that poorly represents the original sound.

5. The sampling rate limit the frequency range of the audio file; to reproduce a given frequency, the sampling rate must be at least twice that frequency. For example, if the audio contains audible frequencies as high as 8,000 Hz, your need a sample rate of 16,000 samples per second to reproduce this audio accurately in digital form. This calculation comes from the Nyquist Theorem, and the highest frequency that can be reproduced by a given sample rate is known as the Nyquist Frequency. CDs have a sampling rate of 44,100 samples per second that allows samples up to 22,050 Hz, which is higher than the limit of human hearing, 20,000Hz.

Ⅱ. Choose the phrase that is closest in meaning to the underlined part.

1. Audio information is one form that is increasingly downloaded, be it <u>a sampler for a band's album</u>, a radio program, or sound as part of a video.

   A. a number of bands playing music

   B. a collection of representative music played by a band

   C. a bundle of sampling songs of a band

   D. a series of music pieces organized in an album

2. In the case of digital audio signals, <u>the amount of digital information needed to accurately reproduce the original PCM samples</u> may be reduced by applying a digital compression algorithm, resulting in a digitally compressed representation of the original signal.

   A. the quantity of digitized data necessary for faithfully reconstructing the PCM signal

   B. the amount of precisely resulted PCM samples in the form of digital information

   C. the original PCM samples that is accurately obtained from the required digital information

   D. the faithful PCM originals reproduced from the large amount of digital information

3. A frame header is attached which contains information <u>required to synchronize to and decode the encoded bit stream.</u>

   A. necessary in synchronization, decoding, and encoding of the data bits

   B. required for the synchronization between the decoded and encoded bit stream

   C. needed to synchronize to the decoded data stream

   D. necessary for the encoded data stream to be synchronized and decoded

4. By applying a digital compression algorithm, resulting in a digitally compressed representation of the original signal, the amount of digital information needed <u>to accurately reproduce the original pulse code modulation samples</u> may be reduced.

   A. to precisely represent the origin of the PCM samples

   B. to reconstruct the signal initially represented by PCM accurately

   C. to accurately regenerate the original pulses of the modulated samples

   D. to resample the pulse code modulation codes correctly

5. In the two-channel mode a rematrixing process <u>may be selectively performed in order to provide additional coding gain,</u> and to allow improved results to be obtained in the event that the two-channel signal is decoded with a matrix surround decoder.

   A. may be selected to produce better coding results

   B. may be chosen in order to gain an additive coding method in the production

   C. may be provided to gain better performance in the additional coding process

   D. may be optionally carried out to enhance the coding gain

6. The main components of the signal can always be extracted using a filter with a sufficiently steep response and a high enough cut-off frequency, <u>as long as the spectral components beyond the cut-off frequency are negligible.</u>

A. provided the cut-off frequency of the spectral contents is to be neglected

B. provided the signal's frequency contents above the cut-off frequency can be neglected

C. so long as the signal spectrum is above the negligible level at the cut-off frequency

D. as long as the spectral density is too small to be greater than the cut-off frequency

7. The modulator generates a varying signal at its output <u>which is proportional in some way to the signal</u> appearing across its input terminals.

A. which is produced in the same way as the signal

B. which comes partially out of the signal

C. which varies in an unknown manner with the signal

D. certain attribute of which varies in proportion to the signal

8. One possible way of classifying multimedia hardware is to differentiate the hardware into <u>media-specific and non-media-specific</u>.

A. special media and ordinary media

B. with and without media specifications

C. media-dependent and media-independent

D. media available and media in need

Unit 10   Digital Image Processing

Images are everywhere. The rapid advances of the computer technology have made digital image processing an increasingly hot research topic as well as an indispensable part of our daily life.

Text

Part I: Two-Dimensional Digital Images

Images are two-dimensional signals representing spatial distribution of some physical parameters, typically light intensity, and more generally any form of energy. Motion pictures and multi-spectral remote sensing images, for example, are three or higher dimensional signals. Modern digital technology has made it possible to manipulate multi-dimensional signals with systems that range from simple digital circuits to advanced parallel computers.[1] The goal of this manipulation can be divided into three categories:

- Image processing: *image in → image out*
- Image analysis: *image in → measurements out*
- Image understanding: *image in → high-level description out*

We will focus on the fundamental concepts of *image processing*. Space does not permit us to make more than a few introductory remarks about image analysis and image understanding. Further, we will restrict ourselves to two-dimensional (2D) image processing although most of the concepts and techniques that are to be described can be extended easily to three or more dimensions.[2]

We begin with certain basic definitions. An image defined in the "real world" is considered to be a function of two real variables, for example, $a(x, y)$ with a as the amplitude (e.g. brightness) of the image at the *real* coordinate position (x, y). An image may be considered to contain sub-images sometimes referred to as regions-of-interest, ROIs, or simply regions. This concept reflects the fact that images frequently contain collections of objects each of which can be the basis for a region. In a sophisticated image processing system it should be possible to apply specific image processing operations to selected regions. Thus one part of an image might be processed to suppress motion blur while another part might be processed to improve color rendition.[3]

The amplitudes of a given image will almost always be either real numbers or integer numbers. The latter is usually a result of a quantization process that converts a continuous range, say, between 0 and 100%, to a discrete number of levels.[4] In certain image-forming processes, however, the signal may involve photon counting which implies that the amplitude would be inherently quantized. In other image forming procedures, such as magnetic resonance imaging, the direct physical measurement yields a complex number in the form of a real magnitude and a real phase. We will consider amplitudes as reals or integers unless otherwise indicated.

A digital image $a[m, n]$ described in a 2D discrete space is derived from an analog image $a(x, y)$ in a 2D continuous space through a *sampling* process that is frequently referred to as digitization.[5] The mathematics of that sampling process will be described later. For now we will look at some basic definitions associated with the digital image. The effect of digitization is shown in Figure 10.1.

Figure 10.1   Digitization

The 2D continuous image $a(x, y)$ is divided into N rows and M columns. The intersection of a row and a column is termed a *pixel*. The value assigned to the integer coordinates $[m, n]$ with $m = 0, 1, 2, \ldots, M–1$ and $n = 0, 1, 2, \ldots, N–1$ is $a[m, n]$. In fact, in most cases $a(x, y)$, which we might consider to be the physical signal that impinges on the face of a 2D sensor, is actually a function of many variables including depth, color, and time.[6] Unless otherwise stated, we will consider the case of 2D, monochromatic, static images in this text.

The image shown in Figure 10.1 has been divided into $N = 16$ rows and $M = 16$ columns. The value assigned to every pixel is the average brightness in the pixel rounded to the nearest integer value. The process of representing the amplitude of the 2D signal at a given coordinate as an integer value with L different gray levels is usually referred to as amplitude quantization or simply *quantization*.[7]

Certain tools are central to the processing of digital images. These include mathematical tools such as *convolution, Fourier analysis,* and *statistical descriptions,* and manipulative tools such as *chain codes* and *run codes.* Here we present these tools without any specific motivation. The motivation will follow in later sections.

Many image processing applications are intended to produce images that are to be viewed by human observers as opposed to, say, automated industrial inspection. It is therefore important to understand the characteristics and limitations of the human visual system — to understand the "receiver" of the 2D signals. At the outset it is important to realize that 1) the human visual system is not well understood, 2) no objective measure exists for judging the quality of an image that corresponds to human assessment of image quality, and 3) the "typical" human observer does not exist.[8] Nevertheless, research in perceptual psychology has provided some important insights into the visual system.

Part II: Digital Images — Definition and Applications

Images are everywhere. No wonder, since we — as human beings — rely on the images we perceive with our eyes more than any other sensory stimulus. Almost all of the information we digest comes to us in the form of an image; whether we look at a photograph, watch television, admire a painting, or read a book, it all makes use of imagery. Images are so natural to us, that we go to great lengths to convert almost any kind of information to images.[1] For example: the TV weather forecast shows the temperature distribution in some geographical area as an image with different colors representing different temperatures, medical scanners can show human metabolism activity as an image where bright spots indicate high activity, *etc.*[2] Moreover, our vision is usually the most efficient of our senses: consider, for example, a computer keyboard. The function of each key is represented by a small image (a character). We could also have identified each key by a specific relief texture, but it would be far less efficient. We could even try to give each key a specific smell, but it is easy to imagine the trouble we would have in typing.

We are also adept at a number of *image processing* tasks. For example, the focusing of our eyes: when we look at something, the first image our eyes send to the brain is probably out of focus. The brain then tries to correct this by adjusting the eye lens, a new image is then sent from the eyes to the brain, and so on. This feedback process is so fast that we aren't even aware of it. Another example is stereo vision: our eyes send two two-dimensional images to the brain, but the brain is able to merge these into one three-dimensional image *virtually instantaneously.*[3]

The science of *image processing* combines this natural way humans use images with the science of mathematics. This provides a unique blend, since images and image processing are described in a rigorous mathematical way without loss of the intuitive character of imagery.[4]

Image processing can be defined as "the manipulation and analysis of information contained in images". This definition is of course very broad, and includes a wide range of natural and artificial processes, from the use of a pair of glasses to automatic analysis of images transmitted by the Hubble telescope. Simple forms of image processing can be found all around us; examples include:

- The use of glasses or contact lenses
- Brightness, contrast, *etc.*, controls on a television or monitor
- Taking and developing a picture using a photo camera
- Natural examples: reflection of scenery on water surface, distortions of scenery in the mist, *etc.*

Examples of the use of advanced image processing include:

- **Forensic science:** enhancement of images of video surveillance cameras, automatic recognition and classification of faces, fingerprints, DNA codes, *etc.*, from images
- **Industry:** checking of manufactured parts, application to CAD/CAM
- **Information processing:** "reading" of handwritten and printed texts (frequently referred to as OCR; optical character recognition), scanning and classification of printed images

A large number of applications of image processing can be found in the medical sciences using one or more medical images of a patient, *e.g.*:

- **Visualization.** For example: before we can make a 3D visualization of a three-dimensional object, we often need to extract the object information first from two-dimensional images.
- **Computer aided diagnosis.** For example: it is now common to regularly make breast radiographs of females above a certain age in order to detect breast cancer in an early stage. In practice, the number of images involved is so large that it would be very helpful to do part of the screening by means of automated computer image processing.[5]
- **Image segmentation,** *i.e.,* division of an image into meaningful structures. For example: the division of a brain image into structures like white brain matter, gray brain matter, cerebrospinal fluid, bone, fat, skin, *etc.* Segmentation is useful in many tasks ranging from improved visualization to the monitoring of tumor growth.
- **Image registration,** *i.e.,* exact alignment of two or more images of the same patient, which is necessary if the information contained in these images is to be combined in a meaningful new image.[6]

Image processing applications can have many purposes. Most of the time, the purpose will be in one or more of these categories:

- **Image enhancement,** *e.g.,* reduction of noise or sharpening of images.
- **Pattern recognition,** *e.g.,* automatic detection of a certain shape or texture in images.
- **Reduction of data** to information that is more easily handled or interpreted, *e.g.,*

the reduction of an image to an "easier" image, to a set of objects or features, or to a set of measurements.[7]

- **Image synthesis,** *e.g.,* reconstructing a three-dimensional scene from two-dimensional photographs.
- **Combination of images.** When images of two different modalities (types) are made from the same scene, combining them involves registration, and, after that, often data reduction and image synthesis.
- **Data compression.** To reduce the size of computer files containing images and speed up image transmission across a network, data compression is often a must.

We concern ourselves only with *digital* image processing, and not analog processing. The reason for this is that analog processing requires special hardware, which makes building a special image processing application a difficult task. Moreover, the use of analog hardware is rapidly becoming obsolete in many image processing areas, since it can often be replaced by digital hardware (computers) which is much more flexible in its use.

But what exactly is a digital image? A schematic of digital image acquisition and processing is shown in Figure 10.2. At the top, there is some imaging device like a video camera, a medical scanner, or anything else that can convert a measure of a physical reality to an electrical signal. The imaging device produces a continuous electrical signal. Since such an analog signal cannot directly be handled with computers, the signal is converted to a discretized form by a digitizer. The resulting image can then directly be used in digital image processing applications.

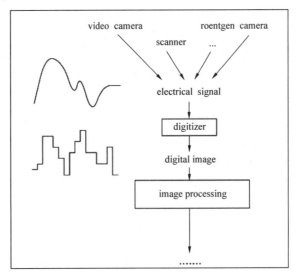

Figure 10.2　Schematic of digital image processing

The digitizer performs two tasks, known as *sampling* and *quantization* (see Figure 10.3). In the sampling process, the values of the continuous signal are sampled at specific locations in the image. In the quantization process, the real values are discretized into digital numbers. After quantization we call the result a digital image. So this answers the question at the beginning of this section: a digital image is nothing more than a matrix of numbers. Each matrix element, *i.e.,* a quantized sample, is called a *picture element* or a *pixel*. In the case of three-dimensional images this is named a *volume element* or *voxel*.

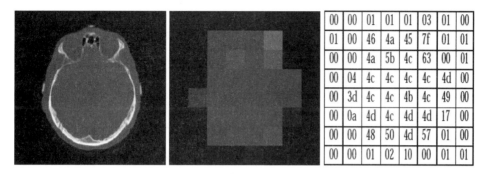

Figure 10.3   Example of sampling and quantization. The left image shows an original scene with continuous intensity values everywhere. After sampling using 8×8 locations (middle image), the image has real intensity values at specific locations only. After quantization (right image), these real values are converted to discrete numbers (here in hexadecimal values).

We can indicate the location of each pixel in an image by two coordinates $(x; y)$. By convention, the $(0; 0)$ pixel, i.e., the origin, is at the top left corner of the image, the x axis runs from left to right, and the y axis runs from top to bottom (see Figure10.4). This may take a little getting used to, because it differs from the conventional mathematical notation of two-dimensional functions[*], as well as from conventional matrix coordinates[†].[8] If a digital image is nothing more than a matrix of numbers, someone might say that digital image processing is merely a collection of mathematical algorithms that operate on a matrix. Fortunately, reality is not nearly as boring as this sound, because in practice we will seldom use the matrix representation shown in Figure 10.3. Instead, we work with the middle image from Figure 10.3, which is in fact the same matrix, but with intensity values assigned to each number — but which usually makes much more sense to a human being.[9] You will find that image processing algorithms will be formulated as mathematical operators working on pixel values or pixel matrices, but the results of these algorithms will also be displayed using images.[10]

Part III: Introduction to Image Processing

Images are produced by a variety of physical devices, including still and video cameras, x-ray devices, electron microscopes, radar, and ultrasound, and used for a variety of purposes, including entertainment, medical, business, industrial, military, civil, security, and scientific. The goal in each case is for an observer, human or machine, to extract useful

---

* In 2D functions, the origin is at the bottom left, and the y axis runs from bottom to top.

† In a matrix, the origin is the top left, the x axis runs from top to bottom, and the y axis from left to right.

information about the scene being imaged.

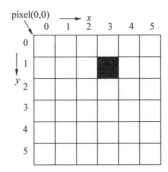

Figure 10.4　Coordinate conventions for images. Pixel (3; 1) is marked in gray

Often the raw image is not directly suitable for this purpose, and must be processed in some way. Such processing is called *image enhancement*; processing by an observer to extract information is called *image analysis*. Enhancement and analysis are distinguished by their output, images vs. scene information, and by the challenges faced and methods employed.

Image enhancement has been done by chemical, optical, and electronic means, while analysis has been done mostly by humans and electronically. Digital image processing, either as enhancement for human observers or performing autonomous analysis, offers advantages in cost, speed, and flexibility, and with the rapidly falling price and rising performance of personal computers, has become the dominant method in use.[1]

The challenge

An image is not a direct measurement of the properties of physical objects being viewed. Rather it is a complex interaction among several physical processes: the intensity and distribution of illuminating radiation, the physics of the interaction of the radiation with the matter comprising the scene, the geometry of projection of the reflected or transmitted radiation from three dimensions to the two dimensions of the image plane, and the electronic characteristics of the sensor.[2] Unlike for example writing a compiler, where an algorithm backed by formal theory exists for translating a high-level computer language to machine language, there is no algorithm and no comparable theory for extracting scene information of interest, such as the position or quality of an article of manufacture, from an image.[3]

The challenge is often underappreciated by novice users due to the seeming effortlessness with which their own visual system extracts information from scenes.[4] Human vision is enormously more sophisticated than anything we can engineer at present and for the foreseeable future. Thus one must be careful not to evaluate the difficulty of a digital image processing application on the basis of how it looks to humans.[5]

Perhaps the first guiding principle is that humans are better at judgment and machines are better at measurement. Thus determining the precise position and size of an automobile part on a conveyer, for example, is well-suited for digital image processing, whereas grading apples or wood is quite a bit more challenging (although not impossible).[6] Along these lines image enhancement, which generally requires lots of numeric computation but little judgment, is well-suited for digital processing.

The problem is further complicated by often severe time budgets. Few users care if a spreadsheet takes 300 milliseconds to update rather than 200, but most industrial applications, for example, must operate within hard constraints imposed by machine cycle times. There are also many applications, such as ultrasound image enhancement, traffic monitoring, and camcorder stabilization that require real-time processing of a video stream.

To make the speed challenge concrete, consider that the video stream from a standard monochrome video camera produces around 10 million pixels per second. For example, a desktop PC can execute 50 machine instructions in the 100 ns available to process each pixel. The set of things one can do in a mere 50 instructions is rather limited.

On top of this, many image processing applications are constrained by severe cost targets. Thus we often face the engineer's dreaded triple curse, the need to design something good, fast, and cheap all at once.

Image acquisition

All image processing applications start with some form of illumination, typically light but more generally some form of energy. In some cases ambient light must be used, but more typically the illumination can be designed for the application. In such cases the battle is often won or lost right here — no amount of clever software can recover information that simply isn't there due to poor illumination.[7]

A camera is any device that converts a pattern of radiated energy into a digital image stored in a random-access memory. In the past this operation was divided into two pieces: conversion of energy to electrical signal, considered to be the camera's function, and conversion and storage of the signal in digital form, performed by a *digitizer*. Now the distinction has become blurred, and cameras can feed directly to computer memory via USB, Ethernet, or IEEE 1394 interfaces.

Camera technology and the characteristics of the resulting images are driven almost exclusively by the highest volume applications, one of which has been consumer television. Thus most video cameras have resolution and speed characteristics established by TV broadcast standards more than a half century ago.

A typical visible light monochrome camera would have a resolution of 640×480 pixels, produce 30 frames per second, and support electronic shuttering and rapid reset (the ability to reset to the beginning of a frame at any time, to avoid having to wait before beginning an image acquisition).[8] It would be based on CCD sensor technology, which produces good image quality but is expensive relative to most chips with a similar number of transistors.

For the first time ever the landscape is changing, as high volume personal computer multimedia applications proliferate. First affected were monitors, which for some time have offered higher-than-broadcast speed and resolution.[9] One would expect cameras to follow*, with high-speed, high-resolution devices driven by consumer digital still camera technology and lower-resolution, ultra low cost units driven by entertainment, internet conferencing, and perceptual user interface applications.[10]

The low cost devices may have the greater influence. These are based on emerging CMOS sensor technology, which uses the same process as most computer chips and is therefore inexpensive due simply to higher process volume.[11] Currently image quality is not up to CCD standards, but that is certain to change as the technology matures.†

Image enhancement

Digital image enhancement algorithms are broadly divided into two classes, point transforms (pixel mapping) and neighborhood operations.

1. Point transforms

Point transforms produce output images where each pixel is some function of a corresponding input pixel. The function is the same for every pixel, and is often derived from global statistics of the image. Point transforms generally execute rapidly but are limited to global transformations such as adjusting overall image contrast.

Point transforms include a large set of enhancements that are useful with scalar-valued pixels. Often these are implemented with a single software routine or hardware module that uses a lookup table. Lookup tables are fast and can be programmed for any function, offering the ultimate in generality at reasonable speed. MMX and similar processors, however, can perform a variety of functions much faster by direct computation than by table lookup, at a cost of increased software complexity. Pixel maps are most useful when the function is computed based on global statistics of the image. One can process an image to have a desired gain and offset, for example, based on the mean and standard deviation, or alternatively, the minimum and maximum, of the input.[12]

Histogram specification is a powerful pixel mapping point transform where an input image is processed so that it has the same distribution of pixel values as some reference image. The pixel map for histogram specification is easily computed from histograms of the input and reference images. Histogram specification is a useful enhancement prior to an analysis step whose goal is some sort of comparison between the input and the reference.

Thresholding is a commonly used enhancement whose goal is to segment an image into *object* and *background*. A threshold value is computed above (or below) which pixels are considered *object* and below (or above) which *background*.[13] Sometimes two thresholds

---

* This has indeed happened as digital cameras have become popular in recent years. While consumer cameras offer high portability with sufficient resolution and good image quality, DSLRs (digital single lens reflection cameras) can produce excellent images comparable with their ancestors, the conventional film SLRs, with powerful control over the camera configuration and post-processing potentials unavailable to films.

† This is also changing. CMOS sensors have already been used in DSLRs.

are used to specify a band of values that correspond to object pixels. Thresholds can be fixed but are best computed from image statistics. Thresholding can also be done using neighborhood operations. In all cases the result is a binary image — only black and white are represented without gray shades.

Color space conversion is used to convert between, for example, the RGB space provided by a camera to the HIS (hue, intensity, saturation) space needed by an image analysis algorithm. Accurate color space conversion is computationally expensive, and crude approximations are often used in time-critical applications. These can be quite effective, but it is a good idea to understand the tradeoffs between speed and accuracy before choosing an algorithm.

Time averaging is the most effective method of handling very low contrast images. Pixel maps to increase image gain are of limited utility because they affect signal and noise equally. Neighborhood operations can reduce noise but at the cost of some loss in image fidelity. The only way to reduce noise without affecting the signal is to average multiple images over time. The amplitude of uncorrelated noise is attenuated by the square root of the number of images averaged.[14] When time averaging is combined with a gain-amplifying pixel map, extremely low contrast scenes can be processed. The main disadvantage of time averaging is the time needed to acquire multiple images from a camera.

2. Neighborhood operations

With neighborhood operations, each output pixel is a function of a set of corresponding input pixels. This set is called a neighborhood because it is usually some region surrounding a corresponding center pixel, for example a 3×3 neighborhood. Neighborhood operations can implement frequency and shape filtering and other sophisticated enhancements, but execute more slowly because the neighborhood must be recomputed for each output pixel.

Linear filters are the best understood of the neighborhood operations, due to the extensively developed mathematical framework of signal theory dating back 200 years to Fourier.[15] Linear filters amplify or attenuate selected spatial frequencies, can achieve such effects as smoothing and sharpening, and usually form the basis of re-sampling and boundary detection algorithms.[16]

Linear filters can be defined by a convolution operation, where output pixels are obtained by multiplying each neighborhood pixel by a corresponding element of a like-shaped set of values called a *kernel*, and then summing those products.[17] The filters can be implemented by direct convolution or in the frequency domain using FFTs. While frequency domain filtering is theoretically more efficient, in practice direct convolution is almost always preferred. Convolution, with its use of small integers and sequential memory addressing, is a better match for digital hardware than FFTs, is simpler to implement and has little trouble with boundary conditions.[18]

Boundary detection has an extensive history and literature, which ranges from simple edge detection to complex algorithms that might more properly be considered under image analysis. We somewhat arbitrarily consider boundary detection under image enhancement because the goal is to emphasize features of interest (the boundaries) and attenuate everything else.[19]

The shading produced by an object in an image is among the least reliable of an object's properties, since shading is a complex combination of illumination, surface properties, projection geometry, and sensor characteristics. Image discontinuities, on the other hand, usually correspond directly to object surface discontinuities (e.g., edges), since the other factors tend not to be discontinuous. Image discontinuities are generally consistent geometrically (i.e., in shape) even when not consistent photometrically.[20] Thus identifying and localizing discontinuities, which is the goal of boundary detection, is one of the most important digital image processing tasks.

Crude edge detectors simply mark image pixels corresponding to gradient magnitude peaks or second derivative zero-crossings. Sophisticated boundary detectors produce organized chains of boundary points, with sub-pixel position and boundary orientation at each point. The best commercially available boundary detectors are also tunable in spatial frequency response over a wide range, and operate at high speed.

Nonlinear filters designed to pass or block desired shapes rather than spatial frequencies have been found useful for digital image enhancement. The first we consider is the median filter, whose output at each pixel is the median of the corresponding input neighborhood. Roughly speaking the effect of a median filter is to attenuate image features smaller in size than the neighborhood and pass image features larger than the neighborhood.

Digital re-sampling refers to a process of estimating the image that would have resulted had the continuous distribution of energy falling on the sensor been sampled differently.[21] A different sampling, perhaps at a different resolution or orientation, is often useful.

Another important class of re-sampling algorithms is coordinate transforms, which can shift by sub-pixel amounts, rotate and size images, and convert between Cartesian and polar representations. Output pixel values are interpolated from a neighborhood of input values. Three methods in common use are nearest neighbor, which is the fastest, bilinear interpolation, which is more accurate but slower and suffers some loss of high frequency components, and cubic convolution, which is very accurate but slowest.[22]

New Words

Part I

parameter	参数	intensity	强度
multi-spectral	多光谱的	manipulate	处理，操作
introductory	介绍性的，引导性的	function	函数
amplitude	幅度	coordinate	坐标

regions-of-interest	感兴趣区	motion blur	运动模糊
rendition	表现，渲染	render	表现，渲染
real number	实数	integer	整数
quantization	量化	discrete	离散的
photon	光子	inherently	内在地，本质上
Magnetic Resonance		phase	相位，相角
Imaging (MRI)	磁共振成像	sampling	采样
digitization	数字化	intersection	交叉点
pixel	像素	impinge	撞击，射到
sensor	传感器，感光器	monochromatic	单色的
round	四舍五入	convolution	卷积
outset	开头，最初	perceptual	感官的

Part Ⅱ

stimulus	刺激	digest	消化，理解
imagery	形象化的描述，比喻	metabolism	新陈代谢
relief texture	凹凸的纹理	adept	熟练的，老练的
out of focus	未聚焦，聚焦不良的	stereo vision	立体视觉
merge	合并	virtually	实际上
instantaneously	瞬时地	blend	混合
rigorous	严格的	character	个性
Hubble telescope	哈勃望远镜	scenery	风景，景物
forensic	司法，法医（取证）的	surveillance	监视
classification	分类	fingerprint	指纹
diagnosis	诊断	radiograph	射线图
screening	筛选，普查	cerebrospinal	脑脊髓的
visualization	可视化，形象化	image registration	图像配准
alignment	对准	enhancement	增强
synthesis	合成，综合	modality	形态，式样
obsolete	过时的，陈旧的	digitizer	数字化仪
voxel	体（像）素	hexadecimal	十六进制的
formulate	表述，用公式表达	operator	算子，算符

Part Ⅲ

autonomous	自治的，自主的	projection	投影
reflected	反射的	transmitted	透射的，发射的
comparable	可比的	underappreciated	认识不足的，被低估的

engineer	设计，策划	spreadsheet	电子表格
conveyer	传输带	time budget	时间限制
constraint	约束，限制	impose	施加
camcorder	手持摄像机	video stream	视频（数据）流
concrete	具体的	dreaded	可怕的
curse	诅咒，咒语	ambient	周围的
resolution	分辨率	shutter	快门
proliferate	激增	mature	成熟
portability	便携性	potential	潜力
map	映射	lookup table	查找表
mean	均值	standard deviation	标准差
histogram	直方图	thresholding	用阈值分割图像
color space	颜色空间	hue	色调
saturation	饱和度	time-critical	对时间要求苛刻的
tradeoff	折中，妥协	fidelity	忠诚，保真度
attenuate	衰减	amplify	放大
convolution	卷积	kernel	核，核心
product	乘积	arbitrarily	任意地
shading	阴影，明暗	discontinuity	不连续性
photometrically	在摄影光度方面	gradient	梯度，渐变的
derivative	导数，微商	zero-crossing	过零点
sub-pixel	亚像素	tunable	可调节的
spatial	空间的	median filter	中值滤波
Cartesian	笛卡儿（坐标）的	polar	极坐标的
interpolate	内插	bilinear	双线性

Notes on the Text

Part I

1. Modern digital technology has made it possible to manipulate multi-dimensional signals with systems that range from simple digital circuits to advanced parallel computers.

   现代数字技术使得处理多维信号成为可能，所使用的系统可从简单的数字电路到先进的并行计算机。

2. Further, we will restrict ourselves to two-dimensional (2D) image processing although most of the concepts and techniques that are to be described can be extended easily to three or more dimensions.

   另外我们将限于讨论二维图像处理，尽管将要描述的大部分概念和方法很容易扩展到三维或更高的维数。

3. Thus one part of an image might be processed to suppress motion blur while another part might be processed to improve color rendition.

于是图像的一部分可以进行抑制运动模糊的处理，而另一部分可以作改进色彩渲染的处理。

4. The latter is usually a result of a quantization process that converts a continuous range, say, between 0 and 100%, to a discrete number of levels.

后者通常是量化的结果，将一个连续的范围如 0~100% 转换为离散的（灰度）级。

5. A digital image $a[m, n]$ described in a 2D discrete space is derived from an analog image $a(x, y)$ in a 2D continuous space through a *sampling* process that is frequently referred to as digitization.

一幅二维离散空间中的数字图像 $a[m, n]$ 是由二维连续空间中的模拟图像 $a(x, y)$ 通过采样得到的。采样过程常称为数字化。

6. In fact, in most cases $a(x, y)$, which we might consider to be the physical signal that impinges on the face of a 2D sensor, is actually a function of many variables including depth, color, and time.

大多数情况下，物理信号射到二维传感器表面而产生的 $a(x, y)$ 实际上是许多变量的函数，包括深度、颜色、时间。

7. The process of representing the amplitude of the 2D signal at a given coordinate as an integer value with L different gray levels is usually referred to as amplitude quantization or simply *quantization*.

将二维信号在给定坐标位置的幅度表示成具有 L 个不同灰度级的整数值的过程通常称为幅度量化，或简称量化。

8. At the outset it is important to realize that 1) the human visual system is not well understood, 2) no objective measure exists for judging the quality of an image that corresponds to human assessment of image quality, and 3) the "typical" human observer does not exist.

一开始就认识到以下几点是很重要的：1)人的视觉系统尚未被充分了解；2)不存在与人眼评价相当的判断图像质量的客观度量；3)不存在所谓"典型"的观察者。

Part Ⅱ

1. Images are so natural to us, that we go to great lengths to convert almost any kind of information to images.

图像对于我们是如此自然，因而总是尽力将几乎任何信息都转换为图像。

- go to great lengths, go (to) all (any) lengths：竭尽全力。

2. For example: the TV weather forecast shows the temperature distribution in some geographical area as an image with different colors representing different temperatures, medical scanners can show human metabolism activity as an image

where bright spots indicate high activity, *etc.*

例如，电视天气预报用图像表示某一地区的温度分布，以不同颜色代表不同的温度；医学扫描装置可将人的新陈代谢活动显示成图像，用亮点表示强的活动性，等等。

3. Our eyes send two two-dimensional images to the brain, but the brain is able to merge these into one three-dimensional image *virtually instantaneously*.

我们的眼睛将两幅二维图像传到大脑，而大脑能在瞬息之间将它们合成为一幅三维图像。

4. This provides a unique blend, since images and image processing are described in a rigorous mathematical way without loss of the intuitive character of imagery.

这就提供了独特的混合，因为可用严格数学方法描述图像和图像处理又不失图像的直观性。

5. In practice, the number of images involved is so large that it would be very helpful to do part of the screening by means of automated computer image processing.

实践中图像数量如此巨大，因而用自动计算机图像处理来完成部分筛选工作十分有益。

6. Exact alignment of two or more images of the same patient, which is necessary if the information contained in these images is to be combined in a meaningful new image.

同一病人的两幅或更多图像应严格对准。若要将这些图像中包含的信息结合起来形成一幅有意义的新图像，这种对准是十分必要的。

7. Reduction of data to information that is more easily handled or interpreted, *e.g.,* the reduction of an image to an "easier" image, to a set of objects or features, or to a set of measurements.

将数据量减少为更容易处置或解释的信息，例如将图像减小为一幅较简单的图像、一组对象或特征、或者一组测量结果。

8. This may take a little getting used to, because this differs from the conventional mathematical notation of two-dimensional functions, as well as from conventional matrix coordinates.

这可能要用一点时间去习惯它，因为它不同于常规的二元函数的数学表示法，也不同于常规的矩阵表示法。

9. Instead, we work with the middle image from Figure 10.3, which is in fact the same matrix, but with intensity values assigned to each number — but which usually makes much more sense to a human being.

而我们则对图 10.3 中间的图像进行处理，这实际上是同一幅图像，但将光强度赋予每一个数，对人而言它通常更有意义。

10. You will find that image processing algorithms will be formulated as mathematical operators working on pixel values or pixel matrices, but the results of these algorithms will also be displayed using images.

你会发现图像处理算法将被描述为数学算子作用于像素值或像素矩阵，这些算法的运算结果也将被用图像形式显示出来。

Part Ⅲ

1. Digital image processing, either as enhancement for human observers or performing autonomous analysis, offers advantages in cost, speed, and flexibility, and with the rapidly falling price and rising performance of personal computers, has become the dominant method in use.

用于观察者的（视觉）增强方法或用于（计算机）自主分析的数字图像处理技术在成本、速度、灵活性方面具有优越性，随着个人计算机价格的急剧下降和功能的快速提升而成了实用的主要方法。

- 本句主要成分：… Digital image processing …offers advantages … and … has become …

2. Rather it is a complex interaction among several physical processes: the intensity and distribution of illuminating radiation, the physics of the interaction of the radiation with the matter comprising the scene, the geometry of projection of the reflected or transmitted radiation from three dimensions to the two dimensions of the image plane, and the electronic characteristics of the sensor.

而是诸多物理因素相互作用的结果：光照强度及其分布、光照与构成景物的物质之间的相互作用、反射或透射的光照从三维到二维图像平面的几何投影以及传感器的电子特性。

- 并列的同位语：the intensity and distribution, the physics, the geometry, and the electronic characteristics

3. Unlike for example writing a compiler, where an algorithm backed by formal theory exists for translating a high-level computer language to machine language, there is no algorithm and no comparable theory for extracting scene information of interest, such as the position or quality of an article of manufacture, from an image.

不像某些其他工作，例如编写编译程序那样以正式理论为基础的算法，可将高级计算机语言翻译成机器语言，不存在从图像中提取感兴趣的景物信息如位置或某一制成品质量的算法和可比的理论。

4. The challenge is often underappreciated by novice users due to the seeming effortlessness with which their own visual system extracts information from scenes.

这种困难常被初学者低估，因为人的视觉系统似乎可轻而易举地从景物中提取信息。

5. Thus one must be careful not to evaluate the difficulty of a digital image processing application on the basis of how it looks to humans.

因此我们必须注意，不要根据人们对某一数字图像处理应用的印象来评估其难易程度。

6. Thus determining the precise position and size of an automobile part on a conveyer, for example, is well-suited for digital image processing, whereas grading apples or wood is quite a bit more challenging (although not impossible).

因此，比方说在传输带上确定一个汽车零件的确切位置和大小很适合于数字图像处理，而要对苹果或木材的质量定级却更具挑战性，尽管不是不可能的。

7. In such cases the battle is often won or lost right here — no amount of clever software can recover information that simply isn't there due to poor illumination.

在这些情况下事情的成败往往就在于此：任何高明的软件都无法将因为照明不良而丢失的信息恢复出来。

8. A typical visible light monochrome camera would have a resolution of 640×480 pixels, produce 30 frames per second, and support electronic shuttering and rapid reset (the ability to reset to the beginning of a frame at any time, to avoid having to wait before beginning an image acquisition).

典型的可见光单色摄像机的分辨率为 640×480px，每秒输出 30 帧图像，并支持电子快门和快速复位（任意时刻回复到一帧初始状态的能力，从而避免在开始捕获一帧新图像前的等待）。

9. For the first time ever the landscape is changing, as high volume personal computer multimedia applications proliferate. First affected were monitors, which for some time have offered higher-than-broadcast speed and resolution.

随着大容量个人计算机多媒体应用的激增情况首次发生了变化。首先受到影响的是显示器，它已有相当一段时间给我们提供了比广播更高的速度和分辨率。

10. One can expect cameras to follow, with high-speed, high-resolution devices driven by consumer digital still camera technology and lower-resolution, ultra low cost units driven by entertainment, internet conferencing, and perceptual user interface applications.

人们可期待照相机/摄像机也随之跟上，包括由民用数字照相机技术所推动的高速度、高分辨率器件，娱乐业、互联网远程会议和用户视觉界面应用所推动的低分辨率和极低价格的设备。

11. These are based on emerging CMOS sensor technology, which uses the same process as most computer chips and is therefore inexpensive due simply to higher process volume.

这些是基于新出现的 CMOS 传感器技术的，其生产工艺与大多数计算机芯片相同，因而得益于生产批量大而价格低廉。

12. One can process an image to have a desired gain and offset, for example, based on the mean and standard deviation, or alternatively, the minimum and maximum, of the input.

人们可以处理一幅图像，在输入信号的均值和标准偏差，或者最小值和最大值的基础上，获得所要求的增益和补偿（偏移）。

13. A threshold value is computed above (or below) which pixels are considered *object* and below (or above) which *background*.

计算阈值，大于（或小于）阈值的就当作对象，否则就是背景。

- 注意后半句省略 are considered。

14. The amplitude of uncorrelated noise is attenuated by the square root of the number of images averaged.

不相关噪声的幅度以参与平均的图像数的平方根为因子被衰减。

15. Linear filters are the best understood of the neighborhood operations, due to the extensively developed mathematical framework of signal theory dating back 200 years to Fourier.

由于有了可追溯到 200 年前 Fourier 信号理论的广泛数学框架,线性滤波器是邻域处理中最容易理解的。

16. Linear filters amplify or attenuate selected spatial frequencies, can achieve such effects as smoothing and sharpening, and usually form the basis of re-sampling and boundary detection algorithms.

线性滤波器有选择地放大或衰减空间频率成分,可达到平滑和锐化等效果,通常是重采样和边缘检测算法的基础。

- 三组动词 amplify or attenuate, can achieve, form 并列。

17. Linear filters can be defined by a convolution operation, where output pixels are obtained by multiplying each neighborhood pixel by a corresponding element of a like-shaped set of values called a kernel, and then summing those products.

线性滤波可用卷积运算定义,其输出像素由邻域内各像素乘以叫做"核"的同样形状区域内的相应值,然后将乘积相加得到。

18. Convolution, with its use of small integers and sequential memory addressing, is a better match for digital hardware than FFTs, is simpler to implement and has little trouble with boundary conditions.

由于使用小的整数运算和时序存储器寻址,卷积比起 FFT 来与数字硬件更加匹配,更容易实现,在边界条件的处理方面几乎没有问题。

19. We somewhat arbitrarily consider boundary detection under image enhancement because the goal is to emphasize features of interest (the boundaries) and attenuate everything else.

我们可以有点随意地将边缘检测看成是一种图像增强,因为其目的是突出感兴趣的边缘特征,而将其他一切都衰减掉。

20. Image discontinuities, on the other hand, usually correspond directly to object surface discontinuities (e.g., edges), since the other factors tend not to be discontinuous. Image discontinuities are generally consistent geometrically (i.e., in shape) even when not consistent photometrically.

另一方面,图像中的不连续区通常直接对应于目标表面的不连续性(例如边缘),因为其他因素不易导致不连续性。图像中的不连续性即使在光度学方面不一致,在几何(即形状)方面通常也是一致的。

21. Digital re-sampling refers to a process of estimating the image that would have resulted had the continuous distribution of energy falling on the sensor been

sampled differently.

数字重采样是指照射到传感器上的能量连续分布被重新采样的情况下估计图像的过程。

22. Three methods in common use are nearest neighbor, which is the fastest, bilinear interpolation, which is more accurate but slower and suffers some loss of high frequency components, and cubic convolution, which is very accurate but slowest.

三种常用方法是：速度最快的最近邻法，更精确但速度较慢而且会损失一些高频分量的双线性法，非常精确但是最慢的三次卷积法。

Technical Tips

Sampling theorem

The Nyquist-Shannon sampling theorem is a fundamental result in the field of information theory, in particular telecommunications and signal processing. Sampling is the process of converting a signal (for example, a function of continuous time or space) into a numeric sequence (a function of discrete time or space). The theorem states that exact reconstruction of a continuous-time baseband signal from its samples is possible if the signal is bandlimited and the sampling frequency is greater than twice the signal bandwidth.

Convolution

Convolution is a mathematical operator which takes two functions f and g and produces a third function that in a sense represents the amount of overlap between f and a reversed and translated version of g. The convolution of f and g is written $f * g$. It is defined as the integral of the product of the two functions after one is reversed and shifted. As such, it is a particular kind of integral transform:

$$f(t) * g(t) = \int_a^b f(\tau) g(t - \tau) \mathrm{d}\tau$$

Supplementary Readings

1. Medical Image Processing

A digital image is characterized by its lattice and by the corresponding picture elements. The lattice is typically a rectangular grid of dimension 2 or 3, corresponding either to 2 or 3 spatial coordinates (planar or volumetric data), or to 2 coordinates plus time (images sequence); in general, the dimension of the lattice is n, with $n \geqslant 2$. In the 2D case, individual elements may have four or six nearest neighbors, corresponding respectively to rectangular or hexagonal arrangements. In the 3D case the lattice is usually parallelepipedic, with six neighbors. The values of those picture elements, called pixels in 2D and voxels in 3D, can be single data such as a density, pairs of data such as relaxation times in MRI, triples such as trichromatic values, etc.

Image manipulation encompasses several types of processing techniques, collectively known as digital imaging. Image synthesis (or computer graphics) consists in assigning a value for each of the above pixels or voxel, the end product being a 2D or 3D image with (generally) some semantic and/or pictorial content. Image synthesis has always been closely associated with human-computer interaction. Most reference textbooks and publications describe interactive computer graphics and not just image synthesis per se. The ability to change pixels rapidly leads naturally to interactive generation of static and dynamic pictures. The full exploitation of the computer as a medium for image synthesis is thus only achieved in a dynamic, interactive environment.

Conversely, image analysis consists of a picture to parameters transformation, starting with image(s) for which each element has a known value. It is customary to subdivide this domain into image processing, image analysis, and computer vision (or image understanding, scene analysis). Image processing consists in transforming one image into another image, often with the same support; the purpose is typically to eliminate or enhance some features. Image analysis goes one step further by extracting parameters and analyzing them; classical domains of application are medical imaging or industrial robotics. Finally, computer vision is a field of study which aims at designing computer systems mimicking the human sense of sight.

A more restricted goal for computer vision is to provide a symbolic description of an image or scene. Computer vision methods usually encompass both numeric and symbolic processing of optical data, which is for example obtained from multi-camera input. By extension, "computer vision" is often used in place of "image analysis" and even "image processing", as soon as the algorithms involved exceeds a certain level of complexity. It could be argued that medical imaging relates more to image analysis than to computer vision; recent developments in medical imaging show however that this distinction is becoming thin.

There are various motivations for using digital image processing methods in medicine:

- New modalities and multimodal analysis: foremost comes certainly the possibility of exploring new imaging modalities, leading to new anatomical or functional insights; further, image analysis will support the combined evaluation of data from different modalities.

- Morphometry: the use of computerized techniques allows better precision and repeatability, with, as a consequence, improved objectivity of measurement of morphometric parameters like size, area, volume, circumference, etc.

- Improved interpretation: the sensitiveness of those new imaging modalities coupled with the power of recent visualization techniques enable more refined diagnosis than with using conventional exploratory methods.

- More accurate prediction: a consequence is the ability of providing more finely tuned medical treatment, for example lower doses in radiation therapy or more accurate positioning in head surgery.

- Process automation: many medical operations can benefit from the reliability provided by automatic processing, from the screening of biological specimen to vision guided surgery.
- Understanding of volume data: recognition of structures from volume data is not a spontaneous visual task and will benefit from computerized processing and visualization.

Medical applications of image synthesis techniques are mostly for 2D and 3D visualization purposes. Typical examples are in diagnosis or planning, for example for surgery or radiotherapy. Graphical methods can also be employed for simulation, typically by means of computer animation techniques. It is worth noting that other theoretical concepts usually perceived as pertaining to computer graphics play an important role in computer vision. The links between these two kindred fields are numerous. It is hard to conceive a physician's workstation without methods originating from both.

The history of image analysis in medicine is older than the one of image synthesis (1960's versus 1980's). The early works were concerned with applications such as chromosome pairing, morphological classification and counting of particles, coding for image compression, storage and communication. More recently, the advent of new imaging technologies has led to methods exploring 3D structures and dynamic changes of objects, usually starting from slice data or possibly from time sequences of 2D or 3D images. Extraction of 3D morphological structures is a very active research area, possibly using artificial intelligence methods. Complex computer vision techniques are also being used in domains such as medical robotics. Although 2D analysis still receives considerable interest, the trend is now to directly analyze volume data by 3D methods.

2. Video Surveillance: Challenge and Solutions

Automated visual surveillance is currently a hot topic in computer vision research, and with good reason. Surveillance cameras are cheap and ubiquitous, but the manpower required to supervise them is expensive. Consequently video from these cameras is usually monitored sparingly or not at all. In fact it is often used merely as a record to examine an incident once it is known to have taken place. Surveillance cameras are far more useful tools if instead of passively recording footage they can detect events requiring attention as they happen, and alert a human supervisor in real time.

The nature of the application may vary according to the sort of decisions and actions a surveillance system is to make. For instance, a recent survey indicated that high priorities for a public transport surveillance system are to detect congestion in restricted areas, and "individual delinquency" (e.g. violence against oneself or others). Detecting congestion requires only a simple description of each person in a scene, maybe just enough to count the number of people present, whereas the detection of delinquent behavior requires a much richer description of an individual, possibly including a history of their overall motion, limb movements and gaze direction.

Although the exact requirements vary between surveillance systems, there are issues common to all. Usually, an operator is interested only in certain objects in the scene. For instance, in surveillance of a public area, one may be interested only in monitoring the people within it rather than the entire scene. Isolating each person in each frame, and tracking them over time, is a problem of object detection, classification and tracking. Once these objects of interest have been identified, a subsequent problem is that of behavior analysis: describing their activity in such a way that a course of action can be decided upon in software.

Object identification and tracking, and behavior analysis, are core problems of automatic surveillance, but they are affected by a number of practical problems. Surveillance networks contain many cameras, which need to be coordinated in order to track an object over an extended distance and period of time. The video obtained from these cameras is often of low resolution and low frame rate, and varies in quality as environmental conditions such as lighting change over time. As well as arriving from many cameras, video may come from various types of camera, including infrared and night-vision. To be useful, surveillance software usually needs to make decisions in real time, which further constrains the amount of processing that can be applied. It is important to take each of these issues into account when designing a surveillance system.

Rather than advocate a set of "best practices" for the main problems in surveillance software, we present a range of approaches to each issue. This is for two reasons: first, the problems of object detection, tracking, identification and analysis from video are still open; and second, solutions to these problems tend to be highly domain specific.

An indication of the difficulty of creating a single general-purpose surveillance system comes from the development of one of the most ambitious surveillance projects: the VSAM (Video Surveillance and Monitoring) project at CMU and other institutions. It is intended for automated surveillance of people and vehicles in cluttered environments, using a range of sensors including color CCD cameras, thermal cameras and night vision cameras. This was intended as a general surveillance system, but has instead become a collection of separate algorithms selected on a case-by-case basis.

There is in general a tradeoff in the choice of approaches to detection and tracking between primitives that are easy to detect, but difficult to track consistently such as corner features, and those that are easier to track but difficult to detect such as higher-level shape models. Surveillance generally demands that objects are tracked over long periods of time, and in varying conditions. This raises difficulties such as tracking in very different lighting conditions, across a cluttered and dynamic background, and in the presence of shadows.

The need to automatically detect suspicious objects, such as a suitcase left in an airport lounge, has led to the development of systems for detecting objects that come to rest for a period of time. This has been solved by regularly computing a measure of the background exhibited in a video sequence of a busy scene using histogram methods, and detecting whether changes to the background have occurred that indicate a new static object has entered the scene. Such a system has obvious additional application in the detecting of blocked road tunnels and illegally parked vehicles.

Object recognition is a classic computer vision problem, which has been tackled in a variety of ways. Surveillance footage usually has quite poor resolution, and objects of interest may span only a few pixels in each frame. This lack of information means that generally coarse color histogram techniques are most applicable on a frame-by-frame basis. On the other hand, footage is available over a long period of time, which enables an informative model of motion to be constructed.

Object detection, tracking and classification, though unsolved problems in themselves, can be seen as precursors to the main problem in automated surveillance: the description of the activity taking place in the scene, which is usually termed behavior analysis.

The difficulty of the tasks of object detection, tracking and analysis is compounded by a number of practical problems. These include keeping track of objects as they move between camera fields of view, ensuring that video is delivered and processed in real time, dealing with video of varying quality, and evaluating the success or otherwise of a surveillance system.

If a good laboratory solution to a key problem in surveillance is to be translated into a commercial system, a good deal of further work is likely to be necessary to achieve suitable robustness in performance. For example, referring back to the problem of detecting objects posited in a busy airport lounge, a commercial system will need to have a very low false-negative rate (we rarely overlook a suspicious object), perhaps at the expense of a slightly elevated false positive rate (we sometimes mistakenly detect an object). This in turn will require that excellent system performance can be maintained in the face of difficult and fluctuating operating conditions. Illumination variation presents particular difficulties in practice, especially in monitoring outdoor scenes. Shadows may need to be isolated and ignored, and illumination changes associated with moving clouds, the onset of rain, setting of the sun, etc., may need to be handled. Indoor lighting changes can also present considerable problems when there are windows, intermittent light-source occlusions, reflections, doors opened, saturation effects due to bright lights, etc. Commercial systems clearly need to be as immune as possible to these types of problems in so far as they arise in the domain of application.

A common assumption in multi-camera surveillance systems is that the fields of view (FOVs) of each camera overlap. This can be quite a severe restriction, especially when monitoring a wide area or one where lines of sight are often occluded. Camera handoff is a term commonly used to describe algorithms for keeping track of an object across multiple camera FOVs, in order to overcome this limitation.

The surveillance of traffic is well suited to cameras with non-overlapping FOVs, because traffic generally follows well-defined paths and these paths extend over long distances which it is impractical to monitor entirely. A system using cameras situated about 2 miles apart along a highway is described. Cars are identified as they enter each camera's field of view based on both their appearance and positional information from views through which they have previously passed.

Surveillance analysis software is usually more useful if it can run in real time, and is therefore able to act on what it sees as it is happening. Although increases in CPU and memory speed have enabled far more sophisticated techniques to be executed in real time, there remains a network bandwidth bottleneck: video streams from several sources need to be collected over a network and moved to where they can be accessed by a CPU. Care therefore needs to be taken to minimize network traffic within a surveillance system. For example, only frames in which some activity is present need to be transmitted and processed.

Surveillance systems tend to be quite domain specific, meaning that the best test of the merit of a system is usually to test it extensively in the environment in which it is to be used. However this is not always possible, and some work has been done on quantitative testing procedures using Receiver Operating Characteristic (ROC) curves.

In addition to real-time surveillance of events, there is an evident need for after-the-event analysis of stored video. Public cameras are now ubiquitous to the extent that a person going about their business in a typical large city can expect to be video-taped hundreds of times per day. As a consequence, when an event such as a robbery takes place, it is common for police to scan (by eye) numerous video tapes from suitably positioned closed-circuit television (CCTV) systems in search of images of an offender. As video repositories switch increasingly from tape to digital form, this presents a variety of challenges for automated surveillance, some of which relate to the field of video mining. For example, a system may be required to search a video repository's last few days' footage for instances of violent behavior, or examples of where a car passed unusually quickly through the field of view.

Despite recent progress in computer vision and other areas, there are still major technical challenges to be overcome before the dream of reliable automated surveillance is realized. These technical challenges, including object identification, tracking and analysis, are compounded by practical considerations such as the physical placement of cameras, the network bandwidth required to support them, installation cost, privacy concerns and robustness to unfavorable weather and lighting conditions. However progress is being made ever more rapidly. The demand for automated surveillance continues to increase in areas ranging from crime prevention, public safety and home security to industrial quality control and military intelligence gathering.

Exercises

I. Translate the following sentences into Chinese.

1. They are transmitting high-resolution full color images at the rate of 30 images per second, a transfer speed that enables full size full quality image viewing in real time.

2. An image is a 2-dimensional distribution of energy, typically of visible electromagnetic radiation (light) but can also be of x-rays, ultraviolet, infrared or other radiation: electrons, acoustic waves or even nuclear particles.

3. High resolution and full color are important for such examinations of standard prepared specimens, but resolution and colors may be reduced for freeze section service as these specimens are low in details and growth pattern is the prevailing feature analyzed.

4. Image discontinuities, on the other hand, usually correspond directly to object surface discontinuities (e.g., edges), since the other factors tend not to be discontinuous. Image discontinuities are generally consistent geometrically (i.e., in shape) even when not consistent photometrically.

5. In a television scanning generator using a pair of free-running relaxation oscillators, free-running frequencies of the oscillators are set slightly below the horizontal and vertical pulse rates, and the stripped pulses are used to trigger the oscillators prematurely and thus to synchronize them to the line and half-frame rates.

6. The need for individual treatment of images makes strong demands on the methodology, but the fact that different features are important in different applications also opens new possibilities regarding data reduction.

II. Choose the phrase that is closest in meaning to the underlined part.

1. In fact, in most cases $a(x, y)$, which we might consider <u>to be the physical signal that impinges on the face of a 2D sensor</u>, is actually a function of many variables including depth, color, and time.

    A. to be a physical distribution resulting from the face of a 2D sensor

    B. to be the physically generated signal that is impinged by a 2D sensor

    C. to be a signal obtained on the face of a 2D sensor illuminated by certain physical energy

    D. to be physically impinged by the signal on the face of a 2D sensor

2. Image processing algorithms will be <u>formulated as mathematical operators working on pixel values or pixel matrices</u>, but the results of these algorithms will also be displayed using images.

    A. expressed as mathematical manipulations operating on pixels or arrays of pixels

    B. represented by mathematical relations between pixel gray levels and matrices

    C. manifested mathematically as operations of pixel gray values and matrices

    D. obtained in a mathematical form as operators of pixels and matrices

3. For the first time ever the landscape is changing <u>as high volume personal computer</u>

multimedia applications proliferate.

A. since applications of personal computer multimedia becomes widespread

B. as the numbers of personal computers and multimedia applications greatly increase

C. as the volume of PC multimedia applications has progressed

D. with the profile of large scale PC multimedia applications

4. Consequently, electronic equipment is constantly subjected to unwanted sources of energy and is constantly producing energy that adjacent equipment is not designed to accept.

A. continually making unaccepted interference to adjacent equipment

B. continuously causing neighboring equipment not to accept expected energy

C. constantly producing energy that is acceptable only to neighboring equipment

D. ceaselessly generating energy that is considered acceptable in the design of adjacent equipment

5. Programs exist that can, given enough time and money, take a description of a problem in logical notation and find the solution to the problem, if one exists.

A. make a logical problem to be described and seek its solution

B. describe a problem using logical expressions and obtain its solution

C. obtain the solution of a logical problem with description of it

D. take a descriptive expression of a problem that is found to be solvable

6. Some of the capture devices, keyboards in particular, also fall into this category.

A. like special keyboards

B. with particular keyboards

C. specifically keyboards

D. specific keyboards

7. The need for individual treatment of images makes strong demands on the methodology, but the fact that different features are important in different applications also opens new possibilities regarding data reduction.

A. displays additional opportunities regarded as data fusion

B. makes public possible new approaches of data mining

C. makes possible data reduction techniques available

D. provides new prospects in the area of data compression

8. The smallness of the optical wavelength allows for the miniaturization of transmit and receive modules, which should allow considerable reduction in size, weight, and cost of optical communication systems with respect to microwave/radio wave counterparts.

A. enables manufacturing of multi-purpose transmitter and receiver within single modules

B. permits minimization of transmit and receive subsystems

C. makes possible to construct small-sized transmit and receive units

D. allows transmitters and receivers to be mixed into single modules

Unit 11

Biometrics Technology

Biometrics is the study of methods for uniquely recognizing humans based upon one or more intrinsic physical or behavioral traits. Examples are fingerprints, hand geometry, retina and iris patterns, facial geometry, and signature and voice recognition. Biometric identification may be preferred over traditional methods such as passwords, smart cards because its information is virtually impossible to steal.

Text

Part I: Fingerprint Identification

Among all the biometric techniques, fingerprint-based identification is the oldest. Everyone is known to have unique, immutable fingerprints. A fingerprint is made of a series of ridges and furrows on the surface of the finger. The uniqueness of a fingerprint can be determined by the pattern of ridges and furrows as well as the minutiae points. Minutiae points are local ridge characteristics that occur at either a ridge bifurcation or a ridge ending.

Fingerprint matching techniques can be placed into two categories: minutiae-based and correlation based. Minutiae-based techniques first find minutiae points and then map their relative placement on the finger as shown in Figure 11.1. However, there are some difficulties when using this approach. It is difficult to extract the minutiae points accurately when the fingerprint is of low quality. Also this method does not take into account the global pattern of ridges and furrows. The correlation-based method is able to overcome some of the difficulties of the minutiae-based approach. However, it has some of its own shortcomings. Correlation-based techniques require the precise location of a registration point and are affected by image translation and rotation.

Fingerprint matching based on minutiae has problems in matching different sized (unregistered) minutiae patterns. Local ridge structures cannot be completely characterized by minutiae. We can try a different representation of fingerprints that will capture more local information and yield a fixed length code for the fingerprint. The matching will then hopefully become a relatively simple task of calculating the Euclidean distance between the two codes.

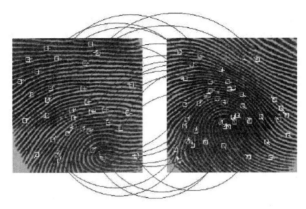

Figure 11.1   Minutiae-based fingerprint matching

It is important to develop algorithms that are more robust to noise in fingerprint images and deliver increased accuracy in real-time.[1] A commercial fingerprint-based authentication system requires a very low false rejection rate (FRR) for a given false acceptance rate (FAR).[2] This is very difficult to achieve with any single technique. We can pool evidence from various matching techniques to increase the overall accuracy of the system. In a real application, the sensor, the acquisition system and the variation in performance of the system over time is critical.[3] To evaluate the system performance, field-test on a limited number of users over a period of time is necessary.

Large volumes of fingerprints are collected and stored everyday in a wide range of applications including forensics, access control, and driver license registration. An automatic recognition of people based on fingerprints requires that the input fingerprint be matched with a large number of fingerprints in a database. To reduce the search time and computational complexity, it is desirable to classify these fingerprints in an accurate and consistent manner so that the input fingerprint is required to be matched only with a subset of the fingerprints in the database.[4]

Fingerprint classification is a technique to assign a fingerprint into one of the several pre-specified types already established in the literature providing an indexing mechanism. Some fingerprints belonging to different classes are shown in Figure 11.2. These are whorl, right loop, left loop, arch, and tented arch. Fingerprint classification can be viewed as a coarse level matching of the fingerprints. An input fingerprint is first matched at a coarse level to one of the pre-specified types and then, at a finer level, it is compared to the subset of the database containing that type of fingerprints only.

Figure 11.2　Fingerprints of different classes

A critical step in automatic fingerprint matching is to automatically and reliably extract minutiae from the input fingerprint images. However, the performance of a minutiae extraction algorithm relies heavily on the quality of the input fingerprint images. In order to ensure that the performance of an automatic fingerprint identification/verification system will be robust with respect to the quality of the fingerprint images, it is essential to incorporate a fingerprint enhancement algorithm in the minutiae extraction module.[5] A fast fingerprint enhancement algorithm can adaptively improve the clarity of ridge and furrow structures of input fingerprint images based on the estimated local ridge orientation and frequency, as illustrated in Figure 11.3.[6] Experiments show that incorporating enhancement algorithms can significantly improve the verification accuracy.

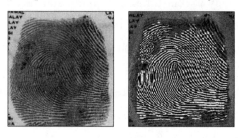

Figure 11.3　Fingerprint enhancement

Part Ⅱ: Introduction to Speaker Identification

Introduction

Modern-day security systems are wide-ranging and usually have multiple layers to get through before they can be properly cracked. Aside from the standard locks and alarm systems, there are very complex methods to protect important material. Many of these are methods that can allow or disallow a specific individual to access the material — a computer system has to be able to successfully detect a fingerprint, read an individual's eye patterns, or determine the true identity of a speaker. This last point is the focus of our topic — speaker identification, which is often confused with other similar terms. The exact definitions of some of these terms are explained below.

- Speaker recognition: Determining who is speaking.
- Speaker identification: The speaker is initially unknown, and must be determined after being compared to templates. There can often be a large number of templates

involved.

- Speaker verification: Determining if the speaker is who he or she claims to be. The speaker's voice is compared to only one template — the person who he or she is claiming to be.[1]

- Speech recognition: Recognizing the actual words being said, in other words, recognizing what is being said rather than who is speaking. Often confused with voice recognition, which recognizes an individual speaker.

Key problems

The issues with speech recognition in general are complex and wide-ranging. One of the main problems lies in the complexity of the speech signal. In such signals as shown in Figure 11.4, it is difficult to interpret the large amounts of information presented to a system.

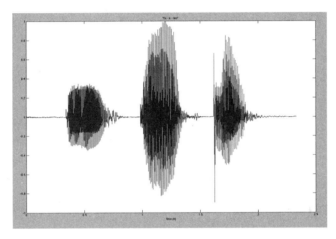

Figure 11.4   The word "Di-a-blo" with DC offset removed

An evident problem is the jaggedness of the signal. A natural speech signal fluctuates throughout. Another naturally occurring property of speech patterns is the fluctuation in the volume, or amplitude, of the signal. Different people emphasize different syllables, letters, or words in different ways. If two signals have different volume levels, they are difficult to compare. Speech signals also have a large number of peaks in a short period of time, corresponding to the syllables in the words being spoken. Comparing two signals becomes much more difficult as the number of peaks increases, as it is easy for results to be skewed by a higher peak, and, consequently, for those results to be interpreted incorrectly.[2] The speed at which the input single is given is also an important issue. A user saying their name at a speed different from the speed at which they normally speak can change results, as two versions of the same pattern are compared.[3] The problem is, the time over which they are spoken is different, and must be accounted for.[4] Finally, when examining the signal in terms of speech verification, an individual may attempt to mimic the speech of another person. If the speaker has a good imitation, it would be possible for the speaker to be accepted by the system.

To deal with the jaggedness of the signal and the noise introduced to the signal through the environment, you have to pass all signals through a smoothing filter. The filter will accomplish two tasks: getting rid of any excess noise and getting rid of the high frequency jaggedness and leaves behind simply the magnitude of the signal.[5] As a result, you get a clean signal that is fairly easy to process.

To account for the different volumes of speakers, the signals must be normalized to the same volume before they are examined. Each signal is normalized about zero such that all signals have the same relative maximum and minimum values.

To examine each of the individual peaks, an envelope function is used after the signal is smoothed to detect peaks in the signal. If a signal passes a certain threshold, it will be examined and compared with the corresponding signal in the database. This will not be an analysis of the entire signal, but rather a formant analysis. The individual formant, or vowel sounds, in the signal will be examined and used to verify the speaker.

To handle varying speeds of inputs, both the formant analysis and the envelope functions will be used. The envelope of the peak will determine which vowels are available, and the actual formants themselves will be relatively unchanged.

To account for imitating speech patterns, once again, the formants of the individual signals are analyzed to actually determine if a speaker is who he claims to be. In most cases, the imitating formants do not match up closely with those stored in the database, and the imitator will be denied.

Envelope detection

Once the system actually reads in the values from a voice signal, the most important thing is to figure out how the signal is broken up. An obvious method is to break a word or series of words into syllables. Although syllables are somewhat difficult to read, as they still have consonants, the vowel sounds make up the majority of the syllables, not to mention the louder part of these signals.[6] As a result, breaking the words into syllables is a good start.

After we pass the signal through a smoothing filter, there is a clear definition of the peaks. However, the question still remains — how do you pick up one of these peaks? In essence, the goal is to choose a correct threshold to start reading signals. The most important thing is managing to differentiate the numerous peaks while at the same time being able to keep the peaks for each and every signal. For example, with a threshold that is too low, noise may get picked up. More likely, however, is that with a threshold too high, some syllables may be ignored.[7]

This ends up a fairly nice solution to our problem — the threshold cuts off the signal at sample values, not time values. We need time values to analyze the actual frequencies of the results so we can look at the formant sounds within each syllable. Thus, we go back to our initial timed signal rather than the sampled signal, and we get our desired results as shown in Figure 11.5 in which the start and end points of each envelope correspond to the start and end points of the syllables.[8]

Thus, most of the signal is preserved, and all vowel sounds are preserved as well — most of what is cut off by the signal is a consonant.[9] Now, we have multiple signals, each of which is almost entirely vowel sounds from our syllables. However, we have to go back to our initial problem — how do you analyze the vowel? How do you even interpret a signal like this?

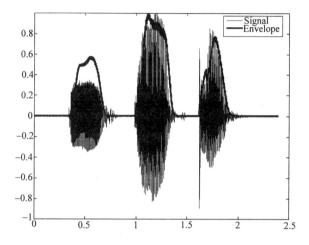

Figure 11.5　Speech signal with an envelope

Formant analysis

Interpreting this signal first begins with determining an actual equation for the signal. The best way to do that is by using an autoregressive model. An autoregressive model is simply a model used to find an estimation of a signal based on previous input values. The actual equation for the model is as follows:

$$X_t = c + \sum_{i=1}^{p} \varphi_i X_{t-i} + \varepsilon_t$$

The model consists of three parts: a constant part, an error or noise part, and the autoregressive summation. The summation represents the fact that the current value of the input depends only on previous values of the input. The variable p is the order of the model. The higher the order, the more accurate a representation it will be. As the system order approaches infinity, we get almost an exact representation of the system.

This system looks almost exactly like a differential equation. In fact, this equation can be used to find the transfer function for the signal.

Finding the formants

Once you have the transfer function, you merely need to get your enveloped syllables and pass them through this transfer function.[10] Once you take the frequency response of the transfer function, you can get a very nice plot as its output. This gives us something we can actually interpret. Specifically, you can clearly see the formants of the vowel — that is, you can see the peak values of the frequency response. These peaks are what differentiate vowel sounds from one another. For instance, looking at these vowel sounds from the same person, there is a clear discrepancy in their appearances (see Figure 11.6).

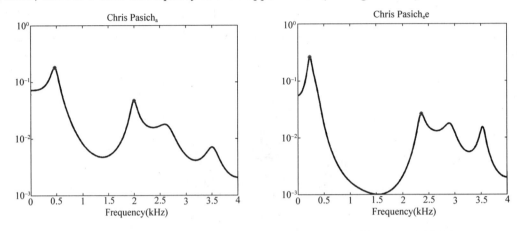

Figure 11.6   Sample formants of different vowels "a" (left) and "ee" (right)

Examining the first two formants, there are clear differences between where they occur and their magnitude in each vowel sound.[11] These peak values will also be different from person to person, even for the same vowel. For instance, compare the sound "a" (as in cat) for different speakers (see Figure 11.7). Even though the structure of the frequency responses are similar, the vowel sounds each have slightly different formants, both in the frequency at which they occur and the height that they attain.[12] So finally, we have some way to analyze our signal. All that remains is the final step — comparing these formants to the formants of the whole group.

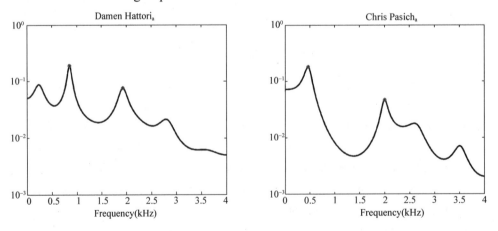

Figure 11.7   Speaker vowel comparisons: "a" sound of two speakers

The final step: identifying the speaker

After everything is broken down, all that is left for the system to do is the easy part —

make a simple comparison between the input formants and the formant in the database. The first step is in determining which vowel is actually being spoken. This is simply an examination of the location of the first two formant peaks. If they both fall within the range of a specific vowel's first two formants, they represent that vowel. That range is stored within the database. These ranges are very well defined for each individual vowel and are adjusted to the members of the group. For example, the first formant of a vowel has a range that will include formants at frequencies just above the highest frequency first formant in the group and just below the lowest frequency first formant.[13] If it does not fall in the range of the vowel, that vowel is not the correct one, and it continues to try the next vowel. It repeats this process until either it finds a vowel or goes through all vowel sounds in the database. If the formants do not fall within any particular formant range, the vowel sound will be ignored.

The second step is the actual comparison. The frequency response of the input vowel sound is multiplied in a dot product with each member's previously stored frequency response for the vowel. This is the vowel that was determined in the first step. A resulting score matrix is produced from the dot product. The score matrix will output a value from 0 to 1, with 1 being a perfect match and a 0 being an entirely incorrect match.[14]

This process is repeated for each vowel sound in the word. The score matrices are then added together, and the system identifies the speaker as the individual with the highest score. If, however, that individual does not pass a threshold value, then the system determines there is no match.

New Words

Part I

biometrics	生物统计学	immutable	不可变更的
ridge	脊	furrow	沟，皱纹，辙
minutia	细节（minutiae）	bifurcation	分叉
correlation	相关	registration	对准
translation	平移	Euclidean distance	欧几里德距离
robust	稳健的，鲁棒的	authentication	认证，确认
pool	共享，汇聚	field-test	现场测试，实地测试
forensic	法医的，司法取证	subset	子集
the literature	文献（总称）	indexing mechanism	索引机制
whorl	涡	identification	识别
verification	确认	module	模块
adaptive	自适应的	orientation	方向

Part Ⅱ

wide-ranging	范围广的	crack	使爆裂
speaker recognition	说话人识别	speech recognition	语音识别
speaker identification	说话人辨识	speaker verification	说话人确认
template	模板，样板	offset	偏移量
jaggedness	起伏不平，不规则	fluctuate	起伏
volume	音量	amplitude	幅度
syllable	音节	skew	歪斜
version	版本	pattern	模式
mimic	模仿	imitation	模仿，仿效
imitator	仿冒者	magnitude	大小，数量
normalize	归一化，标准化	envelope function	包络函数
threshold	阈值，门限	formant	语音的共振峰
vowel	元音	consonant	辅音
autoregressive model	自回归模型	variable	变量
infinity	无穷大	differential equation	微分方程
transfer function	传递函数	differentiate	区分
discrepancy	差异	attain	达到
multiply	相乘	dot product	点积，标量积
score	得分	matrix	矩阵

Notes on the Text

Part I

1. It is important to develop algorithms that are more robust to noise in fingerprint images and deliver increased accuracy in real-time.
研发对于指纹图像中噪声更稳健并能实时提供更高精度的算法是重要的。

   * 注意 in real-time 的用法。

2. A commercial fingerprint-based authentication system requires a very low false rejection rate (FRR) for a given false acceptance rate (FAR).
商用指纹（身份）认证系统对给定的错误接受率要求具有很低的错误拒绝率。

   * false rejection rate (FRR)：错误拒绝率，错误地将身份合格者当作不合格者的概率。

   * false acceptance rate (FAR)：错误接受率，错误地将身份不合格者当作合格者的概率。

3. In a real application, the sensor, the acquisition system and the variation in performance of the system over time is critical.
在实际应用中，传感器、采集系统、性能随时间的变化是关键因素。

4. To reduce the search time and computational complexity, it is desirable to classify these fingerprints in an accurate and consistent manner so that the input fingerprint is required to be matched only with a subset of the fingerprints in the database.

为了缩短搜索时间、降低计算复杂度，要以准确而一致的方式将这些指纹分类，从而使输入的指纹只需与数据库某一子集中的指纹进行比对。

- in ... manner: 以……方式。

5. In order to ensure that the performance of an automatic fingerprint identification/verification system will be robust with respect to the quality of the fingerprint images, it is essential to incorporate a fingerprint enhancement algorithm in the minutiae extraction module.

为确保自动指纹识别或确认系统的性能对于不同指纹图像质量具有稳健性，必须在细节提取模块中加入指纹增强算法。

6. A fast fingerprint enhancement algorithm can adaptively improve the clarity of ridge and furrow structures of input fingerprint images based on the estimated local ridge orientation and frequency, as illustrated in Figure 11.3.

快速指纹增强算法能根据对局部指纹脊方向和频率（密度）的估计自适应地改善输入指纹图像中脊和沟结构的清晰度，如图 11.3 所示。

Part Ⅱ

1. Determining if the speaker is who he or she claims to be. The speaker's voice is compared to only one template — the person who he or she is claiming to be.

确定说话者是否就是他（她）自称的那个人。仅将说话者的话音与一个样板进行比对，即他（她）自称的那一个。

2. Comparing two signals becomes much more difficult as the number of peaks increases, as it is easy for results to be skewed by a higher peak, and, consequently, for those results to be interpreted incorrectly.

尖峰的增加使两个信号的比较变得更为困难，因为结果容易偏向于高的峰值，导致对那些结果的解释发生错误。

- as 说明原因。

3. A user saying their name at a speed different from the speed at which they normally speak can change results, as two versions of the same pattern are compared.

使用者说自己的名字时语速不同于他们平常的讲话速度，这可以改变识别结果，因为这时是将同一模式的两个不同版本进行比较。

- 主语很长：A user saying their name at a speed different from the speed at which they normally speak，是带定语从句的-ing 短语。

4. The problem is, the time over which they are spoken is different, and must be accounted for.

问题在于他们讲话经历的时间长短不同，这必须考虑在内。

- 后半句省略：The time over which they are spoken must be accounted for.

- account for：说明理由（provide an explanation or justification for），构成主要因素（constitute the governing or primary factor in）。这里取后一种解释。

5. The filter will accomplish two tasks: getting rid of any excess noise and getting rid of the high frequency jaggedness and leaves behind simply the magnitude of the signal.

   滤波器要完成两项任务：消除过度的噪声和消除高频起伏，仅仅保留信号的大小。

   - 主语 filter 有两个宾语：The filter will accomplish … and leaves …

6. Although syllables are somewhat difficult to read, as they still have consonants, the vowel sounds make up the majority of the syllables, not to mention the louder part of these signals.

   尽管因为音节中仍含有辅音而有些难以解读，但元音（总是）构成音节的主要部分，更不要说信号中较响亮的部分了。

7. More likely, however, is that with a threshold too high, some syllables may be ignored.

   不过更有可能的是在阈值取得太高的情况下某些音节可能被忽略掉。

   - More likely is that … 省略了 "What is"：What's more likely is that …

8. Thus, we go back to our initial timed signal rather than the sampled signal, and we get our desired results as shown in Figure 11.5 in which the start and end points of each envelope correspond to the start and end points of the syllables.

   于是回到最初的时间（时域）信号而不是采样信号，我们得到如图 11.5 所示的所需结果，其中每个包络的起点和终点对应音节的起点和终点。

9. Thus, most of the signal is preserved, and all vowel sounds are preserved as well — most of what is cut off by the signal is a consonant.

   这样一来，信号的大部分被保留，所有的元音也被保留，信号中去掉的大部分都是辅音。

10. Once you have the transfer function, you merely need to get your enveloped syllables and pass them through this transfer function.

    一旦有了传递函数，就只需要取出包络所包含的音节，使它们通过这一传递函数（所代表的滤波器）。

11. Examining the first two formants, there are clear differences between where they occur and their magnitude in each vowel sound.

    观察前两个共振峰，对每个元音它们的频率和大小有明显的差异。

    - … where they occur：它们出现的位置，频率轴上的位置就是频率。

12. Even though the structure of the frequency responses are similar, the vowel sounds each have slightly different formants, both in the frequency at which they occur and the height that they attain.

    即使频率响应的结构相似，（不同讲话人所发的）元音各自具有稍微不同的共振峰，在出现的频率和达到的高度方面有所不同。

13. For example, the first formant of a vowel has a range that will include formants at

frequencies just above the highest frequency first formant in the group and just below the lowest frequency first formant.

例如元音的第一个共振峰落在某一范围内，此范围包括组内恰好高于最高频率的第一共振峰和恰好低于最低频率的第一共振峰。

14. The score matrix will output a value from 0 to 1, with 1 being a perfect match and a 0 being an entirely incorrect match.

得分矩阵将输出一个介于 0 和 1 之间的值，1 表示完全匹配，0 表示完全不匹配。

Technical Tips

Biometrics

Biometrics is the study of methods for uniquely recognizing humans based on intrinsic physical or behavioral traits. The rapid advancements in networking, communication and mobility increased the need of reliable ways to verify the identity of any person. Identity verification is mainly performed in two ways:

- **Possession-based:** the whole security is based on a "token" the user has (such as a credit card or a document). If it is lost, somebody else might use it to falsify his identity.
- **Knowledge-based:** using a password. A short password is simple to guess, while a complicated one is difficult to remember. If one keeps the password written somewhere, it can be lost or stolen.

The weaknesses of standard validation systems can be avoided if our own body becomes the key. Particular characteristics of the body or habits are much more complicated to forge than a string. Using biometrics adds complexity to identification systems that would be hard to reach with a password-based approach. The main advantages of biometrics over a standard system are:

- Biometric traits cannot be lost or forgotten.
- Biometric traits are difficult to copy, share and distribute.
- They require the person being authenticated to be present at the time and point of authentication.

Biometric characteristics can be divided in two main classes:

- **Physiological** are related to the shape of the body. The oldest traits are fingerprints. Other examples are face recognition, hand geometry and iris recognition.
- **Behavioral** are related to the behavior of a person. The first characteristic to be used is the signature. More modern approaches are the study of keystroke dynamics and of voice.

Strictly speaking, voice is also a physiological trait, but voice recognition is mainly based on the study of the way a person speaks, which is why it is commonly classified as behavioral.

A biometric system can provide the following three functions:

- **Verification:** Is he the person he claims to be? We want to extract new biometric info from the person and check if those are matching with the ones we have. It's 1:1 match verification.
- **Identification:** Who is he? We extract biometric info from a person and compare them with our database. It is more difficult than verification because we have to compare the info with all the other database entries. It is 1:N match verification.
- **Screening:** Does he belong to the watch-list? We want to check if the person belongs to a group. It works like identification, but the number of people in the database is much smaller. It's 1:n match verification, where $n \ll N$ of the previous case.

Supplementary Readings: Biometrics Overview

One of the biggest challenges facing society today is confirming the true identity of a person. There are several identification verification schemes that exist today but the most accurate identification schemes are in the area of biometrics. Take the simple example of an ATM card. When a person wishes to use their ATM card, they are required to enter in a personal identification number (PIN) in order to begin their transaction. This type of identification verification is given by what that person has (their card) and what that person knows (their PIN). There may be a potential problem to the ATM scheme given above. The card could be stolen for instance. It would be difficult for the thief to be able to use this ATM card unless he/she knew the PIN. The PIN is vulnerable to theft especially if someone is looking over your shoulder while you are entering your PIN. This example shows that it is practical to use two types of identity verification methods. Biometrics, alone or used with another type of identification verification method, could be an ideal identification verification system.

Some examples of identifying biometric characteristics are fingerprints, hand geometry, retina and iris patterns, facial geometry, and signature and voice recognition. Biometric identification may be preferred over traditional methods such as passwords, smart cards because its information is virtually impossible to steal. Although in some cases it may become possible to impersonate a biometric, e.g., replicating legitimate user's fingerprints to fool the fingerprint scanner.

Two interesting properties of biometric identification are:

- The person to be identified is required to physically be present at the point of identification, and
- Identification based on biometric techniques does not depend on the user to remember a password or carry a token.

There are two distinct functions for biometric devices:

- To prove you are who you say you are, and
- To prove you are not who you say you are not.

The purpose of the first function is to prevent the use of a single identity by multiple people. In this case it is important that the biometric device be able to differentiate between a live biometric presented to the scanner, (i.e. a real finger) or a spoofed biometric trying to fool the scanner (i.e. a photograph of a legitimate user used to fool a facial scanner). The second function is used to prevent the use of multiple identities by a single person. It would have to be ensured that the biometric system either automatically crosschecks the enrolled characteristics for duplicates, or otherwise does not allow a person to register their biometric (i.e. fingerprint) under two different names.

For positive identification, there are also multiple supplemental technologies such as passwords, tokens, and cryptographic keys. An enticing feature of biometric identification is that it could take the place of millions of passwords (e.g. long, hard to remember passwords used to gain access to sensitive information stored on a computer in a large corporation). To improve security, biometrics could be used in addition to these alternative technologies and would provide us with the information needed to achieve continuous authentication.

Biometrics has been around for many years. The French anthropologist, Alphonse Bertillon, devised the first widely accepted scientific method of biometric identification in 1870. His system was not based on fingerprinting but rather relied on a systematic combination of physical measurements. These measurements included measurements of the skull width, foot length, and the length of the left middle finger combined with hair color, eye color, as well as face and profile pictures. By grouping the data, any single person could be placed into one of 243 distinct categories. For the next thirty years, this was the primary method of biometric identification. Another example of biometrics in practice was a form of finger printing being used in China in the 14th century, as reported by explorer Joao de Barros. He wrote that the Chinese merchants were stamping children's palm prints and footprints on paper with ink to distinguish the young children from one another.

Fingerprints are unique to each individual and each individual has their own pattern in their fingerprints. This type of identification has been successfully used by the police to capture criminals and to find missing children. A fingerprint records the patterns found on a fingertip. There are a variety of approaches to fingerprint verification. The traditional method used by police matches minutiae (details of the fingerprint). Some other approaches are pattern matching, and moiré fringe* patterns. There are some verification approaches that can detect if a live finger is presented, but not all of these approaches can provide this type of information. If fingerprint-scanning techniques were to be incorporated into the

---

* Moiré fringe is a method used to determine 3D profile information of an object or scene, using interference of light stripes and ultrasonics.

flight deck to provide continuous authentication, liveness detection or testing would be a requirement for the system.

Fingerprints serve to reveal an individual's true identity and the practice of using fingerprints as a means of identification has been a helpful aid to those who chose to use this type of identification. Fingerprints are unique in the sense that there has not been any type of pattern duplication by two different people. Not even a single instance has been identified or discovered at this time. This uniqueness also applies to identical twins. One good thing about fingerprints is that any type of burn (superficial), abrasions, or cuts do not affect the ridge structure, thus the fingerprint pattern is unaffected.

Hand geometry involves analyzing and measuring the shape of the hand. This type of biometric offers a good balance of performance characteristics and is relatively easy to use. The ease of integration into other systems and processes, coupled with ease of use, makes hand geometry an obvious first step for many biometric projects. Unlike fingerprints, the human hand is not unique. One drawback for this type of identification is that individual hand features are not descriptive enough for identification. Hand geometry is the granddaddy of the modern biometrics by virtue of a 20-year history of live applications. There have been six different hand-scanning products developed over this span, including some of the most commercially successful biometrics to date. Hand geometry biometric is by far less accurate than other biometric methods.

A retina-based biometric involves analyzing the layer of blood vessels situated at the back of the eye. This technique uses a low-intensity light source through an optical coupler to scan the unique patterns of the retina. Retinal scanning can be quite accurate but does require the user to look into a receptacle and focus on a given point. This technique may pose a problem if the subject wears glasses or if the subject is concerned with having close contact with the retinal reading device. It is also unknown what types of results are presented in a situation when the user has an eye disease such as cataracts.

Retina scan is actually one of the oldest biometrics as 1930's research suggested that the patterns of blood vessels on the back of the human eye were unique to each individual. However, technology has taken more time than the theory to be usable.

An iris-based biometric involves analyzing features found in the colored ring of tissue that surrounds the pupil. This biometric has the potential for higher than average template-matching performance. Ease of use and system integration has not traditionally been strong points with iris scanning devices but as new products emerge, improvements should be expected. The idea of using iris patterns for personal identification was originally proposed in 1936 by Frank Burch. By the 1980's the idea had appeared in James Bond films, but it still remained science fiction and conjecture. In 1987 Aran Safir and Leonard Flom patented this idea, and in 1989 they asked John Daugman (then teaching at Harvard University) to try to create actual algorithms for iris recognition. These algorithms, which Daugman patented in 1994 and are owned by Iridian Technologies, are the basis for all current iris recognition systems and products.

Facial recognition analyzes facial characteristics such as overall facial structure, which includes the distance between the eyes, nose, mouth, and jaw edges. This works in conjunction with a digital video camera that captures the image of the face. This biometric has been widely, and perhaps wildly, touted as a fantastic system for recognizing potential threats, whether terrorist, scam artist, or known criminal, but so far has been unproven in high-level usage. It is currently used in verification only systems with a good deal of success. The development stage for facial recognition began in the late 1980s and commercially available systems were made available in the 1990s. While many people first heard about facial recognition after September 11th, 2001, football fans were introduced to it at the Super Bowl several months earlier.

Biometric signature verification goes beyond visual signature comparison in its analysis of the way a user signs his/her name. Signing features such as speed, velocity, and pressure are as important as the finished signature static shape. Signature verification devices are reasonably accurate in operation and obviously lend themselves to applications where a signature is an accepted identifier. Every person has a unique signature but that signature is still vulnerable to duplication. If one person tries to "forge" a signature, they will study the victim's signature and practice that style of writing. However, since speed, velocity, and pressure play a role in signature verification, an attacker would need to know these characteristics prior to attempting to forge a biometric signature.

In the past, simply looking at two or more samples of a person's signature to see if they matched was signature verification. By performing digital signature verification, matching is done by comparing the movement of how one signs his/her name as mentioned above.

Voice authentication allows the user to use his/her voice as an input device to the system. Voice commands to computers began with applications that were trained by the user to recognize certain words that were spoken such that the user could, for example, speak to a word processor instead of actually typing the words out. Poor quality and ambient noise can affect verification. Certain voice-scan technologies are resistant to impostor attacks to a lesser degree than finger scan systems.

When deciding on a biometric device for use in a practical application, we want to include the best level of security possible, within the physical and operational limits inherent to the environment and we want to be very confident that the device will give us the intended level of security as well as accuracy and near real time results. Current metrics for comparing biometric technologies, such as the crossover error rate[*] and the average enrollment time[†], are limited because they lack a standard test bed on which to base their

---

[*]　Generally stated as a percentage, at which the false rejection rate and the false acceptance rate are equal.

[†]　Defined as the time in which a biometric feature is saved as a personal reference either de-centrally on a chip card or PC, or centrally in a database.

values. Several groups, including the US Department of Defense's Biometrics Management Office, are developing standard testing methodologies.

Along with the positive aspects of biometrics, each method also has its own drawbacks. There are various situations that must be taken into consideration when deciding on a feasible method for a particular use. It is surprising to see that some of these biometric methods have been used for some time now and the immense growth of technology has made it possible to improve upon these methods.

Most of us are familiar with or have used many of the types of identification methods mentioned above. These are examples of the simplest types of identification methods that we use everyday such as driver's license and employee identity cards. Biometrics is not a new concept, we all have been subject to it in some way or another and some of us actually prefer to provide identification via biometrics. Others may have security concerns when it comes to storing their biological trait information in a central database somewhere or even allowing that information to be contained in a little chip on an ID or credit card. Designers of biometric systems must keep in mind that personal biological trait information is sensitive and must be safeguarded with the appropriate security mechanisms.

Continuous authentication takes biometrics one step further. Of all biometric technologies in current use, none of them mention the term "continuous authentication," the authentication process is a one-time event, i.e., placing your palm on a palm reader so that you are allowed to enter a certain area of a building. One major break-through in the world of biometric technology would be to offer a mechanism that would provide continuous authentication for a given amount of time needed.

Exercises

I. Translate the following sentences into Chinese.

1. Although some native speakers have problems in pronouncing some sounds they are perceived as native speakers based on their prosody and vocabulary.

2. A more adaptable technique is edge finding, which detects the regions of high rate of change of tone in an image, on the basis that these are likely to indicate edges of objects or ROI.

3. Many of these early systems had advantages that seemed exciting and intuitive when demonstrated with "toy" programs, but ran into difficult problems when attempts were made to extend them to more realistically-sized programs.

4. Referring to the figure, we see that signal processing techniques are needed for preprocessing, pattern recognition techniques are needed for segmentation, feature extraction, and classification, and artificial intelligence techniques are needed for structure analysis, knowledge-acquisition and representation (world model), and control structure (interaction among the blocks).

5. The picture elements across a line are converted to the video signal and low-pass filtered with an electrical filter. This smoothing removes the discrete structure in the horizontal dimension.

6. These products use commercially available speech toolkits, such as the IBM's ViaVoice, Dragon's Naturally Speaking, or L&H's VoiceXpress, which were created for building voice-enabled applications for native speakers rather than for teaching foreigners.

7. The three major forms of electronic documents mentioned above have a significant impact on the ways in which users select to manage the documents' life cycle comprising creation or reception from an outside entity, processing, storage, retrieval and publishing.

8. Unfortunately in most applications scene shading is such that objects cannot be separated from background by any threshold, and even when an appropriate threshold value exists in principle it is notoriously difficult to find it automatically.

Ⅱ. **Choose the phrase that is closest in meaning to the underlined part.**

1. To reduce the search time and computational complexity, it is desirable to classify these fingerprints in an accurate and consistent manner so that the input fingerprint is required <u>to be matched only with a subset of the fingerprints in the database</u>.

   A. to be identical to those fingerprints in a subset of the fingerprint database

   B. to be compared with a certain portion of the fingerprint

   C. to find a match only within a part of the fingerprint collection

   D. to be checked for identity in part against the fingerprint collection

2. Comparing two signals becomes much more difficult as the number of peaks increases, <u>as it is easy for results to be skewed by a higher peak</u>, and, consequently, for those results to be interpreted incorrectly.

   A. since a higher peak tends to cause a biased result

   B. with a higher peak present, the results may be blurred

   C. while distortion is likely to remove the peak on the higher end

   D. like the skewed results toward the higher part of the peak

3. Even though the structure of the frequency responses are similar, the vowel sounds each have slightly different formants, both <u>in the frequency at which they occur and the height that they attain</u>.

   A. in the occurrence the reached height of the frequency

   B. in the frequency of the formants and in the height of the formants

   C. in the occurred frequency and the attained height of it

   D. at the frequency that the formants reach their height

4. As speech exists originally in the space, <u>it is multidimensional in nature</u>. In other words, a speech signal is a function of four variables — three space variables and time.

    A. it is multidimensional in the nature

    B. it is mainly multidimensional

    C. its characteristic is multidimensional

    D. it is naturally multidimensional

5. Rather than classify hardware on the basis of application characteristics one can rely on <u>the intrinsic functionality</u> of the hardware.

    A. the intelligent properties

    B. the inherent capabilities

    C. the interesting attributes

    D. propagation property

6. The interdisciplinary field of cognitive science <u>brings together computer models from artificial intelligence and experimental techniques from psychology</u>, and tries to construct precise and testable theories of the human mind.

    A. combines computer models with AI, and experimental techniques with psychology

    B. models artificial intelligence with computers and performs experiments in psychology

    C. establishes computer models for AI with techniques used in psychological experiments

    D. combines computer-based AI models with psychological experimental methods

7. The purpose of this book is twofold: to shed light on <u>the state of the art on this new frontier</u>, and to establish common understanding among researchers.

    A. the artistic state of this new front area

    B. the newest development on this current forefront

    C. the art status of this new advanced field

    D. the sophisticated statement on this new boundary

8. What is fascinating about all this from the perspective of computer architecture is that, on the one hand, the basic building blocks for today's computer miracles are virtually the same as those of the IAS computer from 50 years ago, while on the other hand, the techniques for <u>squeezing the last iota of performance out of the materials at hand</u> have become increasingly sophisticated.

    A. achieving tiny improvement from existing materials

    B. making the final effort with the first hand materials

    C. inserting available materials into the final performance

    D. showing the performance with existing materials

Unit 12　Information Security

Information security is the process of protecting data from unauthorized access, use, disclosure, destruction, modification, or disruption. A secure information system must ensure confidentiality so that only those authorized to see the information have access to it, integrity so that accuracy and completeness of the information is safeguarded, and availability so that authorized users have access to information when they need it.

Text

Part I: Information Security — Introduction and a Brief History

Information security is the process of protecting data from unauthorized access, use, disclosure, destruction, modification, or disruption. The terms information security, computer security and information assurance are frequently used interchangeably. These fields are interrelated and share the common goals of protecting the confidentiality, integrity and availability of information; however, there are some subtle differences between them. These differences lie primarily in the approach to the subject, the methodologies used, and the areas of concentration. Information security is concerned with the confidentiality, integrity and availability of data regardless of the form the data may take: electronic, print, or other forms.

Heads of state and military commanders have long understood the importance and necessity of protecting information about their military capabilities, number of troops and troop movements. Such information falling into the hands of the enemy could be disastrous. Governments, military, financial institutions, hospitals, and private businesses amass a great deal of confidential information about their employees, customers, products, research, and financial status. Most of this information is now collected, processed and stored on computers and transmitted across networks to other computers. Should confidential information about a businesses customers or finances or new product line fall into the hands of a competitor, such a breach of security could lead to lost business, law suits or even bankruptcy of the business.[1] Protecting confidential information is a business requirement, and in many cases also an ethical and legal requirement. For the individual, information security has a significant effect on privacy, which is viewed very differently in different cultures.

Since the early days of writing, heads of state and military commanders understood that it was necessary to provide some mechanism to protect the confidentiality of written correspondence and to have some means of detecting tampering. Persons desiring secure communications have used wax seals and other sealing devices since the early days of writing to signify the authenticity of documents, prevent tampering, and ensure confidentiality of correspondence.

Julius Caesar is credited with the invention of the Caesar cipher to prevent his secret messages from being read should a message fall into the wrong hands.[2]

World War Ⅱ brought about many progresses in information security and may mark the beginning of information security as a professional field. WWⅡ saw advancements in the physical protection of information with barricades and armed guards controlling access into information centers. It also saw the introduction of formalized classification of data based upon the sensitivity of the information and who could have access to the information.[3] During WWⅡ background checks were also conducted before granting clearance to classified information.[4]

The end of the 20th century and early years of the 21st century saw rapid advancements in telecommunications, computing hardware and software, and data encryption. The availability of smaller, more powerful and less expensive computing equipment made electronic data processing within the reach of small business and the home user.[5] These computers quickly became interconnected through a network generically called the Internet or World Wide Web.

The rapid growth and wide spread use of electronic data processing and electronic business conducted through the Internet, along with numerous occurrences of international terrorism, fueled the need for better methods of protecting these computers and the information they store, process and transmit.[6] The academic disciplines of computer security, information security and information assurance emerged along with numerous professional organizations — all sharing the common goals of insuring the security and reliability of information systems.[7]

Part Ⅱ: Basic Principles of Information Security

For over twenty years information security has held three key concepts form the core principles of information security: confidentiality, integrity and availability. These are known as the CIA Triad.

Confidentiality

It is virtually impossible to get a drivers license, rent an apartment, obtain medical care, or take out a loan without disclosing a great deal of very personal information about ourselves, such as our name, address, telephone number, date of birth, Social Security number, marital status, number of children, mother's maiden name, income, place of employment, medical history, etc. This is all very personal and private information, yet we are often required to provide such information in order to transact business. We generally take it on faith that the person, business, or institution to whom we disclose such personal information have taken measures to ensure that our information will be protected from unauthorized disclosure, either accidental or intentional, and that our information will only be shared with other people, businesses or institutions who are authorized to have access to the information and who have a genuine need to know the information.[1]

Information that is considered to be confidential in nature must only be accessed, used, copied, or disclosed by persons who have been authorized to access, use, copy, or disclose the information, and then only when there is a genuine need to access, use, copy or disclose the information. A breach of confidentiality occurs when information that is considered to be confidential in nature has been, or may have been, accessed, used, copied, or disclosed to, or by, someone who was not authorized to have access to the information.[2]

For example: permitting someone to look over your shoulder at your computer screen while you have confidential data displayed on it would be a breach of confidentiality if they were not authorized to have the information. If a laptop computer, which contains employment and benefit information about 100,000 employees, is stolen from a car (or is sold on eBay) could result in a breach of confidentiality because the information is now in the hands of someone who is not authorized to have it. Giving out confidential information over the telephone is a breach of confidentiality if the caller is not authorized to have the information.

Confidentiality is a requisite for maintaining the privacy of the people whose personal information the organization holds.

Integrity

In information security, integrity means that data cannot be created, changed, or deleted without authorization. It also means that data stored in one part of a database system is in agreement with other related data stored in another part of the database system (or another system).[3] For example: a loss of integrity can occur when a database system is not properly shut down before maintenance is performed or the database server suddenly loses electrical power. A loss of integrity occurs when an employee accidentally, or with malicious intent, deletes important data files. A loss of integrity can occur if a computer virus is released onto the computer. A loss of integrity can occur when an on-line shopper is able to change the price of the product they are purchasing.[4]

Availability

The concept of availability means that the information, the computing systems used to process the information, and the security controls used to protect the information are all available and functioning correctly when the information is needed.[5] The opposite of availability is denial of service (DOS).

Conclusion

Information security is the ongoing process of exercising due care and due diligence to protect information, and information systems, from unauthorized access, use, disclosure, destruction, modification, or disruption.[6] The never ending process of information security involves ongoing training, assessment, protection, monitoring and detection, incident response and repair, documentation, and review.[7]

In 1989, Carnegie Mellon University established the Information Networking Institute, the United State's first research and education center devoted to information networking. The academic disciplines of computer security, information security and information assurance emerged along with numerous professional organizations during the later years of the 20th century and early years of the 21st century.

Entry into the field can be accomplished through self-study, college or university schooling in the field, or through week long focused training camps.[8] Colleges, universities and training companies offer many of their programs on-line. The profession of information security has seen an increased demand for security professionals who are experienced in network security auditing, penetration testing, and digital forensics investigation.[9]

Part Ⅲ: Intrusion Detection System

An intrusion detection system (IDS) generally detects unwanted manipulations to computer systems, mainly through the Internet. The manipulations may take the form of attacks by crackers. The IDS is used to detect many types of malicious network traffic and computer usage that cannot be detected by a conventional firewall. This includes network attacks against vulnerable services, data driven attacks on applications, host based attacks such as privilege escalation, unauthorized logins and access to sensitive files, and malware (viruses, Trojan horses, and worms).[1]

An IDS is composed of several components: sensors which generate security events, a console to monitor events and alerts and control the sensors, and a central engine that records events logged by the sensors in a database and uses a system of rules to generate alerts from security events received. There are several ways to categorize an IDS depending on the type and location of the sensors and the methodology used by the engine to generate alerts. In many simple IDS implementations all three components are combined in a single device or appliance.

Types of intrusion-detection systems

In a network-based intrusion-detection system (NIDS), the sensors are located at choke points in the network to be monitored, often in the demilitarized zone (DMZ) or at network borders. The sensor captures all network traffic and analyzes the content of individual packets for malicious traffic. In systems, protocol-based intrusion detection system (PIDS) and application protocol-based intrusion detection system (APIDS) are used to monitor the transport and protocol's illegal or inappropriate traffic or constricts of language (say SQL).[2] In a host-based system, the sensor usually consists of a software agent, which monitors all activity of the host on which it is installed. Hybrids of these two systems also exist.

- A network intrusion detection system is an independent platform which identifies intrusions by examining network traffic and monitors multiple hosts. Network Intrusion Detection Systems gain access to network traffic by connecting to a hub, network switch configured for port mirroring, or network tap. An example of a NIDS is Snort.

- A protocol-based intrusion detection system consists of a system or agent that would typically sit at the front end of a server, monitoring and analyzing the communication protocol between a connected device (a user PC or system).[3] For a Web server this would typically monitor the HTTPS protocol stream and understand the HTTP protocol relative to the Web server/system it is trying to protect.[4] Where HTTPS is in use then this system would need to reside in the "shim" or interface between where HTTPS is un-encrypted and immediately prior to it entering the Web presentation layer.[5]

- An application protocol-based intrusion detection system consists of a system or agent that would typically sit within a group of servers, monitoring and analyzing the communication on application specific protocols. For example, in a Web server with database this would monitor the SQL protocol specific to the middleware/business-login as it transacts with the database.[6]

- A host-based intrusion detection system consists of an agent on a host which identifies intrusions by analyzing system calls, application logs, file-system modifications and other host activities and state.

- A hybrid intrusion detection system combines two or more approaches. Host agent data is combined with network information to form a comprehensive view of the network. An example of a Hybrid IDS is Prelude.

Passive system vs. reactive system

In a passive system, the intrusion detection system (IDS) sensor detects a potential security breach, logs the information and signals an alert on the console and/or owner. In a reactive system, also known as an intrusion prevention system (IPS), the IDS responds to the suspicious activity by resetting the connection or by reprogramming the firewall to block network traffic from the suspected malicious source.[7] This can happen automatically or at the command of an operator.

Though they both relate to network security, an intrusion detection system (IDS) differs from a firewall in that a firewall looks outwardly for intrusions in order to stop them from happening. Firewalls limit access between networks to prevent intrusion and do not signal an attack from inside the network. An IDS evaluates a suspected intrusion once it has taken place and signals an alarm. An IDS also watches for attacks that originate from within a system.

This is traditionally achieved by examining network communications, identifying heuristics and patterns (often known as signatures) of common computer attacks, and taking action to alert operators.[8] A system which terminates connections is called an intrusion prevention system, and is another form of an application layer firewall.

Physical intrusion detection systems (passive) are distinguished by their ability to pinpoint the absolute location of an intrusion attempt to within a few feet.[9] The system reports the coordinates of the attempted breach, which can be used for activating corresponding PTZ camera presets or for personnel dispatch.[10]

IDS evasion techniques

Intrusion detection system evasion techniques bypass detection by creating different states on the IDS and on the targeted computer.[11] The adversary accomplishes this by manipulating either the attack itself or the network traffic that contains the attack.

New Words

Part I

unauthorized	未被授权的	disclosure	披露
disruption	瓦解，扰乱	interchangeably	可互换地，不区分地
confidentiality	机密性	integrity	完整性
subtle	细微的，微妙的	disastrous	灾难性的
amass	聚集，堆积	competitor	竞争对手
breach	破坏，违反	law suit	司法诉讼
ethical	伦理的，道德的	correspondence	通信，信件
tamper	损害，篡改	signify	表示，象征
authenticity	真实性	Julius Caesar	朱利叶斯·恺撒
credit	归功于，相信	cipher	密码，暗号
professional field	专业领域	barricade	路障
sensitivity	敏感性，灵敏度	clearance	许可，清除
classified information	机密信息	encryption	加密
interconnected	互联的	terrorism	恐怖主义
fuel	燃起，燃料	discipline	学科，纪律
assurance	保障，保险	emerge	出现，浮现

Part II

core	核心	triad	三个一组，三合一
marital	婚姻的	maiden name	婚前的姓，娘家的姓
transact	办理，交易	faith	新任，忠实

genuine	真的	in nature	性质上
laptop computer	膝上电脑，笔记本电脑	benefit	利益，福利
caller	电话接听者	requisite	必需品，必要条件
in agreement with ...	与……一致，不冲突	database	数据库
server	服务器	malicious	恶意的
virus	病毒	denial	否认，拒绝
ongoing	正在进行的	due	应得的
diligence	勤奋	assessment	评估
focused training	强化训练	profession	职业
professional	专业人员	auditing	审计，查账
penetration	穿透，入侵	forensics	司法，法医，取证

Part Ⅲ

intrusion	入侵	manipulation	操作，处理
cracker	破译者，攻击者	network traffic	网络数据流
firewall	防火墙	vulnerable	易受攻击的
host	主机	privilege	特权
escalation	扩大，增大	login	登录
malware	恶意软件	Trojan horse	特洛伊木马
worm	蠕虫	sensor	传感器
console	控制台	alert	使警觉
appliance	用具，器具	choke	窒息，阻气门
demilitarized	解除武装的	packet	（数据）包
protocol	协议	constrict	收缩
hybrid	混合，混合物	hub	中心，网络集线器
platform	平台	agent	代理
reside	驻留	shim	填片
prior to ...	在……之前	presentation layer	表示层
middleware	中间件	transact	处理，交易
prelude	序言	passive	被动的，无源的
reactive	反应的，反动的	block	阻止，阻塞
outward	向外	originate	来源于
heuristic	启发的，启发程序	signature	签字，标识
terminate	终止	pinpoint	准确地定位
coordinate	坐标	PTZ camera	PTZ 摄像机
pan-tilt-zoom	平摇、俯仰、变焦	dispatch	派遣
evasion	逃避	adversary	对手，敌手

Notes on the Text

Part I

1. Should confidential information about a businesses customers or finances or new product line fall into the hands of a competitor, such a breach of security could lead to lost business, law suits or even bankruptcy of the business.

   万一有关商业客户、财务状况或新生产线的机密信息落入竞争者手中，这样的安全事故就可能导致商业损失、商务诉讼，甚至企业破产。

   - should 用于表示假设，通常语气较强，可译作"万一""竟然"。

2. Julius Caesar is credited with the invention of the Caesar cipher to prevent his secret messages from being read should a message fall into the wrong hands.

   据信是朱利叶斯·恺撒发明了恺撒密码，用来防止他的机密消息万一落入敌人手里时被解读。

   - should 同上。

3. It also saw the introduction of formalized classification of data based upon the sensitivity of the information and who could have access to the information.

   它也见证了数据形式化分类的引入，这种分类建立在信息敏感性和谁能接触这些信息的基础上。

4. During WW II background checks were also conducted before granting clearance to classified information.

   第二次世界大战期间还在准许（当事人）接触机密信息以前进行背景审查。

5. The availability of smaller, more powerful and less expensive computing equipment made electronic data processing within the reach of small business and the home user.

   人们容易获得体积较小、功能较强、价格较低的计算装置，使得电子数据处理能够被小公司和家庭用户所用。

6. The rapid growth and wide spread use of electronic data processing and electronic business conducted through the Internet, along with numerous occurrences of international terrorism, fueled the need for better methods of protecting these computers and the information they store, process and transmit.

   电子数据处理和互联网电子商务的迅速增长和扩展，同时伴随大量国际恐怖事件的发生，激起了寻求更好的（保障信息安全）方法的需求，以保护这些计算机及其存储、处理、传输的信息。

7. The academic disciplines of computer security, information security and information assurance emerged along with numerous professional organizations — all sharing the common goals of insuring the security and reliability of information systems.

   出现了计算机安全、信息安全、信息保障这些学科领域以及各种专业机构，都以保证信息系统的安全性和可靠性为共同目标。

Part Ⅱ

1. We generally take it on faith that the person, business, or institution to whom we disclose such personal information have taken measures to ensure that our information will be protected from unauthorized discloser, either accidental or intentional, and that our information will only be shared with other people, businesses or institutions who are authorized to have access to the information and who have a genuine need to know the information.

我们通常信任向他们透露这种个人信息的人员、公司、机构会采取措施确保我们的信息将得到保护，不会无意或有意向未被授权者披露，同时这些信息将仅仅被有权并且真正需要得知该信息的人所分享。

2. A breach of confidentiality occurs when information that is considered to be confidential in nature has been, or may have been, accessed, used, copied, or disclosed to, or by, someone who was not authorized to have access to the information.

当被认为是具有机密性质的信息已被（或者可能已被）未受权接触该信息的人所接触、使用、复制、披露时，即发生了泄密。

3. It also means that data stored in one part of a database system is in agreement with other related data stored in another part of the database system (or another system).

这也意味着存储在数据库系统中某一部分的数据与存放在该系统另一部分（或另一系统）的其他有关数据是一致的。

4. A loss of integrity can occur when an on-line shopper is able to change the price of the product they are purchasing.

当网上购物者能修改他们所购买产品的价格时，信息的完整性就被破坏了。

5. The concept of availability means that the information, the computing systems used to process the information, and the security controls used to protect the information are all available and functioning correctly when the information is needed.

信息可用性是指当需要某一信息时，信息本身、用来处理信息的计算机、保护信息的安全控制都处于有效可用的状态，并且功能正常。

6. Information security is the ongoing process of exercising due care and due diligence to protect information, and information systems, from unauthorized access, use, disclosure, destruction, modification, or disruption.

信息安全是一个以应有的关注和认真态度对信息和信息系统不断进行（保护）的过程，使之不被非授权者接触、使用、披露、破坏、修改、扰乱。

- destruction: the act of destroying or state of being destroyed.
- disruption: the act or result of the act of bringing something into disorder to prevent it from continuing normally: disruptions in routine, disruption of communications.

7. The never ending process of information security involves ongoing training, assessment, protection, monitoring and detection, incident response and repair, documentation, and review.

信息安全这一永无休止的过程包含不断的训练、评估、保护、监视和检测、对事件的响应和修复、形成文档、检查。

8. Entry into the field can be accomplished through self-study, college or university schooling in the field, or through week long focused training camps.

可通过自学、高等院校学习、为期一周的强化训练营进入这一领域。

9. The profession of information security has seen an increased demand for security professionals who are experienced in network security auditing, penetration testing, and digital forensics investigation.

信息安全职业对安全专业人员的需求日增，这些专业人员具有网络安全审核、入侵测试、数字取证调查方面的经验。

Part Ⅲ

1. This includes network attacks against vulnerable services, data driven attacks on applications, host based attacks such as privilege escalation, unauthorized logins and access to sensitive files, and malware (viruses, Trojan horses, and worms).

这包括针对脆弱业务的网络攻击，由数据驱动的对应用程序的攻击，基于主机的攻击，如特权扩大、非授权登录并访问敏感文档、恶意软件（病毒、特洛伊木马、蠕虫）。

2. In systems, protocol-based intrusion detection system (PIDS) and application protocol-based intrusion detection system (APIDS) are used to monitor the transport and protocol's illegal or inappropriate traffic or constricts of language (say SQL).

在系统中使用基于协议的入侵检测（PIDS）和基于应用协议的入侵检测（APIDS）来监测传输和协议的非法或不当数据流，或者语言（如 SQL）的收缩。

  • SQL: structure query language，结构化查询语言。

3. A protocol-based intrusion detection system consists of a system or agent that would typically sit at the front end of a server, monitoring and analyzing the communication protocol between a connected device (a user PC or system).

基于协议的入侵检测系统包含一个系统或代理，典型情况下该系统或代理位于服务器前端，监视并分析连接设备（用户 PC 或系统）之间的通信协议。

4. For a Web server this would typically monitor the HTTPS protocol stream and understand the HTTP protocol relative to the web server/system it is trying to protect.

对于 Web 服务器，典型情况下这就会监测 HTTPS 协议流，并理解相对于它所要保护的 Web 服务器或系统的 HTTP 协议。

5. Where HTTPS is in use then this system would need to reside in the "shim" or interface between where HTTPS is un-encrypted and immediately prior to it

entering the Web presentation layer.

在使用 HTTPS 的地方该系统需要驻留在 HTTPS 未加密和进入 Web 表现层之前之处的"垫片"或接口中。

6. For example, in a web server with database this would monitor the SQL protocol specific to the middleware/business-login as it transacts with the database.

例如，在一个带有数据库的 Web 服务器中，当它访问数据库时，将监测中间件/ 商务登录的特定 SQL 协议。

7. In a reactive system, also known as an intrusion prevention system (IPS), the IDS responds to the suspicious activity by resetting the connection or by reprogramming the firewall to block network traffic from the suspected malicious source.

在一个反向系统（又称为入侵防止系统 IPS）中，IDS 对可疑行为做出反应，将连接复位或重新对防火墙编程以阻止网络数据流受到疑似恶意来源的影响。

- to block network traffic from … source 阻止网络数据流免受……源的影响

8. This is traditionally achieved by examining network communications, identifying heuristics and patterns (often known as signatures) of common computer attacks, and taking action to alert operators.

这在传统上通过检查网络通信，确定常见计算机攻击的启发和模式（常称为标识），采取警示操作者的方法来实现。

9. Physical intrusion detection systems (passive) are distinguished by their ability to pinpoint the absolute location of an intrusion attempt to within a few feet.

物理入侵（被动）检测系统以其几英尺精度准确定位入侵企图绝对地点的能力来区分。

10. The system reports the coordinates of the attempted breach, which can be used for activating corresponding PTZ camera presets or for personnel dispatch.

系统报告企图入侵突破的坐标位置，可用于激活相应的监控摄像机预置状态或人员派遣。

- PTZ (pan-tilt-zoom camera) camera：可水平摇动、俯仰倾斜、变焦的监控摄像机

11. Intrusion detection system evasion techniques bypass detection by creating different states on the IDS and on the targeted computer.

入侵检测系统的规避技术通过对 IDS 和目标计算机制造不同的状态来躲过检测。

- creating states on … and on …，两个 on 并列。

Technical Tips

Cryptography

Information security uses cryptography to transform usable information into a form that renders it unusable by anyone other than an authorized user; this process is called encryption. Information that has been encrypted (rendered unusable) can be transformed back into its original usable form by an authorized user, who possesses the cryptographic key, through the process of decryption. Cryptography is used in information security to protect information from unauthorized or accidental disclosure while the information is in transit (either electronically or physically) and while information is in storage.

Steganography

Steganography is the art and science of writing hidden messages in such a way that no one apart from the intended recipient knows of the existence of the message; this is in contrast to cryptography, where the existence of the message itself is not disguised, but the content is obscured. Quite often, steganography is hidden in pictures. The detection of steganographically encoded packages is called steganalysis.

Supplementary Readings: Hidden Communication

The rise of the Internet and multimedia techniques in the mid-1990s has prompted increasing interest in hiding data in digital media. Early research concentrated on watermarking to protect copyrighted multimedia products (such as images, audio, video, and text). Data embedding has also been found to be useful in covert communication, or steganography. The goal was and still is to convey messages under cover, concealing the very existence of information exchange.

Compared to watermarking, steganography has drawn less attention until recently, as computer specialists, signal-processing researchers, and multimedia product vendors concerned about information security have recognized that illicit use of the technique might become a threat to the security of the worldwide information infrastructure. Researchers have thus begun to study steganalysis, or the detection of embedded information. Detecting secret data hidden in millions of multimedia items downloadable from online sites is recognized as an especially difficult task.

The idea and practice of hiding the occurrence of information exchange can be dated back hundreds of years. Old techniques of steganography, meaning *covered writing* in Greek, ranged from tattooing the shaved head of a trusted messenger in ancient times, to using invisible ink during the two World Wars. Modern steganography employs digital media contents as camouflage, uses powerful computers and signal processing techniques to hide secret data, and distributes stego-media through the vast cyberspace, posing a serious challenge to scientists and professionals in the fields of information security.

Steganography, watermarking, and cryptography

As two major branches of information hiding, steganography and watermarking have many things in common. However, they differ in a number of important aspects such as purpose, specifications, detection/extraction methods, etc. A fundamental difference is that the object of communication in watermarking is the host signal, with the embedded data providing copyright protection, whereas in steganography the object to be transmitted is the embedded message, and the cover signal merely serves as an innocuous disguise chosen fairly arbitrarily by the user based on its technical suitability. In addition, the existence of a watermark is often openly declared, and any attempts to remove or invalidate the embedded content will render the host useless, while the most crucial requirement for steganography is the perceptual and algorithmic undetectability. Robustness against malicious attacks and signal processing is not of primary concern as for watermarking.

Steganography also differs from cryptography, which does not conceal the communication itself but only scrambles the data to prevent understanding of the contents by eavesdroppers. There are various methods and implementations in cryptography. Steganography, on the other hand, is a fairly new area of study. Practically, steganography and cryptography may be considered complementary and "orthogonal": one can always apply a cryptographic algorithm to the data before being embedded to achieve additional security. In any case, however, once the presence of hidden information is revealed or even suspected, the purpose of steganography is defeated, despite that the message content may not be extracted or deciphered.

Steganographic techniques

We consider steganography in digital images, which can be stored in a straightforward bitmap format such as BMP, or in a compressed format such as JPG. Palette images are usually in the GIF format. Information hiding can be accomplished either in the space domain or the frequency domain. In terms of insertion schemes, several methods can be used such as substitution, addition, and adjustment. One adjustment approach, for example, is the quantization index modulation (QIM). Although a simple and unified method for classifying the techniques does not exist, the following lists some popular approaches that are frequently used in downloadable steganographic tools or found in the literature.

LSB-modification techniques. They are based on modifying the least significant bits of the pixel values in the space domain. In a basic implementation that replaces the entire LSB-plane with the stego-data, on average, 50% of the LSBs are flipped (see Figure 12.1). It can be shown that fidelity of the stego-image measured in peak-signal-to-noise ratio (PSNR) with respect to the cover is 51.1dB, representing a very high degree of imperceptibility compared to the lower bound of 39dB proposed for invisible watermarks.

Masking approaches. They are similar to visible watermarking in which pixel values in masked areas are raised or lowered by a certain percentage. Reducing the increment to a certain degree can make the mark invisible.

Transform domain techniques. Candidate transforms include DCT, DWT, DFT, etc. By embedding in the transform domain, the hidden data can reside in more robust areas and spread across the entire image, leading to better resistance against signal processing.

Techniques incorporated in compression algorithms. The idea here is to integrate the data embedding with an image compression algorithm such as JPEG. For example, a steganographic tool, Jpeg-Jsteg, takes a lossless cover-image and the message to be hidden to generate a JPEG stego-image.

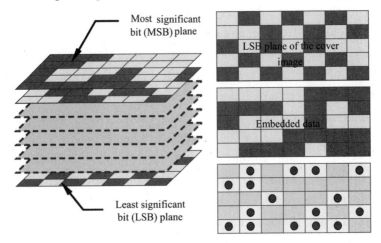

Figure 12.1   Basic LSB approach. Bit-planes of a grayscale image are sketched on the left. The LSB plane of the cover image is shown on the top-right, which is replaced with the hidden data in the middle. The bottom-right map indicates differences between LSB planes of the cover and stego images. Circles represent the flipped bits.

Spread spectrum techniques. The hidden data is spread throughout the cover-image based on spread spectrum techniques such as frequency hopping. A stego-key is used for encryption to randomly select the frequency channels.

It is impossible to mention all the techniques here. Nonetheless, there do exist some basic requirements that have to be satisfied for any steganographic system, of which the following are of the most importance:

- Security of the hidden communication
- Size of the payload
- Robustness against malicious and unintentional attacks

Detection of steganographic contents — steganalysis

Despite the fact that steganographic tools only alter the most insignificant image components, they inevitably leave detectable traces in the stego-image so that successful attacks are possible. The primary goal of attacks against steganography is to detect the presence of hidden data, although in some cases it may also include extraction and/or destruction of the embedded data. Steganalysis in this article refers to detection of the presence of hidden information in a given image. Also, assume that the cover-image is not available to the steganalyst (stego-only detection). In general, there are two major types of steganalytic techniques: visual analysis and statistical (algorithmic) analysis.

Visual analysis tries to reveal the presence of secret communication by inspection, either using the naked eye or with assistance of a computer. It is expected that any unusual appearance in the display of the LSB-plane will announce the existence of hidden information. Visual inspection can be quite successful when secret data are inserted in relatively smooth areas with pixel values near saturation.

Statistical analysis is more powerful since it reveals tiny alterations in the image's statistical behavior caused by steganographic embedding. As there are various approaches of embedding, each modifying the image in a different way, unified techniques for detecting hidden information in all types of stego-images are difficult to find.

The effects of a simple LSB steganographic operation are illustrated in Figure 12.2. The stego-image visually identical to the cover is shown in (a). The LSB plane of the cover shown in (b) contains some noticeable features corresponding especially to the areas with flat and saturated colors. This plane is partially replaced with embedded data, scrambled and spread all over the bit-plane, as displayed in (c), with an embedding capacity of 0.52 bits per color channel. The original features have become vague as they are masked by the embedded data. If the data are embedded sequentially, the map given in (d) results, in which the message data only occupy the red and a portion of the green planes, with the rest of the LSB plane padded with zeros. More sophisticated embedding schemes, such as selecting busy areas and padding unoccupied space with a random sequence possessing the same statistical property as the cover will make direct analysis of the LSB plane more difficult.

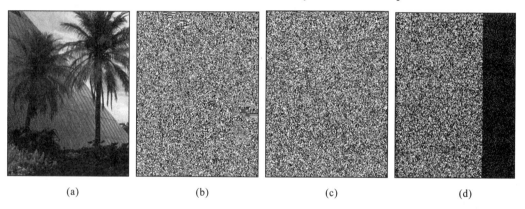

| (a) | (b) | (c) | (d) |

Figure 12.2   Effects of simple LSB embedding. (a) The stego-image visually indistinguishable from the cover. (b) LSB-plane of the cover in which some features are visible. (c) LSB-plane of the stego-image with embedded data of 0.52 bits per color channel scrambled and evenly spread. The original features are blurred. (d) LSB-plane of the stego-image.

For palette-based images such as those in the GIF format, replacing LSB with the embedded data will cause significant color singularities since neighboring indices in a palette may point to very different colors. There are also techniques that simply shuffle the palette according to a key with the image itself intact. These methods can be defeated through analysis of the palette to find unusual ordering as normal software products arrange the palette based on such attributes as color components, luminance, etc. A peculiar palette itself is sufficient to arouse suspicion.

With a steganographic tool at hand, the choice of cover-images is at the discretion of the user. Images stored in the JPEG format are abundant because of the bandwidth limitation and the widespread use of digital cameras, and therefore are likely to be chosen as covers for hidden communications. However, because the JPEG algorithm performs quantization on block DCT coefficients, some known structures are inherent in these images. Slight modification will therefore leave traces incompatible with the JPEG signature, making the stego image vulnerable to analysis.

Generally speaking, blind detection of hidden information in apparently innocuous digital media is more challenging than data embedding, since a steganalyst always works in a passive mode. Another important consideration in a steganalysis is to keep the computational complexity sufficiently low so that screening a large quantity of suspected images is feasible. The computation limitation may be less stringent for steganography, since in practical applications the embedding algorithm is executed only on a few images taken from a large database.

Conclusions

A new round of information warfare has already begun, which is characterized by the use of state-of-the-art computer-based technologies and, in particular, rapid development of the Internet as an increasingly important channel of information dissemination. The battle between steganography and steganalysis is an important part of 21st century cyber warfare that will have profound influence on the crucial issue of information security.

The two sides of the battle are the attempts of transmitting secret messages under the cover of innocuous multimedia signals and the efforts to detect or prevent such hidden communications. Various steganographic tools have been developed, many available online. In a sense, some simple methods are already defeated due to the relentless endeavors of the steganalysts. Meanwhile, countermeasures against steganalysis are also emerging. Tools that can withstand, to some extent, both visual and statistical attacks are being introduced. For example, in data embedding, much attention has been paid to the preservation of statistical characteristics of the cover media. To combat steganalytic tools based on analyzing the increase of unique colors in the image, new embedding methods may be devised in which creation of new colors is avoided. Alternatively, modifications leading to detectable artifacts may be compensated for after embedding, while keeping the secret message extractable to the intended recipients.

As this process goes on, we can expect more and even faster technological advances in both steganography and steganalysis. Apart from their law enforcement/intelligence and anti-terrorist significance, steganographic techniques also have peaceful applications: in-band captioning, integration of multiple media for convenient and reliable storage, management and transmission, embedding of executables for function control, error correction and version upgrading, to name a few. In the years to come, computer specialists, signal processing and information security professionals, and software developers will have a great deal to do in the challenging area of information hiding and detection.

Exercises

I. Translate the following sentences into Chinese.

1. A solid network design is crucial for maintaining a secure network. From perimeter firewalls to locking down endpoint devices and controlling user access, these resources help you build a secure layered network and identify vulnerabilities to prevent attacks.

2. Intrusion management is more than a tool or a person — it is also a process. These resources arm you with the knowledge you need to implement and maintain an intrusion management life cycle.

3. Several classes of human error have been identified and studied, and conditions that increase the likelihood of error can be specified in advance.

4. Similar attempts in other industries have failed because their reports were submitted through a chain of authority that included the person's supervisor or plant management — people who have biases to sanitize the report or to form negative judgments of the reporter.

5. The preceding chapters have described how the automatic computer performs, but have not described how the automatic computer can be put to use to do data handling work to serve an organization, nor why such work is done in the way that it is.

6. The sources of the information are often reports in the media, reports that are incomplete, usually written before all relevant information is gathered, and subject to other sources of inaccuracies and biases.

7. The threat is also placed in a theoretical political context by examining how it relates to paradigm-shifting technologies of the past, what its attractions and deterrents are, and how it would be analyzed and addressed within traditional realist/liberal national security schools.

8. While the subject of coding often carries with it an air of secrecy, a more important motive in many coding systems is the improved efficiency in conveying information.

II. Choose the phrase that is closest in meaning to the underlined part.

1. <u>Julius Caesar is credited with the invention of the Caesar cipher</u> to prevent his secret messages from being read should a message fall into the wrong hands.

 A. Julius Caesar is believed to be the inventor of the Caesar cipher

 B. Julius Caesar actually made the invention of the Caesar cipher

 C. Julius Caesar is the person who was on credit of inventing the Caesar cipher

 D. Julius Caesar is charged as the inventor of the Caesar cipher

2. It also means that data stored in one part of a database system is <u>in agreement with other related data stored in another part of the database system</u> (or another system).

    A. equal to other data that is related to the database system

    B. similar to other data in relation to another section of the database system

    C. consistent with related data stored in a different part of the database

    D. identical to other related data else where in the database system

3. In a reactive system, also known as an intrusion prevention system (IPS), the IDS responds to the suspicious activity by resetting the connection or by <u>reprogramming the firewall to block network traffic from the suspected malicious source</u>.

    A. reprogramming the firewall for the block of data stream coming from the malicious source

    B. changing the firewall program to stop data originating from the presumably hostile source

    C. reconfiguring a block of the firewall to control the network steam against hostile data

    D. reprogramming so that the firewall takes a block of network data to combat malicious attacks

4. As the US Department of Defense urgently wanted military command and control networks that could survive a nuclear war, ARPA <u>was charged with</u> inventing a technology that could get data to its destination reliably even if arbitrary parts of the network disappeared without warning as a result of a nuclear attack.

    A. was accused to be

    B. was asked to pay for

    C. was given the task of

    D. was forced to consider

5. Are they better able to do <u>logical reasoning</u> than people, but less intuitive to do the everyday task?

    A. inference

    B. reason finding

    C. proving

    D. recognizing logically

6. In such a fiber rays traveling at larger angles with respect to the axis <u>have to traverse a longer path</u> and hence take a longer time than those rays which propagate with smaller angles to the axis.

    A. have transmitted over a longer distance

    B. are bound to treat a longer way

    C. must travel through a longer route

    D. must deal with a longer trace

7. The electronic equipment must operate in conjunction with other equipment <u>without causing malfunction or degradation</u> of any of the associated equipment.

A. without making faulty operation or degeneration

B. without bringing about displacement or trouble

C. without inducing manufacturing problem or disadvantage

D. without introducing unknown function or difficulty

8. Recent advances will permit mixed working thus permitting some sites to use their equipment capable of operating at 384kbps and higher resolution, and at the same time <u>allowing smaller sites to be part of the conference</u> with their equipment only operating at 128kbps.

A. agreeing that less important sites can partly become the conference

B. letting insignificant participants join the conference

C. permitting smaller network nodes to partly attend the entire conference

D. making possible that smaller audiences can take part in the conference

Unit 13

Telemedicine and Biomedical Signal Processing

Bioengineering is the application of life science, physical science, information technology, mathematics, and engineering principles to solve problems in biology, medicine, health care and related fields. It applies principles and discoveries in the biological sciences to engineering design and development of new products and services such as medical imaging, bioinformatics, biomaterials, etc.

Text

Part I: Telemedicine

Telemedicine may be as simple as two health professionals discussing a case over the telephone, or as complex as using satellite technology and video-conferencing equipment to conduct a real-time consultation between medical specialists in two different countries.[1] It can also involve the use of an unmanned robot. Telemedicine generally refers to the use of communications and information technologies for the delivery of clinical care.

Care at a distance (also called in absentia care), is an old practice which was often conducted via post; there has been a long and successful history of in absentia health care, which has metamorphosed into what we know as modern telemedicine thanks to the modern communication technology.[2]

In its early manifestations, African villagers used smoke signals to warn people to stay away from the village in case of serious disease. In the early 1900s, people living in remote areas in Australia used two-way radios, powered by a dynamo driven by a set of bicycle pedals, to communicate with the Royal Flying Doctor Service of Australia.

The terms e-health and telehealth are at times wrongly interchanged with telemedicine. Like the terms "medicine" and "health care", telemedicine often refers only to the provision of clinical services while the term telehealth can refer to clinical and non-clinical services such as medical education, administration, and research.[3] The term e-health is often, particularly in the UK and Europe, used as an umbrella term that includes telehealth, electronic medical records, and other components of health IT.

Types of telemedicine

Telemedicine is practiced on the basis of two concepts: real time (synchronous) and store-and-forward (asynchronous).

Real time telemedicine could be as simple as a telephone call or as complex as robotic surgery. It requires the presence of both parties at the same time and a communications link between them that allows a real-time interaction to take place. Video-conferencing equipment is one of the most common forms of technologies used in synchronous telemedicine. There are also peripheral devices which can be attached to computers or the video-conferencing equipment which can aid in an interactive examination.[4] For instance, a tele-otoscope allows a remote physician to "see" inside a patient's ear; a tele-stethoscope allows the consulting remote physician to hear the patient's heartbeat. Medical specialties conducive to this kind of consultation include psychiatry, internal medicine, rehabilitation, cardiology, pediatrics, obstetrics and gynecology and neurology.

Store-and-forward telemedicine involves acquiring medical data (like medical images, biosignals etc.) and then transmitting this data to a doctor or medical specialist at a convenient time for assessment offline. It does not require the presence of both parties at the same time. Dermatology, radiology, and pathology are common specialties that are conducive to asynchronous telemedicine. A properly structured Medical Record preferably in electronic form should be a component of this transfer.

Telemedicine is most beneficial for populations living in isolated communities and remote regions and is currently being applied in virtually all medical domains. Specialties that use telemedicine often use a "tele" prefix; for example, telemedicine as applied by radiologists is called teleradiology. Similarly telemedicine as applied by cardiologists is termed as telecardiology, etc.

Telemedicine is also useful as a communication tool between a general practitioner and a specialist available at a remote location.

The focus of telemedicine has mainly been consultative, meaning a general practitioner consulting a specialist or a specialist consulting another specialist. Monitoring a patient at home using known devices like blood pressure monitors and transferring the information to a caregiver is a fast growing emerging service. These remote monitoring solutions have a focus on current high morbidity chronic diseases and are mainly deployed for the First World. In developing countries a new way of practicing telemedicine is emerging better known as Primary Remote Diagnostic Visits whereby devices examine a patient and a connected doctor residing in another location virtually examines the patient and treat him.[5] This new technology and principle of practicing medicine holds big promises to solving major health care delivery problems in for instance Southern Africa because Primary Remote Diagnostic Consultations not only monitors an already diagnosed chronic disease, but has the promise to diagnosing and managing the diseases a patient will typically visit a general practitioner for.[6]

Teleradiology

Telemedicine is the delivery of healthcare and exchange of health care information across distance. Teleradiology is the ability to send radiographic images (x-rays) from one location to another. For this process to be implemented, three essential components are required, an image sending station, a transmission network, and a receiving / image review station.

The teleradiology process begins at the image sending station. The radiographic image and a modem are required for this first step. The image is scanned and then sent to the modem.

The transmission network can be wire, fiber optics, or microwave. After the digital information has been sent to the modem, electrical impulses are sent along to the transmission network to the receiving/image review station. The receiving/image review station consists of a modem, a computer with sufficient storage capabilities, a display, and sometimes a printer to provide hard copies to the end user. The electrical impulses created through the transmission network are received by the modem on the review station. These impulses are converted back to the original digital image once it reaches the review station. This image is then stored and can be viewed on the display for diagnostic purposes. A hard copy can be printed for more convenience.

Clearly with the number of companies focusing on telemedical devices and the specialization of these companies one can expect telemedicine to become a significant way that physicians, hospitals, and veterinarian offices operate in the near future.

Part II: Computerized Tomographic Imaging

Tomography refers to the cross-sectional imaging of an object from either transmission or reflection data collected by illuminating the object from many different directions. The impact of this technique in diagnostic medicine has been revolutionary, since it has enabled doctors to view internal organs with unprecedented precision and safety to the patient. The first medical application utilized x-rays for forming images of tissues based on their x-ray attenuation coefficient. More recently, however, medical imaging has also been successfully accomplished with radioisotopes, ultrasound, and magnetic resonance; the imaged parameter being different in each case.

There are numerous non-medical imaging applications which lend themselves to the methods of computerized tomography. Researchers have already applied this methodology to the mapping of underground resources via cross-borehole imaging, some specialized cases of cross-sectional imaging for nondestructive testing, the determination of the brightness distribution over a celestial sphere, and three-dimensional imaging with electron microscopy.[1]

Fundamentally, tomographic imaging deals with reconstructing an image from its projections. In the strict sense of the word, a projection at a given angle is the integral of the image in the direction specified by that angle, as illustrated in Figure 13.1. However, in a loose sense, projection means the information derived from the transmitted energies, when an object is illuminated from a particular angle; the phrase "diffracted projection" may be used when energy sources are diffracting, as is the case with ultrasound and microwaves.[2]

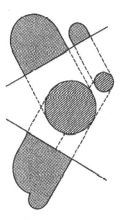

Figure 13.1   Two projections are shown of an object consisting of a pair of cylinders

Although, from a purely mathematical standpoint, the solution to the problem of how to reconstruct a function from its projections dates back to the paper by Radon in 1917, the current excitement in tomographic imaging originated with Hounsfield's invention of the x-ray computed tomographic scanner for which he received a Nobel prize in 1979.[3] He shared the prize with Allan Cormack who independently discovered some of the algorithms. His invention showed that it is possible to compute high-quality cross-sectional images with an accuracy now reaching one part in a thousand in spite of the fact that the projection data do not strictly satisfy the theoretical models underlying the efficiently implementable reconstruction algorithms.[4] His invention also showed that it is possible to process a very large number of measurements (now approaching a million for the case of x-ray tomography) with fairly complex mathematical operations, and still get an image that is incredibly accurate.

It is fair to say that the breakneck pace at which x-ray computed tomography images improved after Hounsfield's invention was in large measure owing to the developments that were made in reconstruction algorithms.[5] Hounsfield used algebraic techniques, and was able to reconstruct noisy looking 80×80 images with an accuracy of one part in a hundred. This was followed by the application of convolution backprojection algorithms, first developed by Ramachandran and Lakshminarayanan and later popularized by Shepp and Logan, to this type of imaging. These later algorithms considerably reduced the processing time for reconstruction, and the image produced was numerically more accurate. As a result, commercial manufacturers of x-ray tomographic scanners started building systems capable of reconstructing 256×256 and 512×512 images that were almost photographically perfect (in the sense that the morphological detail produced was unambiguous and in perfect agreement with the anatomical features).

Given the enormous success of x-ray computed tomography, it is not surprising that in recent years much attention has been focused on extending this image formation technique to nuclear medicine and magnetic resonance on one hand; and ultrasound and microwaves on the other. In nuclear medicine, our interest is in reconstructing a cross-sectional image of radioactive isotope distributions within the human body; and in imaging with magnetic resonance we wish to reconstruct the magnetic properties of the object. In both these areas, the problem can be set up as reconstructing an image from its projections of the type shown in Figure 13.1. This is not the case when ultrasound and microwaves are used as energy sources, although the aim is the same as with X-rays, viz., to reconstruct the cross-sectional image of, say, the attenuation coefficient.[6] X-rays are non-diffracting, i.e., they travel in straight lines, whereas microwaves and ultrasound are diffracting. When an object is illuminated with a diffracting source, the wave field is scattered in practically all directions, although under certain conditions one might be able to get away with the assumption of straight line propagation; these conditions being satisfied when the inhomogeneities are much larger than the wavelength and when the imaging parameter is the refractive index.[7] For situations when one must take diffraction effects (inhomogeneity caused scattering of the wave field) into account, tomographic imaging can in principle be accomplished with the algorithms based on the Fourier diffraction theorem.

New Words

Part I

telemedicine	远程医疗	professional	专业工作者
video-conferencing	视频会议	consultation	咨询
unmanned	无人的	robot	机器人
clinical	临床的	in absentia	缺席的
metamorphose	使变形，变态	manifestation	显示，证明
dynamo	发电机	bicycle pedal	自行车的脚蹬子
e-health	电子保健	telehealth	远程保健
administration	行政，管理	umbrella term	有多种含义的名词，涵盖性术语
component	成分，组成部分	synchronous	同步的
asynchronous	非同步的	forward	转发，转送
robotic surgery	机器人外科	peripheral	外围设备
tele-otoscope	远程耳镜	otology	耳科学
tele-stethoscope	远程听诊器	physician	内科医生
conducive	有益的，有助的	psychiatry	精神病学

internal medicine	内科学	rehabilitation	康复
cardiology	心脏病学	pediatrics	小儿科
obstetrics	产科	gynecology	妇科学
neurology	神经病学	acquire	获取
biosignal	生物医学信号	offline	离线的，非实时的
dermatology	皮肤病学	radiology	放射学
pathology	病理学	virtually	实际上
teleradiology	远程放射学	general practitioner	全科医生
caregiver	护理人员	morbidity	发病率
chronic disease	慢性病	whereby	（关系副词）靠那个
consultation	咨询	radiographic	射线图像
diagnostic	诊断的	veterinarian	兽医

Part Ⅱ

tomography	断层成像术	transmission	透射
reflection	反射	diagnostic	诊断
unprecedented	前所未有的，空前的	attenuation	衰减
coefficient	系数	radioisotope	放射性同位素
resonance	共振	lend oneself to	有助于，适宜于
borehole	钻孔	celestial	天空的
integral	积分	diffract	衍射，绕射
cross-sectional	断面的，截面的	breakneck	极快的，很危险的
algebraic	代数的	backprojection	反向投影
unambiguous	不模糊的，不含糊的	anatomical	解剖学的
cylinder	柱体，圆柱	isotope	同位素
viz. (拉丁语 *videlicet*)	就是说(可读作 namely)	scatter	散射
inhomogeneity	不均匀性	refractive index	折射率
variation	变种	avalanche	雪崩
bibliography	参考书目	cite	引述，引用

Notes on the Text

Part I

1. Telemedicine may be as simple as two health professionals discussing a case over the telephone, or as complex as using satellite technology and video-conferencing equipment to conduct a real-time consultation between medical specialists in two different countries.

远程医疗可以简单到两名医务工作者通过电话讨论病情，或者复杂到通过卫星技术和视频会议系统在两个不同国家的医学专家之间进行实时的医疗咨询。

2. There has been a long and successful history of in absentia health care, which has metamorphosed into what we know as modern telemedicine thanks to the modern communication technology.

缺席医疗服务具有漫长而成功的历史，由于有了现代通信技术，它已发展成为现在我们所了解的现代远程医疗。

3. Like the terms "medicine" and "health care", telemedicine often refers only to the provision of clinical services while the term telehealth can refer to clinical and non-clinical services such as medical education, administration, and research.

就像医疗和保健两个词有所不同一样，远程医疗通常仅指提供临床服务，而远程保健可以指临床和非临床的服务，后者如医学教育、行政管理和研究。

- 注意 such as 是举例说明 non-clinical services 的。

4. There are also peripheral devices which can be attached to computers or the video-conferencing equipment which can aid in an interactive examination.

另外还有外部设备可以接到计算机或视频会议设备上，在交互检查中提供帮助。

- 这里 aid 是不及物动词。

5. In developing countries a new way of practicing telemedicine is emerging better known as Primary Remote Diagnostic Visits whereby devices examine a patient and a connected doctor residing in another location virtually examines the patient and treat him.

在发展中国家正在出现一种新的远程医疗实施方法，常称为"基本远程诊断访问"，通过该系统用设备对病人进行检查，而实际上由另一个国家的联线医生来进行检查和治疗。

6. This new technology and principle of practicing medicine holds big promises to solving major health care delivery problems in for instance Southern Africa because Primary Remote Diagnostic Consultations not only monitors an already diagnosed chronic disease, but has the promise to diagnosing and managing the diseases a patient will typically visit a general practitioner for.

这一新的医疗实践技术和原则对于解决为诸如南部非洲这样的地区提供基本保健服务的问题是一大希望，因为基本远程诊断咨询不仅可监测已诊断出的慢性病，还可对病人通常会求助于全科医生的疾病进行诊断和管理。

- the diseases a patient will typically visit a general practitioner for：病人通常会求助于全科医生的疾病（ = the diseases for which a patient will typically visit a general practitioner）

Part Ⅱ

1. Researchers have already applied this methodology to the mapping of underground resources via cross-borehole imaging, some specialized cases of cross-sectional imaging for nondestructive testing, the determination of the brightness distribution over a celestial sphere, and 3D imaging with electron microscopy.

研究者已经将此方法用在许多方面，例如通过钻孔成像测绘地下资源，无损检测中断面成像的某些特殊案例，确定天球面上的亮度分布，以及电子显微镜三维成像。

- … applied this methodology to 后面跟了一连串的宾语：the mapping of …, some specialized cases …, the determination of …, and three dimensional imaging …。翻译时增加"用在许多方面，例如……"，读起来更顺口一些。

2. However, in a loose sense, projection means the information derived from the transmitted energies, when an object is illuminated from a particular angle; the phrase "diffracted projection" may be used when energy sources are diffracting, as is the case with ultrasound and microwaves.

然而在宽泛的意义上，投影是指物体从某一角度受到照射时由发出的能量所形成的信息。若辐射源是衍射性的，如超声波或微波，可使用"衍射投影"一词。

3. Although, from a purely mathematical standpoint, the solution to the problem of how to reconstruct a function from its projections dates back to the paper by Radon in 1917, the current excitement in tomographic imaging originated with Hounsfield's invention of the x-ray computed tomographic scanner for which he received a Nobel prize in 1979.

虽然从纯数学的角度，对于如何根据投影数据重建图像这一问题的解要追溯到 1917 年 Radon 的论文，但当前在断层成像方面令人激动的成就源自 Hounsfield 发明的 X 光 CT 扫描，他因此项发明而于 1979 年获得了诺贝尔奖。

4. His invention showed that it is possible to compute high-quality cross-sectional images with an accuracy now reaching one part in a thousand in spite of the fact that the projection data do not strictly satisfy the theoretical models underlying the efficiently implementable reconstruction algorithms.

他的发明显示，尽管投影数据并未严格满足有效实现重建算法赖以成立的理论模型，仍有可能得到精度达千分之一的高质量断面图像。

5. It is fair to say that the breakneck pace at which x-ray computed tomography images improved after Hounsfield's invention was in large measure owing to the developments that were made in reconstruction algorithms.

可以说自从 Hounsfield 的发明以来 X 光 CT 成像技术的改进在很大程度上要归功于重建算法方面的发展。

6. This is not the case when ultrasound and microwaves are used as energy sources, although the aim is the same as with x-rays, viz., to reconstruct the cross-sectional image of, say, the attenuation coefficient.

尽管其目的和 X 光（CT）相同，即重建某一参数（例如衰减系数）的断层图像，用超声波和微波作能源时情况有所不同。

7. When an object is illuminated with a diffracting source, the wave field is scattered in practically all directions, although under certain conditions one might be able to get away with the assumption of straight line propagation; these conditions being satisfied when the inhomogeneities are much larger than the wavelength and when the imaging parameter is the refractive index.

当使用衍射源照射物体时，波实际上向四面八方散射，尽管当波场的不均匀范围远大于波长，并且用折射率作为成像参数时，可以假定它是直线传播。

- get away with the assumption: 直译为"作此假设而没有不良后果"。

Technical Tips

E-health

E-health is an emerging field in the intersection of medical informatics, public health and business, referring to health services and information delivered or enhanced through the Internet and related technologies. In a broader sense, the term characterizes not only a technical development, but also a state-of-mind, a way of thinking, an attitude, and a commitment for networked, global thinking, to improve health care locally, regionally, and worldwide by using information and communication technology.

E-health describes the application of information and communications technologies across the whole range of functions that affect the health sector, from the doctor to the hospital manager, via nurses, data processing specialists, social security administrators and, of course, the patients.

Videoconference

A videoconference is a set of interactive telecommunication technologies which allow two or more locations to interact via two-way video and audio transmissions simultaneously. It has also been called visual collaboration and is a type of groupware. It differs from videophone in that it is designed to serve a conference rather than individuals.

The core technology involved is digital compression of audio and video streams in real time. The hardware or software that performs compression is called a codec (coder/decoder). The resulting digital stream of 1's and 0's is subdivided into labeled packets, and transmitted through a digital network such as ISDN and IP. The other components required include:

- Video input: video camera or webcam
- Video output: computer monitor, television or projector
- Audio input: microphone
- Audio output: usually loudspeaker associated with the display device or telephone
- Data transfer: analog or digital telephone network, LAN or Internet

Supplementary Readings: Biomedical Signal Processing

In biomedical signal processing, major progress has been made due to a better understanding of the underlying physiological processes, the further development of high-quality measurement techniques, and the evolving algorithms. Improvements were achieved with regard to the measurement of biomedical signals. For example, high quality biopotential amplifier and recording systems have been developed for a signal-to-noise ratio up to 40 dB. Also, today, we have a better understanding of the source-field relationship, in particular for the human brain and heart. Such an understanding is very important in order to apply the proper mathematical tools and to understand the limitations of the applied approaches. Beside statistical approaches, model-based signal processing techniques have been developed. In general, these approaches are based on a biophysical model of the underlying physiological process. Formulating a linear or a nonlinear input-output relationship is the basis for these model-based approaches, which are powerful techniques also in the case of very complex and noisy signals, like the magneto- (MEG) and electroencephalogram (EEG).

Today, biomedical signal processing is further developed at an organ level and, in particular, on a cellular and subcellular level. Traditional signal processing techniques, like time-frequency domain or wavelet analysis, are also applied to biomolecular data. For instance in microarray analysis or in the analysis of mass spectrometric data, statistical and model-based approaches are just on the way to be introduced for a better and more specific analysis.

Some outstanding works are briefly introduced in the following, which are dedicated to the analysis of transcranial Doppler ultrasound data for embolus identification, the segmentation of the EEG signal waves, the analysis of spinal somatosensory evoked potentials, the determination of the complexity of EEG signals for measuring the depth of anesthesia, and the reconstruction of neural activity from MEG data. All these works deal with biomedical signal processing at an organ level.

Blood flow in the middle cerebral artery can be monitored by transcranial Doppler ultrasound. It may be used to detect cerebral emboli in patients with an increased stroke risk and during invasive cardiovascular examinations and operations. A paper by Fan et al. describes an interesting approach for a quantitative interpretation and analysis of transcranial Doppler ultrasound data for automated embolus identification. An automatic system was developed that replaces the so-called human expert (HE).

Doppler signal patterns were analyzed in both the time domain and frequency domain. The system was trained and tested on Doppler signals recorded during the dissection and recovery phases of carotid endarterectomy. The results were compared with the results obtained by HEs. The automatic system displayed a high sensitivity and specificity.

From a technical point of view, the applied frequency and time domain evaluation has several advantages. It makes pattern recognition much more stable than a pure time domain approach. Also, this approach can handle noisy ultrasound data, which often is the case in a clinical environment. From a clinical perspective, transcranial Doppler ultrasound has several significant benefits. The technique is noninvasive, painless and safe. The procedure is quick and with training, 30-40 minutes is sufficient for acquisition and analysis. The instrumentation is inexpensive and portable. The most crucial aspect in applying transcranial Doppler ultrasound is to develop good operator techniques. With training and experience, reproducibility between operators is good.

Another work involves segmentation of EEG data for tracking the delta, theta, alpha, sigma, beta and the gamma wave. An adaptive recursive band-pass filter is employed for estimating and tracking the center frequency associated with each of these waves. The main advantage is that the employed adaptive filter has only one unknown coefficient to be updated. This coefficient represents an efficient distinct feature for each EEG specific wave. The approach is simple and accurate in comparison with other multivariate adaptive approaches. It can be applied to on-line EEG data and was used for the detection of sleep spindles.

Evoked potentials have been used to detect the integrity of spinal cord function during spinal surgery to minimize the possibility of spinal cord injury. Traditional methods for evoked potential monitoring use only amplitude and latency measurements to indicate potential injury to the spinal cord. However, spectral changes in evoked potentials also occur during neurological injury. An investigation of various time-frequency analysis techniques has been conducted to detect both temporal and spectral changes in the evoked potentials waveforms. The time-frequency distributions (TFDs) computed using these methods were assessed and compared. As shown, short-time Fourier transform with a 20-point length Hanning window provides the best result for spinal somatosensory evoked signals.

The monitoring of depth of anesthesia is an important aspect for patients during interventions and operations. Several methods for automatic segmentation, classification and compact presentation of suppression patterns in the EEG have been developed. A new approach for quantifying the relationship between brain activity patterns and depth of anesthesia has been presented. The spatio-temporal patterns in the EEG were analyzed. Twenty-seven patients undergoing vascular surgery were studied under general anesthesia. The EEG was recorded and patients' anesthesia states were assessed according to the responsiveness component of the observer's assessment of alertness/sedation score. Complexity of the EEG was quantitatively estimated by the Lempel-Ziv complexity measure $C(n)$. The study shows that $C(n)$ is a very useful and promising EEG-derived parameter for characterizing the depth of anesthesia under clinical situations.

Analysis of the MEG for reconstructing neural electrical activity and pattern recognition in the temporal or frequency domain has been a subject of research in the recent years. The work involves the analysis of MEG data and is an important contribution to enhance contrast in the reconstructed images. The basic idea of applying the beamformer technique to this approach is very promising and might give a significant improvement for source localization. A method for reconstructing spatio-temporal activities of neural sources extends the adaptive beamformer technique to incorporate the vector beamformer formulation in which a set of three weight vectors is used to detect the source activity in three orthogonal directions. Both spatial resolution and output signal-to-noise ratio of the proposed beamformer are significantly higher than those of the minimum variance-based vector beamformer. The proposed beamformer has been applied to two sets of auditory evoked MEG data. The results clearly demonstrated the method's capability of reconstructing spatio-temporal activities of neural sources. In reconstructing neural electrical activity, one of the key problems is that we still do not have a proper and physically based source model available. The beamformer technique may overcome this limitation, in particular for the imaging of independent electrical sources.

On an organ level there are various research areas in which novel methodology is developed. Examples are the imaging of electrical function within the human brain and heart from observations on the body surface from electric potential (e.g., EEG) or magnetic field mapping (e.g., MEG) data, the non-invasive and real-time beat-to-beat monitoring of stroke volume, blood pressure, total peripheral resistance and for assessment of autonomic function by measuring ECG, blood pressure and thorax impedance, and the classification of biosignals like EEG or MEG.

Signal processing methods developed at an organ level are further developed also for the application to biomolecular data. Recently, in the signal processing community, terms like genomic signal processing came up. Under genomic signal processing we understand problem solving in making use of the well-established theory, tools, and methodologies from the field of biomedical signal processing. Fields of research are clustering, detection, prediction, and classification of gene expression data, signal transforms and statistical models for the interpretation of biological sequences and statistical and dynamical modeling of gene networks. Sequence analysis techniques including hidden Markov models, wavelet analysis, and artificial neural networks are on the way being introduced.

From a biomedical signal processing point of view it is very challenging to see that mathematical approaches developed for traditional signals like the EEG are now further developed for the application to data on a molecular level. It will be fascinating to see the wide spectrum of biomedical signal processing from an organ to a subcellular level and the similarities of the signal processing approaches used for these different scaling dimensions.

Exercises

I. Translate the following sentences into Chinese.

1. Telemedicine has proven to be effective as a disaster response, a meaningful aid for the third world, care for the elderly and chronically ill in their homes, as well as a provider of health care to remote or isolated areas.

2. The continued surgical procedure is in certain cases dependent on this type of

pathology service, and hospitals without access to frozen section service cannot treat such patients, but has to refer them to another hospital.

3. The importance of early brain development in setting the foundations for language is apparent in babies younger than 6 months.

4. These are typical cases where use of telediagnostics would strongly benefit the patients, and at the same time reduce costs and free medical resources.

5. Whether telemedicine will be a general success will to a large extent depend on whether or not one manages to meet the real challenge — to make such systems work as close to the standard methods as possible, employing telecommunication systems available on a general basis, and with acceptable quality and costs.

6. A telediagnostic approach would require approximately 20 randomly selected images with standard resolution in black and white (512×512 pixels with 8 bit resolution per pixel) which can be transferred over a standard ISDN channel within less than six minutes.

II Choose the phrase that is closest in meaning to the underlined part.

1. In developing countries a new way of practicing telemedicine is emerging whereby devices examine a patient and a connected doctor residing in another location virtually examines the patient and treat him.

    A. an online doctor in a different place actually provides examination and treatment to the patient

    B. a related doctor in a separate location provides virtual service to examine and treat the patient

    C. a doctor concerned in another place does simulated checks and treatment for the patient

    D. a doctor connected to another place makes simulations of tests and operations to the patient

2. This new technology and principle of practicing medicine holds big promises to solving major health care delivery problems in for instance Southern Africa because it not only monitors an already diagnosed chronic disease, but has the promise to diagnosing and managing the diseases a patient will typically visit a general practitioner for.

    A. solving the problems of careful health insurance for places such as Southern Africa

    B. providing health care mainly to the areas like Southern Africa

    C. treating the majority of health care problems in Southern Africa

    D. dealing with the problem of providing health care in places like Southern Africa

3. His invention showed that it is possible to compute high-quality images with high accuracy in spite of the fact that the projection data do not strictly satisfy the theoretical models underlying the reconstruction algorithms.

    A. do not completely fit the models in theory under the algorithm for reconstruction

    B. do not rigorously agree with the theory that is the basis of the reconstruction algorithm

    C. do not meet the requirement of underlying algorithm for image reconstruction in theory

    D. do not consist of the theoretical models under the reconstructed algorithm

4. Changes were made to add key missing features and to enable more efficient implementation by eliminating some instructions and <u>relaxing the specification to eliminate some troublesome special cases</u>.

    A. making specific problems less troublesome

    B. loosen technical requirements to reduce troubles

    C. reducing special difficulties by eliminating

    D. removing special troubles by relating the specifications with the instructions

5. It is possible to compute high-quality cross-sectional images <u>with an accuracy now reaching one part in a thousand</u>.

    A. precisely without causing errors equal to one thousand

    B. accurately enough so that the error is on the order of one thousandth

    C. with a precision of one thousand times better than the reached part

    D. being accurate in part so that it reaches one thousand

6. Not until recently had anyone demonstrated a unified approach that not only allows previously obtained complicated results to be simplified both analytically and computationally but also permits new results to be obtained for special cases <u>that had resisted solution in a simple form</u>.

    A. that had resistance against formality of sample solutions

    B. that had prevented people from obtaining simple-form solutions

    C. that had restricted solution to a simple form

    D. that had resolved in the form of simplified solution

7. <u>Off-the-shelf multimedia platforms</u> reduce various tailor made components facing end users by packaging the needed functionality into a single product.

    A. Specially manufactured multimedia platforms

    B. Multimedia platforms mounted on the shelf

    C. Readily available multimedia platforms

    D. Multimedia platforms that are taken from the shelf

8. These are typical cases where use of telediagnostics would strongly benefit the patients, and at the same time <u>reduce healthcare costs and free medical resources</u>.

    A. make the healthcare less costly and medical resources free of charge

    B. reduce the free medical resources in terms of healthcare costs

    C. lower the expenses of healthcare and make medical resources available to more people

    D. let the healthcare cost less and even use no medical resources

Unit 14　Computers and Networks

Computers are the future whether we like it or not. Computers are not exactly the easiest tools to work with, but they are the most rewarding. Computer networks are everywhere: neither big nor small firms can live without them, not to mention computer departments, public offices, and even private users. Internet is nothing more than a vast set of interconnected smaller networks.

Text

Part I: Evolution of Computers

The evolution of computers and information technology

The birth of computers and information technology goes back many centuries. The development of mathematics led to the development of tools to help in computation. Blaise Pascal, in 17th century France, was credited with building the first calculating machine. In the 19th century, the Englishman Charles Babbage, generally considered the father of computing, designed the first "analytical engine." This machine had a mechanical computing "mill" and, like the Jacquard loom of the early 19th century, used punch cards to store the numbers and processing requirements. Ada Lovelace worked on the design with him and developed the idea of a sequence of instructions — a program. The machine was not complete at Babbage's death in 1871.

Almost a century later, the ideas re-emerged with the development of electro-mechanical calculating machines. In 1890, Herman Hollerith used punch cards to help classify information for the United States Census Bureau. At the same time, the invention of the telegraph and telephone laid the groundwork for telecommunications and the development of the vacuum tube. This electronic device could be used to store information represented as binary patterns — on or off, one or zero.

The first electronic digital computer, ENIAC (Electronic Numerical Integrator and Computer, see Figure 14.1), was developed for the U.S. Army and completed in 1946. Von

Neumann, a Princeton mathematics professor, developed the idea further. He added the idea of a stored computer program. This was a set of instructions stored in the computer memory, which the computer obeyed to complete the programmed task.

Figure 14.1   ENIAC: the first electronic digital computer

From this stage, computers and computer programming evolved rapidly. The move from vacuum tubes to transistors significantly reduced the size and cost of the machines, and increased their reliability. Then came integrated circuit technology, which has reduced the size (and cost) of computers. In the 1960s, the typical computer was a transistor-based machine that cost half a million dollars, and needed a large, air-conditioned room and an on-site engineer. The same computer power now costs $2,000 and sits on a desk. As computers became smaller and cheaper, they also became faster – made possible by a single integrated circuit called a chip.

The evolution of microprocessors and microcomputers

The evolution of microcomputers follows the evolution of integrated circuit (or chip) technology. This technology allows computer logic to be "burnt into" the layers of a chip. A 5 mm^2 chip can contain all the logic needed for a computer processor to run programs. This technological breakthrough made possible a massive reduction in the size of computers, especially compared to transistor-based logic, where components were wired onto boards.[1] The size reduction enabled logic switching at many millions of times a second.

Large-scale integrated circuits appeared in the early 1970s. The development that allowed the processor to fit on a chip also allowed chips to be used for memory, replacing the expensive ferrite core memory. These advances led to the birth of the microcomputer (or personal computer), initially aimed at the hobbyist market. By the early 1970s, machines were being produced for home and office use. Of all the early microcomputers, the Apple and IBM (Figure 14.2) families of machines have survived to become the major players in the market.

Figure 14.2   IBM's personal computer

The operating system is the software that provides an interface between the hardware (the computer itself) and the user. It manages the hardware and enables the user to control the computer. Microsoft developed the first operating system for IBM machines, MS DOS (Microsoft Disk Operating System), the grandfather of the current DOS and Windows systems. Many manufacturers developed clones (or copies) of the IBM machines that could run with MS DOS. The IBM family is based on the Intel 8086 family of chips, which evolved into the high-speed Pentium chips later. At the same time, the Apple Computer Company started its family of machines. They first became popular with the launch of the Apple 2E computer, followed by the Macintosh series; all based on the Motorola 68000 family of microprocessor chips.

As the technology evolved, the number of circuits that could go on a chip grew. Very large-scale integration (VLSI) chip switching rates were measured in hundreds of millions of switchings per second. VLSI technology has enabled personal computers to have a processing speed hundreds of times faster than the early chips.

This additional processing power was paralleled by a growth in the capacity and speed of memory chips. Again, automation of manufacturing and miniaturization were the key factors. Peripheral devices (hardware components that provide the means for input, output and storage) also developed in speed and other capabilities to keep pace with the increased function of the computers themselves.[2] Monitors, printers and storage devices all evolved rapidly with both improved application of existing technology and the introduction of new technologies. There were even new classes of peripheral devices, such as scanners and sound synthesizers, which further enhanced and broadened the ways in which computers could be used.

For example, there was a transition from early monochrome monitors for output display of text only to color monitors with graphics capability. The storage capacity of disk drives has increased dramatically, from drives whose capacity was measured in kilobytes (1000 bytes), to those whose capacity is measured in gigabytes (1,000,000,000 bytes).

The motherboard is the main component of any computer, containing the microprocessor and memory chips. It also contains the bus, a high-speed link that enables all the peripheral devices attached to your machine to communicate with each other and the microprocessor. Some peripherals are in the form of circuit boards that plug into the motherboard bus, while others are external devices which connect using a cable. Most peripherals have some onboard logic.

Most remarkable in this massive increase in the power and versatility of microcomputers is the fact that it has been achieved at no price increase to the user, because of manufacturing improvements made possible by automation and miniaturization.[3] A state-of-the-art personal computer costs about the same today as it did in 1980 — less if you account for inflation.

As computers have become more powerful, much of this additional computing power has been used up by software that makes computers easier to use.[4] Mass marketing of personal computers relies on a product for the work place or home that does not require the user to undergo extensive training. The software evolution began with the XEROX Company, which developed a graphical interface and a mouse to select the operations to perform, rather than using command keys. The idea of a graphical user interface (GUI) was taken on by the Apple Company and used on its Mac range of computers. These "point-and-click" machines set a standard for usability that was emulated by the Windows GUI now used on every personal computer.

Microcomputer technology is still evolving. Later computers were enabled to accommodate voice input and output. The development and widespread use of powerful communications tools for computers led to the mass popularization of the Internet, which is fueling another growth spurt in the industry and its technology.[5] Continuing success in the market place depends on the continual development of software to make machines both easier to use and more versatile. Microcomputer software is developing in the direction of artificial intelligence. One example of this is "smart" business software that helps the user make decisions by analyzing data for patterns of behavior and then applying those patterns to new situations.[6]

Using microcomputers

The first tools to be used widely on microcomputers were word processors, spreadsheets, and database systems. The "big three" enabled the computer to become useful very quickly, as users did not need specialized programming knowledge. The word processor has grown from a simple letter-writing tool to a product capable of desktop publishing. The spreadsheet has grown to incorporate standard tools for statistical and financial analysis, custom programming, and producing high-quality graphics. The microcomputer database has grown from a simple file-management tool to one that handles complex applications across multiple files.[7]

Integrated packages like Microsoft Office enable the application modules to "talk to each other." With these packages, you can develop a report in a word processor that includes graphs from spreadsheets that were developed from data selected from database records.[8] Further to that, you can now create a "living" document. As data in the spreadsheet changes, the report changes. Links between the tools are embedded in the document. The Microsoft version of this is called "Object Linking and Embedding." You may add other pictures from graphical libraries and import materials via the Internet using built-in communications software. The whole document is professionally presented using a word processor or multimedia presentation manager. The word processor can also check spelling and grammar, as well as create the table of contents and indexes. An integrated package may include a professional presentation manager that allows you to develop slide shows that can then be delivered on the computer or any screen.

Client/server technology allows different microcomputers to share information, access files, printers, etc., and communicate with each other. A parallel development, called workgroup computing, has focused on software that automates the flow of information in an organization to facilitate electronic conferencing and similar activities.

In addition, there are a vast number of more specialized applications packages such as Corel Draw for graphics; AutoCAD for design drawings; and financial software such as ACCPAC for automating bookkeeping and accounting functions. New uses for computer technology are found daily, in medicine, education, the arts and every other field of human endeavor.

Issues of compatibility between platforms are being resolved. Most major software products can now process the data created using the major competitors' products. Users need a smooth transition from older software products to new ones, as they often have a significant investment in the records that exist on their computers. In general, newer software can automatically translate documents produced in earlier software applications.

Part II : Local Area Networks

The need for LANs

Perhaps the driving force behind the widespread use of LANs is the dramatic and continuing decrease in computer hardware costs, accompanied by an increase in computer hardware capability. Year by year, the cost of computer systems continues to drop dramatically while the performance and capacity of those systems continue to rise equally dramatically. This ongoing technological revolution has enabled the development of applications of astounding complexity and power. For example, desktop applications that require the great power of today's microprocessor-based systems include the following:

- Image processing
- Speech recognition
- Video conferencing
- Multimedia authoring
- Voice and video annotation of files

Workstation systems now support highly sophisticated engineering and scientific applications, as well as simulation systems, and the ability to apply workgroup principles to image and video applications.[1] In addition, businesses are relying on increasingly powerful servers to handle transaction and database processing and to support massive client/server networks that have replaced the huge mainframe computer centers of yesteryear.[2]

All of these factors lead to an increased number of systems, with increased power, at a single site: office building, factory, operations center, and so on. At the same time, there is an absolute requirement to interconnect these systems to share and exchange data among systems, and to share expensive resources.

The need to share data is a compelling reason for interconnection. Individual users of computer resources don't work in isolation. They need facilities to exchange messages with other users, to access data from several sources in the preparation of a document or for an analysis, and to share project-related information with other members of a workgroup.[3]

The need to share expensive resources is another driving factor in the development of networks. The cost of processor hardware has dropped far more rapidly than the cost of mass storage devices, video equipment, printers, and other peripheral devices. The result is a need to share these expensive devices among a number of users to justify the cost of the equipment. This sharing requires some sort of client/server architecture operating over a LAN that interconnects users and resources.

LAN applications

The variety of applications for LANs is wide. To provide some insight into the types of requirements that LANs are intended to meet, the following sections discuss some of the most important general application areas for these networks.

Personal computer LANs

A common LAN configuration is one that supports personal computers. With the relatively low cost of such systems, individual managers within organizations often independently procure personal computers for departmental applications, such as spreadsheet and project management tools, and for Internet access.[4]

But a collection of department-level processors won't meet all of an organization's needs; central processing facilities are still required. Some programs, such as econometric forecasting models, are too big to run on a small computer. Corporate-wide data files, such as accounting and payroll, require a centralized facility but should be accessible to a number of users. In addition, there are other kinds of files that, although specialized, must be shared by a number of users. Further, there are sound reasons for connecting individual intelligent workstations not only to a central facility but to each other as well.[5] Members of a project or organization team need to share work and information. By far the most efficient way to do so is to establish a network.

Certain expensive resources, such as a disk or a laser printer, can be shared by all users of the departmental LAN. In addition, the network can tie into larger corporate network facilities. For example, the corporation may have a building-wide LAN and a wide area private network. A communications server can provide controlled access to these resources.

LANs for the support of personal computers and workstations have become nearly universal in organizations of all sizes. Even those sites that still depend heavily on the mainframe have transferred much of the processing load to networks of personal computers. Perhaps the prime example of the way in which personal computers are being used is to implement client/server applications.

For personal computer networks, a key requirement is low cost. In particular, the cost of attachment to the network must be significantly less than the cost of the attached device. Thus, for the ordinary personal computer, an attachment cost in the hundreds of dollars is desirable. For more expensive, high-performance workstations, higher attachment costs can be tolerated. In any case, this suggests that the data rate of the network may be limited; in general, the higher the data rate, the higher the cost.

Back-end networks and storage area networks

Back-end networks are used to interconnect large systems such as mainframes, supercomputers, and mass storage devices. The key requirement here is for bulk data transfer among a limited number of devices in a small area. High reliability is generally also a requirement. These are some typical characteristics:

- High data rate. To satisfy the high-volume demand, data rates of 100 Mbps or more are required.
- High-speed interface. Data transfer operations between a large host system and a mass storage device are typically performed through high-speed parallel I/O interfaces, rather than slower communications interfaces. Thus, the physical link between station and network must be high speed.
- Distributed access. Some sort of distributed medium access control (MAC) technique is needed to enable a number of devices to share the medium with efficient and reliable access.
- Limited distance. Typically, a back-end network will be employed in a computer room or a small number of contiguous rooms.
- Limited number of devices. The number of expensive mainframes and mass storage devices found in the computer room generally numbers in the tens of devices.[6]

Back-end networks are commonly found at sites of large companies or research installations with large data-processing budgets. Because of the scale involved, a small difference in productivity can mean millions of dollars.

Consider a site that uses a dedicated mainframe computer. This implies a fairly large application or set of applications. As the load at the site grows, the existing mainframe may be replaced by a more powerful one, perhaps a multiprocessor system. At some sites, a single-system replacement won't be able to keep up; equipment performance growth rates will be exceeded by demand growth rates. The facility will eventually require multiple independent computers. Again, there are compelling reasons for interconnecting these systems. The cost of system interrupt is high, so it should be possible — easily and quickly — to shift applications to backup systems.[7] It must be possible to test new procedures and applications without degrading the production system. Large bulk-storage files must be accessible from more than one computer. Load leveling should be possible to maximize utilization and performance.

Obviously, some key requirements for back-end networks are the opposite of those for personal computer LANs. High data rates are required to keep up with the work, which typically involves the transfer of large blocks of data. The equipment for achieving high speeds is expensive. Fortunately, given the much higher cost of the attached devices, such costs are reasonable.[8]

A concept related to that of the back-end network is the storage area network (SAN). A SAN is a separate network to handle storage needs. The SAN unties storage tasks from specific servers and creates a shared storage facility across a high-speed network. The collection of networked storage devices can include hard disks, tape libraries, and CD arrays. Most SANs use fiber channels. In a typical large LAN installation, with a number of servers and perhaps mainframes, each has its own dedicated storage devices. If a client needs access to a particular storage device, it must go through the server that controls that device. In a SAN, no server sits between the storage devices and the network; instead, the storage devices and servers are linked directly to the network. The SAN arrangement improves client-to-storage access efficiency, as well as direct storage-to-storage communications for backup and replication functions.

High-speed office networks

Traditionally, the office environment has included a variety of devices with low- to medium-speed data transfer requirements. However, new applications in the office environment have been developed for which the limited speeds (up to 10 Mbps) of the traditional LAN are inadequate. Desktop image processors have increased network data flow by an unprecedented amount. Examples of these applications include fax machines, document image processors, and graphics programs on personal computers and workstations. Consider that a typical page with 200 picture elements, or pixels (black or white points), per inch resolution (which is adequate but not high resolution) generates 3,740,000 bits (8.5 inches × 11 inches × 40,000 pixels per square inch).[9] Even with compression techniques, this generates a tremendous load. In addition, disk technology and price/performance have evolved so that desktop storage capacities in the gigabyte range are typical. These new demands require LANs with high speed that can support the larger numbers and greater geographic extent of office systems as compared to back-end systems.[10]

Backbone LANs

The increasing use of distributed processing applications and personal computers has led to a need for a flexible strategy for local networking. Support of premises-wide data communications requires a networking service that is capable of spanning the distances involved and that interconnects equipment in a single (perhaps large) building or a cluster of buildings.[11] Although it is possible to develop a single LAN to interconnect all the data-processing equipment on the premises, this is probably not a practical alternative in most cases. There are several drawbacks to a single LAN strategy:

- Reliability. With a single LAN, a service interruption, even of short duration, could result in a major disruption for users.
- Capacity. A single LAN could be saturated as the number of devices attached to the network grows over time.
- Cost. A single LAN technology is not optimized for the diverse requirements of interconnection and communication. The presence of large numbers of low-cost microcomputers dictates that network support for these devices can be provided at low cost. LANs that support very low cost attachment will not be suitable for meeting the overall requirement.

A more attractive alternative is to employ lower-cost, lower-capacity LANs within buildings or departments and to interconnect these networks with a higher-capacity LAN. This latter network is referred to as a backbone LAN.

Factory LANs

The factory environment is increasingly being dominated by automated equipment: programmable controllers, automated materials-handling devices, time and attendance stations, machine vision devices, and various forms of robots. To manage the production or manufacturing process, it is essential to tie this equipment together. And, indeed, the very nature of the equipment facilitates this.[12] Microprocessor devices have the potential to collect information from the shop floor and accept commands. With the proper use of the information and commands, it is possible to improve the manufacturing process and to provide detailed machine control.

The more a factory is automated, the greater the need for communications. Only by interconnecting all the devices and by providing mechanisms for their cooperation can the automated factory be made to work.[13] The means for interconnection is the factory LAN. Key characteristics of a factory LAN include the following:

- High capacity
- Ability to handle a variety of data traffic
- Large geographic extent
- High reliability
- Ability to specify and control transmission delays

Factory LANs are a niche market requiring, in general, more flexible and reliable LANs than are found in the typical office environment.

Summary

LANs are used to support a wide variety of requirements and a range of applications, as we have just seen. However, the basic technology used for these various purposes is the same. This common technology and the use of standards have promoted the widespread proliferation of LANs in a broad range of settings.

New Words

Part I

analytical	分析的	mill	作坊，工厂
loom	织布机	punch card	穿孔卡片
census	人口普查	vacuum	真空，真空的
integrator	积分机	breakthrough	突破
massive	巨大的	ferrite core memory	铁磁芯存储器
clone	克隆	switching rate	切换速度
parallel	平行，相比	miniaturization	小型化
peripheral	外围	keep pace with …	与……保持一致的步伐
synthesizer	合成器	monochrome	单色的
motherboard	母板	onboard logic	（电路）板上逻辑
versatility	多用途，多样性	state of the art	最新的
inflation	通货膨胀	used up	竭尽全力的，用尽了
useability	可用性	emulate	效法，模仿
popularization	大众化，流行	spurt	冲刺，喷射
artificial intelligence	人工智能	word processor	文字处理软件
spreadsheet	电子表格	embed	嵌入
professionally	专业地	slide show	幻灯放映
client/server	客户/服务器	automate	使自动
facilitate	使容易，促进	conferencing	举行会议
bookkeeping	簿记	accounting	会计学，记账
endeavor	努力，尽力	compatibility	兼容性
competitor	竞争者，竞争对手	investment	投资

Part II

ongoing	进行中的	astounding	令人惊骇的
speech recognition	语音识别	multimedia authoring	多媒体制作
annotation	注释，评注	transaction	办理，交割
mainframe	中央主机	yesteryear	去年，以往，不久前
compelling	强制的	justify	证明是必要的

architecture	建筑，结构	configuration	配置
procure	获得，取得	payroll	工资单，员工清单
intelligent	智能的	corporate	公司的，合伙的
corporation	公司	universal	普遍的，宇宙的
attachment	添加，附加	back-end	后端
supercomputer	超级计算机	bulk	大块，体积
interface	接口	distributed	分布式的，分散的
Medium Access		contiguous	邻接的
Control (MAC)	媒体访问控制	research installation	研究机构
budget	预算	dedicated	专用的，奉献的
multiprocessor	多处理器	interrupt	中断
backup	备份，后备	utilization	利用
load leveling	负载平衡	untie	解开，松开
tape library	磁带库	fiber	纤维，光纤
replication	复制	transfer	迁移，传递
inadequate	不够的	unprecedented	前所未有的
resolution	分辨率	compression	压缩
backbone	骨干，基干	flexible	灵活的
premises	（经营）场地	cluster	群，族
drawback	缺点	duration	期间
saturate	饱和	diverse	多变化的，多元的
dictate	口授，说明	dominate	支配，占优势
programmable		time and	
controller	可编程控制器	attendance station	考勤系统
attendance	出席	machine vision	机器视觉
robot	机器人	shop floor	车间现场
mechanism	机制	data traffic	数据流
niche	有利可图的专门市场	promote	促进，推销
proliferation	激增	setting	环境，背景

Notes on the Text

Part I

1. This technological breakthrough made possible a massive reduction in the size of computers, especially compared to transistor-based logic, where components were wired onto boards.

这一技术突破使得计算机的体积大大缩小，特别是相比于元件联接在电路板上的晶体管逻辑电路。

2. Peripheral devices (hardware components that provide the means for input, output and storage) also developed in speed and other capabilities to keep pace with the increased function of the computers themselves.

外围设备（提供输入、输出、存储手段的硬件设备）也在速度和其他功能方面得到发展，以保持与计算机本身功能的同步增长。

3. Most remarkable in this massive increase in the power and versatility of microcomputers is the fact that it has been achieved at no price increase to the user, because of manufacturing improvements made possible by automation and miniaturization.

在微计算机功能和用途的巨大增长中最令人瞩目的事实是：这种增长在不提高用户承担的价格情况下实现，因为自动化和小型化使得制造工艺的改进成为可能。

4. As computers have become more powerful, much of this additional computing power has been used up by software that makes computers easier to use.

随着计算机功能变得更加强大，所增加的大部分功能都被使计算机更易使用的软件用足了。

5. The development and widespread use of powerful communications tools for computers led to the mass popularization of the Internet, which is fueling another growth spurt in the industry and its technology.

计算机强大的通信工具的发展和广泛使用使互联网大为普及，又引起了（计算机）工业和相关技术的新一轮发展高潮。

6. One example of this is "smart" business software that helps the user make decisions by analyzing data for patterns of behavior and then applying those patterns to new situations.

一个例子是"聪明"商务软件，它帮助用户分析行为模式数据并将这些模式用于新的情况，据此作出决策。

   • 注意 analyzing data 和 applying patterns 并列。

7. The microcomputer database has grown from a simple file-management tool to one that handles complex applications across multiple files.

微机数据库已从一个简单的文档管理工具发展成为在多文档之间处理复杂应用的工具。

8. With these packages, you can develop a report in a word processor that includes graphs from spreadsheets that were developed from data selected from database records.

有了这些软件包，你可以在文字处理器中创建报告，其中包括由电子表格所产生的图，电子表格又是根据数据库中选择的数据制作的。

Part II

1. Workstation systems now support highly sophisticated engineering and scientific applications, as well as simulation systems, and the ability to apply workgroup

principles to image and video applications.

现在工作站系统支持极为复杂的工程和科学应用，也支持仿真系统，以及将工作组原则用于图像和视频应用中。

2. In addition, businesses are relying on increasingly powerful servers to handle transaction and database processing and to support massive client/server networks that have replaced the huge mainframe computer centers of yesteryear.

此外，商业事务正在依赖于愈来愈强大的服务器来进行交易和数据库处理，支持已经取代了以往大型中央计算机的大规模的客户/服务器网络。

3. They need facilities to exchange messages with other users, to access data from several sources in the preparation of a document or for an analysis, and to share project-related information with other members of a workgroup.

他们需要拥有手段与其他用户交换信息，在准备文件或作分析时访问多来源数据，与工作组其他成员共享与项目有关的信息。

4. With the relatively low cost of such systems, individual managers within organizations often independently procure personal computers for departmental applications, such as spreadsheet and project management tools, and for Internet access.

由于这种系统相对较低的价格，机构中个别经理人员常为本部门的应用如电子表格和项目管理工具、访问互联网而独立购买个人计算机。

5. Further, there are sound reasons for connecting individual intelligent workstations not only to a central facility but to each other as well.

而且有充足理由将各个智能工作站不仅与中央设备相联，还要彼此相联。

6. The number of expensive mainframes and mass storage devices found in the computer room generally numbers in the tens of devices.

计算机房中昂贵的主机和大容量存储装置的数量一般以几十台计。

   - 第一个 number 是主语，第二个 numbers 是谓语动词。

7. The cost of system interrupt is high, so it should be possible — easily and quickly — to shift applications to backup systems.

系统中断的代价是高昂的，所以应该具有方便而快捷地将应用转移到备份系统的能力。

8. The equipment for achieving high speeds is expensive. Fortunately, given the much higher cost of the attached devices, such costs are reasonable.

实现高速度的设备是昂贵的。幸亏考虑到附加在上面的设备更要贵得多，这种价格还是合理的。

   - given ... 考虑到（这里作介词）

9. Consider that a typical page with 200 picture elements, or pixels (black or white points), per inch resolution (which is adequate but not high resolution) generates 3,740,000 bits (8.5 inches × 11 inches × 40,000 pixels per square inch).

考虑典型的一页（文档）上每英寸 200 个图像单元（像素，即黑白的点）的分辨率（足够但不是高分辨率的），它产生 3,740,000 比特的数据，即 8.8 英寸乘以 11 英寸乘以每平方英寸 40,000 像素。

10. These new demands require LANs with high speed that can support the larger numbers and greater geographic extent of office systems as compared to back-end systems.

这些新的需求对高速局域网提出了要求，相比于后端（备）系统，这种局域网能支持数量更大、地域分布更广的办公系统。

11. Support of premises-wide data communications requires a networking service that is capable of spanning the distances involved and that interconnects equipment in a single (perhaps large) building or a cluster of buildings.

对整个公司范围内数据通信的支持要求具有这样的网络服务，它能够跨越所涉及的距离，并能将一座大楼（或一群楼宇）内的设备相联。

- premises-wide 指整个场所（如 world-wide, nation-wide）。

12. To manage the production or manufacturing process, it is essential to tie this equipment together. And, indeed, the very nature of the equipment facilitates this.

为了管理生产或制造过程，必须将这些设备联在一起。确实是这样，这些设备的性质本身就是能够提供这种互联。

- 注意 equipment 是不可数名词，但应译成复数。

13. Only by interconnecting all the devices and by providing mechanisms for their cooperation can the automated factory be made to work.

只有将所有的设备互联，提供协同工作的机制，才能使自动化工厂运作。

- Only ... can the factory be made to work. 倒装句表示强调。

Technical Tips

Operating system

An operating system (OS) is a set of computer programs that manage the hardware and software resources of a computer. An operating system processes raw system and user input and responds by allocating and managing tasks and internal system resources as a service to users and programs of the system. At the foundation of all system software, an operating system performs basic tasks such as controlling and allocating memory, prioritizing system requests, controlling input and output devices, facilitating networking and managing file systems.

Local area network (LAN)

A local area network (LAN) is a computer network covering a small geographic area, like a home, office, or group of buildings. The defining characteristics of LANs, in contrast to wide area networks (WANs), include their much higher data transfer rates, smaller geographic range, and lack of a need for leased telecommunication lines. Ethernet over twisted pair cabling and Wi-Fi are the two most common technologies currently, but

ARCNET, token ring and many others have been used in the past.

Supplementary Readings

1. The Information Based Society
The development of the information based society

The transition from an agricultural society to an industrial society took centuries, but the change from an industrial society to one based on information is happening in decades. The main engine for the change has been the computer. Mass-production techniques have reduced the cost of computer power so that the machine which cost half a million dollars 30 years ago is now available for $1000 and users no longer need years of specialized training.

Just as the industrial society was based on manufacturing, the information society focuses on the use of information as a resource. The application of computers to business uses is called "information technology." The "knowledge worker" is the person who earns his or her living using information. The "information age" and the increase in knowledge workers began in the 1960s, made possible by the rapid evolution of information technology over the last half century. Many of the jobs that will be available in five years have not yet been invented. New jobs are replacing the old manual labor and clerical jobs, and reducing the large administrative bureaucracies of earlier years.

The ability to record, synthesize, and use information has helped to simplify work processes and to increase productivity. The computer has enabled automation of the plants that manufacture the products people consume. Industrial robots and large-scale automation of manufacturing processes has enabled widespread access to affordable goods. The use of technology to lever performance has led to the re-engineering of business. Computer technology enabled the move from mass production to mass customization. For example, if you want to remodel your kitchen, you can go to a store and work with a computer that will help you design your kitchen, see what it will look like and how much it will cost. This is computer-aided design (CAD). With virtual reality (VR) software, you can "move around" in your proposed kitchen. When you are satisfied with the design, the computer will develop the list of parts, produce the design drawings, and so on. In some applications, this customized-design information is then fed into the manufacturing system (computer-aided manufacturing, or CAM) of automated factories.

The computer also manages the masses of information needed to organize this increased complexity. Markets are now defined in world terms. Increasingly, people are working from home on their desktop computers. Computer-based technologies are being invented to help people cope with the wealth of information now available on desktop computers. Students can do courses in the same way and use the technology to aid in their learning processes. You are participating in this evolution now.

The rapid growth of telecommunications and its merging with computing technology has enabled you to use your computer to communicate world-wide. The infrastructure to allow computers to connect with each other was already in place when the personal computer started to become widespread. The parallel growth of telecommunications has been described as having the roads, garages, and maintenance infrastructure in place when the first mass-produced cars rolled off the assembly line at the Ford plant.

You may gather information from computers in different countries by using the Internet. This gives you a constantly changing perspective on information technology, which would not be possible using a single textbook. Ten years ago, this was an impossible concept. Like any technology, computer is only a tool that amplifies our abilities to do things. Information technology can be used in useful, frivolous, or harmful ways.

Managing information

The key to handling the masses of information needed to manage our complex society is information technology. Banks, utility companies, government and businesses all use computers to record, organize, summarize and synthesize their information. Historically, information management systems have been the largest component of our use of computers, but other, more broadly-based uses are growing rapidly.

Information technology benefits us mainly by speeding up the manipulation of data. It minimizes the handling of information to speed storage and retrieval. It also provides tools that allow the data to be easily queried and summarized. Previously, administrators would be responsible for gathering, filtering, and distributing information. Now, that information is directly available to the front-line users who need it to do their jobs.

The addition of communications technology has made many business operations "distance insensitive." There is no longer the need to travel in order to visit different sites in a geographically dispersed company. Teleconferencing allows people to meet electronically, while computers allow them to share information electronically.

Here are some specific examples of information systems in practical use.

- Utility bills. These are "turn-around" documents. The bill acts as a payment document. It contains machine-readable portions that are returned to the company along with payment. Some utility companies also provide the customer with historical data showing the consumption over the last year. This is presented in graphic form, made possible by the laser technology now used to print bills.

- Credit cards. Again, the input/output aspects are fully automated. The sales clerk swipes your card and enters the transaction amount. The merchant's machine contacts the credit card company's computers. These computers then check your account and either authorize or reject the transaction. They keep a record of the transaction, and wait for the paper to follow from the merchant.

- Banking services. Banks have undergone significant changes to allow you worldwide access to your bank records 24 hours a day, seven days a week. The increase in Automated Teller Machines has enabled this to happen, with a consequential reduction of human teller positions. In some countries, bank machines include visual and audio contact, via small cameras and microphones. However, if you wish, you can talk to and see a real teller, who may be anywhere. In addition, banks now allow customers to bank from home using their computers.

These are a few examples of businesses providing added services to their customers without raising costs. In most cases, this is made possible by reducing human involvement in routine transactions.

It would be inaccurate to depict that all is well in the information age. Increasingly, industries compete in a world market, which means that people everywhere compete for the same jobs. The changes information technology has brought to our business and government organizations have not come easily. Organizations are grappling with fundamental changes to the way they do business. The process of change involves the re-education of every person in an organization, and some personal dislocation occurs as organizations try to adapt. There are successes and failures.

Information technology also affects those who may not even use it directly, and personal privacy is of serious concern. The protective measures needed to guarantee the confidentiality of personal information collected by organizations are of interest to everyone. One needs access to stored information about oneself and wants to be assured that mistakes in the information will be identified and corrected.

Careers in information technology

Information technology presents many career opportunities. The Software Human Resources Council of Canada indicates that there is a significant shortage in software workers. Projections indicate that 325,000 workers will be needed by the year 2100. At current graduation rates, the output from universities and colleges will not meet the demand.

The main sources of careers in information technology are either in a computer department of an organization (an "in-house worker"), a software company, or computer consultant. However, many organizations now "outsource" their information technology services. This allows an organization whose main business is not computer technology to have specialized computer skills available when needed.

Most careers in information technology are in the development, construction and maintenance of applications systems. A systems analyst analyses an organization's business requirements and current practices. Working with the organization and with this knowledge, the analyst develops a design for business systems using computer technology. These are passed on to the programmer, who builds the system. He or she works directly with the technology and the analysts to create the application (to develop and construct systems software). Applications development often relies on specialists in some aspect of the technology; for example, a programmer who is well versed in telecommunications protocols. A systems programmer usually works for a company who manufactures computers or the software tools used by applications builders, that is, the maintenance and support of applications. A range of professional staff maintain technical infrastructure (like computers and networks) or provide help and training to users of the applications. They are key personnel who need both technical and people skills to ensure that applications of the technology are well received and used.

2. Google Unveils "Universal Search"

Google something, anything. Behind the famous search box, you'll find a very different Google at play. The company's hyper-accurate algorithms, (you know, those mathematical formulas that deliver answers in a fraction of a second), now include video, maps, books, news, images and blogs. The additional features are rolled into all Google's search results, ranked by relevancy and presented in a complete list starting on the main home page. Previously, users needed to go to the company's specialized channels like "Video" "Maps" "Books" or "Images" to see results from different kinds of media. Google calls the tweaks to its search engine "universal search." It's all part of an ongoing, fundamental shift for the Internet giant, one the company hopes will enhance the hundreds of millions of searches it performs daily.

"It's essentially the largest revision we've made in the past two or three years," Sergey Brin, Google's co-founder and president of technology, tells TIME. "It's really a significant undertaking." But with a 64% share of the search market, far ahead of rivals Yahoo! (22%) and MSN (9%), according to Hitwise, an online market research firm, why do the world's most visited site and most valuable brand need to toy with a core product that isn't broken?

"We always have to improve our search," Brin says. "It's not something we consider not doing." Besides being a new strategic and technological focus for Google, universal search is designed to make finding things online simpler yet more comprehensive. "When you search for something, you're likely to get the right pieces of information from the right places by going straight to the Google search box," Brin adds. In other words, by going beyond the standard web pages for text-only results, Google is working harder to get you the answers you're after. It's also a way to stay in front of the competition, which has been melding other types of data into search results — though not to the extent that Google claims to be.

As the web continues to grow and more data is digitized, owning the fastest, most accurate and comprehensive navigational tool is essential to keeping users happy. It also makes sense for a company worth $146 billion and driven almost entirely by Internet search advertising revenue to continually seek out additional targeted ad opportunities around different types of search-related content. Universal search coupled with YouTube's vast video assets, purchased by Google last year for $1.65 billion, could mean video ads aren't far off. "It potentially means advertisers will have the ability to do graphical ads and video ads on Google's search results pages," says Danny Sullivan, a longtime search industry watcher and editor of the blog Search Engine Land. "The ability to get advertising on there has really been limited to textual ads, and now because they're putting graphics out there, it really opens up the possibilities."

Google's home page has been subtly redesigned to reflect the changes, too. Type a query into the search box and results automatically appear in whatever form and rank the search engine determines to be most relevant — whether it's text, video or a map — something Google contends its rivals don't do. For example, a search for "Beatles" reveals the best content types and presents them below the search box. In addition to web pages, Google shows us the most relevant results for the band found in "Music" "News" "Groups" "Blogs" and "Images," which appear in tabs. The familiar text-based results are still there, below the new tabs. The revamped search code's new video tab, for example, offers clips of the band's performances, plus a silly YouTube parody entitled "Indian Beatles: some kinda weird bollywood beatles clones."

Including video in search results, especially on the main home page, will probably be the most popular aspect of Google's big upgrade. Fans of Internet video can now fire up Google's powerful algorithms directly from the search box to find videos, including those not hosted by YouTube or Google Video. Results from independent video sites like Metacafe and dailymotion will appear as thumbnail images. From there, viewers can click on those to get to the host sites, while YouTube and Google-owned videos can be played directly from the main search results page.

Meanwhile, another helpful search feature, "Searches Related to..." now shows up more frequently at the end of each results page. This option helps users refine their searches by automatically offering up extra, contextually related topics for further exploration. In the Beatles example, "lyrics" "songs" "bios" and "history" are some of the categories suggested as click worthy.

Still, says Sullivan, it's important to realize these are just first steps. Universal search, introduced last week, is expected to improve over time. "It's not rolled out completely," he says. There is, however, the possibility that users will miss the old Google's clutter-free, text-only design. "It's possible," he noted. "To some degree this is kind of a gamble that they're making. But so far, I haven't heard a big huge screaming reaction from people."

So, will Google's re-tooling make us even more reliant on the world's master of search? "Our goal is not just to get people to spend more time on Google; it's for them to be able to accomplish more with Google," Brin says of the search phenomenon he helped create in 1996 as a grad school research project. "We actually want them to get more tasks done faster."

Exercises

I. Translate the following passages into Chinese.

1. For the first time ever the landscape is changing, as high volume personal computer

multimedia applications proliferate. First affected were monitors, which for some time have offered higher-than-broadcast speed and resolution. One can expect cameras to follow, with high-speed, high-resolution devices driven by consumer digital still camera technology and lower-resolution, ultra low cost units driven by entertainment, internet conferencing, and perceptual user interface applications.

2. If you already have the fastest CPU in a particular family and still want more performance, then it may be more cost-effective to add system RAM or cache RAM than to put in a processor from a different family. Adding system memory can bring significant performance increases at a relatively low cost, assuming you configure the memory correctly. In addition to added cache and system RAM, a faster and larger hard drive can save you time when running applications dependent on heavy drive access and data throughput. Adding a graphics accelerator card can help, too, especially if you are looking for a way to stay awake while your system redraws images.

3. In university environments, MATLAB has become the standard instructional tool for introductory courses in applied linear algebra, as well as advanced courses in other areas. In industrial settings, MATLAB is used for research and to solve practical engineering and mathematical problems. Typical uses include general purpose numerical computation, algorithm prototyping, and special purpose problem solving with matrix formulations that arise in disciplines such as automatic control theory, statistics, and digital signal processing (time-series analysis).

4. Multimedia is a generic term for "multimedia computing" or "interactive multimedia". The computer and software are used to control and navigate through the communications links, not only one at the time, but several simultaneously. Computer systems have been most developed in using vision and hearing to interface between the digital and analogue worlds, e.g., still and moving images, text and graphics use the visual senses, and audio uses hearing. Multimedia is defined as visual, audio and textual information which can be presented, separately or simultaneously, to convey and present information interactively to users. It is technically easy to digitize the analogue forms of these common media and handled by computers now widely available and inexpensive to be accessible to most users.

5. The essential capability of any multimedia computer system is the ability to convert the analogue signal to a digital format and to compress this information using standard algorithms. The power of the CPU will determine whether this process can be carried out in real-time or whether it has to be done off-line. Originally this power only existed in UNIX systems, but more recently it has become available in PCs and Macintosh. The compression process is necessary otherwise the quantity of data to be stored and transmitted would be excessive. Most PCs have until recently depended upon hardware encoding/decoding systems, but the speed of current

processors is such that software compression systems have been developed. The advantage of the software systems is that the compatibility and interoperability issues can be handled more easily, and the cost of the equipment is not raised by the need to purchase expensive hardware devices.

Ⅱ. Choose the phrase that is closest in meaning to the underlined part.

1. Most remarkable in this massive increase in the power and versatility of microcomputers is the fact that it has been achieved at no price increase to the user, because of <u>manufacturing improvements made possible by automation and miniaturization.</u>

   A. improvement in production that makes automation and miniaturization possible

   B. manufacturing improvements in possible automation and miniaturization

   C. improvements in production due to automation and miniaturization

   D. manufacturing process being improved based on possible automation and miniaturization

2. In addition, businesses are relying on increasingly powerful servers <u>to handle transaction and database processing</u> and to support massive client/server networks that have replaced the huge mainframe computer centers of yesteryear.

   A. to deal with business operations and database processing

   B. to treat and process database transmission

   C. to manipulate interaction of database operations

   D. to carry out interchange of data in the database

3. Support of premises-wide data communications requires a networking service <u>that is capable of spanning the distances involved</u> and that interconnects equipment in a single (perhaps large) building or a cluster of buildings.

   A. that can cross long distances of involvement

   B. that involves distance capable of covering the service cost

   C. that is able to support the distant involvement

   D. that can cover the necessary distances for the service

4. A new round of cyber warfare has already begun, which is characterized by the use of state-of-the-art computer-based technology and, in particular, rapid development of the Internet as <u>an increasingly important channel of information dissemination.</u>

   A. a path of information discrimination which is increasing and important

   B. a pathway of information spreading with ever-growing importance

   C. a transmission channel for more and more important information

   D. a channel for the passage of increasingly important information

5. Assembly language is a <u>machine-specific language</u> that uses symbolic instructions rather than the binary equivalents in the machine language for that machine.

   A. language related to a special computer

   B. language applicable to particular processors

   C. language installed in a specific machine

D. language independent of any computer

6. In microprocessors, the addition of new circuits, and the speed boost that comes from <u>reducing the distances between them</u>, has improved performance four- or five-fold every three years since Intel launched its x86 family in 1970.

A. making the difference between microprocessors smaller

B. making the speed of the new circuits closer to the microprocessors

C. making the circuits closer to each other

D. making the distances between microprocessors smaller

7. Many of these early systems had advantages that <u>seemed exciting and promising when demonstrated with "toy" programs</u>, but ran into difficulties when attempts were made to extend them to more realistically-sized programs.

A. showed attractiveness and usefulness for game applications

B. appeared attractive and hopeful when applied to small test programs

C. seemed to be excited and promised when used as demos in game applications

D. showed excitement and promises when executing unrealistic programs

8. Mathematical models of the automobile bodies are fed into the computer. Based upon these models the computer generates <u>the perspective views</u>.

A. the proportional views

B .the three-dimensional views

C. the provable views

D. the prospective views

Unit 15

Artificial Intelligence

Artificial intelligence is the area of computer science focusing on creating machines that can engage on behaviors that humans consider intelligent. The ability to create intelligent machines has intrigued humans since ancient times. Today with the advent of the computer and 50 years of research into AI programming techniques, the dream of smart machines is becoming a reality.

Text

Part I: What Is Artificial Intelligence

Artificial Intelligence, or AI for short, is a combination of computer science, physiology, and philosophy. AI is a broad topic, consisting of different fields, from machine vision to expert systems. The element that the fields of AI have in common is the creation of machines that can "think".

In order to classify machines as "thinking", it is necessary to define intelligence. To what degree does intelligence consist of, for example, solving complex problems, or making generalizations and relationships?[1] What about perception and comprehension? Research into the areas of learning, of language, and of sensory perception has aided scientists in building intelligent machines. One of the most challenging approaches facing experts is building systems that mimic the behavior of the human brain, made up of billions of neurons, and arguably the most complex matter in the universe. Perhaps the best way to assess the intelligence of a machine is British computer scientist Alan Turing's test(Figure 15.1). He stated that a computer would deserve to be called intelligent if it could deceive a human into believing that it was human.[2]

Artificial Intelligence has come a long way from its early roots, driven by dedicated researchers. The beginnings of AI reach back before electronics, to philosophers and mathematicians such as Boole and others theorizing on principles that were used as the foundation of AI Logic. AI really began to intrigue researchers with the invention of the computer in 1943. The technology was finally available, or so it seemed, to simulate intelligent behavior.[3] Over the next four decades, despite many stumbling blocks, AI has grown from a dozen researchers, to thousands of engineers and specialists; and from programs capable of playing checkers, to systems designed to diagnose disease.

Figure 15.1   Alan Turing

AI has always been on the pioneering end of computer science. Advanced-level computer languages, as well as computer interfaces and word-processors owe their existence to the research into artificial intelligence.[4] The theory and insights brought about by AI research will set the trend in the future of computing. The products available today are only bits and pieces of what are soon to follow, but they are a movement towards the future of artificial intelligence. The advancements in the quest for artificial intelligence have, and will continue to affect our jobs, our education, and our lives.

Use AI as it is intended

We have been studying this issue of AI application for quite some time now and know all the terms and facts. But what we all really need to know is what we can do to get our hands on some AI today. How can we as individuals use our own technology?

First, we should be prepared for a change. Our conservative ways stand in the way of progress. AI is a new step that is very helpful to the society. Machines can do jobs that require detailed instructions followed and mental alertness. AI with its learning capabilities can accomplish those tasks but only if the world's conservatives are ready to change and allow this to be a possibility.[5] It makes us think about how early man finally accepted the wheel as a good invention, not something taking away from its heritage or tradition.

Secondly, we must be prepared to learn about the capabilities of AI. The more use we get out of the machines the less work is required by us. In turn less injuries and stress to human beings. Human beings are a species that learn by trying, and we must be prepared to give AI a chance seeing AI as a blessing, not an inhibition.

Finally, we need to be prepared for the worst of AI. Something as revolutionary as AI is sure to have many twists to work out. There is always that fear that if AI is learning based, will machines learn that being rich and successful is a good thing, then wage war against economic powers and famous people?[6] There are so many things that can go wrong with a new system so we must be as prepared as we can be for this new technology.[7]

However, even though the fear of the machines is there, their capabilities are infinite. Whatever we teach AI, they will suggest in the future if a positive outcome arrives from it. AI is like children that need to be taught to be kind, well mannered, and intelligent. If they are to make important decisions, they should be wise. We as citizens need to make sure AI programmers are keeping things on the level. We should be sure they are doing the job correctly, so that no future accidents occur.

The scope of expert systems

An expert system is able to do the work of a professional. Moreover, a computer system can be trained quickly, has virtually no operating cost, never forgets what it learns, never calls in sick, retires, or goes on vacation. Beyond those, intelligent computers can consider a large amount of information that may not be considered by humans.

But to what extent should these systems replace human experts? Or, should they at all? For example, some people once considered an intelligent computer as a possible substitute for human control over nuclear weapons, citing that a computer could respond more quickly to a threat.[8] We cannot overlook the benefits of having a computer expert. Forecasting the weather, for example, relies on many variables, and a computer expert can more accurately pool all of its knowledge. Still a computer cannot rely on the hunches of a human expert, which are sometimes necessary in predicting an outcome.

In conclusion, in some fields such as forecasting weather or finding bugs in computer software, expert systems are sometimes more accurate than humans. But for other fields, such as medicine, computers aiding doctors will be beneficial, but the human doctor should not be replaced. Expert systems have the power and range to aid to benefit, and in some cases replace humans, and computer experts, if used with discretion, will benefit human kind.

Part Ⅱ: Approaches of AI

Humankind has given itself the scientific name *homo sapiens* (man the wise) because our mental capacities are so important to our everyday lives and our sense of self. The field of artificial intelligence, or AI, attempts to understand intelligent entities. Thus, one reason to study it is to learn more about ourselves. But unlike philosophy and psychology, which are also concerned with intelligence, AI strives to build intelligent entities as well as understand them. Another reason to study AI is that these constructed intelligent entities are interesting and useful in their own right. AI has produced many significant and impressive products even at this early stage in its development. Although no one can predict the future in detail, it is clear that computers with human-level intelligence (or better) would have a huge impact on our everyday lives and on the future course of civilization.

AI addresses one of the ultimate puzzles. How is it possible for a slow, tiny brain, whether biological or electronic, to perceive, understand, predict, and manipulate a world far larger and more complicated than itself? How do we go about making something with those properties? These are hard questions, but unlike the search for faster-than-light travel or an antigravity device, the researcher in AI has solid evidence that the quest is possible.[1] All the researcher has to do is to look in the mirror to see an example of an intelligent system.

AI is one of the newest disciplines. It was formally initiated in 1956, when the name was coined, although at that point work had been under way for about five years. Along with modern genetics, it is regularly cited as the "field I would most like to be in" by scientists in other disciplines. A student in physics might reasonably feel that all the good ideas have already been taken by Galileo, Newton, Einstein, and the rest, and that it takes many years of study before one can contribute new ideas. AI, on the other hand, still has openings for a full-time Einstein.

AI currently encompasses a huge variety of subfields, from general-purpose areas such as perception and logical reasoning, to specific tasks such as playing chess, proving mathematical theorems, writing poetry, and diagnosing diseases. Often, scientists in other fields move gradually into artificial intelligence, where they find the tools and vocabulary to systematize and automate the intellectual tasks on which they have been working all their lives.[2] Similarly, workers in AI can choose to apply their methods to any area of human intellectual endeavor. In this sense, it is truly a universal field.

What is AI?

We have now explained why AI is exciting, but we have not said what it is. We could just say, "Well, it has to do with smart programs, so let's get on and write some." But the history of science shows that it is helpful to aim at the right goals. Early alchemists, looking for a potion for eternal life and a method to turn lead into gold, were probably off on the wrong foot. Only when the aim changed, to that of finding explicit theories that gave accurate predictions of the terrestrial world, in the same way that early astronomy predicted the apparent motions of the stars and planets, could the scientific method emerge and productive science take place.[3] Definitions as given in Table 15.1 vary along two main dimensions. The ones on top are concerned with thought processes and reasoning, whereas the ones on the bottom address behavior. Also, the definitions on the left measure success in terms of human performance, whereas the ones on the right measure against an ideal concept of intelligence, which we will call *rationality*. A system is rational if it does the right thing.

Table 15.1　**Four possible goals to pursue in artificial intelligence**

Systems that think like humans	Systems that think rationally
Systems that act like humans	Systems that act rationally

As one might expect, a tension exists between approaches centered around humans and approaches centered around rationality. We should point out that by distinguishing between human and rational behavior, we are not suggesting that humans are necessarily "irrational" in the sense of "emotionally unstable" or "insane". One merely need note that we often make mistakes; we are not all chess grandmasters even though we may know all the rules of chess; and unfortunately, not everyone gets an A on the exam. A human-centered approach must be an empirical science, involving hypothesis and experimental confirmation. A rationalist approach involves a combination of mathematics and engineering. People in each group sometimes cast aspersions on work done in the other groups, but the truth is that each direction has yielded valuable insights. Let us look at each in more detail.

Acting humanly: the Turing Test approach

The *Turing Test*, proposed by Alan Turing, was designed to provide a satisfactory operational definition of intelligence. Turing defined intelligent behavior as the ability to achieve human-level performance in all cognitive tasks, sufficient to fool an interrogator. Roughly speaking, the test he proposed is that the computer should be interrogated by a human via a teletype, and passes the test if the interrogator cannot tell if there is a computer or a human at the other end. Details of the test, and whether or not a computer is really intelligent if it passes the test, will be discussed later. For now, programming a computer to pass the test provides plenty to work on. The computer would need to possess the following capabilities:

- *Natural language processing* to enable it to communicate successfully in English (or some other human language);
- *Knowledge representation* to store information provided before or during the interrogation;
- *Automated reasoning* to use the stored information to answer questions and to draw new conclusions;
- *Machine learning* to adapt to new circumstances and to detect and extrapolate patterns.

Turing's test deliberately avoided direct physical interaction between the interrogator and the computer, because physical simulation of a person is unnecessary for intelligence. However, the so-called *total Turing Test* includes a video signal so that the interrogator can test the subject's perceptual abilities, as well as the opportunity for the interrogator to pass physical objects "through the hatch".[4] To pass the total Turing Test, the computer will need:

- *Computer vision* to perceive objects;
- *Robotics* to move them about.

Within AI, there has not been a big effort to try to pass the Turing test. The issue of acting like a human comes up primarily when AI programs have to interact with people, as when an expert system explains how it came to its diagnosis, or a natural language processing system has a dialogue with a user. These programs must behave according to certain normal conventions of human interaction in order to make themselves understood. The underlying representation and reasoning in such a system may or may not be based on a human model.

Thinking humanly: the cognitive modeling approach

If we are going to say that a given program thinks like a human, we must have some way of determining how humans think. We need to get inside the actual workings of human minds. There are two ways to do this: through introspection — trying to catch our own thoughts as they go by — or through psychological experiments. Once we have a sufficiently precise theory of the mind, it becomes possible to express the theory as a computer program. If the program's input/output and timing behavior matches human behavior, that is evidence that some of the program's mechanisms may also be operating in humans. For example, Newell and Simon, who developed GPS, the "General Problem Solver", were not content to have their program correctly solve problems. They were more concerned with comparing the trace of its reasoning steps to traces of human subjects solving the same problems. This is in contrast to other researchers of the same time, who were concerned with getting the right answers regardless of how humans might do it.[5] The interdisciplinary field of *cognitive science* brings together computer models from AI and experimental techniques from psychology to try to construct precise and testable theories of the workings of the human mind.[6] Although cognitive science is a fascinating field in itself, we are not going to be discussing it all that much. Real cognitive science, however, is necessarily based on experimental investigation of actual humans or animals. We will simply note that AI and cognitive science continue to fertilize each other, especially in the areas of vision, natural language, and learning.

Thinking rationally: the laws of thought approach

The Greek philosopher Aristotle was one of the first to attempt to codify "right thinking", that is, irrefutable reasoning processes. His famous *syllogisms* provided patterns for argument structures that always gave correct conclusions given correct premises. For example, "Socrates is a man; all men are mortal; therefore Socrates is mortal". These laws of thought were supposed to govern the operation of the mind, and initiated the field of *logic*.

The development of formal logic in the late nineteenth and early twentieth centuries provided a precise notation for statements about all kinds of things in the world and the relations between them. (Contrast this with ordinary arithmetic notation, which provides mainly for equality and inequality statements about numbers.) By 1965, programs existed that could, given enough time and memory, take a description of a problem in logical notation and find the solution to the problem, if one existed.[7] (If there is no solution, the program might never stop looking for it.) The so-called *logicist* tradition within artificial intelligence hopes to build on such programs to create intelligent systems.

There are two main obstacles to this approach. First, it is not easy to take informal knowledge and state it in the formal terms required by logical notation, particularly when the knowledge is less than 100% certain. Second, there is a big difference between being able to solve a problem "in principle" and doing so in practice. Even problems with just a few dozen facts can exhaust the computational resources of any computer unless it has some guidance as to which reasoning steps to try first. Although both of these obstacles apply to any attempt to build computational reasoning systems, they appeared first in the logicist tradition because the power of the representation and reasoning systems are well-defined and fairly well understood.

Acting rationally: the rational agent approach

Acting rationally means acting so as to achieve one's goals, given one's beliefs. An *agent* is just something that perceives and acts. (This may be an unusual use of the word, but you will get used to it.) In this approach, AI is viewed as the study and construction of rational agents.

In the "laws of thought" approach to AI, the whole emphasis was on correct inferences. Making correct inferences is sometimes part of being a rational agent, because one way to act rationally is to reason logically to the conclusion that a given action will achieve one's goals, and then to act on that conclusion.[8] On the other hand, correct inference is not all of rationality, because there are often situations where there is no provably correct thing to do, yet something must still be done. There are also ways of acting rationally that cannot be reasonably said to involve inference. For example, pulling one's hand off of a hot stove is a reflex action that is more successful than a slower action taken after careful deliberation.

All the "cognitive skills" needed for the Turing Test are there to allow rational actions. Thus, we need the ability to represent knowledge and reason with it because this enables us to reach good decisions in a wide variety of situations. We need to be able to generate comprehensible sentences in natural language because saying those sentences helps us get by in a complex society. We need learning not just for knowledge, but because having a better idea of how the world works enables us to generate more effective strategies for dealing with it. We need visual perception not just because seeing is fun, but in order to get a better idea of what an action might achieve.

New Words

Part I

physiology	生理学	generalization	普遍化，推广，概括
perception	感觉	sensory	感觉的，传递感觉的
mimic	模仿	neuron	神经元，神经细胞
arguably	可争辩地，有争议地	dedicated researcher	奉献于事业的研究者
deceive	欺骗	intrigue	引起兴趣，吸引
theorize	使……成为理论	checkers	跳棋
stumbling	笨手笨脚的	quest	追求，探索
diagnose	诊断	mental	精神的，智力的
conservative	保守的	heritage	世袭财产，遗产

alertness	警觉	inhibition	禁止，压制
blessing	赐福，祝福	scope	范围
professional	专业人员	virtually	实际上
substitute	代替	overlook	忽视，俯视
pool	把……集中使用	cite	引用，引证
hunch	预感，直觉的想法	discretion	慎重，斟酌处理权

Part II

entity	实体	coin	创造，杜撰
genetics	遗传学	discipline	学科
encompass	包含，包围，完成	reasoning	推理
endeavor	努力	alchemist	点金术士
eternal	永恒的，不灭的	terrestrial	地面的，地球上的
explicit	明显的，明白的	dimension	维，尺度
rationality	合理性，理性	insane	有精神病的，愚蠢的
grandmaster	大师	empirical	凭经验的，经验性的
hypothesis	假设	aspersion	诽谤，中伤
interrogator	询问者，质询者	teletype	电传打字机
adapt	适应	extrapolate	推断，外延
hatch	孵化，舱口	cognitive	认知的
content (v.)	满足，满意	interdisciplinary	跨学科的
fertilize	施肥，滋养	irrefutable	不能反驳的
syllogism	三段论，推演	premise	前提
mortal	人的，不免一死的	exhaust	耗尽
provably	可证明地	reflex	反射，映像
liberation	深思熟虑	comprehensible	可理解的

Notes on the Text

Part I

1. To what degree does intelligence consist of, for example, solving complex problems, or making generalizations and relationships?
   智能在多大程度上包含譬如解决复杂问题、进行概括和建立关系这样的能力？

2. He stated that a computer would deserve to be called intelligent if it could deceive a human into believing that it was human.
   他说，当一台计算机可以骗过人，相信它是一个人而不是机器时便可称得上是智能的。
   - 翻译时增加"而不是机器"，使译文更顺畅。

3. The technology was finally available, or so it seemed, to simulate intelligent behavior.

这项技术终于可用于模拟智能行为了，或者看起来是这样。

4. Advanced-level computer languages, as well as computer interfaces and word-processors owe their existence to the research into artificial intelligence.

先进的计算机语言，以及计算机接口和文字处理软件都要归功于人工智能的研究。

5. AI with its learning capabilities can accomplish those tasks but only if the worlds conservatives are ready to change and allow this to be a possibility.

具有学习能力的人工智能可以胜任那些工作，但只有人们准备改变他们的保守观念使之成为可能才行。

6. There is always that fear that if AI is learning based, will machines learn that being rich and successful is a good thing, then wage war against economic powers and famous people?

总是有那样一种担忧，以为要是人工智能是建立在学习基础上的，那么机器会不会在得知富有和成功是好事后，去发动战争反对经济强国和著名人物呢？

7. There are so many things that can go wrong with a new system so we must be as prepared as we can be for this new technology.

一个新系统有那么多情况可能出错，所以我们必须尽可能为这种新技术做好准备。

8. For example, some people once considered an intelligent computer as a possible substitute for human control over nuclear weapons, citing that a computer could respond more quickly to a threat.

例如有人曾经把智能计算机看成是人对核武器进行控制的替身，说是计算机对于威胁可做出比人更快的反应。

Part Ⅱ

1. These are hard questions, but unlike the search for faster-than-light travel or an antigravity device, the researcher in AI has solid evidence that the quest is possible.

这些是难题，但是与寻求超光速运动或反重力装置不同，人工智能研究者有确凿的证据证明这种探索是可能成功的。

2. Often, scientists in other fields move gradually into artificial intelligence, where they find the tools and vocabulary to systematize and automate the intellectual tasks on which they have been working all their lives.

通常其他领域中的科学家（会）逐渐转移到人工智能研究中来，他们在这里发现了能使他们自己毕生从事的智力工作实现系统化和自动化的工具和语言。

3. Early alchemists, looking for a potion for eternal life and a method to turn lead into gold, were probably off on the wrong foot. Only when the aim changed, to that of finding explicit theories that gave accurate predictions of the terrestrial world, in the same way that early astronomy predicted the apparent motions of the stars and

planets, could the scientific method emerge and productive science take place.

早年寻求长生不老药和点石成金秘诀的点金术士恐怕是迈错了步子。只有改变目标，用早期天文学家预言星宿和行星运动那样的方法寻求能给出人间世界准确预言的明确理论，科学的方法和有成效的科学才会出现。

4. However, the so-called *total Turing Test* includes a video signal so that the interrogator can test the subject's perceptual abilities, as well as the opportunity for the interrogator to pass physical objects "through the hatch".

不过所谓"完全图灵试验"需要包括视频信号，这样询问者就可以对被测试者的感觉能力进行测试，同时也包括询问者"通过舱口"传递实物的可能性。

5. This is in contrast to other researchers of the same time, who were concerned with getting the right answers regardless of how humans might do it.

这和同时期只关心获得正确答案而不管人们会怎样做的其他研究者形成对比。

6. The interdisciplinary field of *cognitive science* brings together computer models from AI and experimental techniques from psychology to try to construct precise and testable theories of the workings of the human mind.

认知科学这一交叉学科领域将人工智能领域中的计算机模型与心理学中的实验技术结合起来，试图构建人类思维精确并可测试的理论。

7. By 1965, programs existed that could, given enough time and memory, take a description of a problem in logical notation and find the solution to the problem, if one existed.

到 1965 年已经有了计算机程序，只要提供足够的时间和存储容量就能以逻辑表达方式描述问题，并且只要有解，就能找到这些解。

8. Making correct inferences is sometimes part of being a rational agent, because one way to act rationally is to reason logically to the conclusion that a given action will achieve one's goals, and then to act on that conclusion.

有时做出正确推断是按照理性行事的智能代理的一部分，因为理性行事的方式之一就是合乎逻辑地推出这样的结论：某一给定的行为将能达到目的，然后照此行事。

Technical Tips

Expert system

An expert system is a computer program that simulates the judgment and behavior of a human or an organization that has expert knowledge and experience in a particular field. Typically, such a system contains a knowledge base containing accumulated experience and a set of rules for applying the knowledge base to each particular situation that is described to the program. Sophisticated expert systems can be enhanced with additions to the knowledge base or to the set of rules. Among the best-known expert systems have been those that play chess and that assist in medical diagnosis.

Deep learning

Deep learning (also known as deep structured learning or hierarchical learning) is the application to learning tasks of artificial neural networks (ANNs) that contain more than one hidden layers. Deep learning is part of a broader family of machine learning methods based on learning data representations, as opposed to task specific algorithms.

Deep learning is a class of machine learning algorithms that:

- use a cascade of many layers of nonlinear processing units for feature extraction and transformation. Each successive layer uses the output from the previous layer as input. The algorithms may be supervised or unsupervised and applications include pattern analysis (unsupervised) and classification (supervised).
- are based on the (unsupervised) learning of multiple levels of features or representations of the data. Higher level features are derived from lower level features to form a hierarchical representation.
- are part of the broader machine learning field of learning representations of data.
- learn multiple levels of representations that correspond to different levels of abstraction; the levels form a hierarchy of concepts.

These definitions have in common (1) multiple layers of nonlinear processing units and (2) the supervised or unsupervised learning of feature representations in each layer, with the layers forming a hierarchy from low-level to high-level features. The composition of a layer of nonlinear processing units used in a deep learning algorithm depends on the problem to be solved. Layers that have been used in deep learning include hidden layers of an artificial neural network and sets of complicated propositional formulas.

Supplementary Readings: AlphaGo

One of the biggest technology news in 2016 is that an artificial intelligence computer program called AlphaGo, developed by Google's Deep Mind research team, has for the first time beaten the best human player of the go game on this planet, Mr. Sedol Lee.

This achievement of computer artificial intelligence is unprecedented and very important. So important that several Google heavyweights, including Chairman Eric Schmidt, co-founder Sergey Brin and legendary Google top engineer Jeff Dean all flew to Seoul to watch the games. The proxy hand sitting across Sedol Lee to play on behalf of Alphago is no ordinary people either. He is Aja Huang, a go player himself and a research scientist in the Deep Mind team.

Why is this human-machine match so important? Because the ancient go game, with very simple rules, is the most complicated two player board game invented. The board is composed of 19×19 grid of 361 possible positions of cross points, with two players alternatively placing one black or white stone at a time, in a strategy to occupy as much territory as possible and preventing the opponent to do the same. At a given step, a player can place a stone at any of the hundreds of possible spots. It is very hard to foresee how a particular move can affect the odd of the ultimate winning or losing. But often times, in hind sight, it can be shown that one fantastic or mistaken move can have deciding impact on the final outcome. Due to the complexity, players must resort to intuition and experience to come up with the right move at each step. Likewise, a computer cannot hope to exhaust all possible moves and pick the correct one. It has to imitate human behaviors and try to guesstimate the "value" of possible moves.

The way for a computer to go from a set of hundreds of complicated inputs to reach a selected few outputs, "intuitively", or based on experience, without going through exact step by step calculations, is called deep learning neural network. The word "deep" means there are many layers of intermediate neurons before the final output is reached. "Deep" also means the complexity of computation grows exponentially as more layers of neutrons are added, even though more neuron layers could lead to better results. For a deep learning artificial neural network based go program, to win the game over the best human player would be a tremendous milestone achieved. Just two years ago, some predicted that such a goal won't be achieved for at least the next ten years. Well it has been achieved today, by the Google AlphaGo team.

In this section, we briefly introduce the past techniques used in computer Go programs, then provide an estimate for why AlphaGo is able to outperform contemporary programs so dramatically. Currently, Monte Carlo tree search (MCTS), minorization-maximization (MM), and deep convolutional neural networks (DCNNs) have demonstrated great success in Go. MCTS was successfully applied to Go in 2006, leading to a significant improvement in playing skill. One year later, MM was applied so that programs may recognize move patterns using supervised learning, with expert game records as the training sample. Though not as revolutionary as MCTS, MM has also had a longlasting impact on Go programs from 2007 up to 2014. In December of 2014, two teams applied DCNNs to Go independently. Clark and Storkey first published a paper that applied DCNNs to Go, which, when given a game position, could estimate how expert human players respond with a prediction rate of 41%-44%, exceeding the rate of previous methods. Meanwhile, DeepMind's method, which was released 10 days later, had a prediction rate of 55%. Among many of DCNN's applications, it has seen success in image and video recognition. When applied to Go, DCNN is able to recognize move patterns at a significantly lower error rate than MM. For this reason, most state-of-the-art computer Go programs use MCTS combined with either MM or DCNN.

AlphaGo is able to perform leaps and bounds above other contemporary programs because of its extensive use of high quality neural networks, which cannot be easily reproduced by other teams due to insufficient experience and/or inadequate hardware resources. To illustrate, let us consider the three main neural networks used in AlphaGo: a supervised learning (SL) policy network, a reinforcement learning (RL) policy network, and the value network. Both the SL policy network and the value network were used in AlphaGo during competitive play; the RL policy network was used only for generating the training samples for the value network. The SL policy network takes a game board position and attempts to guess where expert players will play next. This SL process was performed with 30 million game positions, and involved 340 million training steps, taking a total of three weeks with 50 graphic processing units (GPUs). The SL algorithm tends to mimic what it has learned from game records instead of favoring moves that yield the highest winning rate when given a choice.

To improve on this, the SL policy network was used to train a separate policy network using RL. Training for the RL policy network takes one day with 50 GPUs. The key to AlphaGo's playing skill is its value network, which was trained through RL with 30 million self-play game positions. The training process takes about one week with 50 GPUs, for a total training time of four weeks and a day for all three networks. The most time-consuming and most difficult process to reproduce, however, is not the training of these three networks, but the generation of self-play game positions. For each of the 30 million self-play positions, 100 playouts are performed; for each playout, we assume on average 200 moves until game completion, so a total of 600 billion move data samples need to be generated to train the value network. Let us assume, for the sake of demonstration, that a research team has access to four GPUs. The training of the three networks will take [(4 weeks×7 days/week) + 1 day] ×(50GPUs) / (4GPUs) = 362.5 days. Assuming a processing speed of 720 moves/s for a single GPU (with a batch size of 16), an optimistic estimate for the generation of self-play game samples is $600×10^9$ moves / (4×720 moves/second)≈208 million seconds, which works out to 2411 days or about 80 months. In addition to the total time required for generating and training the networks, we must consider the fact that parameters involved in the entire process are rarely tuned to fit the requirements in a single trial. This includes a wide variety of settings such as the number of layers and neurons in the neural network, the features to use for the Go positions, the collection of expert game records that are used to train the initial SL policy network, etc. This quick estimate of required resources does not even take into account the knowledge and experience that the DeepMind team has acquired since its inception. As a side note, the distributed version of AlphaGo uses 280 GPUs.

AlphaGo's victory over the world champion Lee Sedol in March 2016 will be marked in history as a remarkable achievement. However, this would not have been possible without the considerable time and effort of countless contributors to computer Go in the past. AlphaGo's impact will almost assuredly popularize and improve Go learning worldwide, especially if a personalized version with reduced hardware costs becomes available. Finally, AlphaGo's performance was truly astonishing, and will undoubtedly be a continued source of inspiration for professional Go players and AI researchers around the world.

Exercises

I. Translate the following paragraphs into Chinese.

1. Artificial Intelligence is a branch of science that helps machines find solutions to complex problems in a human-like fashion. This generally involves borrowing characteristics from human intelligence, and applying them as algorithms in a computer friendly way. Computers are fundamentally well suited to performing mechanical computations using fixed rules. This allows machines to perform simple monotonous tasks efficiently and reliably, which humans are not suited to. Unlike humans, however, computers have trouble in understanding specific situations, and adapting to new situations. Artificial Intelligence aims to improve machine behavior in tackling such complex tasks. Humans have an interesting approach to problem-solving, based on abstract thought, high-level reasoning and pattern recognition. Artificial Intelligence can help us understand this process by recreating it, then potentially enabling us to enhance it beyond our current capabilities.

2. An expert system is a computer application that performs a task that would otherwise be performed by a human expert. For example, there are expert systems that can diagnose human illnesses, make financial forecasts, and schedule routes for delivery vehicles. Some expert systems are designed to take the place of human experts, while others are designed to aid them. Expert systems are part of a general category of computer applications known as artificial intelligence. To design an expert system, one needs a knowledge engineer, an individual who studies how human experts make decisions and translates the rules into terms that a computer can understand.

3. The history of AI, like that of any other science, is one that is filled with surprises, false events, and occasional successes. Probably the most important lesson to date from research in AI is that problems that were thought to be easy (i.e., the ones that a two-year-old can handle effortlessly — e.g., recognizing faces) are extremely difficult to mechanize (given the current state of art). Problems that were thought to be hard (i.e., the ones that require years of formal training — e.g., proving theorems in mathematics) are embarrassingly easy to mechanize. Is it really the case that cognition can be fully understood in terms of computation? Are cold logic and rationality sufficient for intelligence? Are they necessary? Do we need anything else? If so, what? AI research meshes with some of the most exciting philosophical questions. It also offers tremendous scientific and technological challenges.

II. Choose the word or phrase that is closest in meaning to the underlined part.

1. Advanced-level computer languages, as well as computer interfaces and word-processors <u>owe their existence to the research into artificial intelligence</u>.

    A. are developed due partly to the advances of AI research

    B. exist in the research of artificial intelligence

    C. are related to the existence of artificial intelligence

    D. are research areas belonging to artificial intelligence

2. There is always that fear that <u>if AI is learning based</u>, will machines learn that being rich and successful is a good thing, then wage war against economic powers and famous people?

    A. if AI has a learning basis

    B. if AI is learning basis

    C. if AI is established on the basis of learning

    D. if AI takes into account of a learning base

3. Often, scientists in other fields move gradually into artificial intelligence, where they find the tools and vocabulary to systematize and automate the intellectual tasks <u>on which they have been working all their lives</u>.

    A. that are the objectives of their live-time research efforts

    B. that are works entirely belonging to their lives

    C. that work all the way through their lives

    D. that take their whole lives in the work

4. It is no easier for an AI practitioner to give a definition of intelligence than for a biologist to give a definition of life. Both are concepts with <u>a complex contextual meaning</u> in everyday conversation, but neither yields a precise, simple, scientific definition.

    A. a difficult understanding of contents

    B. a complicated and situation-related sense

    C. a composite and sophisticated idea

    D. a complicated common gist

5. <u>Mental machines</u> can surprise their designers with their behavior that can be creative, imaginative, and even emotional. In a word, they can behave like the human mind.

    A. Artificial intelligence practitioners

    B. Computer hardware in AI systems

    C. Computer programs having intelligence

    D. Analogies of human brain as in the knitting machine example

6. Artificial intelligence is the attempt to build <u>computational model of cognitive processes</u> or put it another way: in artificial intelligence we make computers perform tasks that would be considered intelligent if done by a human.

    A. computer simulation of pattern recognition

    B. representation of understanding in terms of computer language

    C. computerized characterization of digital processing

    D. mode of performing tasks with computer

7. If you are unable to separate man from machine then, Turing says, we will have <u>to attribute intelligence to the computer</u>.

    A. to make an intelligent computer

    B. to consider the computer as being intelligent

    C. to contribute to the computer with intelligence

    D. to let the computer have intelligence

8. Unfortunately, we will see that it is not as easy to <u>distinguish between psychologically valid and invalid AI programs</u> as it is to distinguish between physically valid and invalid jumper making procedures.

    A. tell whether or not AI programs are of importance to psychology

    B. provide psychological differences between a valid AI program and an invalid AI program

    C. give valid reasons to distinguish psychologically different AI programs

    D. separate psychologically valid AI programs from psychologically invalid ones

Unit 16 Big Data and Cloud Computing

With the fast development of networking, data storage, and data collection capacity, big data is now rapidly expanding in all domains of science and engineering. Big data is an emerging trend, and the need for big data mining is arising. With the big data technology, we will hopefully be able to provide more relevant and accurate social sensing feedback to better understand our society in real-time. The era of big data has arrived.

Text

Part I: Big Data

Currently, a huge explosion of data is observed in the world. Industry analysts and businesses are looking towards big data as the next big thing to provide opportunities, insights, solutions, and a new way to increase profits in business. From social networking sites to records in a hospital, big data is playing important roles to improve businesses and innovation.

Big data is a term for data sets that are so large and complex for traditional data processing software to deal with, as the information comes from multiple, heterogeneous, autonomous sources with complex and evolving relationships, and keeps growing.[1] Challenges of big data include data's acquisition, storage, search, analysis, sharing, transfer, visualization, querying, updating, and privacy protection.

Data sets grow rapidly — in part because they are increasingly gathered by cheap and numerous information-sensing Internet of Things devices such as mobile devices, software logs, cameras, microphones, radio-frequency identification (RFID) readers and wireless sensor networks.[2] The world's per-capita technological capacity to store information has roughly doubled every 40 months since the 1980s; as of 2012, every day 2.5 exabytes (2.5×10^{18}) of data are generated. The amount of data has been increasing and data set analyzing become more competitive.

There is little doubt that the quantities of data now available are indeed large, but that's not the most relevant characteristic of this new data ecosystem. The challenge is not only to collect and manage vast volume and different types of data, but also to extract meaningful value from it, which involves predictive analytics, user behavior analytics and other advanced data analytics methods.[3] The value of big data is now being recognized by many industries and governments. Analysis of data sets can find new correlations to spot business trends, prevent diseases, combat crime and so on.

Big Data Types

Big data comes from a great variety of sources and can be categorized into three general types: structured, semi-structured and unstructured.[4]

- **Structured data:** Data that can be easily sorted and analyzed, e.g. numbers and words. It is mainly generated because of network sensors embedded in electronic devices such as smartphone and global positioning system (GPS) devices. Structured data also include transaction data, sales figures, account balances etc. The data configuration and consistency allow it to respond to simple queries to arrive at usable information, based on an organization's parameters and operational needs.

- **Semi-structured data:** It is a form of structured data that does not conform to an explicit and fixed schema. The data is inherently self-describing and contains tags or other markers to enforce hierarchies of records and fields within the data. Examples include weblogs and social media feeds.

- **Unstructured data:** It comprises of more complex information, such as customer reviews from commercial websites, photos and other multimedia, and comments on social networking sites. These data cannot easily be separated into categories or analyzed numerically. This type of data consists of formats which cannot easily be indexed into relational tables for analysis or querying. Examples include images, audio and video files.

Characteristics of Big Data

Big data requires a revolutionary step forward from traditional data analysis, characterized by its 3Vs fundamental characteristics. The 3Vs include *Velocity* (data are growing and changing in a rapid way), *Variety* (data come in different and multiple formats) and *Volume* (huge amount of data is generated every second).

- **Variety:** In the past, all data that was created was structured data, it neatly fitted in columns and rows. Nowadays, 90% of the data generated is unstructured data. Data today comes in all types of formats — from structured, numeric data in traditional databases to unstructured text documents, email, video, audio, stock ticker data and financial transactions. The wide variety of data requires a different approach as well as different techniques to store all raw data.

- **Volume:** 90% of all data ever created was created in the past two years. From now on, the amount of data in the world will double every two years. By 2020, we will have 50 times the amount of data as that we had in 2011. The sheer volume of the data is enormous, and a very large contributor to the ever expanding digital universe is the Internet of Things with sensors all over the world in all devices creating data every second.[5] The era of a trillion sensors is upon us.

Organizations collect data from a variety of sources, including business transactions, social media and information from sensor or machine-to-machine data. The size of data now is larger than terabytes and petabytes. The grand scale and rise of data outstrips traditional storing and analysis techniques. In the past, the creation of so much data would have caused serious problems. Nowadays, new technologies have eased the burden. With decreasing storage costs, better storage solutions like Hadoop and the algorithms to create meaning from all that data, this is not a problem at all.

Velocity: The Velocity is the speed at which the data is created, stored, analyzed and visualized. In the past, when batch processing was a common practice, it was normal to receive an update from the database every night or even every week. Computers and servers required substantial time to process the data and update the databases. In the big data era, data is created in real-time or near real-time. With the availability of Internet connected devices, wireless or wired, machines and devices can pass-on their data the moment it is created.

The speed at which data is created currently is almost unimaginable. Every minute we upload 100 hours of video on Youtube. In addition, every minute over 200 million emails are sent, around 20 million photos are viewed and 30,000 uploaded on Flickr, almost 300,000 tweets are sent and almost 2.5 million queries on Google are performed. The challenge organizations have is to cope with the enormous speed the data is created and used in real-time.

Lately, more Vs have been added to better describe big data: *Vision* (the defined purpose of big data mining), *Verification* (processed data comply to some specifications), *Value* (business value that gives organization a compelling advantage), and *Veracity* (the quality of captured data can vary greatly, affecting the accurate analysis.)

Big Data Challenges

There are many issues and challenges that enterprises face while storing and handling big data. Proper data management practices, techniques and infrastructure can help overcome these challenges, problems and issues. Research communities from different sectors have been struggling to develop new, fast, dynamic and user-friendly technologies for big data. Nowadays, many open source and proprietary big data solutions are available. The goal is to help decision makers and data scientists take the next best actions based on discovered patterns, data relations and newly extracted knowledge from big data. We presents hereafter some solutions developed to overcome big data challenges at different levels.

A. Big data frameworks and platforms

Big data has the potential to provide insights that can transform every business. Big data has generated a whole new industry of supporting architectures such as MapReduce.

MapReduce is a programming framework for distributed computing which was created by Google using the divide and conquer method to break down complex big data problems into small units of work and process them in parallel.[6]

Several MapReduce frameworks (e.g., Apache Hadoop, Skynet, and FileMap) were developed to handle structured and unstructured massive data. They are based on many solid concepts including distributed storage, massive parallel processing and fault tolerant system, which allow to store and process large volumes of immutable data (like logs or large binary objects) as well as incrementally collected data (like web crawls, user comments on social networks, GPS data or sensors events). Such frameworks are efficient for many use cases, such as log file analysis, scientific simulations or financial predictions.

B. Knowledge discovery from big data

Knowledge discovery from data (KDD) is the process of discovering useful knowledge from a collection of data. Major KDD application areas include marketing, fraud detection, telecommunication and manufacturing. KDD includes a variety of analysis methods as distributed programming, pattern recognition, data mining, natural language processing, sentiment analysis, statistical and visual analysis and human computer interaction.

Statistical analysis is interested in summarizing massive datasets, understanding data and defining models for prediction. Data mining is the analysis step of the KDD process. It is the computing process of discovering patterns in large data sets, involving methods at the intersection of machine learning, statistics, and database systems. The overall goal of the data mining is to extract information from a data set and transform it into an understandable structure for further use. It is an interdisciplinary subfield of computer science. Aside from the raw analysis step, it involves database and data management aspects, data pre-processing, model and inference considerations, interestingness metrics, complexity considerations, post-processing of discovered structures, visualization, and online updating.

C. Privacy and security issues

Big data is shared over many networks, various clusters and data centers, which increases security and privacy risks. It is important to deploy advanced security mechanisms to protect big data exchanged or stored in multiple clusters. However, because of the velocity and huge volumes, it is difficult to protect all large data sets. Hence it is more practical to protect the data value and its key attributes instead of the data itself. In addition, adding security layers may slow system performances and affect dynamic analysis of huge increasing volumes. Several big data security solutions have been developed such as:

- Anonymization techniques: Anonymization is an important approach to protect data privacy. The goal of the current research is to enhance parallelism capacities, the performance and the scalability of anonymization techniques.
- Privacy techniques: Currently, many projects are working to develop new privacy techniques based on privacy preservation aware analysis and scheduling techniques

of large data sets.

- Homomorphic cryptography: It was proposed to ensure information confidentiality. Unlike some traditional techniques for encryption, it allows to do computation on encrypted data.
- Authentication mechanisms: It provides strong authentication for client/server applications by using secret-key cryptography.

Part II: Cloud Computing

Cloud Computing arises as one of the hottest topic in the field of information technology. Cloud Computing is a pay-per-use-on-demand mode that can easily access shared IT resources through the Internet. It is the new technology to enhance the human communication for using the shared resources such as storage, networks, servers, services and applications without physically acquiring them. As a new form of Internet-based computing, cloud computing provides shared computer processing resources and data to computers and other devices on demand. It is a model for enabling ubiquitous, on-demand access to a shared pool of configurable computing resources (e.g., computer networks, servers, storage, applications and services), which can be rapidly provisioned and released with minimal management effort.[1]

Computing infrastructure is imaged as a "cloud" from which individuals and business corporations can extend their access to its application from anywhere and at any time on demand. The main principle of the cloud is offering computing, storage and software as a service.

Basically, cloud computing allows the users and enterprises with various capabilities to store and process their data in either privately owned cloud, or on a third-party server in order to make data accessing mechanisms much more easy and reliable. Data centers that may be located far from the user—ranging in distance from across a city to across the world. Cloud computing relies on sharing of resources to achieve coherence and economy of scale, similar to a utility (like the electricity grid) over an electricity network.

The goal of cloud computing is to allow users to take benefit from all of these technologies without the need for deep knowledge about or expertise with each one of them. The cloud aims to cut costs, and helps the users focus on their core business instead of being impeded by IT obstacles. The main enabling technology for cloud computing is virtualization. Virtualization software separates a physical computing device into one or more "virtual" devices, each of which can be easily used and managed to perform computing tasks. With operating system-level virtualization essentially creating a scalable system of multiple independent computing devices, idle computing resources can be allocated and used more efficiently. Virtualization provides the agility required to speed up IT operations, and reduces cost by increasing infrastructure utilization.

Autonomic computing automates the process through which the user can access resources on-demand. By minimizing user involvement, automation speeds up the process, and reduces labor costs and possibility of human errors. Users routinely face difficult business problems. Cloud computing adopts concepts from Service-Oriented Architecture (SOA) that can help the user break these problems into services. The results of these services are then integrated to provide a solution. Cloud computing provides all of its resources as services, and makes use of the well-established standards and best practices gained in the domain of SOA to allow global and easy access to cloud services in a standardized way.[2]

Cloud computing also leverages concepts from utility computing to provide metrics for the services used. Such metrics are at the core of the public cloud pay-per-use models. In addition, measured services are an essential part of the feedback loop in autonomic computing, allowing services to scale on-demand and to perform automatic failure recovery. Cloud computing is a kind of grid computing; it has evolved by addressing the QoS (quality of service) and reliability problems. Cloud computing provides the tools and technologies to build data/computation intensive parallel applications with much more affordable prices compared to traditional parallel computing techniques.[3]

Deployment Models

There are various deployment models, with variations in physical location and distribution, which have been adopted by the cloud computing. A cloud can be classified as public, private, community, or hybrid based on model of deployment. The client should select the type of cloud depends upon the purpose.

A cloud is called a "public cloud" when the services are rendered over a network that is open for public use. Technically there may be little or no difference between public and private cloud architecture, however, security consideration may be substantially different. Generally, public cloud service providers like Amazon Web Services (AWS), Microsoft and Google own and operate the infrastructure at their data center and access is generally via the Internet.

Private cloud is a cloud infrastructure operated solely for a single organization, whether managed internally or by a third-party, and hosted either internally or externally. Undertaking a private cloud project requires a significant level and degree of engagement to virtualize the business environment, and requires the organization to reevaluate decisions about existing resources.[4] When done right, it can improve business, but every step in the project raises security issues that must be addressed to prevent serious vulnerabilities.

Hybrid cloud is a composition of two or more clouds (private, community or public) that remain distinct entities but are bound together, offering the benefits of multiple deployment models. Hybrid cloud can also mean the ability to connect collocation, managed and/or dedicated services with cloud resources. Varied use cases for hybrid cloud composition exist. For example, IT organizations use public cloud computing resources to meet temporary capacity needs that cannot be met by the private cloud. This capability enables hybrid clouds to employ cloud bursting for scaling across clouds.

Everything as a Service (XaaS)

Though service-oriented architecture advocates "everything as a service" (with the acronyms EaaS or XaaS or simply aas), cloud-computing providers offer their "services" according to different models, of which the three standard models are Infrastructure as a Service (IaaS), Platform as a Service (PaaS), and Software as a Service (SaaS). These models offer increasing abstraction; they are thus often portrayed as layers in a stack: infrastructure-, platform- and software-as-a-service, but these need not be related. For example, one can provide SaaS implemented on physical machines (bare metal), without using underlying PaaS or IaaS layers, and conversely one can run a program on IaaS and access it directly, without wrapping it as SaaS. Cloud computing is service oriented rather than application oriented. The following services play a major role in cloud computing.

A. Software as a Service (SaaS)

It is a model of delivering software over the internet as a service. The client doesn't have to install and maintain software, but simply access it via the Internet. It would reduce the total cost of purchasing the software and the burden of its maintenance. These applications reside on the top of the cloud stack, for example, social networks and 3D online games.

In the SaaS model, users gain access to application software and databases. Cloud providers manage the infrastructure and platforms that run the applications. SaaS is sometimes referred to as "on-demand software" and is usually priced on a pay-per-use basis or using a subscription fee. Cloud providers install and operate application software in the cloud and cloud users access the software from cloud clients. Cloud users do not manage the cloud infrastructure and platform where the application runs. This eliminates the need to install and run the application on the cloud user's own computers, which simplifies maintenance and support. Cloud applications differ from other applications in their scalability — which can be achieved by cloning tasks onto multiple virtual machines at run-time to meet changing work demand.[5] Load balancers distribute the work over the set of virtual machines. This process is transparent to the cloud user, who sees only a single access-point. To accommodate a large number of cloud users, cloud applications can be multitenant, meaning that any machine may serve more than one cloud-user organization.

The pricing model for SaaS applications is typically a monthly or yearly flat fee per user, so prices become scalable and adjustable if users are added or removed at any point. Proponents claim that SaaS gives a business the potential to reduce IT operational costs by outsourcing hardware and software maintenance and support to the cloud provider. This enables the business to reallocate IT operations costs away from hardware/software spending and from personnel expenses, towards meeting other goals. In addition, with applications hosted centrally, updates can be released without the need for users to install new software. One drawback of SaaS comes with storing the users' data on the cloud provider's server. As a result, there could be unauthorized access to the data. For this reason, users are increasingly adopting intelligent third-party key-management systems to help secure their data.

B. Platform as a Service (PaaS)

This approach offers a high level of abstraction to make a cloud easily programmable. Specialized services like data access, authentication and payments are the building blocks to new application. It is a way to rent hardware, storage and operating systems. Examples include Google App Engine and Microsoft Azure service platform.

PaaS vendors offer a development environment to application developers. The provider typically develops toolkit and standards for development and channels for distribution and payment. In the PaaS models, cloud providers deliver a computing platform, typically including operating system, programming-language execution environment, database, and web server. Application developers can develop and run their software solutions on a cloud platform without the cost and complexity of buying and managing the underlying hardware and software layers.[6] With some PaaS offers like Microsoft Azure and Google App Engine, the underlying computer and storage resources scale automatically to match application demand so that the cloud user does not have to allocate resources manually. Even more specific application types can be provided via PaaS such as media encoding as provided by services like bitcodin.com or media.io.

Some integration and data management providers have also embraced specialized applications of PaaS as delivery models for data solutions. Examples include iPaaS (Integration Platform as a Service) and dPaaS (Data Platform as a Service). iPaaS enables customers to develop, execute and govern integration flows. Under the iPaaS integration model, customers drive the development and deployment of integrations without installing or managing any hardware or middleware. dPaaS delivers integration — and data-management — products as a fully managed service.

Under the dPaaS model, the PaaS provider, not the customer, manages the development and execution of data solutions by building tailored data applications for the customer.[7] dPaaS users retain transparency and control over data through data-visualization tools. PaaS consumers do not manage or control the underlying cloud infrastructure including network, servers, operating systems, or storage, but have control over the deployed applications and possibly configuration settings for the application-hosting environment.

C. Infrastructure as a Service (IaaS)

The capability provided to the consumer is to provide processing, storage, networks, and other fundamental computing resources where the consumer can deploy and run arbitrary software, which may include operating systems and applications. The consumer does not manage or control the underlying cloud infrastructure but has control over operating systems, storage, and deployed applications; and possibly limited control of selected networking components (e.g., host firewalls).

According to the Internet Engineering Task Force (IETF), the most basic cloud-service model is that of providers offering computing infrastructure — virtual machines and other resources — as a service to subscribers. Infrastructure as a service (IaaS) refers to online services that abstract the user from the details of infrastructure like physical computing resources, location, data partitioning, security, backup etc. Pools of hypervisors within the cloud operational system can support large numbers of virtual machines and the ability to scale services up and down according to customers' varying requirements.

Containerization offers higher performance than virtualization, because there is no hypervisor overhead. Also, container capacity auto-scales dynamically with computing load, eliminating the problem of over-provisioning and enabling usage-based billing. IaaS clouds often offer additional resources such as a virtual-machine disk-image library, raw block storage, file or object storage, firewalls, load balancers, IP addresses, virtual local area networks (VLANs), and software bundles.

IaaS-cloud providers supply these resources on-demand from their large pools of equipment installed in data centers. For wide-area connectivity, customers can use either the Internet or carrier clouds (dedicated virtual private networks). To deploy their applications, cloud users install operating-system images and their application software on the cloud infrastructure. In this model, the cloud user patches and maintains the operating systems and the application software. Cloud providers typically bill IaaS services on a utility computing basis: cost reflects the amount of resources allocated and consumed.

New Words

Part I

heterogeneous	各种各样的	autonomous	自治的
storage	存储	per-capita	人均地
terabyte	太字节（10^{12}B）	petabyte	10^{15}B
ecosystem	生态系统	predictive	预测的
analytics	分析学	spot	发现
sort	分类	semi-	半
query	查询	inherently	本身固有的
conform	符合	explicit	明确的
revolutionary	革命性的	velocity	速度
volume	量	raw	原始的
era	时代	outstrip	超过
algorithm	算法	unimaginable	难以想象的
enormous	巨大的	unprecedented	前所未有的
timely	及时的	trillion	万亿
veracity	真实性	enterprise	企业

sector	行业领域	proprietary	专有的
immutable	不可改变的	log	日志
sentiment	情感	statistical	统计的
intersection	交叉	interdisciplinary	跨学科的
metric	度量	visualization	可视化
privacy	隐私	anonymization	匿名化
homomorphic	同态的	cryptography	密码学
authentication	认证	confidentiality	机密性

Part Ⅱ

ubiquitous	无处不在的	configurable	可配置的
on demand	按需	minimal	极少的
scale	规模	utility	公用事业
grid	（输电线路、天然气管道等的）系统网络	expertise	专业知识
impede	阻碍	obstacle	障碍
virtualization	虚拟化	scalable	可伸缩的
agility	灵活性	autonomic	自主的
metric	度量标准	infrastructure	基础设施
virtualize	虚拟化	vulnerability	漏洞
hybrid	混合的	collocation	配置
acronym	首字母缩略词	abstraction	抽象
oriented	以……为导向	physical	物理的
install	安装	clone	克隆
transparent	透明的	authentication	认证
tailored	量身定制的	retain	保持
arbitrary	任意的	containerization	集装箱化
patch	修补		

Notes on the Text

Part I

1. Big data is a term for data sets that are so large or complex that traditional data processing application softwares are inadequate to deal with them, as the information comes from multiple, heterogeneous, autonomous sources with complex and evolving relationships, and keeps growing.

大数据一词指庞大或复杂的数据集，由于信息来自关系复杂且不断变化的多个异构的独立源，并且不断增长，传统的数据处理应用软件都不足以处理它们。

2. Data sets grow rapidly — in part because they are increasingly gathered by cheap and numerous information-sensing Internet of Things devices such as mobile devices, software logs, cameras, microphones, radio-frequency identification (RFID) readers and wireless sensor networks.

数据集的快速增长，部分原因是因为数据越来越多地通过众多价格低廉的物联网信息感知设备被收集起来，这些设备包括移动设备、软件日志、摄像机、麦克风、射频识别（RFID）阅读器和无线传感网等。

3. The challenge is not only to collect and manage vast volume and different type of data, but also to extract meaningful value from it, which involves predictive analytics, user behavior analytics and other advanced data analytics methods.

我们面临的挑战不仅是要收集和管理大量不同类型的数据，还要从中获取有效价值，这其中包括了预测分析、用户行为分析和其他高级数据分析方法。

4. Big data comes from a great variety of sources and can be categorized into three general types: structured, semi-structured and unstructured.

大数据来源多种多样，可分为结构化、半结构化和非结构化三大类。

5. The sheer volume of the data is enormous, and a very large contributor to the ever expanding digital universe is the Internet of Things with sensors all over the world in all devices creating data every second.

数据量是如此巨大，而为这个不断膨胀的数字世界提供数据的巨大贡献者正是物联网，它包含无数传感器，存在于遍布全球、每时每刻产生数据的所有设备中。

6. MapReduce is a programming framework for distributed computing which was created by Google using the divide and conquer method to break down complex big data problems into small units of work and process them in parallel.

MapReduce 是一种分布式计算的编程框架，它由 Google 创建，采用分而治之的方法，将复杂的大数据问题分解成小的工作单元并行处理。

Part Ⅱ

1. It is a model for enabling ubiquitous, on-demand access to a shared pool of configurable computing resources (e.g., computer networks, servers, storage, applications and services), which can be rapidly provisioned and released with minimal management effort.

它是一种能够对可配置计算资源共享池进行无处不在、按需访问的模型（资源包括计算机网络、服务器、存储、应用和服务等）。这些资源能够被快速提供，只需投入极少的管理工作。

2. Cloud computing provides all of its resources as services, and makes use of the well-established standards and best practices gained in the domain of SOA to allow global and easy access to cloud services in a standardized way.

云计算将其所有资源作为服务提供，并利用在 SOA 领域中获得的成熟标准和最佳实践，从而以标准方式向全球提供便捷的云服务。

3. Cloud computing provides the tools and technologies to build data/compute intensive parallel applications with much more affordable prices compared to traditional parallel computing techniques.

与传统的并行计算技术相比，云计算为构建数据密集/计算密集型并行应用提供了更廉价的工具和技术。

4. Undertaking a private cloud project requires a significant level and degree of engagement to virtualize the business environment, and requires the organization to reevaluate decisions about existing resources.

实施私有云项目需要相当高的参与程度使业务环境虚拟化，并要求机构重新评估有关现有资源的决策。

5. Cloud applications differ from other applications in their scalability—which can be achieved by cloning tasks onto multiple virtual machines at run-time to meet changing work demand.

云应用程序与其他应用程序的不同之处在于在其可扩展性——云应用程序可以在运行时将任务克隆到多个虚拟机上，以满足不断变化的工作需求。

6. Application developers can develop and run their software solutions on a cloud platform without the cost and complexity of buying and managing the underlying hardware and software layers.

应用程序开发人员可以在云平台上开发和运行其软件解决方案，而无须承担购买和管理底层硬件和软件层所产生的成本和复杂性。

7. Under the dPaaS model, the PaaS provider, not the customer, manages the development and execution of data solutions by building tailored data applications for the customer.

在 dPaaS 模式下，PaaS 提供商（而非客户）通过为客户构建量身定制的数据应用程序来管理数据解决方案的开发和执行。

Technical Tips

Data extraction

Data extraction is the act or process of retrieving data out of (usually unstructured or poorly structured) data sources for further data processing or data storage. The import into the intermediate extracting system is thus usually followed by data transformation and possibly the addition of metadata prior to export to another stage in the data workflow. Typical unstructured data sources include web pages, emails, documents, PDFs, scanned text, mainframe reports, spool files, classifieds, etc. The growing process of data extraction from the web is referred to as Web scraping.

Data visualization

Data visualization refers to the techniques used to communicate data or information by encoding it as visual objects (e.g., points, lines or bars) contained in graphics. A primary goal of data visualization is to communicate information clearly and efficiently via statistical graphics, plots and information graphics. It is one of the steps in data analysis or data science. Numerical data may be encoded using dots, lines, or bars, to visually communicate a quantitative message. Effective visualization helps users analyze and reason about data and evidence. It makes complex data more accessible, understandable and usable. Users may have particular analytical tasks, such as making comparisons or understanding causality, and the design principle of the graphic follows the task. Tables are generally used where users will look up a specific measurement, while charts of various types are used to show patterns or relationships in the data for one or more variables.

Machine learning

Machine learning is a type of artificial intelligence (AI) that allows software applications to become more accurate in predicting outcomes without being explicitly programmed. The basic premise of machine learning is to build algorithms that can receive input data and use statistical analysis to predict an output value within an acceptable range.

Evolved from the study of pattern recognition and computational learning theory in artificial intelligence, machine learning explores the study and construction of algorithms that can learn from and make predictions on data — such algorithms overcome following strictly static program instructions by making data-driven predictions or decisions, through building a model from sample inputs. The processes involved in machine learning are similar to that of data mining and predictive modeling. Both require searching through data to look for patterns and adjusting program actions accordingly.

Many people are familiar with machine learning from shopping on the internet and being served ads related to their purchase. This happens because recommendation engines use machine learning to personalize online ad delivery in almost real time. Beyond personalized marketing, other common machine learning use cases include fraud detection, spam filtering, network security threat detection, predictive maintenance and building news feeds.

Supplementary Readings: Smart City

Smart cities have become one of the most interesting research topics for governments, businesses and researchers in the last few years. Being a smart city implies a competitive edge compared to other cities in terms of economic growth, sustainability, human resources and governance. Therefore, more and more governments pursue the future vision and hop onto the smart city "bandwagon".

Definition of Smart City

A smart city is an urban development vision to integrate information and communication technology (ICT) and Internet of things (IoT) technology in a secure fashion to manage a city's assets. These assets include local departments' information systems, schools, libraries, transportation systems, hospitals, power plants, water supply networks, waste management, law enforcement, and other community services. A smart city is promoted to use urban informatics and technology to improve efficiency of services. ICT allows city officials to interact directly with the community and the city infrastructure, and to monitor what is happening in the city, how the city is evolving, and how to enable a better quality of life. Through the use of sensors integrated with real-time monitoring systems, data are collected from citizens and devices, and then processed and analyzed. The information and knowledge gathered are keys to tackling inefficiency.

Information and communication technology is used to enhance quality, performance and interactivity of urban services, to reduce costs and resource consumption, and to improve contact between citizens and the government. Smart city applications are developed to manage urban flows and allow for real-time responses. A smart city may therefore be more prepared to respond to challenges than one with a simple "transactional" relationship with citizens. Yet, the term itself remains unclear to its specifics and therefore, open to various interpretations. Other terms that have been used for similar concepts include digital city, electronic communities, information city, intelligent city, MESH city, telecity, teletopia, ubiquitous city, and wired city.

Major technological, economic and environmental changes have generated interest in smart cities, including climate change, economic restructuring, online shopping and entertainment, ageing populations, growth of urban population, and pressures on public finances. The European Union (EU) has devoted constant efforts to devising a strategy for achieving "smart" urban growth for its metropolitan city-regions. The EU has developed a range of programmes under "Europe's Digital Agenda". In 2010, it highlighted its focus on strengthening innovation and investment in ICT services for the purpose of improving public services and quality of life. It is estimated that the global market for smart urban services will be $400 billion per annum by 2020. Examples of Smart City technologies and programs have been implemented in Southampton, Amsterdam, Barcelona, Madrid, Stockholm and in China.

Due to the breadth of technologies that have been implemented under the smart city label, it is difficult to distill a precise definition of smart city. There are four factors that contribute to the definition:

- Application of a wide range of electronic and digital technologies to communities and cities
- Use of ICT to transform life and working environments within the region
- Embedding of ICTs in government systems
- Territorialisation of practices that brings ICTs and people together to enhance innovation and knowledge that they offer.

Characteristics of Smart City

It is suggested that a smart city (also community, business cluster, urban region) uses information technologies to:

> (a) Make more efficient use of physical infrastructure (roads, buildings, environments, and other physical assets) through artificial intelligence and data analytics to support a strong and healthy economic, social, cultural development.
>
> (b) Engage effectively with local people in local governance and decision using open innovation processes and e-participation, and improve collective intelligence of the city's institutions through e-governance with emphasis placed on citizen participation and co-design.
>
> (c) Learn, adapt and innovate, and thereby respond more effectively and promptly to changing circumstances by improving intelligence of the city.

They evolve towards a strong integration of all dimensions of human intelligence, collective intelligence, and also artificial intelligence within the city. The intelligence of cities resides in the increasingly effective combination of digital telecommunication networks (the nerves), ubiquitously embedded intelligence (the brains), sensors and tags (the sensory organs), and software (the knowledge and cognitive competence).

Platforms and technologies

New Internet technologies that promote cloud-based services, Internet of Things (IoT), real-world user interfaces, uses of smart phones and smart meters, networks of sensors and RFIDs, and more accurate communication based on the semantic web are opening new ways to collective action and collaborative problem solving.

Online collaborative sensor data management platforms are on-line database services. They allow sensor owners to register and connect their devices to feed data into an on-line database for storage and allow developers to connect to the database and build their own applications based on that data.

In London, a traffic management system known as SCOOT optimizes green light time at traffic intersections by feeding back magnetometer and inductive loop data to a supercomputer, which can co-ordinate traffic lights across the city to improve traffic throughput.

The city of Santander in Cantabria, northern Spain, has 20,000 sensors connecting buildings, infrastructure, transport, networks and utilities. They offer a physical space for experimentation and validation of the IoT functions such as interaction and management protocols, device technologies, and support services such as discovery, identity management and security. In Santander, the sensors monitor the levels of pollution, noise, traffic and parking.

Electronic cards (known as smart cards) are another common platform in smart city contexts. These cards possess a unique encrypted identifier that allows the owner to log into a range of government provided services (or e-services) without setting up multiple accounts. A single identifier allows governments to aggregate data about citizens and their preferences to improve the provision of services and to determine common interests of groups. This technology has been implemented in Southampton.

Smart City in China

The year of 2013 is considered the first year of smart city in China. With the development of informationization and urbanization in China, city diseases (traffic jam, medical problem and unbalanced education) are increasingly more apparent. Smart city is the key to solving these diseases. In 2015, China introduced "Internet plus" action guidance, and promoted the innovative development of cloud computing and big data. At the same time, the smart city policies were issued, such as the third batch of smart city pilot, national green data center pilot, the first national information consumption pilot, and the second batch of broadband China pilot. With the support of national policies, China has seen rapid development of smart city.

There are four trends in the development of smart city in China:

(a) Infrastructure co-construction and sharing. A trend in developing smart city is co-construction and sharing of new generation infrastructures based on cloud-computing data center. Due to privacy and security issues in public cloud services, the government and enterprises usually do not choose a cloud service. However, with the development of the hybrid cloud services, convenience and safety can be integrated into a single cloud service simultaneously. Hybrid cloud is a big integration containing big data and a variety of data types. It merges small independent data centers to become a large cloud data center. The value of data will be further released.

(b) Comprehensive application of big data. With the improvement of infrastructure and an open data environment, big data is becoming a crucial part in smart city, and helps the government make decisions, provide services and encourage innovations. In the future, smart city will become a model of big data, and use data analysis and data mining to deal with various affairs.

(c) Smart application everywhere. With the development of big data technology and smart applications, traditional government departments and industries will have the ability of making people work and live more convenienctly and comfortably. Smart applications interconnect things in a smart city.

(d) Smart city cluster is a new feature of smart city 2.0. In a market economy, the unimpeded flow of people, goods, capital and information provides low cost and efficiency, and optimizes resource allocation. The National Plan on New Urbanization 2014-2020 stresses improvement of spatial layout, requiring coordinated development of cities and small towns based on major city clusters. City clusters will have better efficiency, coordination and integration, and can attract more industries and residents. They are not just simple integration of several cities, but coordination and integration of a number of smart cities. On an advanced development stage, construction of information infrastructure and improvement of intelligence functions will promote coordination and integration of smart cities, and make the smart city more efficienct with optimized structures and better functions.

Exercises

I. Translate the following passages into Chinese.

1. Unstructured data comprises of more complex information, such as customer reviews from commercial websites, photos and other multimedia, and comments on social networking sites. These data cannot easily be separated into categories or analyzed numerically. This type of data consists of formats which cannot easily be indexed into relational tables for analysis or querying.

2. Cloud Computing is a pay-per-use-on-demand mode that can easily access shared IT resources through the Internet.

3. Computing infrastructure is imaged as a "cloud" from which individuals and business corporations can extend their access to its application from anywhere and at any time on demand.

4. There are various deployment models, with variations in physical location and distribution, which have been adopted by the cloud computing.

5. Hybrid cloud is a composition of two or more clouds (private, community or public) that remain distinct entities but are bound together, offering the benefits of multiple deployment models.

6. Cloud providers typically bill IaaS services on a utility computing basis: cost reflects the amount of resources allocated and consumed.

II. Choose the phrase that is closest in meaning to the underlined part.

1. The size of data now is larger than terabytes and petabytes. <u>The grand scale and rise of data outstrips traditional storing and analysis techniques</u>.

   A. The grand scale and rise of data gives up the traditional storing and analysis techniques.

   B. The growth rate of the new data exceeds that of the traditional data.

   C. The grand scale and rise of data gets rid of the traditional storing and analysis techniques.

   D. Traditional store and analysis techniques are unable to handle the grand scale and rise of data.

2. Specialized services like data access, authentication and payments are the <u>building blocks</u> to new application.

   A. built units

   B. basic modules

   C. important parts

   D. obstacles

3. Cloud computing is a pay-per-use-on-demand mode that can easily access shared IT resources through the Internet.

A. The payment of cloud computing is based on the usage on demand

B. Cloud computing charge each user when demanded

C. The payment of cloud computing is based on each user's request

D. The payment of cloud computing is demanding for each user

4. It is a model for enabling ubiquitous, on-demand access to a shared pool of configurable computing resources, which can be rapidly provisioned and released with minimal management effort.

A. omnipresent, available upon request

B. convenient, by-request

C. immediate, required

D. high-speed, by-request

5. The underlying computer and storage resources scale automatically to match application demand so that the cloud user does not have to allocate resources manually.

A. automatically measures the application demand

B. automatically scales up to meet application requirements

C. increase proportionally to the application demand

D. are automatically adjusted to meet application requirements

Unit 17 Internet of Things (IoT)

We are now embracing a new era of Internet of Things (IoT). Generally speaking, IoT refers to the networked interconnection of everyday objects, which are often equipped with ubiquitous intelligence. IoT will increase ubiquity of the Internet by integrating every object for interaction via embedded systems, leading to a highly distributed network of devices communicating with human beings as well as other devices.

Text

Part I: Internet of Things: Concept and Key Technologies

Thanks to the rapid advances in underlying technologies, Internet of Things (IoT) is opening tremendous opportunities for a large number of novel applications that promise to improve the quality of our lives. In recent years, IoT has drawn significant research attention around the world.[1]

IoT comprises billions of intelligent communicating "things" and empowers the connected things with new capabilities. The future of the Internet will consist of heterogeneously connected devices that will further extend the borders of the world with physical entities and virtual components.[2] Depending on various technologies for implementation, the definition of the IoT varies. However, the fundamental of IoT implies that objects in an IoT can be identified uniquely in the virtual representations. Within an IoT, all things can exchange data and if needed, process data according to predefined schemes.

Some preliminary IoT applications have been already developed in healthcare, transportation, and automotive industries. Currently, IoT technologies are at their infant stages; however, many new developments have occurred in the integration of objects with sensors in the cloud-based Internet.[3] The development of IoT involves many issues such as infrastructure, communications, interfaces, protocols, and standards.

The emerging wirelessly sensory technologies have significantly extended the sensory capabilities of devices, and therefore the original concept of IoT is extending to ambient intelligence and autonomous control.[4] To date, a number of technologies are involved in IoT, such as wireless sensor networks (WSNs), barcodes, intelligent sensing, radio frequency identification (RFID), near field communication (NFC), low energy wireless communications, cloud computing, and so on. Evolutions of these technologies bring new technologies to IoT. Figure 17.1 summarizes the enabling technologies for IoT.

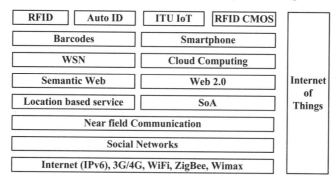

Figure 17.1　Enabling Technologies for IoT

Identification and tracking technologies

The concept of IoT was coined based on the RFID-enabled identification and tracking technologies. A basic RFID system is composed of an RFID reader and an RFID tag. Due to its capability to identify, trace, and track, the RFID system has been widely applied in logistics such as package tracking, supply chain management, healthcare applications. An RFID system can provide sufficient real-time information about things in IoT, which are useful to manufacturers, distributors, and retailers. For example, RFID application in supply chain management can improve inventory management. Some identified advantages include reduced labour cost, simplified business processes, and improved efficiency. The next generation of RFID technology will focus on the item level RFID usage and RFID-aware management issues. Although RFID technology is successfully used in many areas, it is still evolving in developing active systems, inkjet-printing based RFID, and management technologies. Other identified problems need to be solved for applying IoT include collision of RFID readings, privacy protection and integration of RFID and smart sensors.

Integration of WSN and RFID

Many types of intelligent sensors have been developed based on physical principles of infrared, γ-ray, pressure, vibration, electromagnetic, biosensor, and X-ray. Data from those sensors in IoT can be acquired and integrated for analysis, decision-making, and storage. Examples of RFID integrated sensors are On/Off-board locating sensor, sensor tags, independent tag and sensor devices, and RFID reading systems. The integration of sensors and RFID empowers IoT in the implementations of industrial services and the further deployment of services in extended applications. IoT integrating with RFID and WSNs makes it possible to develop IoT applications in healthcare, decision-making of complex systems, and smart systems such as smart transportation, smart city, and smart rehabilitation systems.

Communications

Hardware devices involve diversified specifications in terms of communication, computation, memory, and data storage capacity, or transmission capacities. An IoT application consists of many types of devices. All types of hardware devices should be well organized through the network and be accessible via available communication. Typically, devices can be organized by gateways for the communication purpose over the Internet.

IoT can be an aggregation of heterogeneous networks, such as WSNs, wireless mesh networks, mobile networks, and WLAN. These networks help the things in fulfilling complex activities such as decision-making, computation and data exchange. In addition, reliable communication between gateway and things is essential to make a centralized decision with respect to IoT. The gateway is capable of running complicated optimization algorithms locally by exploiting its network knowledge. The computational complexity is shifted from things to the gateway; the global optimal route and parameter values for the gateway can be obtained. This is feasible since the size of the gateway domain is in the order of a few of tens in comparison with the sizes of things.

Hardware capabilities and the communication requirements vary from one device type to another. The things in IoT can have very different capabilities for computation, memory, power, or communication. For instance, a cellular phone or a tablet has much better communication and computation capabilities than a single-purpose electronic product such as a heart rate monitor watch. Similarly, things can have very different requirements of Quality of Service (QoS), in particular, in the aspects of delay, energy consumption, and reliability. For example, minimizing the energy use for communication/computation purposes is a major constraint for the battery powered devices without efficient energy harvesting techniques; this energy constraint is not critical for the devices with power supply connection.[5]

Networks

There exist a lot of cross-layer protocols for Wireless Networks, Wireless Mesh Networks (WMNs) or Ad Hoc Networks (AHNs). However, they cannot be applied to the IoT due to several reasons. First, the heterogeneity of the IoT due to the fact that things have largely diversified hardware configurations, QoS requirements, functionalities, and goals. On the other hand, nodes in a WSN usually have similar hardware specifications, similar communication requirements, and the shared goal. Second, the Internet is involved in the IoT, from which it inherits a centralized and hierarchical architecture. In comparison, WSNs, WMNs and AHNs have relatively flat network architectures: nodes in these networks communicate in a multi-hop fashion and the Internet is not involved.[6]

Service management

Service management refers to the implementation and management of the services that meet the needs of users or applications. Service-oriented Architecture (SoA) can promote encapsulation of services. Encapsulation allows details of services such as implementation and protocols to be hidden behind the instances of services. SoA allows applications to use heterogeneous objects as compatible services. On the other hand, the dynamic nature of IoT applications requires that IoT can provide reliable and consistent service; it can benefit from an effective service-oriented architecture to avoid failures from dislocations of device or death of battery.

Security and privacy

For IoT, security and privacy are two important challenges. To integrate the devices of sensing layer as intrinsic parts of the IoT, effective security technology is essential to ensure security and privacy protection in various activities such as personal activities, business processes, transportations, and information protection.[7] The applications of IoT might be affected by pervasive threats such as RFID tag attacks and data leakage. In RFID systems, a number of security schemes and authentication protocols have been proposed to cope with security threats. On one hand, low-cost symmetric-key cryptography algorithms, such as Tiny Encryption Algorithm (TEA) and Advance Encryption Standard (AES), have been proposed to protect data exchange. Besides, the low-cost RFID tag has implemented some asymmetric key cryptography algorithm such as Elliptic Curve Cryptography (ECC). On the other hand, the security protocols developed for WSN can be integrated as an intrinsic part of IoT. The following two aspects require further studies: 1) adaption of existing Internet standards for interoperable protocols, and 2) security assurance for composable services. The challenges in security and privacy protection are summarized as resilience to attacks, data authentication, access control, and client privacy.

Part II : IoT Applications

When we crossed the threshold of connecting more objects than people to the Internet, a huge window of opportunity opened for the creation of applications in the areas of automation, sensing, and machine-to-machine communication.[1] In fact, the possibilities are almost endless. The following examples highlight some of the ways IoT is changing people's lives for the better.

The ability to network embedded devices with limited CPU, memory and power resources means that IoT finds applications in nearly every field. Such systems could be in charge of collecting information in settings ranging from natural ecosystems to buildings and factories, thereby finding applications in fields of environmental sensing and urban planning.[2] On the other hand, IoT systems could also be responsible for performing actions, not just sensing things. Intelligent shopping systems, for example, could monitor specific users' purchasing habits in a store by tracking their specific mobile phones. These users could then be provided with special offers on their favorite products, or even location of items that they need, which their fridge has automatically conveyed to the phone. Additional examples of sensing and actuating are reflected in applications that deal with heat, water, electricity and energy management, as well as cruise-assisting transportation systems.

Other applications that the Internet of things can provide is enabling extended home security features and home automation. The concept of an "Internet of living things" has been proposed to describe networks of biological sensors that could use cloud-based analyses to allow users to study DNA or other molecules.[3] However, the application of the IoT is not only restricted to these areas. Other specialized use cases of the IoT may also exist. An overview of some of the most prominent application areas is provided here.

Manufacturing

Network control and management of manufacturing equipment, asset and situation management, or manufacturing process control bring the IoT within the realm of industrial applications and smart manufacturing as well. The IoT intelligent systems enable rapid manufacturing of new products, dynamic response to product demands, and real-time optimization of manufacturing production and supply chain networks, by networking machinery, sensors and control systems together.[4]

Digital control systems to automate process controls, operator tools and service information systems to optimize plant safety and security are within the scope of the IoT. It also extends itself to asset management via predictive maintenance, statistical evaluation, and measurements to maximize reliability. Smart industrial management systems can also be integrated with the Smart Grid, thereby enabling real-time energy optimization. Measurements, automated controls, plant optimization, health and safety management, and other functions are provided by a large number of networked sensors.

The National Science Foundation of United States established an Industry/University Cooperative Research Center on intelligent maintenance systems (IMS) in 2001 with a research focus to use IoT-based predictive analytics technologies to monitor connected machines and to predict machine degradation, and further to prevent potential failures. The vision to achieve near-zero breakdown using IoT-based predictive analytics led the future development of e-manufacturing and e-maintenance activities.

The term IIoT (Industrial Internet of Things) is often encountered in the manufacturing industries, referring to the industrial subset of the IoT. IIoT in manufacturing could generate so much business value that it will eventually lead to the fourth industrial revolution, so the so-called Industry 4.0. It is estimated that in the future, successful companies will be able to increase their revenue through Internet of things by creating new business models and improve productivity, exploit analytics for innovation, and transform workforce. The potential of growth by implementing IIoT will generate $12 trillion of global GDP by 2030.

While connectivity and data acquisition are imperative for IIoT, they should not be the purpose, rather the foundation and path to something bigger. Among all the technologies, predictive maintenance is probably a relatively "easier win" since it is applicable to existing assets and management systems. The objective of intelligent maintenance systems is to reduce unexpected downtime and increase productivity. And to realize that alone would generate around up to 30% over total maintenance costs. Industrial big data analytics will play a vital role in manufacturing asset predictive maintenance, although that is not the only capability of industrial big data. Cyber-physical systems (CPS) is the core technology of industrial big data and it will be an interface between human and the cyber world. Cyber-physical systems can be designed by following the 5C (connection, conversion, cyber, cognition and configuration) architecture, and it will transform the collected data into actionable information, and eventually interfere with the physical assets to optimize processes.[5]

Environmental monitoring

Environmental monitoring applications of the IoT typically use sensors to assist in environmental protection by monitoring air or water quality, atmospheric or soil conditions, and can even include areas like monitoring the movements of wildlife and their habitats. Development of resource constrained devices connected to the Internet also means that other applications like earthquake or tsunami early-warning systems can also be used by emergency services to provide more effective aid. IoT devices in this application typically span a large geographic area and can also be mobile. It has been argued that the standardization IoT brings to wireless sensing will revolutionize this area.

Medical and healthcare

IoT technologies have a number of applications in the health-care sector. They can be used to enhance current assisted living solutions. Patients will carry medical sensors to monitor parameters such as body temperature, blood pressure, breathing activity. These health monitoring devices can range from blood pressure and heart rate monitors to advanced devices capable of monitoring specialized implants, such as pacemakers, electronic wristbands, or advanced hearing aids. Either wearable (e.g., accelerometers, gyroscopes) or fixed sensors will be used to gather data used to monitor patient activities in their living environments. Information will be locally aggregated and transmitted to remote medical centers, which will be able to perform advanced remote monitoring and capable of rapid response actions when needed. The interconnection of such heterogeneous sensors will provide a comprehensive picture of health parameters, thereby triggering an intervention by the medical staff upon detection of conditions that may lead to health deterioration, and realizing preventive care.[6]

Another relevant application sector relates to personalized health-care and well-being solutions. The use of wearable sensors, together with suitable applications running on personal computing devices enables people to track their daily activities (steps walked, calories burned, exercises performed, etc.), providing suggestions for enhancing their lifestyle and prevent the onset of health problems.

Building and home automation

IoT devices can be used to monitor and control the mechanical, electrical and electronic systems used in various types of buildings (e.g., public and private, industrial, institutions, or residential) in home automation and building automation systems. Three main areas are being covered in the literature:

- Integration of the internet with building energy management systems in order to create energy efficient and IOT driven "smart buildings".
- Possible means of real-time monitoring for reducing energy consumption and monitoring occupant behaviors.
- Integration of smart devices in the built environment and how they might be used in future applications.

In this application, a key role is played by sensors, which are used to both monitor resource consumptions as well as to proactively detect current users' needs. Such a scenario integrates a number of different subsystems, and hence requires a high level of standardization to ensure interoperability. Ability to reason in a distributed and cooperative way, and to actuate is also necessary in order to ensure that decisions taken on the resources under control (e.g., switch on/off lighting, heating, cooling, etc.) are in line with the users' needs and expectations.

Transportation

The IoT can assist in integration of communications, control, and information processing across various transportation systems. Application of the IoT extends to all aspects of transportation systems (i.e. the vehicle, the infrastructure, and the driver or user). Dynamic interaction between these components of a transport system enables inter- and intra-vehicular communication, smart traffic control, smart parking, electronic toll collection systems, logistic and fleet management, vehicle control, and safety and road assistance.

Smart Cities

The term "smart city" is used to denote the cyber-physical ecosystem emerging by deploying advanced communication infrastructure and novel services over city-wide scenarios. By means of advanced services, it is indeed possible to optimize the usage of physical city infrastructures (e.g., road networks, power grid, etc.) and quality of life for its citizens. IoT technologies can find a number of diverse application in smart cities scenarios. As a case study, IoT technologies can be used to provide advanced traffic control systems.

Through IoT it will be possible to monitor car traffic in big cities or highways and deploy services that offer traffic routing advice to avoid congestion. In this perspective, cars will be understood as representing "smart objects". In addition, smart parking devices system, based on RFID and sensor technologies, may allow to monitor available parking spaces and provide drivers with automated parking advice, thus improving mobility in urban area.

Moreover, sensors may monitor the flow of vehicular traffic on highways and retrieve aggregate information such as average speed and numbers of cars. Sensors could detect the level of air pollution, retrieve smog information such as the level of carbon dioxide, PM10, etc., and deliver such information to health agencies. Furthermore, sensors could be used in a forensics setting, by detecting violations and by transmitting the relevant data to law enforcement agencies in order to identify the violator, or to store information that will be provided in case of accident for subsequent accident scene analysis.[7]

New Words

Part I

ubiquitous	无所不在的	ubiquity	普遍存在
underlying	基础的	empower	使能够
heterogeneously	不同类地	border	边界
entity	实体	autonomous	自主的
ambient	周围的	identification	识别
RFID	射频识别	preliminary	初步的
healthcare	医疗保健	automotive	汽车的
sensor	传感器	infrastructure	基础设施
interface	接口	protocol	协议
barcode	条形码	logistics	物流
inkjet	喷墨的	tag	标签
manufacturer	制造商	distributor	分销商
retailer	零售商	collision	冲突
rehabilitation	康复	diversified	多样化的
specification	规格	accessible	可访问的
aggregation	集合	heterogeneous	各种各样的
harvesting	获取	cross-layer	跨层
inherit	继承	hierarchical	分层的
multi-hop	多跳	configuration	配置
encapsulation	封装	instance	实体
sensing	感知	intrinsic	内在的
pervasive	遍布的	authentication	认证
cryptography	密码学	encryption	加密
symmetric	对称的	asymmetric	不对称的
interoperable	可互操作的	resilience	快速恢复的能力

Part II

threshold	阈值	highlight	突出
embed	嵌入	ecosystem	生态系统
urban	都市的	specific	特定的

molecule	分子	prominent	突出的
manufacture	制造	plant	工厂
optimize	优化	predictive	预测的
maintenance	维护	breakdown	故障
encounter	遇到	revenue	收益
trillion	万亿	imperative	必要的
applicable	适用于	downtime	停机时间
cyber	信息技术的	cognition	认知
habitat	栖息地	tsunami	海啸
revolutionize	彻底改革	transportation	运输
vehicle	车辆	toll	通行费
fleet	车队	deploy	部署
grid	系统网络	pacemaker	心脏起博器
gyroscope	陀螺仪	trigger	触发
intervention	干预	congestion	拥堵
aggregate	总体的	smog	烟雾
dioxide	二氧化物	forensics	取证

Notes on the Text

Part I

1. In recent years, IoT has drawn significant research attention around the world.
   近年来，物联网在世界范围引起了广泛的研究兴趣。
   - draw significant research attention 是在科技论文写作中引出某一热点主题经常用的经典句型，类似的还有 draw considerable research attentions from academics and industry。

2. The future of the Internet will consist of heterogeneously connected devices that will further extend the borders of the world with physical entities and virtual components.
   未来互联网将由异构连接的设备所组成，这些设备将通过物理实体和虚拟组件进一步扩展世界的边界。

3. Currently, IoT technologies are at their infant stages; however, many new developments have occurred in the integration of objects with sensors in the cloud-based Internet.
   目前，物联网技术处于起步阶段；而在将云网络中的传感器对象集成起来的这一过程中，出现了许多新的发展。

4. The emerging wirelessly sensory technologies have significantly extended the sensory capabilities of devices, and therefore the original concept of IoT is extending to ambient intelligence and autonomous control.

新兴的无线传感技术极大地扩展了设备的感知能力，物联网的最初概念从而扩展到了环境智能和自主控制。

5. For example, minimizing the energy use for communication/computation purposes is a major constraint for the battery powered devices without efficient energy harvesting techniques; this energy constraint is not critical for the devices with power supply connection.

例如，对于无法有效（从外部）获取能量的电池供电设备，使通信和计算的能耗最小化是一个主要制约因素；而这种能量约束对于有电源连接的设备来说并不重要。

6. In comparison, WSNs, WMNs and AHNs have relatively flat network architectures: nodes in these networks communicate in a multi-hop fashion and the Internet is not involved.

相比之下，无线传感器网络、无线网状网和 Ad Hoc 网络具有相对平坦的网络架构：这些网络中的节点以多跳方式进行通信，并且不涉及因特网。

7. To integrate the devices of sensing layer as intrinsic parts of the IoT, effective security technology is essential to ensure security and privacy protection in various activities such as personal activities, business processes, transportations, and information protection.

为了将传感层设备集成为物联网的内在组成部分，有效的安全技术对于确保个人活动、业务流程、运输和信息保护等各种活动的安全和隐私保护至关重要。

Part Ⅱ

1. When we crossed the threshold of connecting more objects than people to the Internet, a huge window of opportunity opened for the creation of applications in the areas of automation, sensing, and machine-to-machine communication.

当我们跨越一道门槛，使得连接到互联网的物多于人时，就在自动化、传感、机对机通信领域为创建各种应用开启了一扇巨大的机会之窗。

2. Such systems could be in charge of collecting information in settings ranging from natural ecosystems to buildings and factories, thereby finding applications in fields of environmental sensing and urban planning.

这些系统可从自然生态系统、建筑物、工厂等环境中收集信息，从而在环境感测和城市规划领域中得到应用。

find applications in the field of ...　在……领域中得到应用。

3. The concept of an "Internet of living things" has been proposed to describe networks of biological sensors that could use cloud-based analyses to allow users to study DNA or other molecules.

"生物互联网"的概念已被提出来，用于描述可用云分析使得用户能研究 DNA 或其他分子的生物传感器网络。

4. The IoT intelligent systems enable rapid manufacturing of new products, dynamic response to product demands, and real-time optimization of manufacturing

production and supply chain networks, by networking machinery, sensors and control systems together.

物联网智能系统通过联网机械、传感器和控制系统，可以快速制造新产品，动态响应产品需求，以及实时优化制造生产和供应链网络。

5. Cyber-physical systems can be designed by following the 5C (connection, conversion, cyber, cognition, and configuration) architecture, and it will transform the collected data into actionable information, and eventually interfere with the physical assets to optimize processes.

信息物理融合系统可按照 5C（连接、转换、网络、认知、配置）架构进行设计，并将收集的数据转换为可操作的信息，最终干预实体资产以优化流程。

6. The interconnection of such heterogeneous sensors will provide a comprehensive picture of health parameters, thereby triggering an intervention by the medical staff upon detection of conditions that may lead to health deterioration, and realizing preventive care.

这些各式各样传感器之间的互连将提供健康参数的全貌，因而在检测到可能导致健康恶化的情况下触发医务人员的干预，从而实现预防性护理。

7. Furthermore, sensors could be used in a forensics setting, by detecting violations and by transmitting the relevant data to law enforcement agencies in order to identify the violator, or to store information that will be provided in case of accident for subsequent accident scene analysis.

此外，传感器可用于取证，通过检测违规行为并将相关数据传送给执法机构，以便识别违规者，或存储信息用于在发生事故的情况下提供后续事故场景分析。

Technical Tips

RFID

Radio-frequency identification (RFID) is a technology to record the presence of an object using radio signals. It is used for inventory control or timing sporting events. RFID is not a replacement for the barcoding, but a complement for distant reading of codes. The technology is used for automatically identifying a person, a package or an item. To do this, it relies on RFID tags. These are small transponders (combined radio receiver and transmitter) that will transmit identity information over a short distance, when asked. The other piece to make use of RFID tags is an RFID tag reader.

RFID tag

An RFID tag is an object that can be applied to or incorporated into a product, animal, or person for the purpose of identification and tracking using radio waves. Some tags can be read from several meters away and beyond the line of sight of the reader. Most tags carry a plain text inscription and a barcode as complements for direct reading and for cases of any failure of radio frequency electronics.

Most RFID tags contain at least two parts. One is an integrated circuit for storing and processing information, modulating and de-modulating a radio-frequency (RF) signal, and other specialized functions. The second is an antenna for receiving and transmitting the signal.

There are generally two types of RFID tags: active RFID tags, which contain a battery, and passive RFID tags, which have no battery.

NFC

Near-field communication (NFC) is a set of communication protocols that enable two electronic devices, one of which is usually a portable device such as a smartphone, to establish communication by bringing them within 4 cm (1.6 inch) of each other.

NFC devices are used in contactless payment systems, similar to those used in credit cards and electronic ticket smartcards and allow mobile payment to replace/supplement these systems. NFC is used for social networking, for sharing contacts, photos, videos or files. NFC-enabled devices can act as electronic identity documents and keycards. NFC offers a low-speed connection with simple setup that can be used to bootstrap more capable wireless connections.

Supplementary Readings: Wireless Sensor Network

The last two decades have seen a series of advances in two directions, namely, wireless communication and electronics. Advances in hardware technology and engineering design of micro/nano electronics have realized the dream of millimeter sized computing devices. Ad-hoc wireless networking, on the other hand, has made it possible for nodes to instantaneously form networks with dynamic topologies and power efficiency. Together, these two directions have resulted in the development of sensor networks.

Wireless sensor networks (WSN) have emerged as a promising tool for monitoring the physical worlds, using self-organizing networks of battery-powered wireless sensors that can sense, process and communicate. A sensor network is controlled through a software core engine. Sensor networks are designed to be self-configuring such that they can gather information about a large geographical area or about movements of an object for surveillance purposes.

A wireless sensor network is a collection of large number of sensor nodes and at least one base station. The sensor node is an autonomous small device that consists of mainly four units that are sensing, processing, communication and power supply. These sensors are used to collect the information from the environment and pass it on to base station. A base station provides a connection to the wired world where the collected data is processed, analyzed and presented to useful applications. Thus by embedding processing and communication within the physical world, WSN can be used as a tool to bridge real and virtual environment.

A sensor node is a tiny device that includes four basic components. A sensing or actuating unit, a processing unit, transceiver unit and power supply unit. In addition to this, the sensor node may also be equipped with location detection unit such as a Global Positioning System (GPS), a mobilizer etc. In sensor networks the different types of sensors such as seismic, thermal, visual, and infrared are used to monitor a variety of ambient conditions such as temperature, humidity, pressure and characteristics of objects and their motion. A basic sensor node consists of four main hardware units, namely sensing unit, processing unit, communication unit and power supply unit. It may also contain one optional unit. Figure 17.2 shows a schematic diagram of the sensor node components.

Each sensing unit is responsible for gathering information from the environment as an input like temperature, pressure, light etc. and produces a related output in a form of electrical or optical signal. The analog signals produced by the sensor are converted to digital signals by analog to digital conversion (ADC) and fed into the processing unit. Sensors are classified according to the type of phenomenon they detect such as thermal, mechanical, optical, electromechanical or acoustic sensors. Recent advances in Micro Electro Mechanical Systems (MEMS) technology has facilitated the development of tiny sensors. These sensors are small, with limiting processing and computing resources, and are inexpensive compared to traditional sensor with integrity of the specifications.

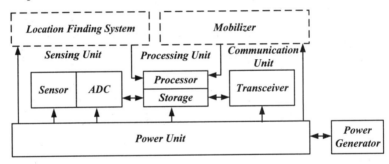

Figure 17.2　Components of a Sensor Node

Sensor nodes often use an ISM (Industrial, Scientific and Medical) band. The ISM bands are defined by ITU-R (International Telecommunication Union - Radio Communications). The use of these bands in individual countries may differ due to variations in national radio regulations. This give free radio, spectrum allocation and global availability. Radio frequency based communication is the most relevant used by most applications in wireless sensor networks. A wireless sensor network uses license free communication frequencies 173, 433, 868 and 915 MHz and 2.4 GHz. Examples of transreceivers are chipcon CC1000 (433～915 MHz) and Bluetooth TI CC 24020 (2.44MHz).

The ZigBee alliance was formed in 2002 as an association of companies with the motive of developing, monitoring and controlling products that are reliable, inexpensive, energy-effective, and can be wirelessly networked using an open global standard. The standard specifies two Direct Sequence Spread Spectrum (DSSS) physical layers and the use of three licensed free frequency bands. One is at 868/915MHz and uses the 868-870MHz band with one channel and the 902~928MHz band with ten channels. That enables data rates of about 20kbps in the 868~870MHz band and 40kbps in the 902~928MHz band. The other is at 2.4GHz and uses the 2.4~2.48GHz frequency band with sixteen channels and data rates of about 250kbps.

Energy consumption of one sensor node is influenced by the structure of protocol layers and the way each layer manages the sensing data. The protocol layers stack used by the sensor nodes and base station within the network includes an application layer, a transport layer, a network layer, a data link layer, a physical layer, a power management plane, a mobility management plane, and a task management plane.

Specifically, the application layer supports different software for applications depending on the sensing task. The transport layer helps maintain the data flow when the application layer is in need. Protocol development on this layer is a real challenge because sensors are influenced by many parameters and constraints such as limited power supply and memory. The network layer allows routing of data through a wireless communication channel. There are several strategies to route data such as routing power cost with available energy based on the energy metric, and data centric routing based on interest dissemination and attribute based naming. The data link layer is responsible for multiplexing of data streams, data frame detection, Medium Access Control (MAC), and error detection and correction. The design issues of the layer protocol must take into account different constraints such as power conservation, mobility management and recovery failure strategies. Lastly, the physical layer is the lowest layer, and is responsible for frequency selection, carrier frequency generation, signal detection, modulation and data encryption.

Wireless sensor networks enable a paradigm shift in the science of monitoring, and constitute the foundation of a broad range of applications related to security, surveillance, military, medical, and environmental monitoring. They can significantly improve accuracy and density of scientific measurements of physical phenomena because a large number of sensors can directly be deployed where experiments are taking place. In a wireless sensor network, the concept of micro-sensing and wireless connection of sensor nodes constitute the foundation of a broad range of applications related to military surveillance, security environment monitoring, medical, home and other commercial application areas. They can significantly improve accuracy and density of scientific measurements of physical phenomena because a large number of sensor can directly be deployed at places where experiments are failing.

With the continued advancement in micro-electro-mechanical systems, miniaturization and increased communication capabilities of sensors has enabled their ubiquitous and invisible deployment anywhere at any time. A sensor network is an infrastructure comprised of sensing (measuring), computing and communication elements that give a user ability to observe instrument and react to events and phenomena in a specified environment. To design and develop protocols or algorithms, some challenges are needed to be understood. The major challenges include limited energy, network lifespan, scalability, lack of global identification, latency, fault tolerance, and so on. Due to scarce energy resources of sensors, energy efficiency is one of the main challenges in the design of protocols for WSNs. The ultimate objective behind the design is to keep the sensors life time as long as possible.

Exercises

I. Translate the following sentences into Chinese.

1. To date, a number of technologies are involved in IoT, such as wireless sensor networks (WSNs), barcodes, intelligent sensing, Radio Frequency Identification (RFID), near field communication (NFC), low energy wireless communications, cloud computing, and so on.

2. Hardware capabilities and the communication requirements vary from one device type to another. The things in IoT can have very different capabilities for computation, memory, power, or communication.

3. To integrate the devices of sensing layer as intrinsic parts of the IoT, effective security technology is essential to ensure security and privacy protection in various activities such as personal activities, business processes, transportations, and information protection.

4. The ability to network embedded devices with limited CPU, memory and power resources means that IoT finds applications in nearly every field.

5. The vision to achieve near-zero breakdown using IoT-based predictive analytics led the future development of e-manufacturing and e-maintenance activities.

6. Industrial big data analytics will play a vital role in manufacturing asset predictive maintenance, although that is not the only capability of industrial big data.

7. Development of resource constrained devices connected to the Internet also means that other applications like earthquake or tsunami early-warning systems can also be used by emergency services to provide more effective aid.

II. Choose the word or phrase that is closest in meaning to the underlined part.

1. Currently, IoT technologies are at their infant stages; however, many new developments have occurred in the integration of objects with sensors in the cloud-based Internet.

    A. IoT technologies are developing at a very fast pace.

    B. IoT technologies are mature and being applied widely.

    C. The development of IoT technologies has come into a new stage.

    D. The development of IoT technologies are still in the beginning.

2. <u>Hardware capabilities and the communication requirements vary from one device type to another.</u>

    A. Hardware capabilities and communication are required for all device types.

    B. Different device types have different hardware capabilities and communication requirements.

    C. Hardware capabilities require communication from one device to another.

    D. Hardware capabilities and communication require various device types.

3. While connectivity and data acquisition are <u>imperative</u> for IIoT, they should not be the purpose, rather the foundation and path to something bigger.

    A. crucial

    B. optional

    C. effective

    D. available

4. IoT can be an aggregation of <u>heterogeneous</u> networks, such as WSNs, wireless mesh networks, mobile networks, and WLAN.

    A. complex

    B. similar

    C. diverse

    D. dynamic

5. The interconnection of such heterogeneous sensors will provide a comprehensive picture of health parameters, thereby <u>triggering an intervention by the medical staff</u> upon detection of conditions that may lead to health deterioration, and realizing preventive care.

    A. making the medical staff intervene

    B. leading to interference with medical staff

    C. interfering with the medical staff

    D. requesting the medical staff to reply

Appendices

Ⅰ. How Should We Read English

我们应该怎样阅读英语 —— 从人工智能得到的启发

英语阅读和人工智能有什么关系？

我们的观点是：绝不要按人工智能（artificial intelligence）的方式阅读，而要用人类智慧（human intelligence，或 human wisdom）。让我们先从什么是人工智能谈起吧。

简单地说，人工智能是用计算机模仿人的大脑进行"智能"活动，例如从照片中识别对象、下棋、文字识别、机器翻译。现在计算机在完成某些高度智能性的工作方面已达到了极高的水平，例如著名的"深蓝"计算机能击败国际象棋大师。可是另一方面，有许多人类轻而易举就能做到的事，计算机却难以胜任，至多只能达到初级水平，例如辨别图片中的特定对象。计算机的优势在于运算能力、准确性、速度、记忆力，这些都是人类望尘莫及的，然而在判断力方面计算机甚至无法与幼儿相比。正因为如此，人工智能在许多实际应用领域中的发展可以说是"路漫漫其修远兮"，还需要人们进行长期的艰苦求索。

那么计算机能不能阅读呢？回答是肯定的。应用光学字符识别技术（Optical Character Recognition, OCR）能从扫描得到的文字图像中识别中外文字符，转换为可以编辑的电子文本。不仅如此，机器还能"读懂"文字，例如在机器翻译中首先就要"理解"原文，然后才能生成译文。

接下来就进入主题了：计算机怎样阅读？我们又应该怎样阅读？

计算机根据程序即预先制定的"规则"行事。为了让计算机阅读英语，必须先输入词典和语法规则。计算机利用词典和语法，通过分析（parsing）来阅读。语法规则可以用树状结构表示，例如主语后面可能是行为动词（do）或联系动词（be），行为动词后面可以跟宾语，也可以不跟宾语，宾语后面又可能有补语、定语或其他成分，等等。"完整"的语法树极为复杂。另一方面，词典的规模也很大，不仅单词数量多，还必须包含各种词义、词性、用法、运用场合、感情色彩、褒义贬义、出现频率等因素，结构也十分复杂。计算机按照程序阅读英语文本的过程就是一个依据层次结构逐步分析的过程。

计算机的记忆力很强，能够准确无误地存储大规模的词典和复杂的语法规则；计算机的运行速度极快，能用很短的时间分析大量的文字。但是计算机的判断能力却很弱，而且不具备情感因素和必要的背景知识，"阅读"时不会产生语感，因此无法"理解"生动、多样的语言内涵。计算机对语言所作的解释是机械、单调、不自然的，而且经常是不恰当甚至错误的。发展至今已有几十年的机器翻译所达到的水平可从一个侧面反映这种状况。

大家知道，人们在阅读母语时是从不进行语法分析的，而是边"扫描"文字边吸收其中所包含的信息、理解作者要传达的意思。我们不仅不必反复分析琢磨每一个句子，有时还可以一目数行地进行快速浏览。除了语言心理学家外，谁也不会对这一复杂过程进行人为的解析，一般人都能凭着对语言的熟练掌握自然地完成阅读。这种阅读能力是通过长期运用语言而形成的，并在大量阅读中不断得到提高。

阅读外语的情况就不同了。许多人在自我评估英语读、写、听、说四种能力时会说自己"阅读没问题"。果真如此吗？这里有一个怎样衡量阅读能力的问题。我们认为最重要的是理解准确性和足够的阅读速度这两条，缺一不可。其中前者可能被广泛认同，对后者却不一定。有两种情况很常见：一是阅读速度很慢，同样内容的文字，看英语所花费的时间可能是看汉语资料的几倍；另一种是读完了全文却未掌握文章的主要内容，脑子里留下的是一片空白，跟没有读过差不多。后一种情况不仅速度不满足要求，理解能力也不合格。这里的问题就在于阅读方法不对。不少人的阅读方式是边看文字边分析语法，他们始终不能丢掉语法这根拐棍。一句复杂的句子往往要看上好几遍，直到将语法关系分析清楚，还不一定正确理解了句子所表达的意思。这种分析过程就好比计算机依靠分析进行阅读的情况。

不具备计算机在速度、记忆、准确性方面所拥有的绝对优势，却采用计算机的分析方法来阅读，其效果可想而知。产生这种情况的根源在于陈旧的英语教学方法。实际上我们长期以来的英语教学就好比是将计算机人工智能的程序（词汇表和语法规则）

输入学生的头脑。是教学生按 artificial intelligence 的方法阅读英语，而不是用 human wisdom。换句话说，教给学生的不是英语本身，而是"关于英语的知识"。教学的过程成了人工智能系统中的训练过程（training）。这种情况从小学一直持续到大学，甚至还要继续下去。不科学的教学方法和错误的应试教学目的，四级、六级、TOEFL 等形形色色的中外考试，使无数学习者的大量时间和精力消耗在无谓的题海和枯燥无味的死记硬背之中，而不是用在广泛的阅读上。尽管学了十几年英语，很多人在大学毕业后还是不具备必要的英语运用能力，包括阅读能力。

因此我们的结论是：若要在英语阅读能力方面有所突破，正确的方法就是大量阅读。语法知识可以作为辅助工具，但在阅读时一定要避免进行语法分析。要用读母语一样的方法去读英语，通过大量阅读培养起正确的语感。用正确的方法进行大量阅读，理解准确性和阅读速度的问题自然能得到解决。不仅如此，大量阅读也有助于写作能力的形成和提高。"熟读唐诗三百首，不会作诗也会吟。"就是这个道理。

参考资料：

[1] C. Krauthammer, Be Afraid: The Meaning of Deep Blue's Victory, *The Weekly Standard*, 2(36), 26 May 1997, http://wright.chebucto.net/AI.html

[2] E. Larson, Rethinking Deep Blue: Why a Computer Can't Reproduce a Mind, Guest Editorial, *Origins & Design*, 18(2), 1997, http://www.arn.org/docs/odesign/od182/blue182.htm

[3] D. Estival, Book Review on "Machine Translation, How Far Can It Go?" *Computational Linguistics*, 16(3), September 1990: 182

[4] 王雪梅. 英语语感的认知阐释——内涵、心理机制及应用. 外语教学，27(1), 2006: 6-13

Ⅱ. Writing Technical English

Write to express not impress. — Robert Gunning

If you can't explain something simply, you don't understand it well. — Albert Einstein

Good writing is based on reading. — Michael Brady

1. Writing in Plain English
用简洁的英语写作

1.1　简洁的英语和难度系数

用简洁平易的语言来写作是近几十年来英美许多著名学者大力提倡的写作风格。我们可将 Robert Gunning 在 *The Technique of Clear Writing*（McGraw-Hill, 1952）一书中的 10 句话作为科技英语写作应遵循的基本原则：

1. Keep sentences short. — 提倡短句

2. Prefer the simple to the complex. — 避繁从简

3. Prefer the familiar word. — 用词朴实

4. Avoid unnecessary words. — 避免冗词

5. Put action in your verbs. — 动词优先

6. Write like you talk. — 文如其言

7. Use terms your reader can picture. — 形象具体

8. Tie in with your reader's experience. — 有的放矢

9. Make full use of variety. — 形式多变

10. Write to express not impress. — 切忌炫耀

为了衡量文章的易读性，Gunning 在书中提出了一个量化指标，称为 fog index，我们姑且将它译作"难度系数"，其定义是：

难度系数 ＝ 0.4 × [每句平均单词数＋多音节单词所占百分比]

这里多音节词是指音节数等于或大于 3 的单词。例如一篇文章中平均每句有 20 个单词，其中 10% 的单词有 3 个或更多的音节，则难度系数=(20+10)×0.4 ＝ 12。下面这段晦涩的文字是一个包含 69 个单词的长句子，有 13 个多音节词，难度系数高达 35：

> In order to eliminate the possibility of errors occurring in the time charges relating to engineering jobs through transposition of numbers or typing errors, each of the Division Planning Offices should set up a file of time cards showing all authorized project numbers and make a daily check of the charges on all time sheets forwarded to the Accounting Department to be sure that only authorized numbers are used.

改写成 plain English，将长句子拆分成 3 句，简化陈腐冗长的表达，尽量采用普通词汇，使多音节词减少到 5 个，单词总数下降为 48，难度系数变为 11：

> It is easy to transpose digits and make typing errors when entering project numbers. We suggest each Division Planning Office set up a file of time cards showing all authorized project numbers. Then all charges should be checked each day before sending timesheets to the Accounting Department.

修改后的文字和原文意思相同，却变得清晰易懂，效果明显改善。又如温斯顿·邱吉尔于 1940 年 6 月 4 日在他的著名演讲中说：

> We shall go on to the end. We shall fight in France. We shall fight on the seas and oceans. We shall fight with growing **confidence** and growing strength in the air. We shall defend our island, **whatever** the cost may be. We shall fight on the beaches. We shall fight on the landing grounds. We shall fight in the fields and in the streets. We shall fight in the hills. We shall never **surrender**.

这段精彩演讲一气呵成，简洁而鲜明，具有强烈的震撼力。整段文字共 10 个短句，75 个单词全部是常用词，其中 3 个多音节词，难度系数仅 4.6。

难度系数约等于能进行顺利阅读的母语读者所受教育的年数，这也就是其中包括乘数 0.4 的原因。例如高中毕业生应能顺利阅读难度系数为 12 的文章。上面邱吉尔的演讲连小学生也能理解。难度系数超过 13 的文章通常较难，需受过高等教育才能顺利阅读。美国著名杂志 *Reader's Digest* 和 *Newsweek* 难度系数分别为 9 和 10，据统计没有一本流行刊物的难度系数超过 13。

难度系数并不能作为衡量文章是否平易简明的唯一标准，但是它给我们提供了如何改进文章可读性、提高文字质量的重要参考依据。简单说来，就是要尽量使用普通单词和控制句子的长度。

1.2　尽量用普通的常用词

要尽量选用词义确切的常用词。实际上我们在用中文写作时也应尽量避免使用生僻词语，何况写英文呢？一定不要用自己也没有把握的词。我们在应付某些英语考试如 TOEFL 时要强记许多单词，其中有些是很冷僻的。如果只是记住了部分词义而没有真正掌握用法，简单地将它们用在文章里就极可能出错，这是写作经验不多的人要注意克服的毛病。在对一种语言尚不能熟练运用的情况下，刻意使用难字偏词必然使写出来的文章矫揉造作，读起来很别扭，不自然。

在汉英词典里找到与中文相对应的英文单词，不了解它的准确含义和用法就直接使用，出错的概率很大，有时甚至南辕北辙，闹出笑话来。译意通之类的电子词典就更不可取了。在本书附录Ⅲ中给出了这样的例子。

我们主张，只要能用简单的常用词，就尽量避免用难的词和短语，更不要用生僻词。如果你的意思是 make，就用 make，而不要用 render。

- 不用：The testing strategy rendered it impossible to find all the faults.
- 而用：The testing strategy made it impossible to find all the faults.

在下表的每两列中，左边的单词应尽量少用，代之以右边的常用词。

宜少用的单词	常用词	宜少用的单词	常用词
endeavor	try	ascertain	determine
terminate	end, stop	essentially	generally
transmit	send	generate	produce
demonstrate	show	portion	part
initiate	begin	ongoing	current
assist	help	signature	characteristics
necessitate	need	commence	start
utilize	use	initiate	begin
facilitate	help	dwelling	house

不少作者喜欢用冗长烦琐的短语，实际上这些短语常可用一个常用词或较简单的短语取代，使得句子结构明晰，语言更加简洁流畅。下面的表中列出了应尽量避免使用的短语和建议使用的简洁表达方式。

避免使用	建议使用	避免使用	建议使用
a majority of	most	a number of	many
a small number of	a few	all of	all
along the line of	like	are found to be	are
are in agreement	agree	are known to be	are
as a consequence of	because of	at the present time	now, at present
by means of	by, with	definitely proved	proved
despite the fact that	although	due to the fact that	because, due to
during that time	while	during the course of	during, while
fall off	decline	first initiated	initiated

续表

避免使用	建议使用	避免使用	建议使用
for a distance of 10 km	10 km	for the purpose of	for, to
for the reason that	because	future plans	plans
give rise to	cause	goes under the name of	is called
has been shown to be	is	has the capability of	can, is able
in our opinion	we think	in all cases	always
in case	if	in close proximity to	near
in connection with	about	in order to	to
in respect to	about	in spite of the fact that	although
in the case of …	in …, for …	in the course of	during, while
in the event that	if	in the near future	soon
in the vicinity of	near	in those areas where	where
in view of the fact that	because	is in a position to	can, may
is known to be	is	it appears that	apparently
it is clear that	clearly	it is likely that	likely
it is often the case that	often	it is possible that	possibly
it is worth pointing out	note	it would appear that	apparently
large amount of	much	large in size	large
large number of	many	located in	in
look after	watch	of great importance	important
on account of	because	on behalf of	for
on the basis of	from, because	on the grounds that	because
original source	source	owing to the fact that	because, due to
past history	history	prior to (in time)	before
referred to as	called	subsequent to	after
take into consideration	consider	the fish in question	this fish
the majority	most	through the use of	by, with (not via)
two equal halves	halves	was of the opinion that	believed
with a view to getting	to get	with the result that	so that

1.3 避免陈旧的表达形式

有人以拗口的法律文书和公文合同中的用语为时尚，这是一个误区。要避免炫耀 (pomposity)，避免某些陈腐用语，例如：forthwith，hereof，thereof，henceforth，hereto，thereat，whereat，herein，herewith，therein，whereon，of the third instance，等等。过去在书面英语中曾被认为是"正式"的一些官样文章，现在已经过时，成为毫无意义的陈词滥调了。例如：

- The said software compiler …，应改为直截了当的表述 The software compiler …
- The aforementioned people have agreed …，应该简单地说 Smith and Jones have agreed …
- It goes without saying that …，可完全删去。

1.4　力求简练

写文章一定要简练，力戒烦琐。例如 this kind of method，应该就说 this method，kind of 是多余的。又如 due to the fact that ... 其实就是 because ...

用短语代替从句往往可使文字更简练：The results which were obtained 可改为 The results obtained。在可长可短的情况下，应尽量用短的：

- The results were inconclusive owing to the fact that ...可简化为 The results were inconclusive because ...
- It is evident that ...就是 Evidently ...
- It will be seen that ... 可以完全删去。

下面是一些烦琐表达形式的例子：

- by making use of ...
- owing to the fact that ...
- a sufficient quantity of ...
- at this point in time ...
- increased by a factor of two
- of the order of magnitude of ...
- in view of the fact that ...
- In the event that ...
- It is often the case that ...
- It has been brought to my attention that...

烦琐的表达	简练的表达
absolutely critical	critical
considerable difficulty	difficulty
utterly wrong	wrong
The product is not of a satisfactory nature.	The product is unsatisfactory.
After specification we are in a position to begin detailed design.	After specification we can begin detailed design.
We are now in the situation of being able to begin detailed design.	We can now begin detailed design.
The printer is located adjacent to the computer.	The printer is adjacent to the computer.
The user can visibly see the image moving.	The user can see the image moving.
The input is suitably processed.	The input is processed.
This is done by means of inserting an artificial fault.	This is done by inserting an artificial fault.
The reason for the increase in number of faults found was due to an increase in testing.	The number of faults found increased because of an increase in testing.
It is likely that problems will arise with regards to the completion of the specification phase.	You will probably have problems completing the specification phase.
Within a comparatively short period we will be able to finish the design.	Soon we will be able to finish the design.

要避免复杂的句子结构，有些不必要的复合句或复杂结构可以简化，下面是几个例子。

烦琐的表达	简练的表达
There is a reasonable expectation that ...	Probably ...
Owing to the situation that ...	Because, since ...
Should a situation arise where ...	If ...
Taking into consideration such factors as ...	Considering ...
Prior to the occasion when ...	Before ...
At this precise moment in time ...	Now ...
Do not hesitate to ...	Please ...
I am in receipt of ...	I have ...

1.5 关于长句和短句

要使难度系数下降，首先要减少长句，有时可将长句分解成几个短句。避免复杂的长句对于英文写作经验不多的新手尤为重要。同时也要注意长句和短句、简单句和复合句搭配使用，使得表达形式多样。多次重复同一句型或措词会令人生厌。一连串的简单短句有时会令人感到单调甚至局促紧张（邱吉尔演讲的目的是激发国民斗志，使用连续的短句取得了极好的效果）。另外段落也不宜过长，一般说来不应超过半页。

过多的长句和复杂结构有可能来源于写作新手卖弄语法知识的倾向。学了十几年的语法，不免要表现一下，于是就出现了连篇的复杂长句。我们有必要重提 Guning 的名言：Write to express not impress. 写作是为了表达思想，科技写作的目的是与读者分享研究成果，而不是为了引人注目。对于自我感觉得意却不能肯定是否适当和得体的用语要坚决舍弃。

英语的写作风格不断演变。在伊丽莎白一世时代平均每句的单词数量多达 40~60个，到 1900 年就下降到了 21 个，1970 年下降到 17 个，现在通常在 12~17 个单词之间[*]。可见语言文字的发展是趋于简洁。Norman Fenton 在 General Principles of Good Writing[†]一文中曾尖锐地指出：

> The English school system produces students who feel ashamed to write short sentences. In my view this is a great failing of our education system. There is nothing clever about writing long, complex sentences. For technical writing it is simply WRONG. You must get used to the idea of writing sentences that are reasonably short and simple.

对并列句也应注意，过多地使用 and、or、while 等连词会导致不必要的长句。逗号的过度使用容易使读者喘不过气来，要用句号将独立的句子截断。文章里应尽量少用括号，必要时可分割为几个句子。特别是要杜绝嵌套括号。下面举一个将长句分解为几个短句的例子：

---

[*] Write to reach your readers – use real words and common sense, BPA Corporate Communications, 1999, http://www.bpa. gov/corporate/kcc/circuit/99ci/ci0299/writetoreach.shtml.

[†] http://www.dcs.qmul.ac.uk/~norman/papers/good_writing/general_.principles.html.

Time division multiplexed systems are basically much simpler, the combination and separation of channels being affected by timing circuits rather than by filters and inter-channel interference is less dependent on system non-linearity, due to the fact that only one channel is using the common communication medium at any instant.

共 49 个单词连成一句，难度系数为 28。其中第一个逗号可直接改为句号。后面的复合句又可拆成两句，并将 due to the fact that 改为 because，其余文字也可简化：

Time division multiplex is much simpler. Channels are combined and separated by timing circuits, not by filters. Inter-channel interference is less dependent on the system non-linearity because only one channel is using the common communication medium at any time.

修改后字数减少到 39 个，难度系数下降为 12.2。

1.6 第一人称和第三人称

过去人们在科技写作中主要使用第三人称或无人称句，而基本不用第一人称，认为只有这样才能体现科学的客观性。持这种观点的人现在已经大为减少，第一人称已被普遍接受。使用第一人称的优点是直截了当，避免了迂回曲折，并且可缩短句子，使文章简练。实际上刻意回避第一人称有时还可能引起误解：

- Recent experiments have resulted in … 未说清楚是谁做的实验，可能是作者，也可能是别人。
- It is not possible to state the exact mode of the operation. 是作者不知道处理模式，还是该处理模式是不可能的，不清楚。

但是应该注意，在正式的科技论文或技术文件中，只能用 we 而不能用 I，即使作者只有一人也是这样。例如：We propose to use a complex representation …。用第一人称时仍要保持客观的语气才能令人信服，不要给人主观武断的印象。有些作者过度使用 our results, our method 等表述，也是不妥的，因为有可能使读者产生无形的排斥心理。

下面的表中给出了几个例子，说明使用第三人称和第一人称的不同。通过比较可看出第一人称有助于使表达简洁、清晰，所以应优先考虑使用。

第三人称	第一人称
The current research work of the author of this report is also described.	We also describe our current research work.
In the previous report of the authors the rationale for the proposed method was discussed in detail.	In our previous report we discussed in detail the rationale for the proposed method.
However, it is the writer's belief that this situation should not have occurred.	However, we believe this situation should not have occurred.
Examination and discussion of the results obtained are necessary before a decision can be taken.	We must examine and discuss the results before we decide.

1.7 动词和名词

在 Gunning 提出的 10 项原则中有一项是 Put action in your verbs. 在动词和表示动

作和行为的名词之间，应优先使用动词，使得意思的表达更为直接清楚，也可缩短句子。下面表中右边各句直接使用了动词而不是表示动作的抽象名词，使结构更加紧凑，表达更加清晰。

用表示行为或动作的名词	直接使用动词
He used to help in the specification of new software.	He used to help specify new software.
Measurement of static software properties was performed by the tool.	The tool measured static software properties.
Clicking the icon causes the execution of the program.	The program executes when the icon is clicked.
The analysis of the software was performed by Fred.	Fred analyzed the software.
The testing of the software was carried out by Jane.	Jane tested the software.
It was reported by Jones that method x facilitated the utilization of inspection techniques by the testing team.	Jones reported that method x helped the testing team use inspection techniques.

1.8　主动语态和被动语态

传统的观点是使用被动语态使科技文章更显"正式"，因而更能被接受。这和坚持用第三人称或无人称句是一脉相承的。这种情况现在也发生了变化。与主动语态相比，被动语态往往使句子和段落的结构更复杂，而且句子较长。现在人们已经愈来愈多地使用主动语态了。

被动语态	主动语态
The report was written by Bloggs, and was found to be excellent.	Bloggs wrote the report, and it was excellent.
The values were measured automatically by the control system.	The control system measured the values automatically.
It was reported by the manager that the project was in trouble.	The manager reported that the project was in trouble.
The precise mechanism responsible for this antagonism cannot be elucidated.	We do not know what causes this antagonism.
The stability of the process is enhanced by co-operation.	Co-operation improves the stability of the process.

2. Examples of Diseased English and the Cure 典型错误剖析

本节围绕例句讨论科技英语写作中存在的一些问题，所举的病句或不当表达均取自编者为刊物改稿时收集的实例。造成这些错误的原因很多，例如：对英语的掌握不够却刻意追求长句和复杂结构；对词义和用法不甚了了却要弃简就繁，专用难词偏词；将中文硬译成英文，不能突破原文束缚，写成中式英语，等等。关于中式英语（洋泾浜）的问题将在附录Ⅲ中讨论。

2.1　用词不当

(1) 用词不当、单词间搭配不当很普遍，仅举一例。

原句：The superiority of rough set in data mining is employed to build cooperation model for MAS.

修改：We build a cooperation model for MAS by taking advantages of rough set in data mining.

评语：Superiority 怎能 employ？显然是从中文硬译过来。

(2) 在许多英汉词典中 apparent 和 obvious 都作"明显的"，但是二者的含义有很大差异。根据 Collins Essential English Dictionary (CEED)：

- If something is obvious, you can easily see it or understand it.
- An apparent situation, quality, or feeling seems to exist, although you cannot be certain that it does exist.

(3) 应该用 derive 的，错用了 deduce，例如：We can deduce the following equation. 此错误很常见。CEED 对这两个词的解释如下：

- If you deduce that something is true, you reach that conclusion because of facts you know to be true.
- If something is derived from another thing, it comes from that thing.

2.2 硬译

(1) 从中文硬译成英语时，往往受到中文的束缚。例如：For the fiber with enough large radius of the core, the attenuation of the optical wave can be ignored. 显然是"纤芯半径足够大的光纤"的硬译。而且多处定冠词均为误用。可改为：For a fiber with a sufficiently large core radius, attenuation of optical waves is negligible.

(2) The changes of its some physical and chemical properties in production were used to research its phase transition process. 这里 some 的位置不对，不能说… of its some properties。另外，research 一词虽无语法问题，但读来别扭，不符合英语习惯。可改为 Changes in some of its physical and chemical properties in the production were used to study its phase transition process.

(3) 逐字硬译：客户信息自然需要用 Oracle 等大型数据库进行管理。

原译：Naturally, the customer information needs to use the large-scale database carries on the management, such as Oracle.

改为：Naturally, it is necessary to use a large-scale database such as Oracle to manage the customer information.

评语：原来的译文中语法关系混乱，几乎是按中文逐字硬套的。

(4) 硬译的另一个实例：近年来信息咨询企业的业务发展迅猛，纸质信息咨询产品的种类愈加繁多，客户数量也成千万地增长。

原译：With the swift and violent development of the information consultant enterprise's service in recent years, the type of paper quality information consultant product are more and more, the customer quantity also became surely growth.

改为：With rapid development of the information consultant service in recent years, the variety of consultant products in hardcopy forms is enormous. The number of customers has been growing very quickly.

评语：将"迅猛"硬译成 swift and violent，"纸质信息"硬译成 paper quality information，另外还有典型的洋泾浜现象。

(5) 硬译而不顾语法。

原句：It shows that the kinetics would influence the dynamic behavior of the Earth's deep interior and need more laboratory data.

改为：This shows that the kinetics would influence the dynamic behavior of the Earth's deep interior, therefore more laboratory data are needed.

评语：原文中 need 一词的主语是什么不清楚，是 it 还是 kinetics？实际上是"我们需要更多的数据"。将后半句改为被动语态。

(6) 又一例不顾语法的硬译。

原句：Optimization of weights using genetic algorithm, is only in order to choose out a better search space from the solution space, and it is depend on BP neural network to accomplish the latter search.

改为：The only purpose of using GA for weight optimization is to choose a better search space in the solution space. The search depends on the BP neural network.

评语：这里 is only in order to 显然是"仅仅是为了……"的硬译。此外 choose out 是"选出"的硬译。depend 词性不对。it 代表什么不清楚，是 optimization 还是 to accomplish the search？只能猜。

2.3 滥用 How to

(1) 用 How to 做主语是一个通病，也是硬译的结果。

原文：How to construct the code book is always a difficult task.

改为：Code book construction is always a difficult task.

评语：就是一个简单句，完全不必用 How to。

(2) 又是一例。

原文：How to develop AMB with independent intellectual property rights and make it cover an area in the field of systematic learning is a rigorous task in front of us Chinese scientists. (Fog index = 18.4)

改为：It is important for Chinese scientists to develop their own AMB and apply it to the field of systematic learning. (Fog index = 12)

评语：避免了 How to，并将难度系数从 18.4 降到 12。

2.4 基本错误成堆

(1) 下面的例子中，句子长且复杂，基本语法错误很多，属于完全不合格的英文写作。

原文：Because it is more complicated that the modes of aerodynamics of SMAV (小飞机) are founded, and there are larger difference between its theoretical modes and practical conditions, it can be not generally used when the control laws of SMAV are designed. We utilize the test method to deal relationship of control forces or moments with movements of rudders of SMAV. Limited to length of the paper, the problems about modeling of its modes will not be detailedly discussed, which will be wholly explained by another paper.

改为：Because modeling the SMAV aerodynamics is complicated, and the theoretical modes greatly differ from the practical situation, these modes cannot be used in designing

SMAV control in general. We use a test method to study the relationship between control forces or moments and the rudder movements. Modeling of the modes will be discussed in a separate paper.

评语：it is that 句型使用不当。there are larger difference between … 比较级使用错误，主谓语单复数对不上。can be not … 不通。deal 后面不能少了 with。生造词组 problems about，detailedly discussed，wholly explained。在 limited to length 中介词 to 不对。修改后单词数量从 85 个减少到 57 个，难度系数从 18 下降为 12。

(2) 短短数行，语病密集。

原文：This article discourses on the method of using the measuring amplifier to abstract the faint bioelectricity signal from the strong interference and how to use the OrCAD PSpice software to simulate and analyse the technology project of carrying out the method and get the satisfactory result.

改为：This paper discusses a method that uses a measuring amplifier to extract faint bioelectrical signal from strong interferences. OrCAD PSpice is used in the simulation. Implementation of the proposed method gives satisfactory results.

评语：不适当的用词和冗词很多。一连串的不当并列使句子长达 46 个单词，语法错误很多。修改后难度系数从 24 下降到 10。

2.5 烦琐而不顾语法

原文：With applying data mining to PDM, it is very meaningful for the thinking and technologies of PDM and the rapid development of the application of data mining. And, it is helpful to improve the development and usage of enterprises' databases.

改为：Application of data mining to PDM is meaningful both to PDM and to the development of data mining itself. Data mining is also useful in developing and applying database in enterprises.

评语：多余的词：With applying …中的 with，very meaningful 中的 very，第二句一开始的 And。用词不当：thinking，technologies，helpful，usage。语法错误多。

2.6 烦琐且不通

原文：According to whether the designed controller depends the time delay or not, the control approaches for time-delay systems may be classified two categories: delay-dependent and delay-independent.

改为：Control techniques used in time-delay systems may be classified into two categories: delay-dependent and delay-independent.

评语：从中文硬译过来。两类控制方法的名称 delay-dependent and delay-independent 已说明是根据什么分类的了，何必再用中式短语"According to whether … or not"？缺少必要的介词。

2.7 烦琐，语义不清

原文：Before we present how to calculate the popularity of a media, we need to define one constant C, which is the limit between partial caching and complete caching, and is to be set in advance, the value of C represents "the medias with which grades should be cached completely".

改为：A predefined constant C is needed in calculating the popularity of a media object. It is a threshold above which complete caching must be used instead of partial caching.

评语：原文烦琐，有多处重复，句子过长。limit between A and B：limit 用词不当，无法理解。修改后难度系数从 20 下降到 10。

2.8 烦琐，用词不当，结构不合理

原文：So the method using high-intensity ultrasonic as a kind of physical refining means to improve solidification structure without pollution is promising.

改为：Therefore high-intensity ultrasound has become a promising physical refining means to improve solidification structure without pollution.

评语：原句中主语 the method 和谓语 is promising 相距太远。a kind of 多余。

2.9 不当并列

原文：Customized and complicated products have the features of high price, very long lifecycle and customers have some maintenance capacity.

改为：Customized and complicated products are usually high-priced. Nonetheless, they have a long lifecycle and provide maintenance to customers.

评语：不对等的句子不能并列。缺点（high price）和优点（long lifecycle）不宜并列。

2.10 乱译

鉴于目前数码显微系统没有针对金属切削刀具的图像分析软件的问题，以 VC++ 为平台开发了专用的分析软件。

原译：According to the present numerical microsystem, there is no specialized microscope that can detect cutting-tool. Special analysis software has been developed through VC++ platform.

改为：As the present digital microscope systems do not include any means for analyzing cutting-tool images, dedicated image analysis software has been developed with VC++.

评语：滥用 According to 是中式英语常见问题之一，见附录Ⅲ。译文与原文意思大相径庭：原文说的是"没有软件"，译文却说"没有显微镜"。原文"没有软件"是状语，英译文将"没有显微镜"变成结果。用词不当：numerical，through。

2.11 长句晦涩难懂

原文：While adopting impact loads with multishocks to make shock experiments for cobalt-base and nickel-base alloy coats on the surface of mild carbon steel or stainless steel, it is found that under the impact force that is only about 11%~43% of the static yield limit of the material, the coat and upper part of base generate micro-plastically deformation.

改为：To perform shock experiments on cobalt- and nickel-based alloy coatings, impact loads of multiple shocks were applied to the surface of mild carbon steel or stainless steel. When the impact force was only 11%~43% of the static yield limit of the material, micro-plastic deformation was found on the coatings and in the upper part of the base.

评语：原句长达 57 个单词，难度系数 30。由 while 引导的从句应可独立成句，说明做一个什么样的实验。原来的主句可改为结构较简单的被动语态，说明实验结果。about 一词多余。基本语法错误：base，plastically。修改后难度系数下降到 12。

2.12 关于状语的位置

原文：Recently, the use of aspect mining techniques as a kind of program comprehension tool may solve the problems of discovering crosscutting concerns partially.

改为：The recent use of aspect mining as a tool for program understanding may partly resolve the problem of discovering crosscutting concerns.

评语：Recently 和 may solve 不配。a kind of 多余，连同放在句末的 partially 成为洋泾浜。不顾语感将副词放在句尾的另一个例子：The values are independent of detuning almost. 宜改为 The values are almost independent of detuning.

2.13 长句可分割

原文：Since Oliver Lodge introduced the biconical antenna in 1898, various types of ultra-wideband antennas have been proposed and applied for many decades, such as Carter's improved match biconical antenna and conical monopole antenna, Schelkunoff's spheroidal antenna, Lindenblad's conical horn element, Brillouin's omni-directional and directional coaxial horn antenna, etc. (Fog index = 31.2)

改为：Since Lodge introduced the biconical antenna in 1898, various ultra-wideband antennas have been proposed and applied. Examples include Carter's improved match biconical antenna and conical monopole antenna, Schelkunoff's spheroidal antenna, Lindenblad's conical horn element, and Brillouin's omni-directional and directional coaxial horn antenna. (Fog index = 20.8)

评语：原文一句长达 48 个词，难度系数 31.2，分成两句，难度系数下降到 20.8。因后一句并列成分多，人名和专用名词均不能避免，所以句子仍较长。

2.14 长句可改短

原文：One of the main features of this antenna is its size reduction with respect to other UWB planar antenna designs found in the literature, such as U-type monopole, elliptical monopole, inverted triangular monopole, knight's helm shape monopole and so on.

改为：A main feature of the antenna is the reduced size compared to other UWB planar antennas such as U-type monopole, elliptical monopole, inverted triangular monopole, and knight's helm shape monopole.

评语：such as 后面不能用 and so on 或 etc. 短语 One of 用得太滥，不必要。多余成分：found in the literature, design。修改后难度系数从 25 下降为 14。

2.15 缩写和省略

不能为了简便而随意使用缩写，在许多情况下应将单词全拼出来，例如不要将 approximately 写成 approx.（很多情况下最好用简单的 about）。论文作者的单位要用全称，但很多人将 University 写成 Univ. 另外，用 etc. 表示省略时，下面的用法是错误的：

- He eats lots of fruits, such as apples, oranges, bananas, etc. (such as 和 etc. 不可同

时使用)

- Jones, etc., proposed a different method. （要用 et al.）

关于 et al.的错误用法也很多：

- H. Morgan, G. Lee, et al. （不宜列举多人再用 et al.）
- et. al. 或 et al （et al. = and others，拉丁文 et alii 的缩写）

2.16 关于论文标题

标题要画龙点睛，重点突出。可用主要结论作标题以引起读者注意。"关于某问题的研究"一类标题现在已很少使用。"的研究"三个字是多余的。国内作者的英文标题使用 Study on 很多，应一律删去。实际上以 On 开头的旧式论文题目现在几乎已经绝迹。以下是两个标题修改的例子。

(1)

原题：A New AC Voltage-Stabilized Source of Base Station Based on Double PWM Technology

改为：Regulated AC Power Supply for Base Station Using Double PWM

评语："稳压电源：应该是 regulated power supply。technology 用词不当，且冗余。PWM (pulse width modulation) 最好给出全文。若由于题目不宜过长，不便用全称，则应在摘要中给出。

(2)

原题：Linear programming method of optimization of systems of partial differential equation

改为：Linear programming for optimizing systems of partial differential equation

评语：删去冗词 method。将名词改为动（名）词

2.17 摘要修改

(1)

原文：The platform of distributed design and resource sharing has been an important method, which medium-sized and smaller companies develop product to win competition. As background of product creation design, we put forward model of product collaborative innovation development (PCID) based knowledge. We analyze the characteristics of the PCID, and research on framework and its key technologies of the PCID platform based knowledge. Through the encapsulation of exist system and interface design, the development platform has been built to support the PCID within KBE (Knowledge-Based Engineering). Applied example indicates that the prototype system has trait of maneuverability and practicability.

改为：The platform of distributed design and resource sharing is important for medium- and small-sized companies in developing products to improve competitiveness. As a background of creative product design, we propose a knowledge model based on collaborative innovation development of products (CIDP). We analyze the characteristics of CIDP, and study the framework and key techniques of the CIDP-platform based knowledge. By integrating the existing system and interface design, a development platform has been built to support the CIDP within knowledge-based engineering (KBE). An example is presented, indicating that the prototype system is flexible and practical.

评语：第一句的主句 platform … has been a method. 不通，platform 不是一种 method。时态也不妥。从句也不通，其中 which 的作用和意义是什么？Product 缺冠词。将用得很滥的 put forward 改为 propose。作者自创的主要专业术语不通，宜改为 collaborative innovation development of products, CIDP。将 research 改为 study。将 technology 改为 technique。应避免难字，尽量用常用词。注意首字母缩写词和全称的表示：先全称，后缩写。避免多余的罕用词（trait：品质，特征）。maneuverable 是机动性，用于本文讨论的"知识框架"等不准确。应该是灵活性：flexible。

(2)

原文：The throughput of mobile ad hoc network (MANET) is limited by collision avoidance. But for CDMA-based MANET, this limitation can be overcome by multiuser detection (MUD) because conventional colliding packets can be detached and detected by MUD so that multi-packet reception (MPR) is possible. In this paper, the principles of MUD algorithm for MANET are given firstly, and then a new adaptive blind MUD algorithm satisfied with given principles is proposed out. Furthermore, a specially designed MAC protocol is brought forward to make MANET work more efficiently by arranging more packets to be sent to a destination simultaneously. The proposed MUD algorithm and MAC protocol builds up a solution for CDMA-based MANET supporting MPR. Simulations show that the throughput performance of MANET is remarkably promoted under this solution.

改为：Throughput of mobile ad hoc network (MANET) is limited by collision avoidance. In the CDMA-based MANET, the problem can be resolved by multiuser detection (MUD) as colliding packets can be separated and detected by MUD so that multi-packet reception (MPR) is possible. This paper introduces the principles of MUD algorithm for MANET, and proposes an adaptive blind MUD algorithm. A special MAC protocol is designed to make MANET more efficient by sending more packets to a destination simultaneously. The proposed MUD algorithm and MAC protocol allow CDMA-based MANET to support MPR. Simulations show a remarkable improvement in the throughput performance of MANET.

评语：原文多处用词不当或冗余，作了适当精简。将被动语态改为主动语态。原文的 firstly … then 是八股，不用。satisfied with given principles, proposed out 语法错误。builds up a solution for 不通。

参考资料

[1] R. Gunning, The Technique of Clear Writing, McGraw-Hill, 1952.

[2] J. Gibaldi, MLA Handbook for Writers of Research Papers（MLA 科研论文写作规范）. 5th Edition. 上海：上海外语教育出版社，2001.

[3] 任胜利. 英语科技论文撰写与投稿. 北京：科学出版社，2004.

[4] 李旭，英语科技论文写作指南. 北京：国防工业出版社，2005.

[5] T. M. Georges, Analytical Writing for Science and Technology, 1996, Online

course, http://mywebpages.comcast.net/tgeorges/write/index.html.

[6] Write to Reach Your Readers — Use Real Words and Common Sense, BPA Corporate Communications, 1999.

[7] Dennis R. Morgan, Dos and Don'ts of Technical Writing, *IEEE Potentials*, Aug./Sept. 2005: 22-25.

[8] R. T. Compton, Jr., Fourteen Steps to a Clearly Written Technical Paper, Reprinted by *IEEE Circuits & Device Magazine*, September 1992.

[9] Victor O. K. Li, Hints on Writing Technical Papers and Making Presentations, *IEEE Transactions on Education*, vol. 42, no. 2, May 1999: 134-137.

[10] Norman Fenton, General Principles of Good Writing, 13 July 2000, http://www.dcs.qmul.ac.uk/~norman/papers/good_writing/general_.principles.html.

III. Avoid Pidgin English

Pidgin English was originally a trade jargon developed between the British and the Chinese in the 19th century, but now commonly and loosely used to mean any kind of 'broken' or 'native' version of the English language. For us, it is also known as Chinese English or Chinglish. Writing technical English without being influenced by the mother tongue is difficult. The only remedy is to establish a strong sense of the English language through extensive practice including reading and writing.

1. Avoid Influence of Mother Tongue on Technical English Writing
科技写作要避免中式英语*

随着国际科技交流日益广泛以及科研水平评价中对学术出版要求的不断提高，用英语发表研究成果的科技人员愈来愈多。语言文字的运用水平是写好英语科技论文的基础。显然，一篇文字表达错误百出的论文是难以将作者的研究方法和学术观点表达清楚的，而且可能使作者的创新成果得不到认同。内容虽好但英文不过关的论文往往被国际学术刊物拒收。

近年来我国科技人员的英语写作水平已经有了很大提高，但英语写作达不到应有水平的仍不在少数。一部分稿件在文字表达方面问题很多，文理不通，甚至还有不少基本语法错误。更多的情况是文字基本可读却或多或少地存在中式英语的毛病，使人读来十分别扭，有时还会引起误解，影响正常的学术交流。这就是英语写作中的母语干扰问题。

以下根据编者多年来从事英文科技论文写稿、改稿的实践，就避免母语干扰，克服中式英语倾向的问题提出一些看法。

1.1 中国英语和中式英语

作为国际交往中使用最多的语言，英语已成为科技界事实上的通用语言载体（Lingua Franca）。在一些大量使用英语的非母语国家中，形成了区别于英国英语和美

---

* 本节主要内容发表在：沈美芳，王朔中. 排除科技英语写作中的母语干扰. 中国科技期刊研究, 18(2), 2007.

国英语，具有本国语言特色的特殊英语，例如中国英语（China English）、印度英语。根据汪榕榕的定义，中国英语是"中国人在中国本土上使用的、以标准英语为核心、具有中国特点的英语"[1]。李文中认为"中国英语是以规范英语为核心，表达中国社会文化诸领域特有事物，不受母语干扰和影响，通过音译、译借及语义再生诸手段进入英语交际，具有中国特点的词汇、句式和语篇。中国英语主要构成包括音译词、译借词以及独特的句式和语篇"[2,3]。中国英语不仅在英语中加入中国特有的政治、经济、文化、生活等方面的概念和词语，如 imperial examinations（科举）、jiaozi（饺子）、four modernizations（四个现代化）等等，还在更高层次丰富了英语，成为表达与中国有关的话题时不可缺少的成分，应该看成是英语的发展。

另一方面，中式英语（Chinese English, Chinglish）不同于中国英语。这是一种受中文干扰、生硬套用英语形式的非规范英语。随着 19 世纪西方列强用武力打开中国大门，英语和各种商品一起涌了进来，首先是广州，接着来到上海。为适应中外贸易的需要出现了所谓洋泾浜英语（Pidgin English）的混杂语言[4]。洋泾浜原为上海的一条小河，后来成为英法租界的分界，位于现在的延安东路。姚公鹤在《上海闲话》一书中说，洋泾浜是"以中国文法英国字音拼合而成，为上海特别之英语"。1860 年即上海开埠后第 18 年，冯泽夫等人汇资出版《英话注解》，标志了洋泾浜英语的诞生。

早期 Buy what thing?之类简单生硬的洋泾浜英语现在已不多见，但是受到中文干扰，不符合英语语法、用词和表达习惯的不规范英语仍然比比皆是，也包括见面就问 How old are you?和 Have you had your lunch?之类违背西方文化传统和思维方式的语句。我们不妨将这些统称为中式英语。

我们知道，自然科学的研究成果和工程技术的进展是没有国界的，一切理论、概念、技术、方法，无论由谁首先提出都是全世界共同的，因此科技写作并不需要中国英语，当然更要拒绝中式英语或洋泾浜。本节主要探讨如何在科技英语写作中克服中文干扰，避免洋泾浜英语的问题。

1.2 科技英文写作中母语干扰的不同形式

许多人有这样的体会：学了多年英文，证书也拿了不少，就是写不出比较地道的英文文章。所谓"地道"，不仅要求语法正确，还要摆脱中文束缚，克服中文式的表达方法，使文章符合英语的自然习惯。这也许是中国人在英文写作中最难做到的。

硬译是导致洋泾浜的重要原因

The calculation formulas according to equal accuracy distribution law are obtained as follows. 其实中文的"计算公式"，翻译成英文就是 formula 或 equation，不必加上 calculation。另外 equal accuracy distribution law 也是洋泾浜。频繁使用 according to 的问题在下节讨论。这一句可改为：The equations are obtained from the law of equal accuracy distribution as follows.

The experimental data also reflect two questions. 显然是根据中文逐字硬译的。英文 question、problem、issue 等都可以译成"问题"。"提两个问题"是 ask two questions，而"反映两个问题"却不能说 reflect two questions。可改为：The experimental results also show two problems. 或者根据上下文用其他单词如 phenomena、aspects 等。

The above problems are analyzed and studied. 中文可以说对某个问题进行"分析研

究"，而英文只要说 are analyzed 就行了。

还有一个例子是将"培养计划"硬译成 cultivation plan。英文 cultivation 的意思是对植物、细菌等的培养。汉语中对人才的培养或栽培实际上都是比喻，成语"揠苗助长"用的也是这个比喻。英文没有这种比喻，西方人见到 cultivation 并不会联想到对人的培养，因此将人才培养硬译成 talent cultivation 听起来感觉很怪。实际上"培养计划""学科建设"是具有中国特色的概念，恰当地译成英文应成为中国英语的一部分。前者可用普普通通的 education program 来表示；后者不妨译作 disciplinary development，而不要用 disciplinary construction，因为学科是不能 construct 的。

However, <u>how to mine valuable information and knowledge from the PDM system</u> becomes the key to improve <u>work efficiency</u> and implement knowledge management of an enterprise. 用 How to … 短语做主语是典型的中式错误。这一句显然是受中文"如何挖掘……有价值的信息和知识已成为关键"的影响。work efficiency 则是"工作效率"的硬译。关于 mine 一词，现在信息技术领域有 data mining 即数据挖掘，是一个新的科技术语，但将 mining 的使用随意推广也是洋泾浜。可改为：However, exploration of valuable information and knowledge from the PDM system has become a key in the improvement of efficiency and implementation of knowledge management in an enterprise.

再举一例。This paper <u>puts forward</u> a design of <u>security identity authentication system</u> with fingerprint identification and <u>contactless</u> IC card <u>technologies</u>, <u>then</u> discusses the specific security mechanism. The principle, main function and the composition of hardware and software of the system <u>are mainly discussed</u>. It has fine safety, high reliability and utility value. 可看出从中文逐字硬译的明显痕迹，其中 put forward，then，are mainly discussed，it has …是典型的中式英语。滥用 technology，不知道它和 technique 的区别也是常见问题。可改为：This paper introduces an ID authentication system based on a non-contact IC card and fingerprint identification. The security mechanism, the system operation and its main functions are discussed. Hardware and software structures are introduced. The described system is highly secure and reliable.

中英文语法和用词搭配的差异

另一类洋泾浜英语是由中英两种语言在用词搭配和语法方面的差异造成的：

Because …, so …，这是受了中文"因为……，所以……"的影响。中文在表示因果、条件、让步等句子中关系词往往成对出现："虽然……，但是……""如果……，那么……"，英文却只用一个词就够了，although 后面不用 but，例如：Although no one can predict the future in detail, it is clear that computers with human-level intelligence would have a huge impact on our everyday lives and on the future course of civilization.[5] 另外 if 后面也不一定跟 then。尽管计算机程序有 if …, then …，但程序语言不是英语。

汉英词典造成的误导

不假思索地直接搬用汉英词典中查到的单词也是产生中式英语的一个原因。汉英词典的基本用途是帮助外国人学习中文，给出的只是中文单词的英文解释，绝不可直接用来"替换"中文。应该使用英美出版的原文词典或有详细用法和例句的英汉词典。有时可先查汉英词典得到启发，再从英语词典或好的英汉词典中找出能确切表达意思的单词或短语。科技文章应朴实无华，避免生僻单词，避免烦琐和不必要的修饰。要尽量选用简短、含义清楚并为人熟知的词语。即使用母语写作也不宜使用生僻词语，更何况用外语写作。尤其是在对一种语言尚不能熟练运用的情况下，刻意使用难字反而显得矫揉造作，使读者感到别扭甚至反感。

关于词典，我们主张尽量使用英语（单语）词典。单语词典是用解释的方法说明单词的意思，使我们能够确切地理解词的含义，并通过例句掌握词的用法。当然也可以使用有详细用法解释和例句的英汉词典。当我们不知道一个中文词或某一概念的英文表达方法，不得不使用汉英词典时，必须再查英语词典或英汉词典进行核对，看是否是符合要表达的意思。

不要卖弄语法及其他

我们都已经学习了多年的语法，语法知识不可谓不多。但是卖弄语法又往往成为产生中式英语的重要原因。要避免复杂的长句子，因为对于作者而言，长句子写到后来会忘记前后关系，顾此失彼产生混乱，出错的比例自然就高；对于读者，过分长的句子会令人抓不住要点，读起来头昏脑胀。

少数中国作者喜欢在学术论文中使用 at home and abroad，our country，developing countries 等词语，也是现代洋泾浜的表现。学术论文的灵魂是创新性，创新是不分中外的，外国已经有的，再做同样的研究就不是创新。

论文题目以 On …或者 Study on …，Research on …开头是陈腐的表达形式，在 19 世纪很流行，现在几乎已绝迹。讨论什么问题就直接用那个问题做题目。可是中国作者的许多文章题目仍在使用 Study on。我们对一批博士论文后面的参考文献清单进行过统计，凡是用 Study on 的，十拿九稳是中国作者写的。实际上在中文题目"某某问题的研究"中，"的研究"三个字也是蛇足，硬译成英语自然就是洋泾浜了。

1.3　中式英语中某些短语的使用频度统计特征

自然语言中字母、单词、短语均有一定的出现频度，明显偏离正常统计特性就不是地道的自然语言。有许多表达方式在语法上并无大错，但在使用习惯、出现频度等方面却不符合英语的规律。此类语句的频繁使用会使文章在语感、风格等方面表现出某些微妙的特征，显得不自然，使人一看就知道是中国作者写的。

这里列举中国作者用得很多的几个典型短语：

- this kind of …
- play an important role
- pay attention to …
- put forward
- according to …
- not only … , but also …
- Firstly …
- more and more

这些短语也被英美等国的母语作者使用，但相比之下却更加受到中国作者的青睐，它们在中国作者所写文章里的出现频度大大高于自然英语中的正常频率，因此可认为是中式英语的一个特征。

　　我们分别选取母语作者和中国作者的两组科技文章进行分析，每组文章包含的单词总数均为 10 万左右。母语作者的文章取自一本信息与通信专业科技英语教材[6]，有课文和课外阅读材料各 20 篇，代表 40 位不同作者。中国作者的论文取自 2004 年 *Journal of Shanghai University* 增刊上发表的全国高等学校制造自动化研究会第 11 届学术年会英文论文 37 篇，以及《声学技术》2003 年和 2004 年英文专刊发表的论文 12 篇，共代表 49 位作者。选取增刊上发表的会议论文是考虑到这些作者来自全国许多省市，因而更具代表性。两组论文涉及的专业领域不尽相同，但是较为接近。统计的结果在下表中列出。中国作者使用这些短语的次数高于母语作者最低为 2.75 倍（not only …, but also …），最高达 10 倍之多（put forward）。

英语短语	在 49 位中国作者的论文中出现次数	在 40 位母语作者的文章中出现次数
play an important role	9	1
pay attention to	8	2
put forward	10	1
according to	96	22
kind of	27	9
not only …, but also …	22	8
Firstly	15	2
more and more	14	2

　　值得注意的是，在母语作者所写的文章中，与 attention 结合使用的动词是多样化的，除了出现两次 pay 以外，还有多处与动词 get，focus，devote，give，draw 配合，例如 In recent years much attention has been focused on extending this image formation technique. 而在我们统计的 49 篇论文中，中国作者无一例外地使用 pay attention to。

　　某些短语使用频率过高的现象与我国的英语教学方法和教材状况不无关系。从小学开始一些表达模式就被当成经典反复向学生灌输，当然也是各种考试中的热门题目，给学生留下了难以磨灭的印象。英语是丰富多彩的，同样的意思可用许多不同方法来表达，这种语言的多样性在教学中没有得到足够重视，导致许多人在写作时不由自主地反复使用少数的固定短语。我们主张在写作时有意识地纠正这种倾向。

1.4　大量实践，克服母语干扰

　　理工专业的科技人员要在英语写作中克服母语干扰，避免洋泾浜英语，根本途径就是大量实践，包括写作和阅读两方面的实践。

　　在写的方面首先应养成直接用英语写作的习惯，尽量不要先写成中文然后再硬译成英文，这样更有利于摆脱中文的束缚。如果一定要由中文翻译，就必须大胆突破中文用语和表达方式的约束，不要简单地逐字直译。其实对自己写的文章完全能做到这一点。只有摆脱了中文的影响，才能写出比较地道的英文。在写作时不可拘泥于语法条文，要根据语感来写。很多人写出来的东西摆脱不了洋泾浜腔调，究其原因就是缺乏正确的语感。

　　英语语感只能经过长期、大量接触英语，在潜移默化中培养起来，因此培养写作能力的实践不能仅限于多写文章，还要包括阅读，必须强调阅读对提高写作水平的重要作用。读书破万卷，下笔如有神，正是这个道理。不仅要读得多，还要特别重视养成良好的阅读习惯，这对于写作水平的提高至关重要。良好的习惯包括在阅读时留心观察，例如我们会注意到 put forward 和 pay attention to 并不像过去的印象中那样广泛流行。

最后，写作必须认真，稿子写成后务必反复多看几遍，根据我们的经验，五遍十遍绝不算多。可以肯定每一遍都会有修改和提高。要仔细推敲语法和用词，直到自己读来顺口，不要把自己都不满意的稿子拿出去。

2. Examples of Chinese English in Technical Writing
中式英语举例

(1) 从中文硬套过来，包含一些典型的 Chinglish 特征：

However, how to mine valuable information and knowledge from the PDM system becomes the key to improve work efficiency and implement knowledge management of an enterprise.

评语：用 How to … 做主语是一部分中国作者的偏爱。汉语中短语"如何……"做主语很常见，但英文却不行。work efficiency 是"工作效率"的硬译。这里的动词 mine 也使用不当，计算机科学中有研究领域称为 data mining，即数据挖掘，但将 mine 的使用随意推广，to mine information and knowledge 就成了洋泾浜。改为：

However, exploration of valuable information and knowledge from the PDM system has become a key in the improvement of efficiency and implementation of knowledge management in an enterprise.

(2) 写中文常有八股倾向，这种毛病也被带到英文里来。例如下面这段文字：

提出了一整套有效的算法，首先采用……进行预处理；然后基于……进行校正；接着提出了……方法，并基于该方法进行……；最后基于……方法进行有效的……

A set of methods used for facial image segmentation and feature extraction is proposed. At first, an adaptive image segmentation based on skin color detection is applied. Then, the image tilt is calibrated by global symmetric correlation. Subsequently, DCT coefficient projection is proposed, and is used for effective segmentation of facial organ. At last, based on different feature detection algorithms, multiple-method fusion scheme is applied to facial feature detection and extraction.

评语：罗列步骤，重复啰唆，用词不当，是中式八股文章的翻版。修改后单词数量从 70 个减少到 50 个，删去重复用语和 at first、at last 等陈词滥调，克服了八股腔：

We propose a set of methods to segment a face image and extract features, including adaptive image segmentation based on skin colors, skew correction with global symmetric correlation, and DCT coefficient projection for organ localization. A fusion scheme is developed to combine several feature detection results to represent facial characteristics.

(3) 从下面这段文字可看出从中文逐字硬译的明显痕迹。

This paper puts forward a design of security identity authentication system with fingerprint identification and contactless IC card technologies, then discusses the specific security mechanism. The principle, main function and the composition of hardware and software of the system are mainly discussed. It has fine safety, high reliability and utility value.

评语：puts forward a design …是中国作者特有的表达方式。IC card 称不上是 technology，只是一种 technique。副词 mainly 的用法是典型的中式英语。最后一句完全不通。修改如下，由 51 个单词减少到 40 个：

This paper introduces an ID authentication system based on non-contact IC card and fingerprint identification. The security mechanism, the system's operation and main functions are discussed. Hardware and software structures are described. The system is highly secure and reliable.

(4) 其他不符合英文表达习惯的中式英文例句。

Owing to the development of nanometer techniques and microelectronics, the trend of the miniaturization of integrated circuits and components towards atomic scale becomes strong and definite.

评语：显然是由中文逐字硬译而成，可改为：

The development of nanometer techniques and microelectronics has led to the miniaturization of integrated circuits and components with sizes toward the atomic scale.

(5)

So the speed of the atoms can be controlled.

评语：频繁地用 so 开头是中文表达习惯的影响，用多了读起来感到很别扭。如果文章里已出现过几处 so，可考虑改用其他表达形式。例如可改为：

Thus the speed of the atoms can be controlled.

(6)

In order for formulas (15) ～ (17) to do numerical calculations, the diffusion coefficients are taken to be …

评语：由谁进行数值计算？是作者还是公式？另外 formulas (15)～(17) 也不对，并非所有名词都可用作序号引导词的，这里应该用 Equation。改为：

In order to evaluate Equations (15)～(17) numerically, the diffusion coefficients are taken to be …

(7)

This results from the increase of temperature mainly.

评语：语法似不错，但语感不对。片面理解了某些教材中关于副词放在后面的"规则"。改为：

This results mainly from the temperature increase.

(8)

Nowadays, paying much more attention to the environmental protection, people have been looking for some ideal methods that not only can decrease the environmental pollution in the manufacturing processes but also can reduce the "contamination" of products.

评语：出现口语化的 nowadays，以及用得过滥的 pay attention to（而且是 much more）

和 not only … but also … ，改为：

With ever increasing environmental concerns, effective methods are being sought that can reduce pollution in the manufacturing process and minimize harmful effects in the end products.

(9)

It is more superior to other kind narrow band filters.

评语：superior to …就是"优于"，不要再用 more。还有语法错误。改为：

It is superior to the other kind of narrow band filters.

(10)

The experimental data also reflect two questions.

评语：reflect questions 是中文"反映了……问题"的硬译。

The experimental results also imply (show, indicate, reveal) two issues (phenomena, problems).

(11)

In this paper, the concepts, basic features, development, theoretical methods, and potential applications are mainly discussed.

评语：这是一篇讨论知识工程论文的第一句话。罗列了一串名词，却没有交代是关于什么问题的，是什么的概念、特征、发展、方法、应用？此外 mainly 的位置也不对，是典型的中式英语。改为：

This paper introduces the concept and theoretical aspects of knowledge-based engineering (KBE), and discusses its development and potential applications.

(12)

After high development of broadband network in residential areas in 2000 and 2001, the task confronting China's ISPs (Internet Service Providers) is how to expand value-added services on the broadband network.

评语：2000 和 2001 显然是指过去的两年。high development 和 confronting 用词不当。首字母缩写应该放在全文后面的括号内。改为：

Having experienced a rapid growth of broadband networks in residential areas during the past two years, China's Internet service providers (ISP) are facing an increased demand of value-added services on the net.

(13)

In practice, the manner in which a programmer gets understanding of a software system varies greatly and depends on the individual, the magnitude of the program and the level of understanding needed.

评语：the manner in which …不通。get understanding of，拐弯抹角，就是简单的 understand。多处用词不当。改为：

In practice, the way in which a programmer understands a software system varies depending on the individual, the scope of the problem, and the required level of understanding.

(14)

However, the problems of understanding the crosscutting concerns are paid little attention.

评语：又是 pay attention。删去 problem。改为主动语态，避免 pay：

However, understanding of the crosscutting concerns has received little attention.

参考资料

[1] 汪榕培. 中国英语是客观存在. 解放军外语学院学报，1991, (1): 1-8.

[2] 李文中. 中国英语与中式英语. 外语教学与研究，1993, (4): 18-24.

[3] 谢之君. 中国英语——跨文化交际中的干扰性变体. 现代英语，1995, (4): 7-11.

[4] 周振鹤. 别琴竹枝词百首笺释—洋泾浜英语研究之一. 上海文化，1995, (3).

[5] S. Russell and P. Norvig, Artificial Intelligence: A Modern Approach, http://www.cs.berkeley.edu/~russell/intro.html.

[6] 王朔中. 信息与通信工程专业科技英语. 北京：清华大学出版社，2004.

Ⅳ. Title of Scientific Papers

英文科技论文标题

论文标题高度概括全文内容，居论文之首，重要性不言而喻。好的标题令读者产生阅读欲望，有利于提高论文的关注度和引用率；反之，标题不当会被读者和检索机构忽略，使论文淹没在浩瀚的文献海洋中，学术影响大打折扣。以下讨论英文科技论文标题有关的几个问题。

1. Keep Concise and Informative
简洁精炼，突出主题

标题凝练论文主题，以简洁为上，一般不超过 20 个单词，因而必须字斟句酌，尽可能删除冗词。中文期刊有时出现"某某技术的研究"这种题目，而英文的 Research on, Study on, technology 等用语通常是多余的，并无信息量，应该删掉。国外早期论文常以 On …开头作为标题，这种陈腐的套路早已过时。当然也不能片面压缩字数而有损对内容的归纳，要确保清晰，有时不得不长一些。

标题应正确体现论文主题，反映内容要点，突出研究成果的特色和原创性。为此必须具体，要包含能体现论文特色的关键性信息，使用有助于检索的通用专业术语，例如：Adaptive limited feedback for sum-rate maximizing beamforming in cooperative multicell systems，读者从这个标题可清楚了解研究内容（波束成形有限反馈技术）、研究目的（最大化系统速率总和）、应用环境（多小区协作系统）和技术特点（自适应）。又如：

- Asymptotic capacity of beamforming with limited feedback
- Fundamental green tradeoffs: progresses, challenges and impacts on 5G networks
- Scenario-based performance analysis of routing protocols for mobile ad-hoc networks
- An overview of smart antenna technology and its application to wireless

communication systems

要避免范围过大的空泛标题。例如针对有非线性相位噪声的信道研究一种基于最大似然和导频辅助的相干光 QPSK 相位估计方法，论文若以 Phase estimation in coherent optical systems 为题就过于笼统了。这样的标题涉及范围太广，因为相干光系统相位估计是一个大问题，无法在一篇论文里进行深入讨论。可改为 Phase estimation in coherent optical QPSK systems with nonlinear phase noise 以突出非线性相位噪声。为了进一步反映论文的独特之处，可在 phase estimation 前加修饰语，确定标题为 Pilot-assisted maximum-likelihood phase estimation in coherent optical QPSK systems with nonlinear phase noise，共 15 个词，准确说明了论文中提出的方法。

2. Composition of Titles
标题构成

科技论文的标题通常是名词性短语而不是完整句子，其核心是名词。要具有明确的针对性就得对主要名词进行限定和修饰，用定语描述概念、方法、事物等的特点和性质，如 location-aware device，decision-aided scheme，adaptive processor，low-complexity algorithm，low-cost printing technique。定语也用来说明效果，如 contrast-enhanced algorithm。标题 Energy-efficient resource allocation in OFDMA networks 强调了论文提出的资源分配方案具有高效节能的优点。

修饰词较多时要注意以下几方面：

- 词序。如前面的例子 Adaptive limited feedback for sum-rate maximizing beamforming，主题是 limited feedback。如果论文主要讨论波束形成，则应改为 Sum-rate maximizing beamforming with adaptive limited feedback。
- 层次。例如 smart antenna technology and its application，智能天线技术和它的应用是并列的，而 application of smart antenna technology 则强调应用，技术只是简单介绍，和应用不在一个层面。
- 表达方式。用名词做定语通常比较简洁，例如 frequency-domain artifacts 比 artifacts in the frequency-domain 更好。但应避免连续多个名词做定语，如果修饰词较多则形式要有变化，正确体现逻辑关系，例如 frequency domain remote-sensing image artifacts，主次不清，读来不得要领，应改为 frequency-domain artifacts in remote-sensing images。

有时可用动名词短语做标题，含有行为的成分：Reducing frequency-domain artifacts of binary image due to coarse sampling by repeated interpolation and smoothing of Radon projections，比起 Reduction of frequency-domain artifacts 来更简洁，而且避免了一连串的 of。

要尽量把体现论文主题的重要词组放在前面，如第 1 部分两个例子中的 Adaptive limited feedback 和 Pilot-assisted maximum-likelihood phase estimation。

标题结构并非千篇一律，也可以不用名词短语形式。报纸杂志文章广泛采用非名词性题目，这不在我们讨论之列。有些科技文章用问句为题，往往更为生动，能吸引读者，这种标题多见于科普文章和网文，或是跨领域科学杂志中的概论和综述文章。例如：

- 5G spectrum: Is China ready?
- What will 5G be?
- How much training and feedback are needed in MIMO broadcast channels?

用问句做标题要确保文章内容围绕题中所问展开，并给出答复，否则文不对题，反而弄巧成拙。

3. What to Avoid
应避免的问题

除避免冗长和空泛之外，标题还应避免使用非广为人知的缩略词、字符、代号，避免出现非文字元素如化学结构式和数学公式。研究论文要避免口语化表达。

标题中并非绝对不能出现缩略词，缩略词的最大优点是简短，缺点是会使一部分读者不知所云。由于多数科技期刊是面向特定专业领域的读者群，只要是该领域普遍知晓的缩略词就可以用。例如在通信工程领域，OFDM、CDMA、MIMO 这些标准缩略词会经常出现在标题中，包含这类缩略词的标题也有助于论文的索引和检索。需要指出，这些缩略词在摘要或正文中第一次出现时仍应给出全称：orthogonal frequency division multiplexing（OFDM），以后再提到时仅用缩略词 OFDM。

最后还要避免使用不必要的修饰词如 novel、unique、innovative、ground-breaking 等，这些并无信息量的自我褒扬不仅不能增加论文的份量，还有可能产生负面作用。

4. Tips for Good Title
标题撰写技巧

在确定标题前可先查阅所投刊物上相近研究领域的论文作为参考，了解大多数作者所用的标题形式，关注广泛使用的专业关键词等，但绝不可抄袭照搬。

许多刊物网站的投稿页面上会提供 Instruction for Authors（投稿须知），作者应仔细阅读里面关于标题格式和字数限制的要求，确保论文标题的类型和风格与该刊物相吻合。

作为全文内容的缩影，标题和摘要一样，虽然位于论文之首，然而在写作顺序上，一般不要急于确定。可以先拟几个备选标题，在论文写成后再定。这是因为通过正文的撰写思路更清晰了，对方法、结果、创新更加明确，再回过头来仔细推敲，才能写出最合适的标题。

Ⅴ. How to Write Abstract

科技论文英文摘要撰写规范

摘要是原始文献的代表；它提供原始文献的信息内容，但不能代替原始文献（即一次文献），因为其内容已大大简化。摘要告诉读者该篇文献包含的主要概念和讨论的主要问题，帮助科技人员决定这篇文献对自己的工作是否有用。

美国《工程索引》（Engineering Index，EI）是世界著名的检索刊物之一，报道世界工程文献摘要，每期有刊录的主题索引与作者索引，每年还出版年卷本和年度索引，年度索引中增加作者单位索引。以下材料是以 EI 对摘要的要求为基础整理的。

1. Types of Abstract
摘要的种类

按 EI 的分类，摘要分为信息性摘要和指示性摘要，或者两者结合的摘要。

信息性摘要（informative abstracts）。包括原始文献重要内容梗概，多用于科技杂志或科技期刊文章、会议论文、专题技术报告。应包括下列几部分内容。

- 目的：写此文章的目的，或主要解决的问题。
- 过程及方法：主要工作过程及所用方法、条件、主要设备和仪器。
- 结果和结论：如可能，尽量提一句所得结果的应用范围和应用情况。

指示性摘要（indicative abstracts）。仅指出文献的综合内容，适用于综述性文献、图书介绍、专著等。这种文献是综述情况而不是某个技术工艺、某产品或某设备的研究过程。包含以下内容：

- 某技术在某时期的综合发展情况。
- 或某技术在目前的发展水平，以及未来展望等。

信息性摘要占绝大部分比例，以下主要这对这一类摘要说明应注意的事项。

2. Length of Abstract
摘要长度

摘要的长度一般不超过 150 个英文单词，不少于 100 个单词。少数情况可例外，视原文文献而定，但主题概念不得遗漏。据统计，如果根据前述几部分写摘要一般都不会少于 100 个单词。翻译摘要可以不受原文摘要的约束。

摘要应简练，缩短摘要的一般方法：

- 只包括新情况、新内容。
- 取消或减少背景情况（background information）。
- 取消过去的研究细节和未来研究计划。
- 取消不必要的字句：如 It is reported…, Extensive investigations show that …, The author discusses…, This paper concerned with…
- 适当简化物理单位及通用词。
- 不说废话，如"本文讨论的研究工作是对过去工艺的一个极大改进"之类不可进入摘要。
- 删除重复成分，如：
  (a) 不用 at a temperature of 250℃～300℃，而用 at 250℃～300℃
  (b) 不用 at a high pressure of 200 MPa，而用 at 200 Mpa
  (c) 不用 Specially designed or formulated，而用 Specially designed
- 摘要第一句话切不可与题目重复；EI 中数据库中将摘要和题目连排，只是题目用黑体排印，可认为是摘要的第一句话。这一点很重要，如有重复必须改写。
  (a) 例如：WAVE FUNCTION FOR THE B CENTER IN LiF. A wave function for the B center in LiF is proposed assuming a linear combination of appropriate molecular orbits. The …
  (b) 改为：WAVE FUNCTION FOR THE B CENTER IN LiF. A linear combination

of appropriate molecular orbits is assumed. The ...

3. Styles
文体风格

摘要必须简明扼要，逻辑性强。句子结构要严谨完整，尽量使用短句，用有限的篇幅把论文的要点阐述清楚。要满足摘要能独立存在、意思完整的要求。在文体风格上应注意下列各项：

- 用标准书面英语，不用口语、俚语、未被普遍接受的用语。
- 删繁从简。例如用 increase 代替 has been found to increase。
- 尽量使用工程领域的通用标准术语。语言朴实无华，不要用文学性描述。
- 用过去时叙述作者的工作（如实验），用现在时叙述结论。例如：The structure of dislocation core in Gap was investigated by weak-beam electro microscope. The dislocations are dissociated into two Shokley partial with ...
- 在可以用动词的情况下，尽量避免用动词的名词形式。例如不用 Measurement of thickness of plastic sheet was made. 而用 Thickness of plastic sheets was measured.
- 尽量用主动语态代替被动语态。例如，A exceed B 优于 B is exceeded by A。
- 注意冠词用法。分清 a 是泛指，the 是专指。例如 Pressure is a function of temperature，不是 Pressure is a function of the temperature. 又如 The refinery operates... 不要遗漏定冠词，写成 Refinery operates ...
- 要避免用一长串形容词或名词作修饰语，可用预置短语分开，或用连字符断开名词词组，作为一个形容词。例如不用 the cholorine containing high melt index propylene based polymer，而用 the cholorine-containing propylene-based polymer of high melt index.
- 使动词尽量接近主语。例如 The decolorazation in solutions of the pigment, which were exposed to 10 h of UV irradiation, was no longer irreversible. 应改为 When the pigment was dissoved, decolorization was irreversible after 10 h of UV irradiation.
- 要用重要的事实开头，避免用辅助从句开头。例如 From data obtained experimentally, power consumption of telephone switching systems was determined. 应将主要名词 Power consumption 移到前面：Power consumption of telephone switching systems was determined from data obtained experimentally.
- 语言要简练，但不可使用电报语言，例如不用 Multipath effect on rate-distortion performance investigation. 而用 Multipath effect on the rate-distortion performance was investigated.
- 摘要中涉及他人的工作或研究成果时，可列出作者名字，但不可引用正文中的文献编号。
- 用英美拼法均可，但篇内应保持一致。

- 题目中尽量不用特殊字符及希腊字母。摘要中也应避免或尽可能少用。特殊字符主要指各种数学符号，对它们的录入 EI 有特殊的规定，因为它们的输入极为麻烦，而且易出错，影响摘要本身的准确性。应尽量用文字表达，如"导热系数 ρ"中的 ρ 可去掉。如涉及数学公式如 $\Phi = A\mu_{s-1}x$ 或更复杂的表达式，应设法指引读者去看原始文献。

Bibliography

1. A. J. Herbert, *The Structure of Technical English*, Longmans, London, 1987.
2. 范仲英. 实用翻译教程. 北京：外语教学与研究出版社，1994.
3. 黄荣恩. 科技英语翻译浅说. 北京：中国对外翻译出版公司，1981.
4. 张培基，等. 英汉翻译教程. 上海：上海外语教育出版社，1986.
5. 阎庆甲. 科技英语翻译方法. 北京：冶金工业出版社，1986.
6. 陈忠华，等，科技英语应用话语分析，武汉：湖北教育出版社，1995.
7. D. Bolinger, D. A. Sears. *Aspects of Language*. 3rd Edition. Harcourt Brace Jovanovich, Inc., New York, 1981.
8. 侯维瑞. 英语语体.上海：上海外语教育出版社，1988.
9. K. Hudson. *The Dictionary of Diseased English*, The MacMillan Press Ltd., London/Basingstoke, 1980.
10. *Oxford Advanced Learner's Dictionary of Current English*. 6th Edition. The Commercial Press and Oxford University Press, 2000.
11. 葛传椝，等. 新英汉词典. 世纪版. 上海：上海译文出版社，2000.
12. *Longman Language Activator*, Longman Group UK Ltd., 1993.
13. Collins COBUILD, *Essential English Dictionary*, William Collins Sons & Co., Ltd., 1988.
14. C. Young. *The New Penguin Dictionary of Electronics*. Penguin Books Ltd., London, 1979.
15. R. L. Freeman. *Telecommunication Transmission Handbook*. 2nd Ed.. John Wiley & Sons, New York, 1991.
16. J. Graham. *Dictionary of Telecommunications*. Penguin Books Ltd., London, 1991.
17. 夏培肃. 英汉计算机辞典. 北京：人民邮电出版社，1984.
18. B. Happé. *BKSTS Dictionary of Audio-Visual Terms*. Focal Press, London, 1983.
19. J. Stein and S. B. Flexner. *The Random House Thesaurus*. Random House, Inc., New York, 1984.
20. 任胜利. 英语科技论文撰写与投稿. 北京：科学出版社，2004.
21. 李旭. 英语科技论文写作指南. 北京：国防工业出版社，2005.
22. J. Gibaldi. *MLA Handbook for Writers of Research Papers*. 5th Ed.. 上海：上海外语教育出版社，2001.
23. T. M. Georges, *Analytical Writing for Science and Technology*, online course, 1996, http://mywebpages.comcast.net/tgeorges/write/.
24. R. Gunning, *The Technique of Clear Writing*, McGraw-Hill, 1952.

25. Norman Fenton, *General Principles of Good Writing*, 13 July 2000, http://www.dcs.qmul.ac.uk/~norman/papers/good_writing/general_principles.html.

26. *Write to Reach Your Readers — Use Real Words and Common Sense*, BPA Corporate Communications, 1999.

27. D. A. Hillson. *Describing Probability: The Limitations of Natural Language*. PMI Global Congress. EMEA Proceedings, Edinburgh, UK, 2005.

28. Some of the text or supplementary readings have used materials from the Wikipedia articles under the GNU Free Documentation License (http://www.gnu.org/copyleft/fdl.html).

29. 王朔中. 信息与通信工程专业科技英语. 北京：清华大学出版社，2004.

30. 沈美芳，王朔中. 排除科技英语写作中的母语干扰. 中国科技期刊研究，18(2)，2007.